The Handbook of Risk Management and Analysis

The Handbook of Risk Management and Analysis

Edited by Carol Alexander
The University of Sussex

JOHN WILEY & SONS
Chichester • New York • Brisbane • Toronto • Singapore

Other Wiley Editorial Offices

John Wiley & Sons, Inc., 605 Third Avenue,
New York, NY 10158-0012, USA

Jacaranda Wiley Ltd, 33 Park Road, Milton,
Queensland 4064, Australia

John Wiley & Sons (Canada) Ltd, 22 Worcester Road,
Rexdale, Ontario M9W 1L1, Canada

John Wiley & Sons (Asia) Pte Ltd, 2 Clementi Loop #02-01
Jin Xing Distripark, Singapore 129 809

Library of Congress Cataloging-in-Publication Data

The handbook of risk management & analysis / edited by Carol
    Alexander.
        p.   cm.
    Includes bibliographical references and index.
    ISBN 0-471-95309-1 (cloth)
    1. Derivative securities.   2. Options (Finance).   3. Risk
    management.   I. Alexander, Carol.
HG6024.A3H363   1996
332.6 — dc20   95-39199
                                                    CIP

British Library Cataloguing in Publication Data

A catalogue record for this book is available from the British Library

ISBN 0-471-95309-1

Typeset in 10/12pt Times by Laser Words, Madras
Printed and bound in Great Britain by Bookcraft (Bath) Ltd
This book is printed on acid-free paper responsibly manufactured from sustainable forestation,
for which at least two trees are planted for each one used for paper production.

Contents

Contents

Contents ———————————————————————————— xi

List of Contributors

CAROL ALEXANDER
University of Sussex, Brighton, UK.

STAN BECKERS
Barra International Ltd, London, UK.

MARK FOX
Emerging Markets Group, Lehman Brothers, London, UK.

M. DESMOND FITZGERALD
Equitable House Investments Ltd, London, UK.

ROBERT JARROW
Johnson Graduate School of Management, Cornell, USA.

DAMIAN KISSANE
Bebag Asset Management AG, Switzerland.

EDMOND LEVY
Specialized Derivatives Group, HSBC Midland, London, UK.

RICCARDO REBONATO
BZW-Barclays, London, UK.

ANDREW STREET
SFA, London, UK.

BRYAN THOMAS
Bank of America, Singapore.

STUART TURNBULL
School of Business, Queen's University, Ontario, Canada.

LEE WAKEMAN
TMG Financial Products, USA.

THOMAS C. WILSON
McKinsey & Company, London, UK, and Zurich, Switzerland.

About the Contributors

CAROL ALEXANDER

Carol Alexander obtained her Ph.D. in Algebraic Number Theory and, after a year as a Bond Analyst at Phillips and Drew (UBS), returned to academic life. Since 1985 she has been based in Brighton, lecturing at the University of Sussex in Algebra and Econometrics. During the past four years she has been consulting in Time Series Analysis for banks, corporates and other financial institutions. She speaks at many international conferences, writes regularly for professional publications and runs training courses specializing in volatility and correlation analysis for Risk Management. She has published widely in international journals and is currently writing a textbook on *Time Series Analysis for Financial Markets*, also for John Wiley.

STAN BECKERS

Stan Beckers received his Ph.D. in Finance from the University of California. He is President of BARRA International Ltd. Stan started BARRA's international operations in London in 1982 after having worked as a consultant to BARRA for four years. Previously Stan was senior economist at Chase Econometric Associates in Philadelphia. He has published articles on a wide range of international investment topics and frequently speaks at financial industry practitioner forums. Stan is currently Professor in Finance at the K.U. Leuven (Belgium) and at various times has taught at the University of California, the European Institute for Advanced Studies in Management (Brussels), London's City University Business School and the Free University of Amsterdam. Major achievements in his life include cycling from London to Paris and a successful ascent to the summit of Kilimanjaro.

Dr M. DESMOND FITZGERALD

Dr M. Desmond Fitzgerald BA (York) Ph.D. (Manchester) is Chairman and Chief Executive of Equitable House Investments Limited, a specialized arbitrage and derivatives trading firm. He is also Chairman of Unique Consultants Limited, a major financial training and risk management consultancy firm. Previously he served as Director, Head of Arbitrage at Mitsubishi Finance International plc, as Chief Economist and Head of Planning at Credit Lyonnais-Alexanders, Laing and Cruickshank and as a Senior Economist with

Chemical Bank. His academic posts have included that of Ernst and Whinney Professor of Finance at the University of Strathclyde, Senior Lecturer and Head of Finance at City University, London, and Associate Professor of Finance at New York University. He has written two standard texts *Financial Futures* and *Financial Options* and numerous articles.

MARK FOX

Mark Fox is Chief European Strategist for Lehman Brothers, Associate Research Fellow ISMA Centre, University of Reading and Member of the UK Bond Commission. Prior to his current role Mark was the Head of Emerging Markets Research, Europe, involved in both selling and designing strategies for emerging markets. In 1991 he set up the emerging markets fund management capability within Lehman Brothers, managing a range of emerging markets portfolios. Mark was a fund manager of both OECD and emerging markets bond and multicurrency portfolios for nine years prior to joining the Lehman Brothers Emerging Markets Group in 1993. He is also responsible for teaching and examining on emerging markets for the ISMA, and has published many articles on a variety of financially related topics.

ROBERT JARROW

Robert Jarrow is the Ronald P. and Susan E. Lynch Professor of Investment Management at the Johnson Graduate School of Management, Cornell University. He is a graduate of Duke University, Dartmouth College and the Massachusetts Institute of Technology. Professor Jarrow is renowned for his pioneering work on the Heath–Jarrow–Morton model for pricing interest rate derivatives. His current research interests include the pricing of exotic interest rate options and other derivative securities as well as investment management theory. His publications include four books, *Options Pricing, Finance Theory, Modelling Fixed Income Securities and Interest Rate Options*, and *Derivative Securities*, as well as over 50 publications in leading finance and economic journals. Professor Jarrow is currently co-editor of *Mathematical Finance* and an associate editor of the *Review of Financial Studies*, the *Journal of Financial and Quantitative Analysis*, and the *Review of Derivatives Research*. He is also a managing director and the director of research at Kamakura Corporation.

DAMIAN KISSANE

Damian Kissane is the Director and Global Investment Manager of Bebag Asset Management AG, a Swiss company specializing in Global Investment Management using its own proprietary stock selection and risk management techniques. Previously he was a Director of UBS Limited, responsible for Structuring and Risk Management in the medium term note and new issue business. He also served as Head of Derivative Marketing for Europe for Mitsubishi Financial International. He holds an MBA from the Manchester Business School.

EDMOND LEVY

Dr Edmond Levy is currently Assistant Director in the Specialized Derivatives Group at HSBC MIDLAND, where he is mainly responsible for the development and risk management of foreign exchange exotic options. The group also covers a wide range of structured equity and capital market products. Prior to joining the HSBC group, he was at BZW-Barclays Bank and Nomura Bank International plc. Edmond came to derivative trading from an academic background. He lectured in Finance at Liverpool University and Econometrics at Southampton University where he received his Ph.D.

RICCARDO REBONATO

Dr Riccardo Rebonato is Director and Head of Research at BZW — Debt Capital Markets — Barclays Bank. His main responsibilities are modelling, pricing and hedging interest rate dependent "exotic" options, with particular emphasis on new products. He frequently talks at conferences and seminars in Europe and America. He has been at BZW for five years, and prior to this he was a Research Fellow in Physics at Corpus Christi College, Oxford. He holds Doctorates in Nuclear Engineering and Science of Materials (Solid State Physics).

ANDREW STREET

Dr Andrew Street received a first class degree in the theoritical physics from Durham and a D.Phil. from Oxford in the theory of many body collisions. He worked briefly at the atomic energy research establishment at Harwell before becoming a financial quantitiative analyst with Barings in the mid 1980's. Research of new products lead to a direct involvement in trading, structuring and risk managing new derivative instruments. He moved to Paribas capital markets in 1989 to become senior trader in OTC equity derivatives. Headhunted to Nomura International in 1991 he headed the European Equity Derivative Trading and Structuring.

In 1992, Mitsubishi Finance International recruited him as, at first, Director and then Executive Director of the Arbitrage Group responsible for equity, bonds, foreign exchange and commodity derivatives in Mitsubishi. In 1995 he was asked to join the Securities and Futures Authority, the UK securities regulator, as Head of the Risk Assessment Group, responsible for overseeing the risk management practices and modelling of the SFA regulated firms.

He is also a partner in the specialist risk management consultancy 'Value Consultants Limited'.

BRYAN THOMAS

Bryan Thomas received a BA in Economics and MBA in Finance and General Management from the University of California, Los Angeles. He worked for three years as a money market trader with Bankers Trust. He then enjoyed ten years with Banque Indosuez, of which three were spent in Paris, learning currency options as the market was developing.

He joined Midland Bank, London, where he developed their Tender-to-Contract-Hedge product. In 1993 he became Head of Global Currency Options Development with the Bank of America in London and these responsibilities have taken him to Singapore where he is setting up a new currency options trading desk. Bryan is a frequent speaker at conferences on exotic options.

STUART TURNBULL

Stuart M. Turnbull is Bank of Montreal Professor of Banking and Finance, Queen's University (Canada), and a Research Fellow, Institute for Policy Analysis (Toronto). He is a graduate of the Imperial College of Science and Technology (London) and the University of British Columbia. He is the author of *Option Valuation*, and (with Robert A. Jarrow) *Derivative Securities*. He has published over 30 articles in major finance and economics journals, and in law and economics journals, as well as many articles in practitioner journals. His current research interests include the pricing of credit derivatives, exotic options, risk management and asset pricing theory. Professor Turnbull is an associate editor of *Mathematical Finance*, and the *Journal of Financial Engineering*, and has served as an associate editor for the *Journal of Finance*.

LEE WAKEMAN

Lee Wakeman is the founder, President and Chief Executive Officer of TMG Financial Products. He has structured derivative products for numerous domestic and international corporations and government entities, and pioneered the development of interest rate collar, compound option and average interest rate option products. Previously Lee Wakeman was a Senior Vice President and Managing Director, Global Risk Management, at Sakura Global Capital. He also served as Managing Director, Treasury, Continental Bank, Head of Interest Rate Arbitrage at Chemical Bank and was responsible for the Bond Research and Risk Management units of Citicorp Investment Bank in London. Lee Wakeman was an Associate Professor of Finance at the University of Rochester and has been a visiting Professor of Finance at the University of California. He attended Cambridge University (BA), Indiana University (MBA) and Massachusetts Institute of Technology (Ph.D. in Economics and Finance). He has published numerous articles on derivative products and finance.

THOMAS C. WILSON

Thomas C. Wilson is a Partner in the Zurich and London offices of McKinsey and Company. His primary focus has been on finance and risk management related issues. Over the past years, he has been actively involved in these areas with clients in the United States, Europe, and the Far East and has published several articles on risk management related issues. Prior to joining McKinsey, Dr Wilson worked at Union Bank of Switzerland in Zurich as systems developer, risk manager and trader in their Swap-option trading department. Dr Wilson has a Ph.D. in International Finance from Stanford University and a BS in Business Administration from the University of California at Berkeley.

Preface

There have been very many international conferences on Banking and Finance during the past few years. These have been so well attended, and with presentations from so many highly informed practitioners, that it seemed only sensible to make a book from this wealth of expertise. I feel very privileged to have brought together such a collection of world famous names in one book, all of whom are far more knowledgeable and eloquent than myself.

In editing each chapter I have not tried to influence the author's own particular style of writing. Neither has a uniform technical level been imposed on each chapter. In fact we trust that readers will benefit from the variety of styles and levels, as in any edited book, although the handbook has been structured according to three unifying themes: financial products, risk measurement, and risk management. A project of this size is bound to miss out on some topics: Equity Derivative Pricing Models, and Optimal Hedging Strategies to name but two. But I very much hope that these areas will be covered in a second edition — or even a second volume — of the handbook.

The handbook is divided into three parts: the first part on FINANCIAL PRODUCTS provides a reference for pricing, hedging and trading some of the new products which have been in common use during the past few years. Chapter 1 on *Equity Derivatives* by **Andrew Street** gives an historical overview of the development of equity derivative markets since exchange trading began in 1973. This chapter emphasizes the managers' perspective, on the efficiency of different types of equity derivatives and the way that markets operate. In contrast, the style of Chapter 2 could not be more different! **Riccardo Rebonato's** chapter on *Interest Rate Option Models: a Critical Survey* is one of the more mathematically complex chapters in the handbook. It is very comprehensive, but accessible to a wide audience of practitioners and academics. The chapter is beautifully constructed, from the essential "no arbitrage" conditions to the critical review of advanced interest rate option pricing models. Then, with the two Chapters 3 and 4 on *Exotic Options* by **Edmond Levy** and **Bryan Thomas**, we have a very complete picture of the new products in this rapidly expanding area of the derivatives business. The risk management aspects of each product are described, and precise details of valuation methods are provided. The authors' relative expertise is reflected in each chapter: Bryan's emphasises risk management applications and Ed's has a higher mathematical content. The last chapter in the financial products section — on *Swaps*, by **Damian Kissane** — describes FRAs and interest rate swaps. This transparent account of swap pricing and hedging should be easily accessible even to those with no background in this area.

The second part of the book, concerning RISK MEASUREMENT, opens with *A Survey of Risk Measurement Theory and Practice*. Again, an historic perspective is taken, with particular emphasis on risk diversification and on factor models. We are privileged to have one of the most knowledgeable experts in this field as the author — **Stan Beckers**. Chapter 7 on *Calculating Risk Capital* represents one of the most complete and informative texts in this area currently available. It is written by **Thomas C. Wilson**, who gives full details of his delta-gamma methods for derivative products, as well as an overview of the common techniques for calculating value-at-risk from market movements. Chapter 8 on *Volatility and Correlation Forecasting* by **Carol Alexander** provides a critical account of this important area of risk management and analysis. Particular emphasis is placed on the relative merits of GARCH models, and on the application of variance and covariance forecasts to value-at-risk models for cash products. Here you will also find a detailed description of the methods currently employed by RiskMetrics™. Value-at-risk models are not complete without accounting for *Credit Risk*, and we are very pleased that the pioneers of this important area have chosen to introduce their methods in Chapter 9 of the handbook. **Robert Jarrow** and **Stuart Turnbull** have written a beautiful account of their pricing methods for credit risky products and of modelling the credit default risk on swaps.

The third and final part of the handbook covers certain aspects of RISK MANAGEMENT. In Chapter 10, risk diversification into *Emerging Markets* is described by **Mark Fox**. All types of emerging market are covered, and the emphasis on Brady bonds and loans reflects Mark's particular expertise. Building on the mathematical methods of Chapter 9, we have an account of *Credit Enhancement Techniques for Derivatives* in Chapter 11. This is written by an expert on the various techniques for mitigating credit risk, the most eloquent and knowledgeable **Lee Wakeman**. And finally, a clear and informative account of the principles of *Volatility Trading* is provided by the universally acclaimed expert, **M. Desmond Fitzgerald**.

Editing this book has not been an easy task, and I am grateful to all the authors for responding to comments, pestering phone calls, faxes and e-mails. Many thanks also to Liz Benson of Sussex University and Lynne Barc of John Wiley, who have provided tireless support both with the authors and with the administrative side of the project.

Carol Alexander
The University of Sussex

Foreword

The true business of financial institutions is not so much to deal in cash and securities as to manage risks. These institutions face not only the potential default of counterparties, but also the price risks associated with volatile assets and liabilities, while their day-to-day business is fraught with a multitude of operational, legal, tax and regulatory considerations — a business, one might add, which grows continuously in volume and complexity but on ever thinner margins.

Given their background, there is a tremendous opportunity for these institutions to provide financial risk management products and services to clients whose main expertise lies elsewhere. The unparalleled growth of financial derivatives over the last twenty years or so is ample proof of the wide-ranging need to manage risks actively. Of course, from a pure profit perspective, derivatives are a zero-sum game: what some win others must lose. But from a risk management perspective, participants who have a clear understanding of what they do should all be winners.

In the context of risk management, derivatives have never been far from the headlines and have been the subject of many books and publications in recent years. Few of these, however, have attempted to address both market and credit risk management based on a detailed discussion of the tools of the trade and of the most up-to-date risk measurement techniques. Carol Alexander has been brave enough to take up this challenge and has succeeded in bringing together contributions from many well-known experts, be they practitioners, consultants or academics. It is an honour to be associated with this publication and a pleasure to congratulate her on her success.

Jacques Pézier
General Controller
Crédit Agricole Lazard Financial Products Bank

PART 1
Financial Products

1

Equity Derivatives

ANDREW STREET

1.1 INTRODUCTION

1.1.1 Aims and Scope of this Chapter

As its title suggests this chapter will focus on equity derivatives and in particular the new products that have been developed in that area over the last few years. To study in detail the precise pay-off formulae of equity derivative (EDs from now on) structures and the methods of their mathematical evaluation, whilst important, would be to miss the big picture with regard to derivatives, and the equity variety in particular. It is often said that financial markets are driven by fear and greed, this is as true of derivative markets as of any others. Derivatives only exist because they enhance economic efficiency, they either save money, make money or prevent its loss. This efficiency extends to the ability either to guarantee or insure results, to avoid taxes, to take advantage of specific legislation or to exploit a new category of risk such as volatility or correlation with the enhanced leverage this offers. The world's equity markets and their respective legal frameworks with regard to ownership rights over different classes of shares and dividend rights are far from standardized or non-arbitragable. Each of these markets has specific quirks which can be exploited with derivatives to the advantage of both the issuers and holders of equity financing. Each of these markets has differing liquidities, dealing and settlement terms, dividend policies and general information with regard to the returns available, both actual and prospective. Derivatives can be designed to reduce or overcome a lot of these problems and to take advantage of the potential returns with limited risk. It is often said that derivatives allow the "bundling" and "unbundling" of risk and return. This is not only true of the so-called "emerging markets" such as Thailand and Pakistan but also highly developed stock markets such as the US or UK.

This chapter is broken down into seven further sections. The remainder of this section looks at how the different types of equity derivatives can be classified depending on their structure, use and form. We will then briefly visit the general pricing assumptions of these types of contracts and securities. In Section 1.2 we look at the historical development of

The Handbook of Risk Management and Analysis. Edited by Carol Alexander
© 1996 John Wiley & Sons Ltd

equity derivatives. Section 1.3 deals with the economic utility of equity derivatives for both borrowers and investors. The role of investment banks in the creation of equity derivatives is examined in Section 1.4. Section 1.5 deals exclusively with stock index-based products, including exchange traded OTCs, hybrids and securities. Applications of equity derivatives for single shares and bespoke indices are covered in Section 1.6. The final section looks at the potential future developments for equity derivatives. A glossary of some of the specialist terms used is included in Section 1.8, and references can be found in Section 1.9.

1.1.2 Classification of Equity Derivatives

So what is an equity derivative? Let's break down the term into its component parts. Equity, in this context, is a share in ownership of a company or corporation. Equities are shares, listed or unlisted on an exchange, which generally carry a voting right at the annual general meeting, an entitlement to a dividend and a pro-rata share in the company's assets at the point of winding up (liquidation) after all other creditors have been paid. Some "equities", for example preference shares, are a kind of half-way house between true equities and debt in that they do not carry full voting rights, but have an enhanced entitlement to dividend payments, which may well be fixed in advance and so are not subject in amount to the vagaries of the company's profit cycle. Derivative is a much used and abused word these days; in this context it refers to either a contract or a security whose pay-off or final value is dependent on one or more features of the underlying equity. In many circumstances it is the price of the underlying equity which determines to a large extent the value of the equity derivative, although other factors like interest rates, time to maturity and strike price can play an equally large role. I used the terms "security" and "contract" and it is important that these are explained. A security (e.g. a government bond or "gilt" in the UK) is an obligation issued by one party to another through the mechanism of listing on a stock exchange. Listing carries with it special obligations through listing conditions which must be satisfied. These conditions vary from exchange to exchange but broadly require production of offering memoranda (which contain such things as details of the issue, audited company accounts and proposed use of funds) and the issue of a fixed number of securities either in definitive or global note form (see glossary). This ensures that new securities cannot be created and destroyed at will, and therefore has consequences for short selling and liquidity squeezes. In general, securities are in finite supply and this has direct consequences for both underlying assets and derivatives themselves. A contract, or more specifically an OTC (literally "over the counter", i.e. privately agreed between two direct counterparts) contract, can be created and destroyed virtually at will and is therefore much less prone to "paper" squeezes which can occur at the time of delivery. In general the underlying equity asset will be a security, whereas the derivative on it may be a contract or a security in its own right. The contract may also be differentiated into standardized, exchange traded contracts and those traded OTC with completely bespoke terms and conditions. These are usually, but not exclusively, agreed under some master document engineered by an industry group such as ISDA (International Swap Dealers Association).

1.1.3 General Features of Pricing Equity Derivatives

The detailed mechanics of simple and exotic option pricing will be discussed in later chapters in much more detail, but it is worthwhile here to focus upon some practical aspects of equity derivative pricing. Generally most derivative pricing takes place in what is usually called the "Black–Scholes" (see Hull (1993), Cox and Rubenstein (1985) and Wilmott, Dewynne and Howison (1994)) universe since this leads to the most readily accessible results (see Special Section Review of Black–Scholes Option Pricing, p. 8). In this universe an instantaneously risk-free portfolio (i.e. a portfolio which yields the risk-free interest rate under all market scenarios when the portfolio is continuously rebalanced) can be constructed out of the derivative, the underlying risky asset and a riskless bond. It is said that the portfolio composed of a special combination of the risky asset and a riskless discount (or zero bond) "replicates" the value characteristics of the derivative. This requires that asset price volatility is constant, interest rates are constant and have a flat term structure, that the market in the underlying risky asset has infinite liquidity (i.e. a zero bid/offer spread in any size bargain) and that the market price of the asset behaves in an entirely random walk and non-trending manner. If you ask anyone who has traded any market, but especially equity, they will tell you that the real world does not work like that! Some of the conditions of the Black–Scholes universe can be relaxed, but the subsequent differential equations become much more complex to solve with practically no gain in real day-to-day usefulness. The problem of accuracy lies as much with the estimation of parameters, typically forward prices and volatilities, as it does with the dynamics and boundary conditions of the price process. The model produced is at best a good guide which must be used carefully and with insight and experience, it being more important to evaluate carefully the factors that the models cannot cope with and to operate a risk management policy based on relative rather than absolute valuation. An example of the latter is when a three-year call option is hedged by a two-year call option on a volatility calendar spread basis (i.e. a long position in two-year volatility is hedged by selling a vega (volatility) weighted amount of three-year volatility) rather than by a pure delta hedging ("replication") strategy; the possible systematic error is potentially much larger in the latter case, since it is much more likely that systematic valuation errors will cancel in the former case.

The equity underlying has specific valuation problems all of its own. In constructing the forward asset price a dividend yield must be assumed or derived from market prices. Information on prospective dividends is seldom published beyond three to six months of the ex-dividend date and the dividend policies of corporates are notoriously fickle. In a sense they have to be, as the dividend represents one of the balancing items in a company's financial health and is often the first thing to be sacrificed in difficult times. Markets in forward prices are thin (i.e. a wide bid/offer spread) for the equity market indices such as the FTSE 100 or S&P 500 (for which the foregoing problems are reduced somewhat due to the portfolio effect of having many diverse equity dividend flows within it) and virtually non-existent for single stocks. Longer dated option valuation on equity underlyings therefore frequently contains substantial unhedgeable risk which must be priced in as a Black–Scholes extra.

Figure 1.1 is a schematic representation of the forward price of an equity index, i.e. its value today for future delivery (one might pay 1.05 times the spot price today for delivery in a year's time). It is worth noting a few significant features of this figure which have been exaggerated for clarity. During the settlement period or "account" the asset (in this case a basket of stocks representing the "current" stock index) can be bought and sold without any cash flows actually taking place, thus there is no difference in price from spot for the asset traded within the account. The UK stock market

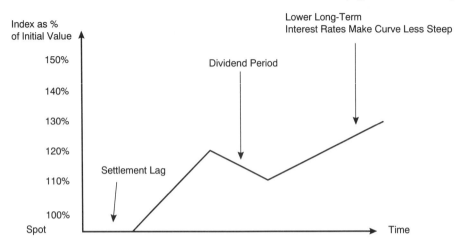

Figure 1.1 Equity index forward price curve

operated a two-week account up until the middle of 1994 when it changed over to rolling ten-day settlement. The French stock market still operates a monthly account for some of its stocks. In general the yield or dividend on the stock index will be less than the prevailing risk-free interest rates; this means that holding the asset will not be self-funding and it will have a negative "cost of carry", i.e. the cost of financing the holding is greater than the dividends received. This is reflected in the positive sloping forward curve. If the dividend flows are concentrated over a particular part of the year, as they are in the French CAC 40 index and the German DAX 30 index or indeed for a single stock, it is possible for the dividend flow to exceed the cost of financing the position over a period of the year. This leads to the negative sloping part of the asset forward curve. If longer-term interest rates are lower than short-term interest rates (i.e. a negative sloping yield curve) the longer-term forward curve will be less steep than the short term.

One further factor with regard to equity forward curves needs to be borne in mind, the mechanism of going "short" the market. "Short" selling is the sale of an asset which one does not already own, it is therefore necessary to borrow the asset to effect the delivery of the sale. This is frequently called stock borrowing/lending or sometimes "repo" (short for "sale and repurchase agreement"), which refers to a contract whereby two parties agree for one to simultaneously buy an asset spot and sell it forward at an agreed price to the other. The net effect is the same as it effectively separates the ownership of an asset (i.e. exposure to price risk) from its "physical" possession or deliverability. The holder (who is not the "owner") of the stock can then deliver the asset in settlement of his sell bargain. The costs of borrowing and lending stock are not constant and are subject to a bid/offer spread. Typically in the UK the cost is around 0.5 per cent to borrow. There is therefore both an offer and a bid forward asset price curve. In some markets, such as the UK, there are legal restrictions on borrowing stock, which mean that only a registered market-maker in that particular equity may actually enter the stock loan market to cover a short position. This can lead to distortions in the forward asset price curve and therefore in derivative pricing, particularly on the short side (e.g. put options on individual shares) as we are not dealing in a free and unstratified market.

An even larger problem than establishing the correct forward for the equity asset is deciding on the appropriate volatility or standard deviation of asset price to use in evaluating the equity derivative. Within the model this factor determines the distribution width characteristic of the random walk of the asset price and therefore the range of the possible values for the derivative. If a liquid market in the derivative exists the implied volatility can be back calculated by using the market prices to arrive at a suitable volatility figure, i.e. one that will give market observed prices when inserted in the model. If one is able to buy at the bid and sell at the offer (i.e. act as market-maker in a liquid market) this may be all that is required to run a successful book of options. However when markets are thin or non-existent the problem of parameter estimation generally falls to forecasting techniques from simple weighted mean reverting volatility models to more sophisticated GARCH (Generalized Auto Regressive Conditional Heteroskedasticity) models, based on historical and market implied volatility data. If the market is illiquid and the parameter has to be forecast, any derivative seller is going to want to build in a generous margin of error into his volatility parameter estimation as insurance against getting it wrong and having to hedge the position over a long time horizon.

One further practical problem of equity derivative valuation is the effect of "market impact" on the price of the contingent claim and the related problem of finite bid/offer spread in the underlying asset in a delta hedge ("replication") strategy. Whenever the equity derivative agreement is made the hedge for that risk must in some way be offset in the market. In a simple case the delta equivalent amount of the risky asset is bought or sold.

Consider a call option struck at 100 ("at the money") with the market trading at 99 bid/101 offer in 25/25 lots (25 units on the bid and the offer). If we buy the delta amount of contracts, say 50, we will buy the first lot of 25 at 101 and possibly the next lot of 25 at 102, giving an average price of 101.5. In this case the price is 1.5 above the mean level of the market due to the bid/offer spread and market impact, i.e. the market rallied because we bought it. Our hedge has now cost us 1.5 more than the theory would suggest! We encounter the same problem in a smaller way for the day-to-day rebalances as these are much smaller in size, but become significant when gamma gets large (e.g. near the barrier of an in-the-money barrier option). Also note we have a similar problem on taking the hedge off at expiry or exercise.

Having established some of the more practical aspects of equity derivative pricing above it is worthwhile to examine briefly the concept of the price of a derivative security as being the present value (i.e. discounted back to today's value) of the expected future pay-off of the derivative. Referring to Figure 1.2, we consider a European call option (value C) on an asset, price S, struck at K with expiry time T (i.e. the pay-off at T is Max(S (at expiry) $- K$, 0). The forward price of the asset at time T will be S_T and the width of the probability distribution of the asset price will be $\sigma\sqrt{T}$. If the risk-free rate of interest is R then the value of the derivative is the integral from K to plus infinity of $(S - K)$ multiplied by the normal probability distribution Φ centred on S_T with width $\sigma\sqrt{T}$ over S, discounted by $e^{(T-t)R}$. Equation (1) is given below:

$$C = \frac{1}{e^{(T-t)R}} \int_K^\infty (S - K)\Phi(S_T, \sigma\sqrt{T})\,dS \tag{1}$$

This concept of the present value of the expected (probabilistic) future value of the derivative pay-off is one of the basic building blocks of derivative pricing and is very

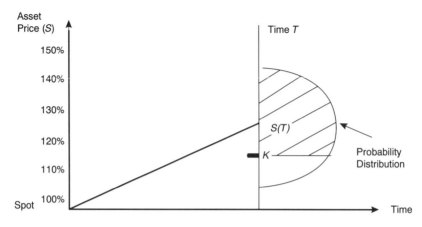

Figure 1.2 Option value as PV of expectation value

useful in looking at more complex pay-off situations where many different scenarios are possible.

Special Section Review of Black–Scholes Option Pricing

Definitions and notations for options in the Black–Scholes universe (Wilmott, Dewynne and Howison (1994)):

- $O(S, t)$ is the value of an option at time t with underlying asset price S
- σ is the price volatility of the underlying asset
- K is the exercise price of the option
- T is the expiry
- R is the risk-free interest rate
- Call option (right to buy asset for K) has terminal value $C(S, T) = \text{Max}(S - K, 0)$
- Put option (right to sell asset for K), has terminal value $P(S, T) = \text{Max}(K - S, 0)$
- Put–call parity ensures $S + P - C = K/e^{(T-t)R}$

Black–Scholes Assumptions:

- The asset price follows log normal random walk
- The risk-free interest rate and volatility are known functions of time
- No transaction costs in hedging portfolio
- No dividends paid during the life of the option
- No arbitrage possibilities, all risk-free portfolios earn the risk-free rate
- Continuous trading of underlying asset
- Underlying asset can be sold short in any size without penalty
- Stochastic differential equation, i.e. the underlying price process of the asset:

$$\frac{dS}{S} = \sigma\, dW + \mu\, dt \tag{2}$$

(where S is the asset price, dS is a small change in price over time dt, σ is the volatility, dW is a random variable from a normal distribution, μ is the drift (risk-free rate) and dt is a small time step)

- Black–Scholes partial differential equation (derived via Ito's lemma and no riskless arbitrage arguments from the above):

$$\frac{\partial O}{\partial t} + \frac{1}{2}\sigma^2 S^2 \frac{\partial^2 O}{\partial S^2} + RS\frac{\partial O}{\partial S} - RO = 0 \qquad (3)$$

- A solution for the above differential equation, with the boundary conditions equivalent to the case of a European call option with no dividends, is:

$$C(S, t) = SN(d_1) - \frac{K}{e^{(T-t)R}}N(d_2) \qquad (4)$$

$$N(x) = \frac{1}{(2\pi)^{1/2}} \int_{-\infty}^{\infty} e^{-1/2y^2}\, dy \qquad (5)$$

$$d_1 = \frac{\ln(S/K) + (R + \sigma^2/2)(T - t)}{\sigma\sqrt{T - t}} \qquad (6)$$

$$d_2 = \frac{\ln(S/K) + (R - \sigma^2/2)(T - t)}{\sigma\sqrt{T - t}} \qquad (7)$$

- The partial derivatives or option price sensitivities, often known as the "Greeks":

$$\text{Delta } \Delta = \frac{\partial C}{\partial S} \qquad (8)$$

$$\text{Gamma } \Gamma = \frac{\partial^2 C}{\partial S^2} \qquad (9)$$

$$\text{Theta } \Theta = \frac{\partial C}{\partial t} \qquad (10)$$

$$\text{Vega (or Kappa) } \kappa = \frac{\partial C}{\partial \sigma} \qquad (11)$$

$$\text{Rho } \rho = \frac{\partial C}{\partial R} \qquad (12)$$

Other higher order derivatives exist (e.g. $\partial^2 C/\partial S\, \partial\sigma$) and have esoteric names such as charm, colour, beauty, etc. Dividend sensitivity has come to be known as omega by some market practitioners.

1.2 HISTORICAL DEVELOPMENT

1.2.1 Listed Equity Derivatives

In considering *listed* equity derivatives (these are derivatives which are "listed" or controlled on a recognized exchange) we need to differentiate between those which are traded as contracts, such as futures and options on the FTSE 100 traded on the London LIFFE exchange, and those which are traded as securities and are either settled domestically or through settlement systems such as EuroClear and CEDEL, such as a FTSE 100 index covered warrant issued by an investment bank or a convertible bond issued by a corporation to raise working capital (e.g. The Burton Group $4\frac{3}{4}$% Convertible due 25/08/01).

The FTSE 100 futures and options type equity derivatives are termed exchanged traded contracts or ETCs and are subject to strict regulatory control, daily marking to market and margining on the basis of each counterpart's exposure. Each day payments have to be made to and from the exchange to maintain the financial cover for the risk on open positions. This margin flow consists of two types, initial margin, paid on each opening of a contract and variational margin, paid or received based on the new closing mark to market value of the open positions. The exchange is the counterpart to all contracts and acts as the guarantor of performance under the obligations entered into therein. In the case of options, with their asymmetric risk profile (i.e. the contract is a *right* to the holder and an *obligation* to the seller), only the option premium needs to be paid by the option buyer at the time of purchase. The holder of the option has no further obligations once the premium has been paid. These contracts on stock indices and individual shares are typically shorter dated futures and simple call and put options with standardized terms and conditions.

Since the exchange traded listed equity derivative, an options contract on an equity, was first traded in 1973 (on the Chicago Board Options Exchange), there has been a rapid expansion of exchanges and equity ETCs world-wide. It was in the 1980s that most of Europe gained ETCs on equity indices and increasingly on individual shares. In London in the mid-1980s, LIFFE listed the FTSE 100 futures, then in the early 1990s the FTSE 250. LTOM (the London traded option market, later merged with LIFFE in 1992) listed options on the FTSE 100 index, and by 1992 also listed options on approximately 80 individual equities, most of whom were components of the FTSE 100 index. This exchange was based on the Chicago pattern of pit trading "open outcry" as were the French exchanges called the MATIF (Marché à Terme International de France) and the MONEP (Marché des Options Negotiables de la Bourse de Paris) which lists the CAC 40 futures and options along with options on approximately 20 individual equities. Other exchanges followed, but not all followed the pattern of open outcry pit trading; the German DTB for example is a pure electronic market, where traders communicate only via an electronic data exchange and terminal. This system creates an electronic pit trading environment where bids can be hit and offers taken via a keyboard, mouse and VDU. The derivative contract terms themselves however remain essentially of the same form the world over. A similar system for after-hours trading in London, called the APT (Automated Pit Trading), also exists.

The pattern of derivatives exchanges being set up to trade listed future and options contracts on the major large capitalization index of the country's stock market has been one that has been repeated many times over the globe, from Australia's All-Ordinaries Index via Hong Kong's Hang-Seng index to Canada's TSE 35 index. This growth can be linked to several underlying factors in global capital markets:

1. Increasing global investment, diversifying home market portfolios to include overseas exposure so as to increase returns and reduce risk.

2. Significant outperformance of equity markets over fixed income in the 1980s, portfolio weightings therefore tilted more towards equity.

3. Structural changes in capital market regulation and the opening of new markets for investment lead to enhanced opportunities overseas, both in established markets such as Europe and also emerging markets in the Far East and South America.

4. The shift in investment management practices so as to reduce costs and comply with more onerous legislation means a greater emphasis on index tracking, tactical asset

allocation (between cash, equity and bonds; in some cases currency and commodity assets also) and the reduction in costs in trading the market portfolio (as represented by a large market capitalization, broadly based index) via the futures market rather than active management through individual stock selection. Stock selection in overseas markets is made expensive and difficult due to lack of data and non-standard accounting methods.

5. The development of portfolio enhancement techniques such as portfolio insurance, yield enhancement and volatility trading.

6. The explosion of "hedge" funds and other high risk/return collective investments.

7. The development of the over-the-counter derivatives market with the associated hedging needs of the investment banks to hedge their risk.

8. The management of credit risk in overseas investment through properly controlled and margined derivatives exchanges, most of which are based on the Chicago model.

These developments along with other factors have led to the rapid growth of exchange traded futures and options on equity stock indices and individual stocks.

Other forms of listed equity derivative exist, ones that are stock exchange listed securities rather than derivative contracts traded and settled on their own exchange. Most of this type of equity derivative are either *warrants* or *convertible bonds*. These types of financing have their origins in the early Eurobond market of the late 1960s and early 1970s. They became much more prevalent in the early to mid-1980s due to the major equity bull trend in global markets. The Japanese market in particular, up to the end of the 1980s, used debt issues with equity warrants attached and convertibles to finance the remarkable growth of the economy. The Japanese stock market contains one of the largest reservoirs of the types of listed equity derivatives detailed below:

• *Warrants* are essentially options on an underlying share or basket of shares or an equity index, which are listed as securities on an exchange. The warrants may be issued by the company upon whose shares the warrants are exercisable or by a third party, such as an investment bank. The warrants are generally of the call option type and in the case of company issued warrants, frequently lead to the issue of new shares on exercise giving rise to some dilution effects which are not present in warrants issued by third parties (e.g. stock index warrants issued by banks), or indeed in the case of exchange traded contracts. The dilution of the share price on issue of new shares can be calculated by considering the overall value of the company to be a constant at time of issue, plus the exercise premium of the warrants, so that the number of shares in issue multiplied by the share price before exercise is equal to the new total number of shares in issue times the "new" (i.e. diluted) share price plus the amount paid by the warrant holders to exercise their warrants. Dilution can have a large effect on option valuation if the total underlying size of the warrant issue is significant, say 10 per cent of total equity.

  Warrants are frequently issued by corporates alongside a bond issue as a way of encouraging investors to buy the issue (the so-called "Equity Kicker") and for accounting advantages due to the off balance sheet treatment of warrant obligations for tax and accounting purposes. These warrants would frequently be just out-of-the-money (i.e. with a strike price set 5 to 10 per cent above the current share price for each year of the life of the warrant). Not least they offer the funding opportunity of issuing something which will only become a "real" debt for the company if the share price performs well and the warrant holders exercise their rights. Clearly the company would be in a good position to cope with the obligation in those circumstances and would welcome the cash injection from the exercise premium. The buoyant share price would also tend to mitigate dilution effects.

Warrants are traded in a secondary, telephone market and are either settled through domestic arrangements or via EuroClear or CEDEL. This mechanism is very similar to the straight Eurobond market.

- *Convertible bonds (CBs)* are similar in some ways to a bond issue with attached (or "wedded") warrants, except that on exercise the whole bond is surrendered for a fixed number of shares without payment of exercise premium. The convertible bond therefore carries a coupon (annual interest payment) which is lower than a standard plain vanilla bond since the embedded equity option has to be paid for by the investor through reduced interest payments. Convertibles therefore have a hybrid characteristic of both debt and equity. When the underlying share price is low and the embedded equity option is deep out-of-the-money, the convertible bond has a price behaviour similar to a "straight" bond; with a high share price the CB has strong equity price characteristics. The convertible's exercise price is typically (for a five-year issue) set approximately 130 per cent above the spot price and convertibility is usually only available on specific anniversary dates. Company issued CBs do produce dilution as new shares are generally issued. The major benefits to the issuer are similar to warrants: reduced funding costs so long as the share price does not outperform, conversion of debt to equity if it does. Convertibles either trade in price like ordinary bonds, i.e. in percentage of face value (this is true of Euro Converts), or alternatively in absolute price as for French Domestic Convertibles.

More complex hybrid securities were created and listed, generally by investment banks in response to a particular client request. Particular examples are the index linked redemption bonds and the coupon linked redemption bonds, frequently linked to the Nikkei 225 index. These are often termed "structured notes", and can be issued under programmes of issuers such as Medium Term Notes (MTNs) or Euro Commercial Paper (ECP). The listing on a stock exchange is often a requirement for the investor as he is frequently operating under trustee constraints of the type of asset that may be held in a fund. The last five years have seen an increase of this type of bespoke derivative creation, frequently the whole issue is "privately placed" with one client and does not trade in a secondary market in the way a normal, widely distributed security would.

1.2.2 Unlisted or "Over-the-Counter" Equity Derivatives

The development of unlisted or over-the-counter equity derivatives is much harder to trace than the listed EDs since they are by their very nature private transactions between two counterparts. It is probably fair to say that apart from some purely matched transactions the development of OTC equity derivatives followed after the development of the interest rate swap market and stemmed from two main areas: the twin concepts of risk management of a portfolio of risk on an unmatched/active basis by the investment banking intermediary and the repackaging/creation of securities such as covered warrants and structured notes. Both of these ideas have their origins in the fixed income markets, the swap book coming from the back-to-back loan market which in turn was driven by exchange controls. Repackaging and creating securities to satisfy particular investor appetite became more feasible once the techniques of risk control and book running had been established, typified by the growth of asset swaps.

Some of the earliest OTC equity derivatives were options on indices embedded in interest rate swap contracts resulting from the creation of index linked bonds, in particular the Nikkei linked redemption bonds issued in the mid 1980s. These bonds were generally privately placed with Japanese life insurance companies and other institutional investors who effectively wrote long dated options on the index in order to earn an enhanced coupon (interest) on the Euroyen bond. Certain accounting standards in Japan, with regard to the tax treatment of capital gains and income, made this approach particularly attractive. Frequently this technique was also used by traditional fixed income investors to gain equity market exposure whilst not contravening trustee boundaries. These options were frequently repackaged and sold as securities in the form of warrants to European investors.

At this time portfolio insurance techniques using dynamic replication strategies by buying and selling futures contracts according to a notional delta became discredited due to the problem of liquidity at the crucial point of market breakdown. The desire of portfolio managers to buy custom protection to exact dates, strikes and in sufficient size to hedge realistic portfolios became much greater, particularly with funds which closely mimic the index portfolio. OTC index options began to be traded by portfolio managers, particularly out-of-the-money puts and "collar" trades (where put protection is financed by selling a call for a net zero premium).

The increase in the use of tactical asset allocation and greater overseas investment led to an interest in derivatives which allow the switching of equity returns for fixed income returns. The equity returns typically include dividend payments which are often subject to special taxation treatment, which can in some circumstances lead to a payment of more than 100 per cent of the gross dividend declared. These derivatives are called *equity swaps* and have become one of the most popular OTC equity derivatives.

Under certain circumstances an investor would wish to express a particular view of the market, but because of credit considerations, for example the investor wishes to sell options and does not have a credit rating, cannot do so via a pure OTC transaction. He may choose to implement it via a structured investment where a security in the form of a "note" or bond would be specially created with pay-off profiles which linked the payment of interest and/or the final redemption amount to the behaviour of some equity underlying. The OTC option would thus be embedded in the structure, the note structure removing the credit risk for the option buyer. The option is thus termed an *embeddo*. These are frequently known as *structured notes* or *equity linked notes* and became increasingly popular in the early 1990s.

In the next section we will look at the utility of equity derivatives for both investors and borrowers.

1.3 THE UTILITY OF EQUITY DERIVATIVES

In this section we will examine the specific aspects of equity derivatives which make them attractive to both investors and borrowers alike. It is the particular utility of the structures rather than the structures themselves that we examine, specific structural examples will be detailed in Sections 1.5 and 1.6.

1.3.1 The Evaluation of Risk and Return

One of the greatest advances made in mathematical finance was the work done on the evaluation of risk and return (Markowitz (1989)). Essentially statistical analysis of historical data of price evolution allows the mean and moments (usually just the first moment, the width of the distribution at FWHM, the standard deviation) of asset performance to be measured over a suitable time scale. Having corrected for the expected risk-free rate of return, a plot of risk and return can be created for different assets, this is the basis of the Capital Asset Pricing Model (CAPM). The problem arises however as to how stable these statistical measures of risk/return will be in the future, i.e. how good is their predictive power? Not surprisingly over relatively short time periods their predictive power is poor as assets tend to perform relative to business cycles, but improves over longer time horizons. At one end of the quantitative sophistication scale, quantitative tactical asset allocators may well use these data (along with the covariance matrix, which shows how returns on different assets are correlated) to decide the composition (weighting) of their portfolio so as to get their optimal risk/return ratio for the fund. At the other end of the quantitative sophistication spectrum an investor may decide that a particular individual equity looks cheap, as it has underperformed the market for reasons which do not seem to be justified. Both investors are making a value judgement as to the prospective risk/return ratio inherent in their investment. If they include cash as an asset within the portfolio they are effectively creating a replicating portfolio of the type discussed in the special Black–Scholes section earlier, with assumptions as to the prospective variability or volatility in the risky assets. They are in fact synthesizing an option-like pay-off, from which one can infer the implied volatility of the replicating portfolio. If options are available, their prices may be used to benchmark this investment strategy through the comparison of the implied volatility in the replicating portfolio and that implied in the options. The investor is thus clearly faced with a choice as to whether to replicate the desired risk/return portfolio on a prospective basis or to go with the guarantee of performance offered by the option, since purchase of the option effectively allows the investor to lock in the variability of returns at the start rather than suffer the possibility that the risk/return forecast is wrong. Clearly in a situation where the implied volatility of the option is below that of the portfolio, it would seem obvious to go with the guarantee offered by purchase of an option and to keep the balance of funds in risk-free assets. It is thus in this situation cheaper to buy rather than to attempt to replicate the desired pay-off profile. Derivatives can therefore have a great role to play in benchmarking all investment decisions since they offer the certainty of outcome at a price, the price of which may be perceived as rich or cheap to the investor's own analysis and therefore may alter their implementation strategy. This is the essence of the "make or buy" argument of derivatives.

1.3.2 Tax Efficiency

The essence of tax efficiency in derivatives usually comes from their ability to convert income to capital gains or vice versa and in their ability to alter the classification of the security as debt or equity. Thus a simple box spread structure in European options (long call, short put both at strike $K1$, long put, short call both strike at $K2$) which is entirely equivalent to a zero coupon bond may actually be taxed as capital gain rather than income in some tax jurisdictions. In the UK for example the zero bond is a deep discount security and is taxed as income. Clearly the trick with tax efficiency is to use corporate structures in differing tax domiciles, linked by derivatives contracts so that less tax is paid overall by the organization; the linkages are often via an investment bank which may have an active or passive role with respect to the tax authorities. The taxation of dividend income from equities is a good example as often a domestic company holding structure may well benefit from tax rebates which are dependent on having income in that tax state; in a few cases no income in that structure is needed to benefit from enhanced tax rebates compared with foreign investors. This has been particularly true for the German equity market. Dividend swaps or more simply equity swaps allow these dividends to be washed through shell companies. The French market dividend wash requires that the shell company has income to offset.

Conversion of debt interest to dividend payments can also attract significant tax benefits in some jurisdictions. In the United States payments (Watson, Farley and Williams (1994)) of interest on instruments that qualify as debt for tax purposes are deductible by the issuer. Payments of dividends on equity stocks are not deductible by the issuer, but corporate holders of equity are generally entitled to deduct a portion of the dividend from their income (typically 70 per cent of the dividend). This leads to various forms of hybrid instruments, many of which are designed not only to be treated as debt for tax purposes, but as equity for financial accounting, regulatory, or rating agency purposes.

There is also industry specific tax legislation which can be exploited using derivative products. In particular the tax treatment of life insurance policies and the contingent liabilities created under these can be used, via a derivative transaction, to lower the costs of longer-term equity investment, especially for the underwriting insurance companies.

1.3.3 Regulatory Efficiency

Regulators such as SEC (Securities Exchange Commission), SFA (Securities and Futures Association) and IMRO (Investment Management Regulatory Organization) apply capital adequacy rules based on "risk models" which seek to make an organization provide sufficient capital to support its liabilities in the case of extreme market movements or a credit default of a counterpart. These regulatory "hair-cuts" can be reduced by efficient hedging using derivatives and certain regulator treatments can be transformed via a derivative trade either to allow a particular strategy or to reduce its capital costs. In some cases a product has to be sold with a "guarantee" of performance, in which case an organization may well have to buy an option structure from a "AAA" (triple A) rated organization to embed in a product. An example might be the Business Expansion Scheme structures where the FTSE index performance is provided by an option bought from a third party, highly rated bank. Other examples include the guaranteed minimum performance bonds issued by various building societies, where a minimum rate of interest is guaranteed plus some upside in the equity market. Frequently a regulator may demand that a very small risk within a product or investment strategy be bought in from a third party in much the same way that the reinsurance market takes on board the very low probability, high cost risks of the insurance market.

Another area in which derivatives have a part to play in regulatory efficiency is in the process of mergers and acquisitions (M&A) of companies. Takeovers of companies are governed by legislation and controlled by groups such as the Panel for Takeovers and Mergers (POTAM) in the UK. There exist trigger levels of *direct* equity ownership which set in train a sequence of events by law, such that a company acquiring say 15 per cent of the total equity of a company is forced either to complete a takeover within a time period or alternatively to back-off for a period of time during which no more shares may be bought or sold. Derivatives can be used in these situations to ensure that the total price paid for the acquisition of the company is hedged via option contracts without direct acquisition of shares which would trigger the M&A rules and thus force through the acquisition in a time scale not necessarily of the buyer's choice. Derivatives allow the company to exercise control over the price of the purchase of the target without triggering the takeover rules and thus forcing the bidder's hand.

For pension and mutual funds, derivatives frequently allow regulatory constraints on investments to be met or circumvented. These constraints can be in the generation of a minimum return or a maximum amount of overseas investment or a minimum amount of the fund to be invested in government bonds. Such regulations exist for funds in countries as diverse as Canada, the Netherlands and Japan.

1.3.4 Leverage

Leverage or the ability to gear up or multiply the risk exposure within an investment strategy is probably one of the best known aspects of derivatives products. It is perfectly possible to buy an option for 20 units, have cash of 80 units and still have the same price exposure to an asset as if one had spent 100 units buying the asset. In this case with 100 units one can gear the investment five times since each one times exposure costs only 20 units. Clearly this is risky as one is five times more likely to win or lose a certain amount of return. The point is that derivative products offer choice as to just how risky or not an investment strategy is when one wishes to implement a position. Again one can replicate this leveraged portfolio effect, but the derivative offers a guarantee of pay-off which may in fact be cheaper due to the different financing rates, the costs and difficulty of shorting stock and the overall level of volatility available for purchase in the market.

1.3.5 Implementation of Specific Investment Views

One of the greatest utilities of derivatives is their ability to bundle and unbundle risks. This means that specific investment ideas can be implemented very cleanly without gaining unwanted exposure or losing an exposure which was actually desired. A good example is where an investor may wish to have an equity exposure within an economy, say for example the US stock market, without necessarily having direct exposure to the US dollar. Currency protected options, forwards and futures allow the exposure without the currency risk. The derivative contract is also generally time bounded and so allows an investor to specify a time horizon for his view which is generally not available in traditional equity investment. In general the more specific the risk profile the smaller the risk/return space, with generally a decrease in the overall cost of implementation.

1.3.6 Efficiency and Cost Effectiveness

The efficiency and cost effectiveness of derivatives stems from the ability to trade individual aspects of risk rather than a bundled product, thus an entire portfolio of equities need not be completely liquidated and new stocks bought just to change an aspect of the risk profile. For example if a portfolio is to be made market neutral, selling index futures is much cheaper than selling the individual equities wholesale and then having to buy them back two weeks later. The bid/offer in the futures market for the round turn may be

50 b.p., whereas selling and buying the entire portfolio may well cost 150 b.p. plus taxes such as stamp duty. Particularly in the case of futures markets, the liquidity available frequently outstrips the cash market and makes trades in the market (index) portfolio cheaper than specific, tilted portfolios. The particular bespoke terms of the OTC derivatives contract allow great efficiency in isolating the particular aspect of the risk/return space required by the investor or borrower to suit their views.

The greater liquidity which the futures markets offer over the cash market means that investment strategies can frequently be implemented more speedily and cheaply via a derivatives trade such as a buy or sell programme trade or by staged use of futures and options over a cash flow cycle to manage the liquidity of funds which have investor cash flows over a time period.

One further aspect of OTC derivatives over their exchange traded counterparts is the credit element. As mentioned above the ETCs require margin and maintenance of that margin via a daily mark-to-market process operated by the exchange. If the counterparts are deemed creditworthy by each other they may well buy or sell contracts on the basis of credit, effectively lending or borrowing a sum of money, the interest and/or the principal redemption of which is linked to an equity index, a basket of equity or even a single stock. This is then just an extension of traditional banking business of borrowing and lending money if the equity risk can be effectively hedged. Frequently the returns on this kind of lending are much higher than the traditional business lines and represent one of the main motivations for well-capitalized banks to enter the derivatives markets. For many organizations, it greatly enhances their efficiency if they can finance on credit terms rather than drain working capital from the business where it will be earning higher returns than the interest cost on the bank financing.

For the non-banking counterpart the lack of daily margining of ETCs which OTCs offer considerably simplifies the cash management and administration of derivative positions, which for even simple ETC positions require daily administration.

1.3.7 The Utility of Equity Derivatives for Borrowers

All borrowers are interested in generating funding for the right term at the lowest possible cost. They are also interested in creating, expanding and maintaining a solid secondary market in their paper as this ensures a good market to tap further in the future and may well reduce borrowing costs if managed well, as investors will lower their expected risk premiums if they perceive that it is easier to trade the debts. Derivatives can help in two main ways:

1. The creation of a security with characteristics of particular interest and therefore value to investors which are therefore popular issues and may also attract classes of new investors.

2. The embedded equity option and/or forward elements in the security may well be sold or bought at a price which when hedged out by the derivative provider may provide a subsidy to the issue and thus give cheaper funding. This technique is frequently called volatility arbitrage or forward arbitrage.

The embedding of an option in a security can allow the investor either to buy or to sell volatility on the underlying asset, which opens up exciting possibilities for investors who may not have a direct method of writing options. A recent example of securities of this type has been the boosted coupon note where the investor effectively sells strips of binary options on an equity index for which they receive an enhanced coupon for the number of days during which the index stays within a certain range or "corridor".

Frequently the price of these embedded options in volatility terms and the implied forward interest rates (the effective discount rates for future coupons derived from the yield curve) are fixed at levels which do allow a subsidy to the issue. The whole "wrap" on these securities means that the individual components of the structured note are difficult to separate and price separately, thus making it harder for the investor to truly identify its value. This does not mean that they necessarily represent bad value, but it must be recognized that the structure has a cost of production which must be covered and the investor must be convinced of the correctness of the view embedded in the note.

1.4 THE ROLE OF THE INVESTMENT BANK IN THE CREATION OF EQUITY DERIVATIVES

Investment banks play a key role in the derivative industry, particularly in the creation of new or repackaged securities and as the creators and primary sellers of OTC derivatives contracts. Clearly theirs is a business enterprise driven by the desire to secure profits from this trade, but also clearly they have a duty and a desire to help all elements involved in the trade, both borrowers and investors, to achieve better results since this is the only way that the bank will truly prosper and survive. As mentioned in the introduction, if derivatives did not help business they would not survive, and yet they prosper. Their prosperity is due in no small part to the role of the investment banks and in particular their contribution in the four main areas of Capital, Credit, Risk Aggregation and Technology.

1.4.1 Capital

In creating and hedging OTC derivative transactions the regulatory authorities (such as the Bank of England, the SFA, the Federal Reserve Board, the SEC) require that the participating institution has sufficient capital to meet its obligations in the event of market movement or credit default by one of its counterparts. In the most sophisticated analysis, valuation models and market movement scenarios are used to establish potential losses, the magnitude of these losses determines the amount of capital (in the form of equity and near equity such as subordinated debt) that the institution must have to support its business. The capital requirement is frequently divided into two parts: one is the price risk requirement (market movement) and the other is the credit risk requirement (default of a debtor). These models along with the capital available determine the size of portfolios of derivative positions that can be sustained subject to regulatory approval and licensing. Thus the effective gearing of the balance sheet is determined by how well risks are offset within the models and how small in magnitude the movements in the scenario analysis are, since these ultimately determine the capital usage. The goal of the investment bank is to maximize its return on its capital whilst minimizing the variance (risk) of the profits; it is therefore in its best interest to use all of its capital in very well-hedged, high margin derivatives trades, where the balance sheet leverage is as high as possible without exceeding its regulatory capital requirements.

1.4.2 Credit

The traditional role of banking institutions is the lending of money for term against taking deposits for sight or short-term money. Lending money without collateral is effectively a question of credit and credit risk. Derivative transactions of all kinds can be used to lend money indirectly and thus establish a credit relationship with the counterparty on which a return is earned for the "credit risk". The advantage of derivatives is however that generally a much bigger margin for credit can be achieved than on simple lending business since ostensibly smaller margins on individual trades are more than compensated by the higher volume of trades available for the same capital usage. The banks provide a network of creditworthy institutions through which netting and credit control is effected.

1.4.3 Risk Aggregation

The two main forms of value risk in derivative portfolios are the price movement risk and credit default risk. The network of creditworthy institutions provides hubs of a multi-hub network of transactions with credit default risk. This risk is either bilateral, as in the case of swaps, or asymmetric, as in the case of normal, premium up-front options. The banks provide a valuable service in risk aggregation whereby risks of these types can be offset by running a portfolio of positions which offset in price risk so that only a small portion of the risk, known as the residual, needs to be actively managed. Credit risk is managed by attempting to write business which offsets exposure and via netting agreements (such as the ISDA master) so that payments due to a defaulting counterpart can be offset against those owed in the event of default. In some cases margin or collateral agreements are put in place. The net effect of risk aggregation is to reduce the overall risk in writing business and thus ultimately leads to a lower overall cost and helps to safeguard the banking system.

1.4.4 Technology

The role that technology has to play in the business of derivatives cannot be overstated. The technology, both hardware and software and the mathematics behind them, is essential to the valuation, risk analysis and portfolio evaluation needed in running derivative positions. The risk manager needs real time position analysis to keep him or her informed as to the current risk being run. The trader needs rapid access to pricing models and the parameters such as interest rates, dividend forecasts and estimates of volatility in order to respond to pricing requests from clients. Capital adequacy models along with scenario analysis need to be run every day so that capital adequacy regulations can be observed and reported. This modelling requires enormous processing since it models the performance of non-linear portfolios in many dimensions (such as price movement, interest rate movement, changes in correlation, etc.) and may frequently take hours for a very complex and large portfolio.

Requests from clients for new solutions to problems demand a lot from the product development teams who frequently have to go back to first principles to gain a solution method. Sometimes these may be analytic, but most of the time a numerical solution to the partial differential equations (PDEs) is required (Wilmott, Dewynne and Howison (1994)). Often industry standard library routines such as the NAG (Numerical Algorithms Group) library are used to find the fastest and most efficient solutions. These techniques are generally of the finite difference type. For more complex, higher dimensional problems the Monte Carlo techniques are favoured. Monte Carlo is frequently used to provide independent pricing verification through replication of the hedge portfolio of the derivative in a dynamic simulation. These simulation techniques are particularly heavy on computation time since they depend on a large number of iterations for accuracy.

1.5 INDEX PRODUCTS

In this section we shall look at some of the equity derivatives structures in use today. Most of these structures are based on a stock index, although in theory the underlying is not restricted to these; in practice it may be due to liquidity and hedging considerations. The great advantage of most index products is the general availability of extremely liquid exchange traded futures (frequently trading on a bid/offer spread a fraction of that in the cash equities markets) and options for the construction of efficient hedges.

1.5.1 Exchange Traded Equity Derivatives

There has been an explosive growth of exchange traded listed equity derivative index products around the world. Usually the underlying stock index is a broadly based, capitalization weighted index, the components of which are reviewed periodically by committees and adjusted, often on a quarterly or annual basis (one major exception being the Nikkei 225 index which is a simple average of prices). The typical index of this kind is the $S + P$ 500, an index which represents a very large part of the entire US equity market, which is a capitalization weighted index of the largest 500 stocks in the US. Listed futures and options exist on this index as do user specified contracts, called "FLEX" options, which are a kind of exchange cleared OTC option. The index and therefore the derivatives on it are used for a range of investment and hedging techniques including index tracking where the use of futures avoids the problems of rebalancing the tracking portfolio as equity weightings change over time. Using futures to track indices has become a very important investment technique owing to its unambiguous performance criteria and low costs and one that has brought much greater liquidity to the futures market itself. Buying and selling a tracking portfolio against the mispriced stock index futures as an arbitrage is also a very popular low risk trading strategy.

The holder or buyer of the futures contract purchases an obligation at a price for the forward purchase of the index, in the case of the $S + P$ 500 in units of the index level multiplied by USD 500. The correct arbitrage price for the future is determined by arbitrage arguments and is equal to the net cost of carry (funding costs less dividends received) of the equivalent index portfolio for the life of the futures contract. The futures contracts are marked-to-market daily by the exchange and a margin cash flow occurs which is equal to the purchase price plus or minus the new settlement price (depending on whether the position is making money or not). This daily cash flow derived from the mark-to-market process is the essential difference between an exchange traded futures contract and a forward contract. The expiry cycles of the futures contract are typically March, June, September and December and contracts may trade out to maturities of two years, although usually liquidity is poor in the back months.

ETC option contracts are usually restricted to simple calls and puts on the index, or in some cases the settlement is in futures contracts rather than being cash settled against the index level at expiry in the same way as the futures contracts. Any variety of option type is generally restricted to the choice of American or European exercise and the expiry cycle is usually like the futures contract with perhaps the addition of contracts on all four nearest months to the spot date.

Investors use ETC futures and options for a range of uses:

1. Hedging downside movement in price by buying puts. This has largely replaced the old replication strategy of portfolio insurance which has been discredited. OTC options are also used for larger trades and to longer time horizons.

2. "Collar" trades whereby downside put protection is purchased by selling an out-of-the-money call. This has the effect of limiting upside gains in reward for limited downside.

3. Yield enhancement of the portfolio by selling out of the money call options.

4. Creating leveraged trading positions to take advantage of market direction movements, sometimes known as "geared futures and options funds".

5. Creating positions in volatility which are market neutral so as to take advantage of changes in the level of volatility.

6. In some markets, for example Germany, the overseas investor may get an enhanced dividend yield through holding deep in the money call options (or futures) over the dividend period rather than actual equity as the derivative will trade at an implied dividend somewhere between the overseas investor rate of 85 per cent and the domestic rate of 156 per cent of announced dividends. It will therefore be cheaper to hold exposure to the market via the derivative over the dividend period rather than the stock.

7. In a takeover situation, a bidder would be able to hedge his overall market risk (systematic) via index products whilst retaining the specific risk of the target company via its shareholding.

8. Index tracking portfolios can use the futures market to manage the regular cash inflow from investors by buying the market via futures in anticipation of full cash investment later. A switch from futures to cash stocks can then be effected at one price, this price is dependent on the futures basis and market liquidity at the time. This switching is known as an "EFP" or exchange for physical.

9. The natural extension of the EFP trade is a programme or portfolio trade where the portfolio is no longer the exact market portfolio but one containing different weightings or "tilts". The price of the programme is the estimate of the unwinding costs of the position against the index futures in the current market conditions. These programmes can be conducted as principal (the bank takes on the risk at a pre-agreed price) or agency (where the execution is best efforts and the fees are commissions plus an incentive fee based on a threshold price for the all-in cost).

10. Global futures markets allow very rapid and cheap deployment of funds in tactical asset allocation since they frequently operate on narrower bid/offers than the cash market and do not require full investment at the time of purchase. This also provides a very efficient method of tracking world indices and switching weighting between countries. When switching weightings between equity and fixed income the greater liquidity of futures provides cost savings.

1.5.2 Over-the-Counter Traded Equity Derivatives

The great advantages of the OTC equity derivative are its complete flexibility as to specification and the ability to operate on a credit basis rather than margin. In general all the features of ETCs can be obtained in OTCs and they can be used as described in the above section. This includes OTC forwards and strips of OTC forwards which are known as equity swaps. However their advantages over the ETCs are bespoke terms and conditions, longer maturities if required and enhanced liquidity which may be offered by a single counterpart handling the whole trade. Moreover many special option types are available OTC which are not available as ETCs. These exotic option types (many of which will be described in more detail in later chapters) such as path dependent options (e.g. barrier options which appear or disappear when the market level crosses the barrier strike), options on more than one asset (e.g. best of two stocks) and options which protect returns in an equity market in a currency not native to that equity market are available over the counter. Not all exotic options are particularly useful with the equity underlying as each asset class has its own unique set of problems. For example the Asian or average rate option is extremely useful in the context of foreign exchange since it mimics the nature of foreign cash flows as they may occur in a business enterprise, e.g. they average exchange rates over a period of, say, three months or a year. So far Asian options have seen little practical interest in the equity sphere, although they are beginning to be incorporated as part of an averaging in and averaging out process in collective investment funds. A brief description of the different kinds of exotic option is given below:

- *Path dependent options* (the value of pay-off is dependent on how the underlying market reaches its final value on the expiry date) include:
  - *Asian* (average strike or average price). Pay-off is the difference between a constant and the arithmetic average of the index.
  - *Lookback* (price lookback or strike lookback). Pay-off is the difference between a constant and the high or low of the asset price over the life of the option.
  - *Delayed strike*. Normal option once the strike price has been set, typically set as an at-the-money option in say one month's time.
  - *Resetting strike*. The option strike price is periodically set to a fixed percentage of the then current market level, freezing the pay-off from the previous period. Known as cliquet or "ratchet" option in France.
  - *Barrier* (up and out, up and in, down and out, down and in). Options which appear or disappear at certain market levels.
  - *Binary* (digital or bet option). Options which pay a fixed amount of money or an amount of an asset and depend on whether the option is in the money or not.

- *MultiAsset* (pay-offs depend on the price performance of more than one risky asset):
  - *Outperformance*. Pay-off is the difference in price of two or more assets.
  - *Best of*. Pay-off is the best performance of one of two or more assets.

- *Currency linked* (pay-offs have an element of risk linked to a FOREX rate):
  - *Quanto* (fixed exchange rate). Pay-off in foreign index has fixed exchange rate in home currency.
  - *Cross option*. Pay-off is the foreign index expressed as a fixed point value in home currency.

- *Compound options.* Options on options, e.g. one month call into a one year put.
- *Special indices.* Options on hybrid indices like the FT World with embedded currency linkage via the index composition.

Equity swaps are bilateral contracts whereby two counterparts are joined so that one party pays an equity index return (either price movement with or without the actual dividends over the period) whilst the other pays a money market return such as a three-month Libor. Depending on the movement of the price index during the period (usually three months) the payment on the equity leg may be either positive or negative. An equity swap can be viewed very simply as counterpart A running an index portfolio on behalf of counterpart B; counterpart A lends B the capital to maintain the position at a rate of interest that B pays to A every quarter. A then buys and maintains the index portfolio. Each quarter any profits are passed from A to B, and losses have to be made good by payment from B to A. The life of an equity swap can range from three months up to about five years and sometimes longer. By swapping the cash flows the currency of returns can be changed, with suitable adjustment to the rates. Indeed both legs of the swap can be pure equity return, e.g. pay FTSE receive S + P 500.

Consider a one-year (four quarterly periods) equity swap on the S + P 500 index versus three-month USD Libor, on a notional amount of USD 10 million. The notional amount is fixed throughout. The starting index level is 100 and three-month USD Libor is 10 per cent at the start. Libor is set in advance and paid in arrears. Counterpart A pays the equity return and receives the money market return from counterpart B. There are no dividends. The cash flows would be as below (in USD):

End of	Index	USD 3m Libor	Party A Pays	Party B Pays	Cash Flow
Q1	110	11%	1,000,000	250,000	750,000
Q2	105	8%	−454,454	275,000	−179,454
Q3	115	9%	952,381	200,000	1,152,381
Q4	120	10%	434,783	225,000	659,783

1.5.3 Hybrid Equity Derivatives

Hybrid products are frequently securities which combine an equity derivative with a bond structure to achieve a specific goal as an investment strategy to a particular target market. Below we describe some of the features of more popular hybrid equity derivatives.

(i) Redemption Linked Bond

This is a coupon bond structure where the total redemption amount (the amount due to the investor at maturity), usually 100 per cent of face, is linked via the sale of an option spread to an equity pay-off. As a result the bond has a boosted coupon due to the premium received for the option spread. Consider a two-year bond with annual coupons of 10 per cent. If the investor chooses to sell a 100 per cent–80 per cent two-year put spread (short the at-the-money option) (100 per cent strike) and long the 20 per cent out-of-the-money option (80 per cent strike) for 10 per cent premium, this will boost the coupon on the bond by approximately 5 per cent per year (ignoring compounding). The downside for the investor is of course that he may end up only receiving 80 per cent of his original investment. If he sells two times the spread, he can boost the coupon to 20 per cent per annum but may lose 40 per cent of his investment at maturity. Clearly this strategy can be geared up to five times at which point total loss of principal at maturity is possible. Similar structures can also be constructed using the cash flows of the coupons to produce a coupon linked structure.

(ii) Equity Linked CDs

CDs are tradable bank debts called certificates of deposit. Generally these trade as zero coupon bonds, the interest element being the difference between the issue price and the final redemption price (usually 100 per cent). If the redemption amount of the CDs is made a function of a stock index price by selling or buying option spreads on an equity index, the pay-off amounts can be greater than or less than 100 per cent dependent on the final level of the index. This is attractive as in certain circumstances the equity return can be treated as debt interest payments for tax purposes. When these structures are issued by corporates as notes and not CDs they are frequently known by a wide variety of names such as PINS (Protected Index Notes) or PERCs (Protected Equity Return Certificates).

(iii) Business Expansion Scheme (BES) Structures

In the UK the government allowed special tax relief at the highest rate to investors in qualifying Business Expansion Schemes for investment in start-up businesses in which the minimum investment term is five years. Several schemes were evolved whereby a guaranteed exit price was obtained via a bank guarantee on a property portfolio. As an alternative to receiving a fixed return over the life of the BES some companies offered structures linked to the FTSE index which offered a locking feature whereby if the FTSE index crosses certain price levels during the five-year period these are locked in and paid at the end. These embedded options are forms of barrier options. The minimum return of the original investment is guaranteed, the interest element thus funds the purchase of the embedded option.

(iv) Cliquets in PEA Structures

The French government introduced tax legislation which allowed tax-free investment over a period greater than eight years. This has led to the creation of structured investments which accumulate returns over an eight-year period. These are known as PEAs (Plan d'Epargne en Actions). Unlike traditional cash based PEAs, these specialist derivative structures use zero coupon bonds to guarantee principal return whilst capturing CAC 40 index growth — and storing it away for the requisite eight years — by using various combinations of conventional, "cliquet" and "lock-in " calls. (Cliquet, or ratchet, options capture growth periodically, perhaps slicing the time series annually, whilst lock-ins capture specific levels of performance; for example, lock-in "rungs" may be set at plus 10 per cent, plus 20 per cent and plus 30 per cent growth.)

1.6 SINGLE STOCKS, BESPOKE INDEX PRODUCTS

Many stock index structures described above can be applied to single stock products. The major demand for single stock equity derivatives is for equity linked redemption bonds or "convertibles", particularly in stocks where there is no company issued paper. As discussed previously there are frequently tax advantages in these structures as they mix equity and debt. Notes can be created which allow the investor the choice as to whether he is long or short gamma (long or short options) in the underlying corporate of his choice via this security.

Mergers and acquisitions can give rise to the need for a bidding corporation either to hedge their overall market exposure with respect to their ownership of target shares, or more specifically, to hedge themselves against further price increases in the stock by buying out of the money call options prior to launching the bid. This area of using equity derivatives in corporate finance applications is increasing as knowledge of what can be done legally develops.

As well as single stocks, small baskets of specific stocks may be of use as a derivative underlying in certain circumstances. One example is the hedging of a portfolio of mortgages against default by the borrowers, this is a particular problem since the housing market for repossessed property is poor and represents an inferior way of guaranteeing the value of the investment. One method around this problem is to construct an index from property stocks and purchase a put option on that specific underlying. Thus a poor mortgage environment leads to poor performance by the property sector stocks and hence an increase in value of the hedge.

1.7 FUTURE DEVELOPMENT FOR EQUITY DERIVATIVES

The key feature of derivatives is their role as risk management building blocks in their ability to bundle and unbundle risk. As more investors and borrowers become aware of this capability the growth of volume in exchange traded contracts is inevitable as the volume of global capital flows increases. Enhanced and standardized reporting and accountancy standards across the world will lead to greater uniformity in assessment of risk and returns and therefore a greater proportion of investment will shift to more global equity investment. Increasingly borrowers will capitalize on the ability to lower funding cost by participating in producing structured equity investment to the specific requirements of the investors. Derivatives will play a leading role in opening up new markets since they are capable of removing unwanted risks from early investment. In mainstream investment the drive to lower costs and to justify investment techniques and goals will lead to a much greater emphasis on indexation and other quantitative methods which will naturally lead to a greater use of derivatives, although perhaps principally only via ETCs rather than OTCs.

Packaged investments with guaranteed minimum returns and locking-in returns on a periodic basis, especially when currency protected, will become an increasingly popular way of investment for the smaller investor, especially if encouraged via government legislation for tax shelters such as PEPs (personal equity plans) in the UK and PEA in France. These products are increasingly being marketed by banks, building societies and other financial institutions.

Structural differences between the tax and regulatory treatment of investments in different domiciles will probably remain for a long time to come and derivatives will continue their role as the primary technique for their exploitation and arbitrage.

The growth and increasing diversity of equity derivatives would seem to be assured for the future as they are not so much individual products but a set of techniques and innovative approaches to real world investment and borrowing goals.

1.8 GLOSSARY OF TERMS

Avoir Fiscal   French domestic holders of cash equity receive an enhanced dividend payment from the state as "holders of physical" shares.

Barrier   Derivative contracts can have appearing or disappearing features which are triggered by the market price crossing the barrier level.

Basis (as in Futures "Basis")   The difference in price between the price of the futures contract and the underlying deliverable.

Borrower   The issuer of debt/equity securities who takes investors' money for use in his business.

Box Spread   Option structure equivalent to a zero coupon bond. Long the market at strike K1, short the market at strike K2 via calls and puts with the same expiry. Value is the present value of K1 minus K2.

Broker   Financial intermediary who introduces two counterparts with an interest in dealing.

Calculation Agent   Third party responsible for ensuring the correct calculation of payments for derivatives contracts at settlement.

Call Option   The holder has the right but not the obligation to buy the underlying asset at the strike price K. The writer assumes an obligation in return for payment of premium. The terminal value at expiry is $\mathrm{Max}(S - K, 0)$.

Capital Guarantee Structure   Investment structure usually linked to an equity underlying, where the terminal value has a guaranteed minimum value. Usually achieved by zero coupon bonds and option spreads.

Cash Basket   A portfolio of shares which is a round lot, for example the index portfolio which can be arbitraged against the stock index futures.

Confirmation   Written confirmation of a deal containing details of the agreement, usually a telex.

Convertible Bond   A bond with an embedded option to exchange the bond for a fixed number of underlying shares. Carries a coupon below the market rate to pay for the option.

Corridor Option   Option composed of strips of binary options (cash or nothing) which pays a fixed amount of money for each period that the market is between two values. Sometimes called "boosts".

Debt   Usually in the form of a security, i.e. a bond. The borrowing of money.

Definitive Note   A physical piece of paper representing an obligation which can be physically delivered.

Dividend   Payment to shareholders as return for investment in the corporation.

Equity   A share in the ownership of a company. Usually carries the right to vote at meetings and a share in the dividends.

Equity Derivative   Derivative based on an equity underlying asset.

Equity Linked CD   Tradable bank loan (certificate of deposit) with redemption linked to an equity underlying.

Equity Swap   A bilateral agreement whereby one counterpart agrees to pay an equity return in payment for a money market return, e.g. pay FTSE plus dividends, receive three-month sterling Libor.

EuroClear/CEDEL   Centralized clearing houses for the settlement of Eurobond securities business. Securities accounts are operated like bank accounts on behalf of members.

Exchange Traded Option   Option traded on a derivatives exchange with centralized settlement and margining.

Expiry   The termination time of a derivatives contract, usually when the final pay-off value is calculated and paid.

Forward   Agreement to buy or sell a commodity at some point in the future at a price agreed today. Different from a future as it is not margined and therefore has a greater credit risk.

Forward/Forward   Agreement for the purchase or sale of an underlying in the future agreed for a delayed start date. For example, an interest rate agreement to borrow three-month money in three months time, known as an FRA (forward rate agreement), the interest rate is known as the three-month/three-month forward/forward rate.

Futures Roll   Buying or selling the near month futures contract in favour of the next period futures contract. Rolls the position out to longer maturities.

Global Note   The representation of the obligation under a security held as a single piece of paper against which holdings are matched at EuroClear and CEDEL. If held under a global note the securities cannot be issued in bearer form.

Interest Rate Swap (IRS)   Bilateral agreement to exchange cash flows one leg of which is a fixed coupon, the other leg of which is a floating reference index, e.g. three-month Libor.

Intermediary   A counterparty which stands between two other counterparts, usually to enhance credit quality.

Investor   Counterpart who has long assets and is looking to earn a return by investment.

ISDA   International Swap Dealers Association. Professional body of market participants with responsibility for increasing the overall efficiency of the business by standardization of agreements, etc.

Jelly Roll   Synthetic futures roll using options.

Knock-out Option   Option which disappears, usually worthless, when a barrier price level of the underlying market is breached.

Leverage   The use of derivatives to generate a market exposure greater than one, so that small market movements can produce very large p + l swings.

Listed Option   Option contract standardized and traded on a derivatives exchange.

Listing   The creation of a security by following stock exchange rules. The security is then included in the official list with closing prices.

Margin (as in profit and initial and variational margin)   Profit margin is the amount of money left after costs have been covered. Initial margin is an amount of money paid on opening a position in an ETC. Variational margin is the amount of money to be paid or received as a result of the daily mark to market of the open ETCs.

Mark-to-Market   The process of evaluating positions at the prevailing market prices to establish p + l and also margin calls.

Master Document   A legal document where general terms and conditions are agreed.

Maturity   The time period of the life of the derivatives contract.

Mezzanine Finance   Intermediate funding which has characteristics midway between debt and equity. Convertible bonds are an example.

Notional   The underlying size of the deal. The notional value determines the point value of the derivatives pay-off. For example, GBP 10 million notional, strike price of 100, gives a point value of GBP 100,000 per point.

Novation   The mechanism whereby one counterpart to an OTC agreement is changed to another counterpart, so that all other terms and conditions remain the same.

One-off Agreement   A single one-off contract to document a deal rather than as a series of deals under a master agreement.

Option   The right to the holder and an obligation to the seller of a contract either to buy (call) or sell (put) an underlying asset at a fixed price for a premium.

OTC Option   Option traded by private treaty between two counterparts.

Par Bond/Swap   A bond or an interest rate swap whose coupon is equal to the current yield to maturity and therefore has a price equal to 100 per cent for the bond and zero for the IRS. Sometimes known as on-the-run.

Path Dependent Option   Derivatives contract whose final value is dependent on how the market behaved prior to expiry.

Principal   A counterpart to an OTC agreement. The amount of money invested, see also Notional.

Put   The right to sell for the holder and the obligation to buy for the writer at a strike price K for the payment of a premium.

Reference Bank   A bank used to establish a fair price to calculate settlement values for derivative contracts.

Risk Management   The process of establishing the type and magnitude of risk in a business enterprise and using derivatives to control and shape that risk to maximize the business objective.

Screen Price   The price indicated on the dealer screen such as Reuters or Telerate.

SEC (Securities Exchanges Commission)   US official body charged with regulation of many financial products in the US.

Securitization   The conversion of an asset into a tradeable security, e.g. a mortgage portfolio transformed into a mortgage backed security (MBS).

Security   A tradeable obligation, usually listed on an exchange.

SFA (Securities and Futures Authority)   UK regulatory body responsible for overseeing a large portion of the derivatives business in the UK.

Spot   The price for immediate delivery of an asset. The shortest delivery period.

Strike Price   The price at which the underlying is bought or sold in an options contract.

Structured Note   Note or bond with pay-off characteristics linked to an equity underlying. A tailor-made investment.

Swapped Deltas   When a option deal is struck, the counterpart may agree to transfer the delta amount of underlying as a hedge for the option; this is swapping deltas.

Unwind   The reversal of an existing contract.

Volatility   The standard deviation of the natural logarithm of the price returns of an asset. The probability factor used in option valuation to determine the range of the random walk of the price process.

Warrant   A security which can be traded and has very similar characteristics to options. Usually longer dated and may be on indices or single stocks.

Zero Coupon Bond (or "Zero")   An obligation which contains only an initial and final cash flow. There are no intermediate cash flows or coupons. Useful as no assumptions have to be made as to the rate at which coupons are reinvested. Frequently used to guarantee a minimum value at maturity in a capital guaranteed product.

1.9 REFERENCES

Bookstaber, R.M. (1991) *Option Pricing and Investment Strategies*. London: McGraw-Hill.
Courtney, D. (1992) *Derivatives Trading in Europe*. London: Butterworths.
Cox, J.C. and Rubinstein, M. (1985) *Options Markets*. New Jersey: Prentice-Hall.

Das, S. (1989) *Swap Financing*. London: IFR Publishing.

Fabozzi, F.J. and Fabozzi, T.D. (1995) *The Handbook of Fixed Income Securities* (4th ed.). New York: Irwin.

Haugen, R.A. (1990) *Modern Investment Theory*. New Jersey: Prentice-Hall.

Hull, J.C. (1993) *Options, Futures, and other Derivative Securities* (2nd ed.). New Jersey: Prentice-Hall.

Hull, J. and White, A. (1991) "Pricing and Hedging Interest-rate Options". Proceeding of the conference, 5–6 September.

Inside The Swap Market (3rd ed.) (1988). London: IFR Books, IFR Publishing Limited.

ISDA Master Agreement, Definitions and Terms (1991, 1993). New York: International Swap Dealers Association Inc.

Markowitz, H.M. (1989) *Mean-Variance Analysis in Portfolio Choice and Capital Markets*. Oxford: Basil Blackwell.

Street, A.M. and Gommo, R.N. (1994) *The Mitsubishi Finance Risk Directory 1995*. London: *Risk Magazine*.

Watson, J. (ed.) (1993) *The Intercapital Equity Derivatives Handbook*. London: Euromoney Books.

Watson, Farley and Williams (Solicitors) (1994) "The US Taxation of Global Derivatives Trading and Hybrid Securities" Private communication.

Wilmott, P., Dewynne, J. and Howison, S. (1994) *Option Pricing: Mathematical Models and Computation*. Oxford: Oxford Financial Press.

2
Interest Rate Option Models:
A Critical Survey

2.1 INTRODUCTION AND OUTLINE OF THE CHAPTER

In every review of the interest rates derivatives markets it appears to be *de rigueur* to present a table, or the ubiquitous bar chart, displaying the exponential-like growth of this type of product in terms of underlying notional, outstanding deals, or some other measure of volume. The correctness of these statistics and the importance of these measures are undeniable; even more significant, however, has been the *qualitative* change in the type of options which have recently begun to be actively traded in the OTC markets.

If one chooses, in fact, to describe as "first generation" those options for which the Black model provides a closed-form solution (caps, floors and swaptions), path dependent and barrier options can be reasonably regarded as "second-" and "third-generation" instruments, respectively. These options have been traded more and more frequently, and in ever increasing volumes, either as self-standing instruments (e.g. knock-out caps), or embedded in swaps or structured notes (e.g. indexed-principal swaps or one-way floaters). In either case they have introduced a whole new dimension to the pricing of options dependent on interest rates. On the one hand, they have required the introduction of models capable of pricing instruments crucially dependent on the correlated movements of different portions of the yield curve. On the other hand, they have highlighted the need to manage the risk of these new exotic options in a manner consistent with the pricing and hedging of the first-generation instruments.

The very concept of the "underlying" instrument has undergone a subtle but important transformation: exotic OTC option traders will often hedge their positions in the "third generation" instrument using not cash instruments (the old "underlying bond") but the proverbially heady cocktail of actively traded, more elementary *options* (e.g. caps or

* Thanks are due to Mike Sherring and Dr Ian Cooper for many useful discussions; to Charles Thompson and Dr Vivian Li for performing some calculations; to Dr Carol Alexander for most helpful editorial comments; and to Dr Thomas Gustavsson, who kindly made available his unpublished thesis. Needless to say, all remaining errors are mine.

The Handbook of Risk Management and Analysis. Edited by Carol Alexander
© 1996 John Wiley & Sons Ltd

European swaptions). Whatever the chosen model, it must therefore yield the same price for the plain vanilla hedging options, priced in the market using a different (usually Black's) model.

In this context, the very success of the Black (1976) model for plain vanilla options has been both the blessing and the bane of more sophisticated approaches. It is, in fact, essential to emphasize that expert practitioners are all too aware of the limitations of the Black model, and that their "doctoring" of *the* one unobservable input (the "implied" volatility) can well recover a desired option price; but *a priori* this procedure does not tell them anything about the 'intrinsic' correctness of the model. In other terms, its virtually universal acceptance in the market does not imply a similar acceptance of the underlying assumptions, since distributional features not accommodated by Black's model (notably mean reversion, leptokurtosis, etc.) are incorporated in an *ad hoc* way by adjusting the Black's implied volatility. The indubitable simplicity and intuitive appeal of the Black approach have therefore given rise to a situation where any more sophisticated model has "at least" to recover the Black prices for plain vanilla instruments, if it is to win any acceptance among practitioners. From this point of view the Black approach has become not an equal ranking model, which might see its predictions challenged by a more "realistic" approach, but a benchmark which more advanced methodologies simply cannot ignore.

The need to go beyond Black's closed form formula (to value, for instance, American options) has always been present, but, as pointed out before, option markets have recently seen the appearance of option pay-offs strongly dependent on the imperfect correlation between rates (e.g. yield spread options), on the path followed by the rates (e.g. indexed principal swap), and/or of a discontinuous nature (e.g. knock-out caps). The first class of pay-offs points to two-factor models as the way forward. The second shifts the emphasis towards Monte Carlo approaches. The latter requires, in numeric implementations, a sampling resolution which seriously stretches even one-factor models. The hard lessons learnt by some market practitioners in attempting to risk-manage instruments such as knock-out indexed principal swaps show that even state-of-the-art model implementations are far from being able to provide black-box solutions.

In order to tackle these problems, so many computational procedures (Monte Carlo simulations, finite differences schemes, lattice methodologies, etc.) have been developed, that it is easy to miss their underlying similarities and the common financial reasoning. In this light, the purpose of this chapter is to:

- give a justification for yield curve models
- clarify the constraints that they must satisfy to be financially viable (no arbitrage)
- show how from these common principles the various approaches naturally follow
- review known and present original results on their theoretical and empirical implications
- highlight the caveats and pitfalls the user might encounter.

The model review presented is not meant to be exhaustive; rather, representative examples have been chosen of those classes of models that have so far encountered favour, or aroused interest, among practitioners.

One of the salient messages from this chapter is that the quality of a model should be assessed on the basis not of the *a priori* appeal of its assumptions (e.g. normal vs. log-normal rates), but of the effectiveness of its hedging performance. This has not only practical but also theoretical appeal, since an option price is, after all, nothing but the cost incurred in running the duplicating hedging portfolio.

Furthermore, I shall stress that the calibration procedure is an integral part of a model specification, and that it makes little sense to talk about the "goodness" or "realism" of a given model, for instance on the basis of its distributional or economic assumptions, without exploring the ease, robustness and reliability of the parameter estimation procedure.

Financial intuition rather than mathematical rigidness has been stressed throughout; references have been provided to allow the more mathematically inclined readers to find rigorous proofs for the sketchy derivations presented in the text.

I would consider my task more than satisfactorily accomplished if, by the end of the chapter, the reader will not be tempted to paraphrase Oscar Wilde's famous book review: "Good in parts, and original in parts; unfortunately, the good parts were not original, and the original parts were not good."

2.2 YIELD CURVE MODELS: A STATISTICAL MOTIVATION

2.2.1 Statistical Analysis of the Evolution of Rates

The behaviour of the yield curve in its entirety can be described in terms of the evolution of a continuum of spot rates of maturity between $0 + \varepsilon$ and T, where ε is the shortest (instantaneous) lending/borrowing period, and T the longest maturity of interest. All these rates are stochastic variables imperfectly correlated with each other, with the degree of correlation normally decreasing with increasing difference in maturity. If one discretizes the maturity spectrum, and a simple drift/diffusion process is assumed for each rate, one is therefore led to write

$$dr_i(t) = \mu_{r_i}(r_i(t), t)\, dt + \sigma_{r_i}(r_i(t), t)\, dz_i \tag{1}$$

with $i = 1, 2, \ldots, n$ sources of uncertainty (normal Brownian motions). These Brownian motions are not independent, since

$$E[dz_i] = 0 \qquad E[dz_i\, dz_j] = \rho_{ij}\, dt$$

A typical example of the degree of correlation observable among changes in rates of different maturities is shown in Table 2.1 for the UK yield curve in the years 1989–1991.

Table 2.1 Degree of correlation for changes in UK rates of different maturities (rate $r1$ = three-month rate, rate $r5$ = 18-month rate) for the 1989–1991 period

	$r1$	$r2$	$r3$	$r4$	$r5$
$r1$	1.000	0.915	0.840	0.783	0.732
$r2$	0.915	1.000	0.984	0.955	0.923
$r3$	0.840	0.984	1.000	0.992	0.974
$r4$	0.783	0.955	0.992	1.000	0.994
$r5$	0.732	0.923	0.974	0.994	1.000

The next step in the analysis is to realize that, given this high degree of correlation, one could look for orthogonal linear combinations $\{y_j\}$ of the changes in rates (i.e. Δr_i)

$$y_1 = \sum_i \alpha_{1i} \Delta r_i,$$

$$y_2 = \sum_i \alpha_{2i} \Delta r_i, \tag{2}$$

$$\ldots$$

$$y_n = \sum_i \alpha_{ni} \Delta r_i$$

such that y_1 is the first eigenvector of the variance–covariance matrix, y_2 the second eigenvector constructed to be orthogonal to the first, and so on up to the nth eigenvector. By construction the first new variable y_1 accounts for the maximum amount of the total variability, the second for the maximum amount of the residual variability, and so on up to the nth new variable, by which time 100 per cent of the total variability must be accounted for. This technique, known as Principal Component Analysis (see Wilson (1994) for a discussion with up-to-date references to recent empirical work), if applied to the term structure of interest rate of most of the major currencies, produces new variables $\{y_i\}$ such that

  (i)   the first principal component is made up by approximately equal weights $\{\alpha_{1i}\}$ of the original variables, and can therefore be intuitively interpreted as the "average level" of the yield curve;

  (ii) the second is made up by weights $\{\alpha_{2i}\}$ of similar magnitude and opposite signs at the opposite end of the maturity spectrum, and therefore lends itself to the interpretation of being the slope of the yield curve;

 (iii) the third is made up by weights $\{\alpha_{3i}\}$ of similar magnitude and identical signs at the extremes of the maturity spectrum, and approximately twice as large and of opposite sign in the middle; this feature warrants the interpretation of the third component as the "curvature" of the yield curve.

These results are for instance borne out by the Principal Component Analysis of the rates in the UK market in the years 1989/1992 (see Tables 2.2 and 2.3), where the eight chosen maturity bins span the spectrum from the three-month to the ten-year rate, and the data were sampled with weekly frequency.

    As for the "explanatory power" of these new variables, in most currencies one then finds that the "level" often accounts for up to 80–90 per cent of the total variance, and that the first three principal components taken together often describe up to 95–99 per cent

Table 2.2 Contributions to the overall explained variance of the different principal components for the UK rate data described in the text

Principal Component	Explained Variance (%)	Total Variance (%)
1	92.170	92.170
2	6.930	99.100
3	0.614	99.714
4	0.240	99.954
5	0.031	99.985

Table 2.3 Weights of the original variables (i.e. changes in rates of maturities 1 to 8) needed to produce the first three principal components

Weights	First Principal Component	Second Principal Component	Third Principal Component
1	0.299	−0.768	0.49
2	0.354	−0.333	−0.352
3	0.365	−0.105	−0.389
4	0.367	0.049	−0.259
5	0.364	0.161	−0.196
6	0.361	0.239	−0.005
7	0.358	0.296	0.0258
8	0.352	0.333	0.557

of the intermaturity variability. *The number of independent rates (or linear combinations thereof) needed to describe the whole yield curve can therefore be drastically reduced with little loss of information.*

In establishing a framework for option pricing, some researchers have therefore adopted a two-variable approach. More commonly, however, a single variable has been chosen to describe the whole yield curve. It must be stressed at this point that this does not mean that the yield curve is forced to move in parallel, but simply that only one source of uncertainty is allowed to affect the different rates. The individual rates can be affected by changes in the driving variable to a different extent, in as complex a way as the richness of the model can allow. One-factor models do, however, imply perfect local correlation between movements in rates of different maturities. The relevance of this will be explored next.

2.2.2 A Framework for Option Pricing

In the light of the above, it has been customary, especially in early approaches, to choose one specific rate, usually the short rate, $r(t)$, as a proxy for the single variable (i.e. the level) that Principal Component Analysis indicates can best describe the movements of the yield curve (notice the approximately constant weights for the various maturity rates in the first column of Table 2.3). In this approach, after allowing the stochastic component of its process to be of diffusive nature only (no discontinuous jumps), one is led to write explicitly, or implicitly to assume,

$$dr(t) = \mu_r(r(t), t)\, dt + \sigma_r(r(t), t)\, dz \tag{1'}$$

In this framework, the price of any contingent claim depending on the yield curve as a whole (not only on the short rate) will be a function of calendar time, t, of its pay-off at expiry or maturity, T, and, via Ito's lemma, of the short rate dynamics only. All the rates of maturity intermediate between the maturity of r and T are accounted for in this framework by the process of the short rates, that "drives" the whole yield curve.

This approach, however, is by no means necessary, or unique. The "modern" or "evolutionary" approach, for instance, pioneered by HJM (Heath, Jarrow and Morton (1987)), has taken a continuum of instantaneous forward rates as the building blocks to describe the dynamics of the whole term structure. Equations formally similar to equation (3) above can then be written for each forward rate (and will be derived in following sections). The

Principal Component Analysis mentioned before can provide the volatility inputs for the dynamics of the forward rates (see Section 2.5.4).

Given either approach, the task of pricing contingent claims on instruments dependent on the yield curve movements can in any case be reduced to the following conceptual "ingredients":

(i) a concrete specification of the process for the driving factor(s) (i.e. for the parameters in equation (3) which describes the dynamics of the short rate);

(ii) a way of translating the deterministic and stochastic movements of the driving variable(s) into the deterministic and stochastic movements of the underlying quantities of interest (bonds, forward rates, etc.);

(iii) a way of relating the possible attainable future values of an asset to its present value, i.e. a discounting procedure.

However, before embarking on the analysis of these different models, a fundamental condition must be imposed concerning point (ii) above, i.e. on the possible "allowable" movements for the prices of the underlying instruments (bonds etc.) which depend on the yield curve. This fundamental condition must be enforced in order to prevent the possibility of arbitrage (as more precisely defined in the following section) between bonds of different maturities, and, more generally, between any two instruments. So many are the possible equivalent formulations of this no-arbitrage condition (Jamshidian (1990) enumerates 14!), that, once again, it is very easy to miss the underlying common reasoning. Different, albeit equivalent, formulations of no-arbitrage are however useful because enforcing the no-arbitrage condition in a particular form for a specific model can be considerably more straightforward and intuitive than if a different formulation had been chosen. The task of presenting the "classical" (Vasicek (1977)) and "modern"(martingale) formulation of the no-arbitrage condition in such a way as to underline their similarity, and to show how they can be directly applied to different types of implementation, is therefore undertaken in the next section.

2.3 THE NO-ARBITRAGE CONDITIONS

2.3.1 Definition of No-arbitrage in a Complete Market

A rigorous definition of the no-arbitrage condition requires, especially in continuous time, comparatively sophisticated mathematical tools. The attempt will instead be made in this section to point out the financial intuition behind the more rigorous treatments and to highlight those results useful for the practical model implementations presented in later sections. No attempt will be made in this section to re-derive the no-arbitrage results, which are already available, for instance, in Gustavsson (1992), Harrison and Kreps (1979), Harrison and Pliska (1983), or, in a more accessible way, in Rebonato (1996). The most important results will, however, be presented, with a special focus on their relevance for model implementation.

The intuitive idea behind the term "no-arbitrage" is that no riskless strategy of zero set-up cost should yield with certainty a positive return. A rigorous definition requires careful handling of several concepts: a self-financing strategy, an attainable contingent claim, an implicit price system and a complete market. Loosely speaking, the no-arbitrage idea is formalized by (i) showing, within suitable market assumptions, the correspondence between a contingent claim and a zero-set-up cost replicating strategy (whence the attainability condition, the self-financing requirement for the strategy, and the completeness of the market); and (ii) by shifting the no-arbitrage requirement from the contingent claim itself to the replicating portfolio. When this "transfer" is accomplished, one can then translate the intuitive requirement that it should not be possible to gain something for nothing into the condition

$$E_o[\Theta(T)\mathbf{S}(T)] > 0 \Rightarrow \Theta(0)\mathbf{S}(0) > 0,$$

or, equivalently,

$$\Theta(0)\mathbf{S}(0) = 0 \Rightarrow E_o[\Theta(T)\mathbf{S}(T)] = 0,$$

where the vector Θ indicates the holdings of the different assets in the strategy, $\mathbf{S}$ designates the vector of the asset prices, and $E_o[]$ indicates expectation taken conditional upon information up to and including time 0. In words, *any contingent claim with strictly positive pay-offs must cost something today; and if a portfolio has zero cost today the expectation of the possible pay-offs of the associated contingent claim is also zero.*

2.3.2 The Condition of No-arbitrage: Vasicek's Approach

In the context of explicit interest rate models, the constraints on the bond price processes were derived as early as 1977 by Vasicek (1977). The derivation, sketched in the following, is extremely simple and intuitively appealing. Its main result, i.e. the maturity independence of the market price of risk, directly leads to the PDE approach, which can then be tackled either by explicit analytic solutions, or by the finite differences methods (see Section 2.4.3).

The more modern (martingale) approach has a wider scope, in that it does not start from an explicit process for the short rate, and enjoys greater generality by directly allowing a variety of possible numeraires, as described below. It leads naturally to lattice methodologies (Section 2.4.1) and MC simulations (Section 2.4.2). Due to its greater mathematical complexity it will be dealt with, albeit in a qualitative way, after presenting the Vasicek approach.

The "classic" treatment is well known, and similar in spirit to the Black and Scholes (Black and Scholes (1973)) approach: starting from a general Brownian process for the short rate, $r(t)$, of drift $\mu_r(t)$ and instantaneous variance per unit time $\sigma_r(r, t)^2$,

$$dr(t) = \mu_r(r, t)\, dt + \sigma_r(r, t)\, dz, \tag{1}$$

with dz a standard Brownian motion ($E[dz] = 0$ and $E[dz^2] = 1$).

Ito's lemma yields for the process of a discount bond of maturity T, $P(t, T)$

$$dP(t, T) = [\partial P/\partial r\, \mu_r + \partial P/\partial t + 1/2\sigma_r^2\, \partial^2 P/\partial r^2]\, dt + \sigma_r\, \partial P(t, T)/\partial r\, dz$$

$$\equiv \mu(t, T)\, dt + \upsilon(t, T)\, dz \tag{2}$$

A portfolio Π is then created, composed of θ_1 units of bond T_1, and θ_2 units of bond T_2, ($\theta_1 + \theta_2 = 1$, without loss of generality), with the weights so chosen as to cancel the stochastic component of the process for the portfolio:

$$d\Pi = [\theta_1\mu(t, T_1) + (1 - \theta_1)\mu(t, T_2)]\, dt$$

$$+ [\theta_1\, \partial P(t, T_1)/\partial r\, \sigma_r + (1 - \theta_1)\, \partial P(t, T_2)/\partial r\, \sigma_r]\, dz \equiv \mu_\Pi\, dt + \sigma_\Pi\, dz \tag{3}$$

$$\sigma_\Pi = 0 \Rightarrow \theta_1 = (\partial P(t, T_2)/\partial r)/(\partial P(t, T_2)/\partial r - \partial P(t, T_1)/\partial r)$$

$$= v(t, T_2)/[v(t, T_2) - v(t, T_1)] \tag{3'}$$

Since the portfolio return is no longer stochastic, it can only earn, over time dt, the spot rate $r(t)$:

$$\mathrm{d}\Pi/\Pi = r(t)\,\mathrm{d}t \tag{4}$$

Therefore, rearranging equation (3) and substituting for θ_1 from equation (3'), one obtains

$$[\mu(t, T_1) - r\,P(t, T_1)]/v(t, T_1) = [\mu(t, T_2) - r\,P(t, T_2)]/v(t, T_2) \equiv \lambda(t) \tag{5}$$

i.e. *the expected return $(\mu - r)$ per unit risk $(1/v)$ is a constant across maturities.* (The result (5) is easily seen to be identical to Vasicek's if one assumes percentage volatility and drift.) Notice that equation (5) imposes a *drift* condition across different discount bonds, which embodies the fact that, in this one-factor universe, investors are "correctly" compensated for their accepting more risk with a longer-maturity bond by an expected return scaled with the riskiness (instantaneous standard deviation) of the bond itself. The maturity-independent quantity $\lambda(t)$ is therefore aptly described as the *market price of risk*.

Furthermore, making use of result (5) one can easily derive the PDE describing the dynamics of a bond of maturity T as a function of the driving factor by equating the coefficients of the drift term:

$$[\partial P/\partial r\,\mu_r + \partial P/\partial t + 1/2\sigma_r^2\,\partial^2 P/\partial r^2] = r\,P + \lambda\sigma_r\partial P/\partial r \tag{6}$$

Finally, recognizing that no special use has been made in the derivation of the fact that $P(t, T)$ represents a discount *bond* price, one can conclude that the same PDE, supplemented with the appropriate terminal conditions, has to be obeyed by any asset traded in the economy, if arbitrage is to be avoided. Different (one-factor) models will produce PDEs of identical structure to equation (6) above, but with different μ_r and σ_r inputs. This is therefore the fundamental equation that analytic or finite difference methods have set out to solve.

2.3.3 The Condition of No-arbitrage: the Martingale Approach

One of the main advantages of the martingale approach is the direct and natural link afforded between the market price of risk, the discounting procedure (choice of numeraire) and the underlying equivalent measures. It is this link, of great conceptual and practical importance, that ultimately justifies the mathematically rather complex set up, which could otherwise be regarded as an unnecessarily complicated formalism. This and the following three sections report in a concise form those results obtained in Gustavsson (1992) which are of direct relevance to the implementation and analysis of the yield curve models presented further on. For ease of reference, Gustavsson's notation has been retained as much as possible.

Crucial to the treatment is the choice of a numeraire, defined as the common unit on the basis of which the prices of all the N securities can be expressed. Any of the N assets can be chosen as numeraire, as long as it has strictly positive pay-offs at all times and in all states of the world. Assets prices expressed as a function of this numeraire (arbitrarily chosen to be asset 1) can then be written as

$$Z_n{}^*(t) = S_n(t)/S_1(t) \tag{1}$$

Each distinct choice of numeraire will give rise to a different set of relative prices.

Three theorems then constitute the cornerstones of no-arbitrage pricing: the first gives the necessary and sufficient conditions for the process of relative prices if arbitrage is to be avoided; under the Brownian assumption for the stochastic process, the second provides the explicit martingale form for the relative price processes; the third will enable us to relate processes obtained using different choices of the numeraire. More precisely:

Theorem (1) A complete market is arbitrage-free if and only if there exists a measure Q^*, equivalent to Q, such that the relative prices $Z^*(t)$ become martingales, i.e.

$$E_t^*[Z^*(T)] = Z^*(t) \tag{2}$$

where $E_t^*[.]$ denotes expectation taken at time t with respect to the measure Q^*, contingent on all past and present information up to time t. A few remarks can enhance the financial intuition behind this theorem: saying that a measure Q^* (i.e. loosely speaking, a law associating to events a "probability") is *equivalent* to another measure Q means that events impossible in one measure are also impossible in the other. Therefore no-arbitrage results only stem from the "impossibility regions" of different measures. Furthermore, the statement that, in the new equivalent measure, the relative price process should be a martingale is tantamount to requiring that the expectation of any relative price at any later time should be the same as its price today. This requirement of zero drift might seem surprising, since it seems to imply no expected return from an asset, but, by recalling the definition of $Z^*(T)$ as *ratios* of traded assets, it can be seen that the martingale requirement is equivalent to imposing the *same* return from both assets. But this is very similar to the old Black and Scholes (1973) results, where all assets earn the same (riskless) rate of return. It will become apparent in the next section that it is even more similar, nay identical, to the result obtained using the classic (Vasicek) approach: it will in fact be shown that in the risk-neutral world every bond earns exactly the spot rate. In other words, the change of measure from Q to Q^* tilts the playing field in such a way that the return from each unnormalized asset is the same as the return from the numeraire asset. It can be immediately seen that, since there is no unique choice for the latter, the type and extent of the "tilting" will have to be different for each numeraire choice.

Theorem (2) then states that, under the Brownian assumption for the arrival of information, any martingale $Z^*(t)$ can be represented as

$$dZ_n^*(t) = \sigma_n(t)Z_n^*(t)\,dW^*(t) \tag{3}$$

where $W^*(t)$ is *the* Wiener process in the measure Q^*. (Extension to several processes is straightforward.)

For the sake of concreteness, Theorem (3) will be reported at the end of the section, after introducing actual examples of numeraires.

The importance of these rather abstract beginnings can be appreciated by considering two specific choices for the numeraire, namely (i) by discounting each asset pay-off at time T, $S(T)$, by a discount bond maturing at T, $P(t, T)$, or (ii) by dividing the asset price by a rolled-up-money-market account (for brevity a money-market account in the following), where £1 is reinvested at the prevailing short rate from t up to time T. Both choices correspond to different ways to present-value future cash flows and, implicitly, to construct one's hedged position.

2.3.4 First Choice of Numeraire: the Money Market Account

If one defines the money market account as the value of £1 instantaneously reinvested at the current short term rate

$$B(t) = \exp\left[\int_o^t r(s)\,ds\right] \tag{1}$$

the relative prices with respect to this numeraire are given by

$$Z'_n(t) = S_n(t)/B(t) \tag{2}$$

By Theorem (1), a unique equivalent measure Q' must exist such that the drift of the cash assets and of the money market account are identical, i.e. such that the relative prices are martingales:

$$E'_t[Z'_n(T)] = E'_t[S_n(T)/B(T)] = S_n(t)/B(t) = Z'_n(t) \quad \forall T \geq t \tag{3}$$

Specializing equation (3) to the case where the original asset price is today's price of a bond of maturity $T, P(0, T)$, one readily obtains

$$P(0, T) = E'_t[1/B(T)] = E'_t\left[\exp\left[-\int_0^T r(s)\,ds\right]\right] \tag{4}$$

(since $P(T, T) = 1$), i.e. *today's price of a T-maturity bond is equal to the expectation under Q' of the reciprocal of the money account*. It is instructive to compare equation (4) with the well-known result for a bond price in the case of deterministic interest rates, i.e. with the result that would apply if the future path of the short rate were assumed to be known with certainty at time 0. In this case imposing no-arbitrage implies that $P(t, T) = P(t, s)P(s, T)$. Furthermore, since the instantaneous forward rate, $f(t, T)$ is given by

$$f(t, T) = \partial[\ln(P(t, T))]/\partial T$$

and $r(s) = f(s, s)$ one can write

$$P(0, T) = \exp\left[-\int_o^T r(s)\,ds\right] \tag{4'}$$

where $r(s)$ is now a deterministic quantity. Clearly it is the non-linearity of the discounting operator that brings about the difference between equations (4) and (4').

The crucial importance of result (4) will be appreciated in the context of lattice methodologies. It will suffice for the moment to say that it is by enforcing condition (4) that these numerical procedures ensure that expectations of future option pay-offs are taken with respect to the correct, but *a priori* unknown, measure Q'.

Moving one step further, from equations (1) and (2) one can obtain that

$$dS_n(t)/S_n(t) = r(t)\,dt + \sigma_n(t)\,dW'(t) \tag{5}$$

i.e. *in the measure Q' the return on any asset is identical* (there is no index n in the drift term) *and is equal to the riskless rate*, thus justifying the name of "risk neutral" for this particular measure. That all the returns should turn out to be identical should come as no surprise, after the qualitative remarks which followed Theorem (1); the specific result that this rate of return must be the riskless rate is specific to the particular choice of numeraire. Result (5) also applies, in particular, to the price of discount bonds, with $P(t, T)$ replacing $S_n(t)$. This result will be of crucial importance in the implementation of lattice methodologies by means of Green's functions.

Furthermore, remembering that the time-t forward rate from time T' to time T'' can be written as

$$f(t, T', T'') = (\ln(P(t, T')) - \ln(P(t, T'')))/(T'' - T') \tag{6}$$

and applying Ito's lemma to $\ln(P(.))$ one easily obtains in the measure Q' for a log-normal bond price process

$$df(t, T', T'') = [v(t, T'')^2 - v(t, T')^2]/(2(T'' - T'))\, dt$$
$$+ [v(t, T') - v(t, T'')]/(T'' - T')\, dw'(t) \tag{7}$$

or, by taking the limit as $T'' \to T'$,

$$df(t, T) = \partial v(t, T)/\partial T\, v(t, T)\, dt - \partial v(t, T)/\partial T\, dw'(t) \tag{8}$$

This expression shows that, *in the measure Q', forward rates are* not *martingales*, and, formally, one could argue that they could be turned into a martingale process by defining a new measure Q^*, where

$$dW^*(t) = dW'(t) - \partial v(t, T)/\partial T\, v(t, T) \tag{9}$$

It is shown in the following section that this *ad hoc* construction exactly creates the measure defined by choosing as numeraire the price of a discount bond.

2.3.5 Second Choice of Numeraire: a Discount Bond

With this choice of numeraire, one can write for the new relative prices

$$Z_n''(t, T) = S_n(t)/P(t, T) \tag{1}$$

By Theorem (1), to any discount bond $P(t, T)$ there corresponds a measure Q'', equivalent to the real-world measure Q, such that relative prices become martingales, i.e.

$$E_t''[Z_n''(u, T)] = E_t''[S_n(u)/P(u, T)] = Z_n''(t, T) = S_n(t)/P(t, T) \quad \forall T \geq u \geq t \tag{2}$$

From definition (1) and equation (2) one can obtain the rate of return on an asset $S(t)$:

$$dS(t)/S(t) = -dP(s, t)/P(s, t) + dZ''(t)/Z''(t); \tag{3}$$

Once again, notice that there is no dependence on the specific asset n on the right-hand side. One can therefore draw the first conclusion that *all assets earn the same percentage return, given by the return on a bond maturing at time t*. This expression can be further clarified by remembering that, since a bond of maturity t and the instantaneous forward rates $f(0, t)$ are linked by

$$P(0, t) = \exp\left[-\int_o^t f(0, s)\, ds\right], \tag{4}$$

differentiation and substitution in equation (5) gives for Brownian processes

$$dS(t)/S(t) = f(0, t) \, dt + \sigma''(t) \, dW''(t) \tag{5}$$

i.e. the rate of return on any asset in Q'' equals the t-maturity forward rate.

In addition, it is possible to show that, for this choice of numeraire, *forward rates and forward prices are driftless (martingales).* It is clear that financially this way of discounting cash flows corresponds to hedging options by taking positions in *forward* assets, whereas the money market discounting is equivalent to rolling one's positions at the instantaneous short rate. For a single-horizon (European) option, the former approach is clearly more appropriate, since it does not expose the holder to the "reinvestment" risk. This strategy, however, would be unsuitable for multiple-exercise or American options, where no single horizon can be *a priori* defined. Notice that this subtle distinction, crucial to interest rate options, does not arise in the original Black and Scholes treatment, which can be indifferently cast in either numeraire, since, within that approach, rates are assumed to be deterministic.

2.3.6 The General Link Between Different Measures

Section 2.3.4 has shown that the link between the two measures Q' and Q'' is via a drift transformation like equation (9) in Section 2.3.4. For Wiener processes, this result is actually of general validity, and constitutes the third "cornerstone" (Girsanov's theorem) mentioned in Section 2.3.3. More precisely, it can be shown that, taking any two equivalent measures, Q' and Q, any Wiener process $W'(t)$ in the original measure Q' is transformed into

$$W(t) = W'(t) - \int_o^t q(s) \, ds \tag{1}$$

where $q(s)$ is a suitable function (the Radon–Nykodin derivative). The specific functional form of the function $q(s)$ is, for the purposes of our discussion, less important than the fact that equation (1) describes a *drift* transformation between measures. The link with the "classical" (Vasicek) approach can in fact now be made: the market price of risk equation (5) in Section 2.3.2 is seen to be the change of measure which transforms the *a priori* unknown drift $\mu(t, T)$ in the real world (described by measure Q) into the riskless rate under Q'.

A simple example can perhaps make the above discussion more concrete. Consider the case of the evaluation of a simple caplet of maturity T. With Black's model, which implies discount-bond discounting, each final pay-off is probability-weighted by the log-normal distribution and then discounted by a bond of maturity T. Notice that, given this choice of numeraire, no drift is assumed for the caplet forward rate. Notice also that large pay-offs (corresponding to high realizations of the forward rate, and weighted by their log-normal probability distribution) are discounted using the same discount bond as lower rate pay-offs. Let us consider, on the other hand, a lattice approach, such as the BDT model presented later, which discounts each final pay-off by the actual path followed by the short rate to reach the appropriate state of the world at maturity, i.e. using a rolled-up money market account. By so doing large pay-offs are discounted using larger realizations of the money market account. *Yet lattice approaches give the same value as Black's model for the caplet.* This can only occur because of a different implicit drift associated with the rolled-up numeraire. How the implicit drift of the forward rate can actually be obtained will be shown in Section 2.5.1, but it is important to notice that it is this change in drift that exactly compensates for the different discounting (i.e. numeraire) in the two approaches.

The message of this section can therefore be summarized as follows: the process of discounting pay-offs plays a central role in option pricing, and each numeraire implies a different no-arbitrage measure, under which different quantities have different drifts. In particular, a common choice of numeraire, i.e. a pure T-maturity discount bond, has the computational advantage of implying no drift for the T-maturity forward rate and price, thereby making the evaluation of non-compounded European options very straightforward. The discounting in this measure, however, must be carried out all the way from option expiry to today, without "stopping along the way" to impose, for instance, a compound option exercise condition. It is exactly in order to be able to tackle non-European pay-offs that a different type of numeraire, i.e. the money market account, is employed. The price to be paid is that forward rates are no longer martingales, and their drift must be obtained, either explicitly (e.g. via the HJM evolutionary approach), or implicitly (e.g. via the construction associated with a computational tree such as BDT's). Showing how this is accomplished will be one the central tasks of the sections devoted to these types of models.

2.4 THE IMPLEMENTATION TOOLS

2.4.1 Lattice Approaches: Justification and Implementation

Ho and Lee (1986) (HL in the following) and Black, Derman and Toy (1990) (BDT in the following) pioneered the use of arbitrage-free computational lattices for the evaluation of interest rate options. Their methodology has enjoyed vast popularity due to the in-built capability of their models to price exactly any received market set of discount bonds, and for the intuitional appeal of their approaches which bear formal, if not very deep, similarities to the Cox–Ross–Rubinstein binomial model. In this section it will be shown how their prescription can be rigorously justified, and that it can afford, combined with the techniques of forward and backward induction, a very efficient computational tool. The results of Section 2.2 will be heavily drawn upon, both to justify the procedures, and to construct the necessary Green's functions.

The starting point for one-factor yield curve lattice models is an exogenous set of discount bond prices $\{P_i(.)\}$ observed in the market. The assumption is also made that the driving factor is the short rate, and that it can be described by a Brownian process. The value of the short rate today, i.e. at time 0 and in state 0, $r(0, 0)$, is known from the price of $P(0, 0, 1\Delta t)$:

$$r(0, 0) = - \ln P(0, 0, \Delta t)/\Delta t \tag{1}$$

(where $P(i, j, T)$ indicates the price in state i and at time j of a bond of maturity T). It is further assumed that the user knows the time-dependent (absolute or percentage) volatility of the short rate. No explicit knowledge is required about its drift. The short rate itself (HL) or its logarithm (BDT) are then allowed, from today's value, to move up or down with equal probabilities to two, as yet undetermined, states $r(1, 1)$ and $r(1, -1)$ (where, again, the first index denotes the time and the second the state). Given the Brownian assumption, their separation, i.e. $r(1, 1) - r(1, -1)$, can be immediately determined from the knowledge of the volatility at time $t(0)$, $\sigma(0)$, by remembering that the standard deviation of two quantities A and B is simply given by $|A - B|/2$. For the BDT and the

HL case one therefore easily obtains

$$r(1, 1) = r(1, -1)\exp(2\sigma\Delta t) \quad \text{(log-normal (BDT) case)} \tag{2}$$

$$r(1, 1) = r(1, -1) + 2\sigma\Delta t \quad \text{(normal (HL) case)} \tag{2'}$$

respectively. What remains to be determined is the absolute level of the two rates, a unique function, via equations (2) and (2') of either rate. In order to determine, say, $r(1, -1)$ the following procedure can be employed: construct an additional tree representing bond prices in the same states of the world described by the short rate tree, and extending one extra time step (i.e. in the example treated so far, up to time $2\Delta t$) (see Figure 2.1). If one considers a bond of maturity $2\Delta t$, which therefore pays with certainty £1 in all states of the world at time $2\Delta t$, one can ask for the price of this bond at time $1\Delta t$ in state, say, 1, i.e. for $P(1, 1, 2\Delta t)$. From the results of Section 2.2, if we discount using a market account, this is given by

$$P(1, 1, 2\Delta t) = E'_{t=\Delta t}\left[\exp - \left(\int_{\Delta t}^{2\Delta t} r(s)\,ds\right)\Big| r(\Delta t) = r(1, 1)\right] \tag{3}$$

(A slight liberty has been taken with the notation, since "r" denotes the short rate both in the continuous, $r(t)$, and in the discrete, $r(i, j)$, case.) Given the Brownian assumption this expectation is given in discrete time by

$$E_{t=\Delta t'}[1\exp(-r(1, 1)\Delta t] = \exp(-r(1, 1)\Delta t)(1\tfrac{1}{2} + 1\tfrac{1}{2}) \tag{3'}$$

where the non-linear function exp[.] has been taken out of the expectation operator because, at time 1 and in state 1, $r(1, 1)$ is a known quantity. Let us call $P(1, 1, 2\Delta t; r(1, 1))$ and $P(1, -1, 2\Delta t; r(1, -1))$ the value at time 1 of a discount bond maturing at time $2\Delta t$ in the 1 (up) and -1 (down) states of the world, respectively (the parametric argument $r(i, j)$ specifies on which rate(s) the discount bond price depends). The expectation as of today of the price of a $2-\Delta t$ maturity discount bond $P(0, 0, 2\Delta t; r(1, 1), r(1, -1), r(0, 0))$ must then be given by

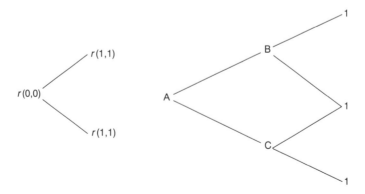

Figure 2.1 $r(0, 0)$ is known at time 0 from equation (1); the value of the short rate in the up state at time $1\Delta t$, $r(1, 1)$, is linked to $r(1, -1)$ by equation (2) or (2'); B is given by $1/2(1 + 1)\exp[-r(1, 1)\Delta t]$; C is given by $1/2(1 + 1)\exp[-r(1, -1)\Delta t]$; A is given by $1/2(B + C)\exp[-r(0, 0)\Delta t]$

$$P(0, 0, 2\Delta t; r(1, 1), r(1, -1), r(0, 0))$$

$$= E'_{t=0}\left[P(1, 2\Delta t)\exp\left[-\int_0^{\Delta t} r(s)\,ds\right] | r(0) = r(0, 0)\right]$$

$$= \exp[-r(0, 0)\Delta t]1/2\{P(1, 1, 2\Delta t) + P(1, -1, 2\Delta t)\} \tag{4}$$

(Again the equivalence between the continuous, $P(t, T)$, and discrete-time, $P(i, j, T)$, notation should be clear.) The notation employed for the first term in equation (4) emphasizes that the discount bond price $P(0, 0, 2\Delta t)$ depends on $r(0, 0)$, $r(1, -1)$ and $r(1, 1)$. Since, however, $r(0, 0)$ is known from equation (1), since the prices $P(1, \pm1, 2\Delta t)$ are related to $r(1, 1)$ and $r(1, -1)$ by equation (3), and since the two rates at time 1 $r(1, 1)$, $r(1, -1)$ are linked by the relationships $(2, 2')$ above, the price $P(0, 0, 2\Delta t)$ can be seen to be a function of $r(1, 1)$ (or $r(1, -1)$) only. This function of a single variable can now be equated to the observed market price of a two-year discount bond, thereby uniquely determining the value for $r(1, 1)$ (or $r(1, -1)$). The resulting solution admits close solution for the HL model, or requires a simple numerical algorithm (e.g. Newton–Raphson) for the BDT approach.

It is easy to see that the extension of the rate tree by one time step will introduce a single new unknown and one more equation. All the rates in the various states of the world j at time i are in fact linked by

$$r(i, j + 1) = r(i, j - 1) + 2\sigma\Delta t \quad \text{(HL, normal case)} \tag{5}$$

$$r(i, j + 1) = r(i, j - 1)\exp[2\sigma\Delta t] \quad \text{(BDT, log-normal case)} \tag{5'}$$

and, therefore, given the value of the volatility at time $(i-1)\Delta t$, they can all be expressed as a function of, say, $r(i, -i)$. The unit pay-offs from a bond maturing at time $i+1$ can then be discounted to time i using all and only the rates $r(i, j)$ (all a function of $r(i, -i)$), and from time i to time 0 using *already determined rates*. This model value for an $(i+1)\Delta t$-maturity bond can then be compared with the corresponding market value, and the single unknown, $r(i, -i)$, adjusted accordingly.

By the way lattice methodologies have been described it is clear that the commonly made statement that models like BDT or HL "do not depend on the market price of risk" should actually be rephrased as "do not require an *a priori* explicit knowledge of the market price of risk". The tree fitting procedure described above, in fact, actually endows the unknown function describing the market price of risk with as many degrees of freedom as there are market discount bonds, and implicitly determines the values of this function which allow exact pricing of the market bonds.

It is also apparent, from the "naive" presentation given above, that fitting further time slices of the interest rate tree as suggested entails traversing the same portions of the lattice over and over again. But, thanks to the no-arbitrage conditions obtained before, there is a way to avoid this duplication of labour. As shown before, in the measure associated with the money market account, all assets, and hence discount bonds, earn the short rate over a time step Δt. To see how this can be of assistance in the construction of the tree, let us define $G(i, j, s, t)$ as the value at time j and state i of a security paying £1 in state s and time $t(t > j)$. These quantities are known in financial literature as Arrow–Debreu prices (see e.g. Jamshidian (1991)), and bear an obvious discrete-time similarity to the Green's functions of physics, which describe the response to the unit (delta) stimulus for linear systems. Notice that the completeness assumption in Section 2.2 ensures the possibility of actually constructing these single pay-off securities by linear combinations of traded assets. A special case of these Arrow–Debreu prices is today's value of a security paying £1 at (s, t), $G(0, 0, s, t)$. Given the assumed market completeness and absence of arbitrage, the price today, $V(0, t)$, of a generic security paying £$v(s, t)$ in state s at a future time t must be given by

$$V(0, t) = \sum_s G(0, 0, s, t)v(s, t); \tag{6}$$

in particular, for a discount bond maturing at time T, equation (6) must reduce to

$$P(0, T) = \sum_s G(0, 0, s, T) \tag{6'}$$

Therefore, *knowledge of the Arrow–Debreu prices completely determines the value of a discount bond.* Furthermore, in the computational trees so far considered, knowledge of the Green's function for time t, $G(0, 0, (.), t)$ immediately determines the value of the Green's function at the next time step, $G(0, 0, (.), t + \Delta t)$. Remembering in fact that *all* assets earn the short rate over time Δt, from Figure 2.2 it is easy to see that the price of a security paying £1 in state j at time $t + \Delta t$ and £0 everywhere else is given by

$$G(0, 0, j, t + \Delta t) = 1/2(0 + 1)\exp[-r(j + 1, t)\Delta t]G(0, 0, j + 1, t)$$
$$+ 1/2(1 + 0)\exp[-r(j - 1, t)\Delta t]G(0, 0, j - 1, t) \tag{7}$$

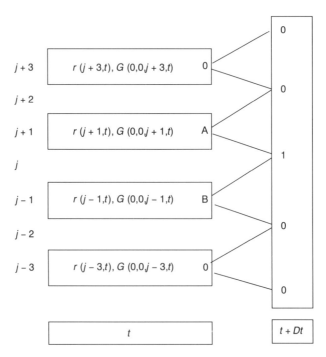

Figure 2.2 The Green's function $G(0, 0, j, t + \Delta t)$ is given by the sum of A $G(0, 0, j + 1, t)$ and B $G(0, 0, j - 1, t)$; A and B are given by $1/2(0 + 1)\exp[-r(j + 1, t)\Delta t]$ and $1/2(1 + 0)\exp[-r(j - 1, t)\Delta t]$, respectively; $G(0, 0, j + 1, t)$ and $G(0, 0, j - 1, t)$ are known

Therefore, *knowledge of the Arrow–Debreu prices and of the short rates at time t completely determines all the Arrow–Debreu prices at time $t + \Delta t$.* Furthermore, as shown above, all rates at time t are a unique function, via the volatility, of a single value of the short rate. Therefore, by virtue of equation (6) not only can one express a model bond price as a function of a single unknown rate, as shown before, but the traversing of already fitted portions of the lattice can be avoided by simple multiplication by the appropriate Green's functions. *The computational savings afforded by this technique reduce the number of operations from $O(N^3)$ to $O(N^2)$.*

Once the rate tree has been constructed, the pricing of any security of known terminal pay-off, be it a discount bond or a contingent claim, is easily accomplished by following the backward induction procedure used in the building of the tree: the value at node $(i - 1, j)$ is obtained by averaging the values at nodes $(i, j - 1)$ and $(i, j + 1)$ and discounting them at the short rate prevailing at $(i - 1, j)$. What has been accomplished by the forward induction tree-fitting procedure is to ensure that the short rate process displays the correct drift *for a given choice of the volatility function*. From Section 2.3 one can recall that this drift is *a priori* unknown, but also that the value of any discount bond is given by the expectation, in the appropriate measure, of the reciprocal of the money market account. By forcing, via the fitting procedure, the model and market price for the discount bond to coincide, one is effectively implicitly imputing *the* drift that, for any given choice of the process variance, characterizes the measure under which *all* expectations (i.e. expectations of *any* future pay-off) have to be taken if arbitrage is to be avoided. Indeed the drift can often be explicitly obtained, either *a priori* for Gaussian models, or once the tree has been constructed for log-normal models. It will be shown in the following how this can be of more than academic interest, if one is interested, or forced, to carry out a Monte Carlo simulation consistent with a given lattice model.

Notice carefully, however, that the perfect match of model and market prices of discount bonds tells one nothing about the appropriateness of the chosen volatility function. The argument is rather subtle: bond prices depend not only on future expectations of rates, but also on future volatility, via the non-linear expectation operator in equation (4) of Section 2.3.4. A lattice construction of the kind described above therefore creates an expectation of rates (i.e. an implicit drift term for the short rate) which is a function of an unknown quantity, i.e. the chosen volatility function itself. The impasse can only be broken by further forcing correct simultaneous pricing of volatility-dependent instruments, such as caps and floors. It is the correctness of the pricing of the latter, in fact, which ensures that the "correct" (given the model assumptions) contributions to the curvature of the term structure are provided by rate expectations and future volatilities.

This extremely important point will be visited again in the discussion of analytic models, which limit *a priori* the possible deterministic path followed by the short rate (Section 2.5.3). Further sections will also explore the methodological strengths and weaknesses of lattice approaches with respect to MC (Section 2.4.2) and PDE methods (Section 2.4.3).

2.4.2 Monte Carlo (MC) Approaches

It was pointed out in the introductory section that an increasing number of actively traded OTC interest rate options display path-dependent features. Although skilful, if rather cumbersome, implementations (Hull and White (1993)) often make these problems tractable using lattice methodologies, the most direct and general route towards their evaluation remains the MC approach, first introduced in the option-pricing context by Boyle (1977). Furthermore, recently introduced techniques for MC methodologies (Clewlow and Carverhill (1994)) can give valuable help in the evaluation of the risk statistics that have until recently been very arduous to determine. Further impetus has been given to research into efficient implementations of MC methods by the intellectual and practical appeal of the HJM (evolutionary) approach (see Section 2.5.4), which has so far defied evaluation using recombining lattices.

The idea behind the technique is extremely simple and it amounts to the numerical evaluation of integral (4) in Section 2.3.4: selected stochastic quantities are evolved through time using pre-assigned drifts and volatilities and the Brownian increment dz, which is obtained from a random draw ε from a Gaussian distribution as $dz = \varepsilon\sqrt{\Delta t}$; during the course of each realization, whichever path-dependent statistics are needed to evaluate the final pay-off can be collected; the option value at expiry thus determined is then appropriately discounted to today; the average of a (very) large number of runs is then computed, to give the required expected value of the discounted pay-off. As usual, the conceptually crucial part of the calculation is to ensure that the correct terminal distribution is achieved (i.e. that expectations are taken in the correct measure). Since each different way of discounting implies a different measure, the term "correct" only makes sense once the discounting procedure is specified. In principle, discounting by a discount bond could be employed, as long as quantities such as forward rates or prices were assigned the correct (zero) drift. However, the martingale condition only holds for pay-offs occurring at the bond maturity. Therefore, with this type of discounting no pay-off-sensitive manipulations can be accomplished along the path. In other words, in this framework MC offers no more than a cumbersome (and expensive) way of performing numerically the integral given analytically for European options by Black's result. If, however, one discounted using the money market account, and used the appropriate (non-zero) drifts for forward rates, any intermediate condition can be imposed along the path. The drawback is that the terminal pay-offs must be present-valued (*before* averaging) using the specific path followed by the short rate, and that the forward rate drifts are not known *a priori*.

After the decision has been taken to tackle a specific problem using MC techniques, several choices still remain to be made: first of all, MC being a technique rather than a model, its "ingredients" (i.e. drifts and variances) must be obtained from the separate choice of a no-arbitrage model. A later section, for instance, will show how to obtain the drift consistent with the BDT model; or, to give a different example, with the HJM approach, also reviewed in the following, the forward rate drifts turn out to be simply related to discount bond variances. In any case, once the desired model has been chosen, specific quantities will have to be evolved over time. One knows, from the results of Section 2.3, that, using a money market account as numeraire, all *assets* grow with a drift equal to the short rate, $r(t)$, and that forward rates display a drift given by equation (8) in Section 2.3.4. In addition, the money market account will have to be reinvested along each path in order to provide the necessary discount factor. To this effect the process for the short rate must also be known. Equation (3′) of Section 2.5.1 or equations (7) and (8) of Section 2.3.4 provide the relevant expressions for the BDT and HJM models, respectively.

The MC technique therefore is yet another route to perform the numerical integration of the final pay-off function times the appropriate probability distribution. In this respect, its similarities with lattice or PDE methodologies (in turn even more closely related) are quite apparent. The methodological differences, however, are the sources of both its strengths and its weaknesses. To begin with, in a binomial lattice methodology the probability of reaching the topmost node after n steps is 0.5^n; for a weekly tree extending out to five years this implies that the topmost path has a probability of occurrence of 5×10^{-79}; in turn, this implies that the highest and lowest values of the short rate sampled by a realistic weekly BDT tree of this maturity can be as high and as low as 10100 per cent and 0.0060 per cent, respectively, for the example above (GBP curve, May 94, 20 per cent vol.). For this same tree the short rate spacing around the forward rate can be as coarse as 40 b.p. Clearly, a BDT-like lattice methodology affords a very inefficient procedure to take the expectation of any function likely to vary rapidly around the centre of the distribution, as is the case with barrier options. To compound the problem, if one wants to achieve a finer sampling in rate space, one is forced, within a tree framework, to increase the number of time steps as well, thereby paying an n^2 price, despite the fact that the accuracy of the integration is known to depend mainly on the fineness of the r-space sampling, and not on a high number of time steps.

The MC approach is free from all these problems: time steps can be tailor made; the sampling of the distribution is finest around the forward rate (or price, as appropriate); each path has the same probability of occurrence of 1/(number of realizations). Furthermore, it is known that, if one wanted to tackle a multi-factor model, MC is probably *the* method to perform high-dimensional numerical integrations.

These advantages are not without price, at least for "naive" implementations: to begin with, in order to increase by a factor n the accuracy of the MC estimate, n^2 as many simulations have to be carried out. Furthermore, deltas and gammas are arduous to obtain, since they are numerically obtained as differences of noisy quantities. Finally, American early exercise opportunities cannot be evaluated, since at time t the expectation of a pay-off occurring at a later time (obtainable in trees using backward induction) is not available.

The well-known antithetic technique (see, e.g. Boyle (1977) or Hull and White (1988)), whereby to each path obtained with the stream of Brownian increments $\{dz_i\}$ the mirror path is added, obtained with the stream $\{-dz_i\}$, can substantially reduce the variance of the estimate. In addition, evaluating using the same stream of random numbers used to price the option of interest another security of analytically known value can provide a way to correct the option estimate (contravariate technique) (Boyle (1977)).

As for deltas or other statistics, a useful procedure consists of using the same series of random numbers to evaluate the option values for two slightly different initial values of the quantity with respect to which differentiation is sought. By this procedure, biases in each individual realization should to a large extent cancel when taking the difference between the "up" and "down" simulation. It is actually not rare to obtain, for relatively simple problems, deltas more accurate than the prices.

These techniques are neither very new nor very complicated. In addition, very recently the Martingale Variate Control technique (Clewlow and Carverhill (1994)) has been proposed, which claims to be able to reduce computational time by an order of magnitude; the actual suitability and power of the technique for interest rate options remains to be explored.

Despite these useful ancillary techniques MC procedures are only beginning to achieve great popularity, since, for realistic interest rate applications, a very large number of variables have to be evolved through time: the processes are in fact needed for the short rate and for as many forward rates as resets and pay-off indices affect the pay-offs, plus the "up" and "down" states for all of these quantities. Due to the resulting substantial computation burden, even "clever" implementations therefore often tend to be regarded as "tools of last resort".

2.4.3 PDE Approaches: Finite Differences Schemes and Analytic Solutions

In Section 2.3.2 it was shown that no-arbitrage arguments can lead directly to the PDE obeyed by any contingent claim. Historically this has indeed been the first line of approach to the valuation of interest rate options: as early as 1977 Vasicek introduced a normal mean-reverting model, followed by CIR's square-root-volatility process for the mean-reverting rate (Cox, Ingersoll and Ross (1985)), and Brennan and Schwartz's two-factor model (Brennan and Schwartz (1982)). Lately the approach has enjoyed a renewed interest due to the LS model (Longstaff and Schwartz (1992)), and to the HW extended-Vasicek approach (Hull and White (1990a)), reviewed in Sections 2.5.3 and 2.5.2, respectively.

As shown in Section 2.3.2 the common feature of these models is that the set of parameters (e.g. reversion speed, volatility, etc., collectively denoted in the following by $\{\alpha_i\}$), which describe the "real-world" process for the short rate, enter the PDE for an interest rate-dependent instrument together with the market price of risk. Therefore, estimating the $\{\alpha_i\}$ from time-series analysis of rates observed in the "real-world" measure is not sufficient in order to determine the coefficients of the PDE: access is needed to market instruments (e.g. bonds) which price the risk connected with the variability of the underlying factor(s). This is the route followed, among others, by LS: by making use of the time-series estimates of the "real-world" parameters $\{\alpha_i\}$, they obtain an estimate of the market price of risk by cross-sectional best fit to the observed bond prices on a given day.

Alternatively, one can dispense with the time-series analysis altogether, and attempt to determine the non-linear *combinations* of the $\{\alpha_i\}$ and of the market price of risk that cross-sectionally best account for the observed bond prices. Since a discount bond price is given by the expectation of the discounted maturity pay-off

$$P(t, T) = E'_t \left[\exp \left[- \int_t^T r(u) \, du \right] \right]$$

and since the discounting function is non-linear in the short rate, in general the yield of a T-maturity bond will depend not only on expectations of the future rates but also on future volatility. If the model were correctly specified and the "market noise" not too severe it would, of course, be immaterial whether the former or the latter route were followed. In practice, attempting an exclusively cross-sectional estimate of the PDE coefficients has inherent dangers: if the deterministic part of the short rate process is too simple to allow for complex patterns of expectations of rates, an inordinate burden would be put on the shoulders of the volatility component in order to attempt to recover the observed term structure. Humped yield curves have been known to create problems with simple approaches such as CIR or Vasicek. But it should always be remembered that even "rich" models which allow for more complex yield curve shapes can give no guarantee that the correct apportioning will be accomplished by a cross-sectional procedure between yield curvature arising from rate expectations and from future yield volatility.

In order to gain confidence about the reliability of the coefficients, a time-series inspection of their daily cross-sectional estimates is often very useful. Due to the fact that the

$\{\alpha_i\}$ are often estimated in conjunction with the *a priori* unknown market price of risk, it can be difficult to say anything very precise from the numerical values themselves, but such tell-tale indications as wildly fluctuating estimates over consecutive days can often point to a mis-specified or mis-estimated model.

Once reasonable confidence has been obtained that reliable coefficients have been estimated, if the functional form of the factor's process gives rise to a PDE which admits closed-form solution for the required boundary conditions, the computational advantages are obvious. Less obvious, but just as important, is that considerable computational savings can be accomplished with closed-form models even if numerical methods, such as finite differences, have to be employed to check, for instance, for early exercise opportunities: since at each node both the coefficients and the state variables are known, all quantities, in fact, such as swap rates, which can be expressed as a function of linear combinations of discount bonds, can be evaluated analytically on a node-by-node basis.

The preferred numerical procedures for the integration of the PDE have tended to be linked to finite differences schemes, either in the implicit (IFD) or the explicit (EFD) formulation. In both approaches, a rectangular grid is first set up containing different values of the state variable on one axis, and time on the other (for helpful graphical illustrations of the geometry of the problem see, e.g. Press et al. (1990)). The desired initial conditions, $v(., T)$, are first applied at expiry time T. As for the time derivative, it is evaluated as a *forward* difference, i.e. using the known value $v(i, T)$ and the unknown $v(i, T - 1)$. In the EFD scheme, the required first- and second-order space derivatives at node $(i, T - 1)$ (where i denotes the space (rate) co-ordinate and $T - 1$ the time) are then approximated by finite differences computed using the *known* values at nodes $v(i+1, T)$, $v(i, T)$, $v(i-1, T)$. In this approach, therefore, a single unknown quantity appears at each node (the value $v(i, T - 1)$ in the time derivative), and locally the PDE can therefore be recast in terms of a linear equation in a single unknown of the form:

$$v(i, T - 1) = \text{A } v(i - 1, T) + \text{B } v(i, T) + \text{C } v(i + 1, T) \tag{1}$$

This expression lends itself to a suggestive interpretation: if one defines $\text{A}' = \text{A } (1 + r\Delta t)$, $\text{B}' = \text{B } (1 + r\Delta t)$ and $\text{C}' = \text{C } (1 + r\Delta t)$ one can "read" the procedure as implying that the value $v(i, T)$ can move up, straight or down to values $v(i - 1, T)$, $v(i, T)$, $v(i + 1, t)$ with probabilities A', B' and C', respectively. For this interpretation to make sense the three coefficients must all be positive and add up to one. A more careful discussion of the stability issues shows that, for the type of parabolic PDE at hand, these are indeed the conditions (see Ames (1977), Nelson (1990)) for the stability of the numerical procedure. In general, however, the implicit drift of the short rate might be such that, for a given choice of Δt and Δx (where x denotes the "space" (i.e. rate) variable), the above stability conditions might not be satisfied. The problem can be circumvented by allowing the possibility of an upward or downward branching, from (i, j) to $(i + k - 1, j + 1)$, $(i + k, j + 1)$, $(i + k + 1, j + 1)$, with k equal to the smallest integer for which the stability conditions are met. The EFD scheme thus modified is the approach advocated by HW (Hull and White (1990b)) for their extended-Vasicek and -CIR approaches.

The IFD scheme, which "simply" differs in that the space derivatives at time $T - 1$ are approximated by a *centred* expression involving $v(i + 1, T - 1)$, $v(i, T - 1)$ and $v(i - 1, T - 1)$, does not suffer from these stability constraints; the appearance of a value, $v(i, T - 2)$, belonging to the time slice being updated implies, however, that no simple expression such as equation (1) is available, and one is forced to solve a linear system of equations; its solution is trivial, since the associated matrix is tri-diagonal, but the appealing intuitional features associated with the EFD scheme are lost. This is certainly one of the reasons why the EFD approach, with the modifications outlined above, has become very popular among practitioners. Despite the formal similarities between this method and lattice approaches, the EFD procedure is intrinsically more "delicate": to begin with, in order to ensure faster convergence and better stability, it is useful to transform the original space (i.e. rate) co-ordinate to a new variable, such that the coefficients of the PDE can be made time-independent (Hull and White (1990b) present a general procedure to accomplish this task). Careful handling of the boundary conditions is in general very important, particularly if more than one state variable is used; in this latter case, a mixture of implicit and explicit approaches (using, for instance, the Hopscotch method (Gourlay and McKee (1979))) is recommended. Furthermore, the "pseudo-probabilities" A', B' and C' can be made time-independent, but are always space-dependent, and have to be determined during the calculation (a lattice approach such as BDT's, instead, simply assumes $\frac{1}{2}$ and $\frac{1}{2}$ probabilities for the up and down states).

On the other hand, the closely linked trinomial tree technology, developed by HW in conjunction with their extended-Vasicek model reviewed later, supplies the user with an additional degree of freedom, with respect to binomial lattice methods, to fit an extra market variable; in particular, the approach can overcome the limitations of the BDT model by allowing the user to specify at the same time both the future volatility of the short rate and the term structure of volatility. Whether this should be regarded as an intrinsically positive feature is a debatable point and is discussed in Sections 2.5.1 and 2.5.2.

2.5 ANALYSIS OF SPECIFIC MODELS

2.5.1 BDT: Model Implications and Empirical Findings

The BDT model (Black, Derman and Toy (1990)) is a one-factor model algorithmically constructed in such a way as to price exactly any set of market discount bonds without requiring any explicit specification of investors' risk preferences. As a consequence, (plain vanilla) swap rates, which can be expressed as linear combinations of discount bonds, can be priced exactly for any volatility input. Whilst these features are shared by the HL model, the BDT approach further assumes a log-normal process for the short rate. Besides preventing negative rates, this assumption allows the volatility input to be specified as a percentage volatility, thereby following market conventions and making model calibration to cap prices much easier. This latter point is less trivial than it might seem, at least for non-flat term structure, as discussed in connection with the HW model (Section 2.5.2). Therefore, *simultaneous* fitting to the yield curve *and* to cap (or swaption) volatilities is conceptually straightforward and computationally very easy to achieve.

The price to be paid for all these positive features is, on the one hand, numerical (log-normal distributions hinder analytic tractability), and, on the other hand, conceptual: by the very fact that the model is specified algorithmically, it is rather "opaque" as to its implications and hidden assumptions, regarding, for instance, the nature of its mean reversion. It is therefore useful to unravel the implicit features of the BDT model, with a view to understand better the strengths and weaknesses of its performance.

The continuous-time equivalent of the BDT short rate process can be written in the form

$$r(t) = u(t) \exp(\sigma(t)z(t)), \tag{1}$$

where $u(t)$ is the median of the short rate distribution at time t, $\sigma(t)$ the short rate volatility, and $z(t)$ a standard Brownian motion. Unlike the case for the HL model, the median $u(t)$ is not obtainable analytically for log-normal processes. Some insight can, however, be obtained by converting equation (1) to its stochastic incremental form: after applying Ito's lemma to $r = r(t, z(t))$, with $z(t) = [\ln(r(t)) - \ln u(t)]/\sigma(t)$, one easily obtains

$$dy(t) = \{c(t) + a(t)[w(t) - y(t)]\} \, dt + \sigma(t) \, dz \tag{2}$$

with

$$y(t) = \ln[r(t)]$$

$$w(t) = \ln[u(t)]$$

$$c(t) = \partial \ln w(t)/\partial t$$

$$a(t) = \partial \ln[\sigma(t)]/\partial t$$

(Similar expressions are known in the literature; equation (2) above, however, makes explicit the link with the median of the distribution, important for MC implementations; the median, in turn, can be readily obtained from the built tree.) As the expression above shows, if the volatility is assumed to be constant, the model does not display any reversion speed: the logarithm of the short rate evolves by diffusion with a drift which follows the logarithm of the median, as implicitly determined by the forward induction tree-fitting procedure. If, on the other hand, the volatility is decaying with time, for instance according to the simple law

$$\sigma(t) = \sigma(0) \exp(-vt), \quad v > 0 \tag{3}$$

then equation (2) can be rewritten as

$$dy(t) = \{c(t) + v[w(t) - y(t)]\} \, dt + \sigma(t) \, dz \tag{3'}$$

clearly displaying the reversion of the logarithm of the short rate to a time-dependent reversion level, roughly given by the level of the (logarithm of) the forward rates. It is by this feature that the BDT model can simultaneously recover a series of market (Black) cap (or swaption) prices, obtained with a declining implied volatility. The equations obtained above can prove very useful in order to carry out MC simulations consistent with a given BDT implementation. This, in turn, is very important if one wants to risk-manage individual path-dependent options in a portfolio of ordinary options priced using the conventional tree methodology.

From equation (3) and (3') one can see that the assumption of decaying short rate volatility is required to prevent the unconditional variance of the short rate, $\sigma(t)^2 t$, from increasing with t without bounds, which would be inconsistent with the mean-reverting character of the short rate process. By allowing greater flexibility for the $\sigma(t)$ function, the prices of as many caps as desired can be simultaneously and easily obtained. It is important to notice that it is also possible, although slightly more cumbersome, to obtain simultaneous fitting to the prices of a series of options to enter, at different times, the same-maturity swap. It is in general, however, not possible to match at the same time cap and swaption prices; this is no specific shortcoming of the BDT model, but rather reflects the intrinsic limitation of any one-factor model, which, as such, implies perfect instantaneous correlation between different rates: whilst, in fact, a cap is a portfolio of independent options (caplets), a swaption is an option on a portfolio of rates, and, therefore, dependent on the imperfect correlation between them. Yield spread options would be similarly beyond the reach of the BDT approach. Only two-factor models can satisfactorily accommodate this feature.

A feature which is instead specific to the BDT model, as opposed to one-factor models in general, is the fact that the term structure of volatility is completely determined by the specification of the future volatility of the short rate. This simply stems from the fact that the reversion speed, which by and large determines the volatility of rates of different maturities, is not an independent parameter (as, for instance, in the HW model) but is a unique function of the short rate volatility (see equation (2) above). Figure 2.3 shows the volatility of yields of maturities from three months to ten years for a recent market USD curve, for different values of the decay constant v, and for a value of $\sigma(0)$ similar to what is observed at the short end of the cap market. For positive values of the decay constant, as implied by declining Black volatilities, yields of long maturities display less variability than short-maturity yields, in overall agreement with market observations.

With these limitations clearly in mind, it is important to assess the overall "realism" of the model, with a view to the ultimate acid test, i.e. the hedging performance. Within

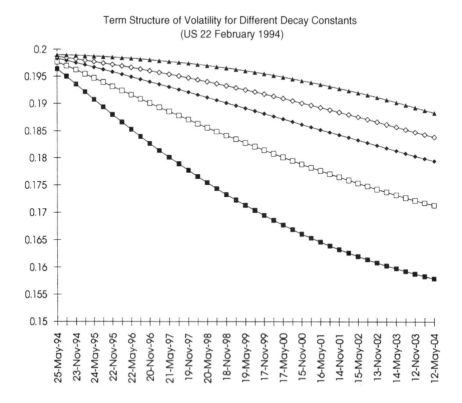

Figure 2.3 Volatility of yields of different maturities (USD 22nd February 1994) with decay constant v (top to bottom) $= 0$, 0.02, 0.04, 0.08, 0.16, and $\sigma_0 = 20$ per cent

the framework of any approach hedging can be accomplished "within the model", i.e. by attempting to neutralize the exposure to the model driving factor(s), or "outside the model", i.e. by obtaining price changes with respect to rate changes virtually not allowed by the model itself, e.g. rigid yield curve shifts. The latter procedure is clearly conceptually inconsistent, but a lot of confidence is needed to embrace the first, since, within the framework of any one-factor model, one could hedge an exposure to a ten-year yield with an overnight deposit! Technically, obtaining in-model hedge parameters is straightforward. By evolving backwards in the tree any two assets, A and B, to time $1\Delta t$, one can obtain their relative sensitivity through their sensitivities to the short rate:

$$\frac{A(\text{up}) - A(\text{down})}{B(\text{up}) - B(\text{down})} = \frac{\{[A(\text{up}) - A(\text{down})]/[r(\text{up}) - r(\text{down})]\}}{\{[B(\text{up}) - B(\text{down})]/[r(\text{up}) - r(\text{down})]\}} \tag{4}$$

Gammas can be similarly obtained by considering the asset prices at time $2\Delta t$, and the corrections for the small theta effect introduced are, in practical applications, both small and straightforward. To see more clearly the conceptual implications of the procedure, one can (Black, Derman and Toy (1990)) follow the strategy of buying a coupon-bearing bond, selling a call on the bond itself struck at X and purchasing a put, also struck at X. The value of this portfolio must equal the sum of the strike price X and the certain pay-offs from the strategy, i.e. the coupons intervening between today and the option expiry. If the present values of these known cash flows, correctly priced by the model by construction, are denoted as $\{Z(i)\}$, one must be able to write

$$\text{Put}(0) - \text{Call}(0) + \text{Bond}(0) = \sum_i \{Z(i)\}; \tag{5}$$

differentiating each term with respect to the bond price, one obtains

$$\Delta_{\text{call}} - \Delta_{\text{put}} = 1 - \partial \left[\sum \{Z(i)\}\right] \Big/ \partial \text{Bond} \tag{6}$$

The last term on the right-hand side represents the sensitivity of the portfolio of discount bonds to changes in the bond price. This term is absent in any Black-like price model, since, in such a framework, forward bond prices can change without any accompanying change in the discounting. Clearly, the effect becomes significant only when the option expiry is similar to the maturity of the bond.

From equation (4) above, one can easily derive the sensitivity of bond prices (and hence yields) of different maturities to changes in the short rate. In contrast with the term structure of volatilities, these sensitivities in general show little dependence on the decay constant v. They are instead strongly dependent on the shape of the yield curve, as displayed by Figure 2.4 for several market yield curves. Upward sloping term structures (e.g. USD and GBP in 1994) produce an elasticity above 1; the reverse is true for declining yield curves (e.g. ITL and ESP in the last quarter of 1993). This should come as no surprise, given the percentage nature of the BDT volatility. With these sensitivities, one can carry out what is probably one of the most stringent tests of a model's "realism". Armed with the yield sensitivities obtained using equation (4) above and with the foreknowledge of the day-by-day actual experienced changes in the short rate, one can predict the changes in yields of any maturity, and compare the model answers with the market outcome. This analysis, carried out for several currencies for

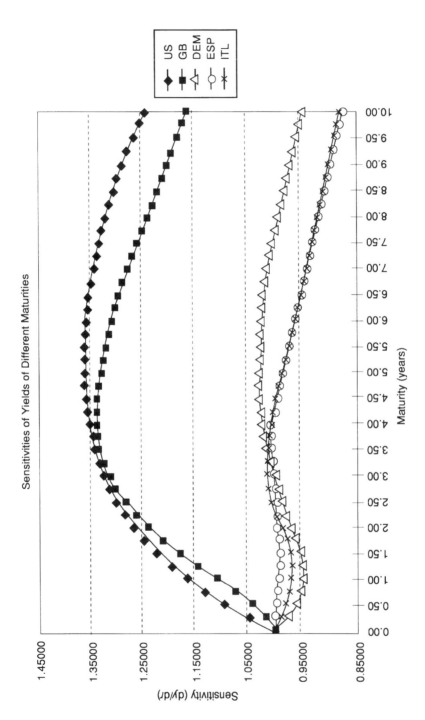

Figure 2.4 Sensitivity of yields of different maturities to a change in the short rate, for the yield curves of USD, GBP, DEM, ITL, ESP (24th February 1994, top to bottom at the right-end extreme). On this date, the GBP and USD yield curves were upward sloping, the DEM curve humped, and the ITL and ESP curve inverted

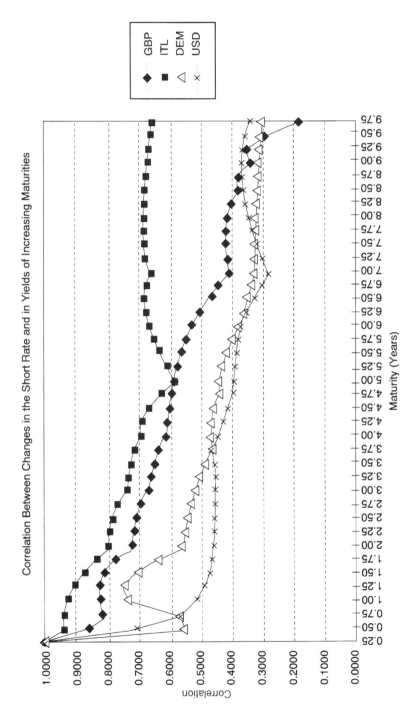

Figure 2.5 Correlation between experienced and model yield changes for increasing yield maturity using a choice of σ_0 and ν to give a good fit to cap prices: top to bottom ITL, USD, DEM, GBP

the period 1990–1993 with decay constant chosen to give an overall acceptable fit to market cap prices, obtained the results summarized in Figure 2.5. The correlation between experienced and predicted yield changes is, by construction, perfect at the short end, and decreases with yield maturity.

Whenever a yield curve displays steepening or flattening the agreement between observed and experienced yield changes is obviously poor, given the one-factor nature of the model. This important test therefore strongly cautions, in such environments, against blind in-model hedging.

The BDT model has therefore been shown to enjoy several positive features (among which the ease of calibration should not be underestimated) but to suffer from two important shortcomings: substantial inability to handle conditions where the impact of a second (tilt) factor could be of relevance; and inability to specify the volatility of yields of different maturities independently of the future volatility of the short rate. The former is unavoidable for any one-factor model; if one felt that the latter could be of relevance for a specific option (e.g. a long-maturity swap with principal determined by a short-maturity index), one could turn to approaches such as the HW model, reviewed in Section 2.5.2.

2.5.2 Extended Vasicek (HW): Model Implications and Empirical Findings

The previous section has highlighted how the mean-reverting features of the BDT model (on which the term structure of volatilities depends) cannot be divorced from the specification of the future volatility of the short rate. Hull and White (HW in the following) circumvent this problem by an approach that naturally combines the "classical" (PDE) approach and lattice methodologies. The process for the short rate, in fact, is explicitly given as

$$dr(t) = a(t)[\theta(t) - r(t)]\,dt + \sigma(t)r^\beta\,dz \qquad (1)$$

where the reversion level $\theta(t)$ is always a function of time, β is equal to 0 or $\frac{1}{2}$ to mirror the Vasicek or the CIR approach, respectively, and the volatility and reversion speed functions can, but need not, be time-dependent. The very elegant numerical strategy proposed by HW (1994) for the numerical solution of the accompanying PDE is a version of the Explicit Finite Difference method, modified, as explained in Section 2.4.3, to ensure numerical stability. In an earlier paper, HW (1990b) advocated a procedure whereby the choice was made on a node-by-node basis of whether normal, upward or downward branching should be effected. In a more recent paper (Hull and White (1994)) they have shown that the time step and the level at which switching from normal to modified branching occurs can be determined *a priori* from the model parameters, thus lightening the computational burden. It should be noticed that, after the switching time step, the resulting tree displays downward branching in the upper (high rates) region, upward branching in the lower region, and normal branching in the middle. Therefore, once switching has occurred, the overall "width" of the tree does not increase, thereby avoiding the wasteful sampling of very high and very low rates occurring with negligible probabilities in conventional (BDT-like) lattice approaches.

As for a comparison with the Vasicek/CIR approach, the salient difference is that, by allowing $\theta(t)$ to change with time, yield curves of arbitrary complex shapes can be exactly fitted. In this respect, therefore, the HW approach (Hull and White (1990a)) shares the same advantages and the same conceptual characteristics as the BDT approach. In addition, if the reversion speed is allowed to be time-dependent, the volatility of the yield of any maturity can be exactly recovered. The price to be paid for this *exact* match is that expressions for bond and bond option prices are no longer analytically obtainable even for the normal (Vasicek, $\beta = 0$) case, and for constant volatility. In earlier papers, Hull and White (1990a, 1993) show in detail the numerical procedure to employ in order to achieve the volatility match. Exact fitting to the term structure of volatilities, however, tends to produce, day by day, $a(t)$ functions that bear little resemblance to each other, and that imply implausible behaviour for the future term structure of volatilities. As Carverhill (1994) shows, the drawback of the BDT approach of imposing a potentially undesirable behaviour to the future behaviour of the short rate, rather than disappearing is shifted to the volatility term structure. In view of these considerations, the precise-fitting approach has been abandoned by practitioners, and by HW themselves in later papers, and the model is normally implemented with constant reversion speed. As a consequence, unlike BDT, it does not exactly reproduce the prices of an arbitrary set of caps. It is therefore customary to estimate, often using a least-square-fit procedure, the value of the reversion speed that best approximates the observed cap prices. If a constant volatility function is also chosen, the fitting is rendered particularly simple by the availability of analytic expressions for bond options: HW (1990a) in fact prove that, for the normal, constant-reversion-speed (a), constant-volatility (σ) model, a call option C expiring at time T and struck at X on a discount bond $P(0, s)$ maturing at time s is given by the Black-like expression

$$P(0, T)[P(T, s)N(h) - XN(h - \sigma_P)] \qquad (2)$$

where

$$P(T, s) = P(0, s)/P(0, T)$$
$$\sigma_P = v(0, T)B(T, s)$$
$$v(0, T)^2 = \sigma^2(1 - \exp[-2aT])/(2a)$$
$$B(t, T) = (1 - \exp[-a(T - t)])/a$$
$$P(t, T) = A(t, T)\exp[-B(t, T)r]$$
$$h = (\ln[P(T, s)/X] + \tfrac{1}{2}\sigma_P^2)/\sigma_P$$
$$\ln A(t, T) = \ln[P(0, T)/P(0, t)] - B(t, T)$$
$$- \sigma^2(\exp[-aT] - \exp[at])^2(\exp[2at] - 1)/(4a^3)$$
$$- B(t, T)\partial \ln[P(0, t)]/\partial t$$

Equation (2) highlights the similarity with the Black formula, since $P(0, T)$ plays the role of the discounting bond (the numeraire), and the option struck at X is seen to be a call on the *forward* bond price.

The cap-fitting procedure is, however, not quite as straightforward as one might surmise, both from the technical and from the conceptual point of view. Cap prices and (percentage!) volatilities, in fact, are quoted in the market on the basis of the Black model, which assumes log-normal rates. Since the normal distribution of rates implied by the HW/Vasicek model is fitted to the first two moments of the log-normal distribution, very little price difference is to be found for at-the-money strikes. Moving away from at-the-money strikes, however, the normal assumption begins to play a more important role. For a non-flat term structure of rates and a given strike, however, not all the caplets can be at-the-money. *In matching prices of caps of different maturities it is therefore essential to disentangle the price effects arising from the mean-reverting character of the short rate process* (approximately translated, in a Black framework, by assigning percentage volatilities declining with increasing maturities), *and from the different distributional assumptions.* Large errors in the estimate of the reversion speed can otherwise be made.

More seriously, a declining *percentage* volatility does not automatically imply a declining *absolute* volatility, as displayed by any sharply upward sloping curve. If one takes as a proxy for the absolute volatility the product of the relevant forward rate and its percentage volatility, it is easy to see that commonly observed market yield curves, such as the USD and GBP curves in 1994, coupled even with sharply declining percentage forward rate volatilities, fail to produce a positive (absolute) reversion speed for the normal HW model. Conversely, for declining yield curves, fitting to cap prices which imply a declining percentage volatility will tend to obtain a very strong normal reversion speed. Humped yield curves pose serious problems.

This feature, *per se*, simply indicates that some caution is needed when one is comparing the implications for mean reversion of log-normal and normal models. In the long run, all yield curves should become reasonably flat, and, therefore, a positive mean reversion must prevail in order to price very long caps. If one is interested in intermediate maturities, however, which can still be as long as eight or ten years for recent USD market yield curves, any positive reversion speed could seriously fail to account for their prices.

The situation is clearly illustrated by Figures 2.6 to 2.9. For a textbook case of a flat term structure of interest rates (10 per cent), the HW approach obtains with excellent accuracy the Black cap prices obtained not only with a flat term structure of volatilities (20 per cent, Figure 2.6), but also with a declining volatility (Figure 2.7). Notice that in the first case the optimal reversion speed and absolute volatility turn out to be almost exactly 0 and 0.02 ($= 20\% \cdot 10\%$) (This need not *a priori* have been the case, given the different distributional assumptions). For the second case of a declining percentage volatility, the reversion speed that gives overall best fit is positive (0.0991) and the absolute volatility similar, although not identical, to the product of the Black volatility $\sigma(0)$ (20 per cent) and *the* one rate (10 per cent). It is interesting to note that, in both cases, for at-the-money options the distributional differences play a very minor role.

For a decaying term structure of interest rates the fit to the cap prices obtained using the *same* declining percentage volatility is still acceptable (Figure 2.8), but now the estimated reversion speed is more than five times as large (0.548). Finally, Figure 2.9 shows that for a rising term structure of rates and the same declining term structure of volatilities not only is the fit rather poor, but the estimated "best" reversion speed turns out to be *negative* ($\sigma = 0.0197$, $a = -0.128$).

If one were only interested in these short-to-intermediate maturities, and therefore ready to accept the resulting model inconsistencies with very long maturity instruments, a normal negative reversion speed could be acceptable. From the implementation point of view, however, a negative mean reversion does create additional problems: the trinomial branching switching from "normal" to "upwards" or "downwards", described in detail in Hull and White (1994) and briefly touched upon in Section 2.4.3, totally fails to occur for negative reversion speeds; unfortunately, as discussed in the section devoted to the PDE/trinomial approach, it is indeed the switching that affords a potentially attractive construction in order to avoid the wasteful sampling of rate space effected by a model like BDT.

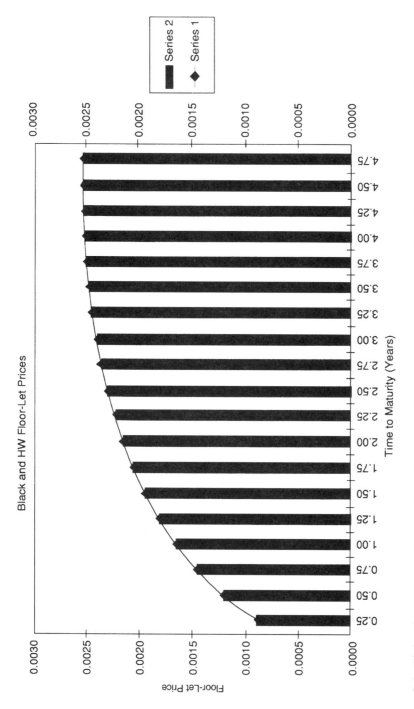

Figure 2.6 Fitting the HW parameters σ and α to log-normal floor prices for at-the-money strikes with flat term structures of interest rates (10 per cent) and of volatilities (20 per cent) for a variety of times to expiry (x-axis in years). The bars indicate the Black floor prices, and the continuous line the HW prices. Optimized reversion speed $a = 0$, $\sigma = 0.02$

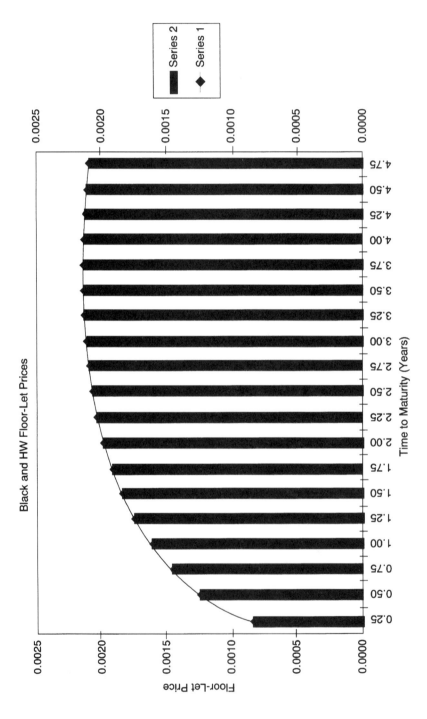

Figure 2.7 Same as Figure 2.6 with Black volatility starting at 20 per cent and declining by 0.20 per cent every quarter. The absolute volatility and the reversion speed were χ^2-optimized to minimize the sum of the squares of the differences between "market" (Black) and model option prices. Optimized reversion speed $a = 0.0991$, $\sigma = 0.02072$

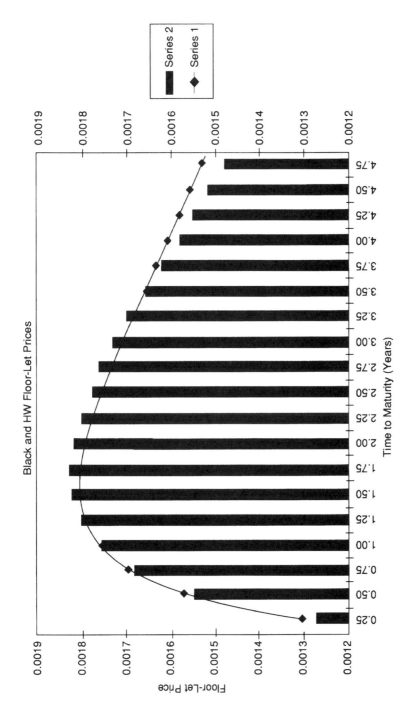

Figure 2.8 Same as Figure 2.7 but with term structure of rates declining from 10 per cent to 7.25 per cent over five years. Optimized reversion speed $a = 0.548$, $\sigma = 0.0231$

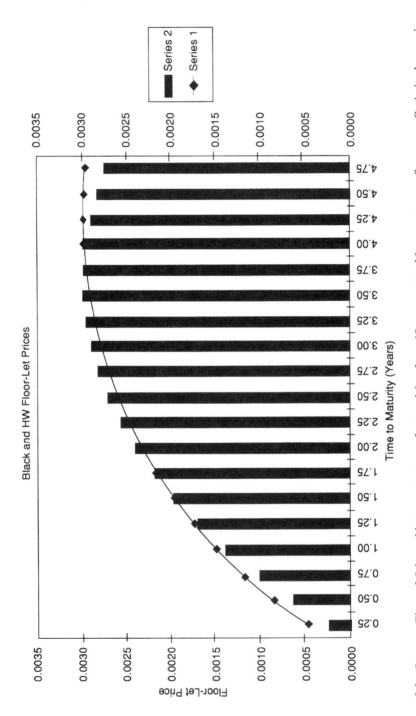

Figure 2.9 Same as Figure 2.8 but with term structure of rates rising from 10 per cent to 16 per cent over five years. Optimized reversion speed $a = -0.1275$, $\sigma = 0.0197$

At the present state of development, the HW approach therefore requires very careful handling. If these shortcomings are recognized, the existence of analytic solutions for bond and bond option prices makes the model of great appeal, if judiciously and carefully implemented. It should be recalled, in fact, that the HW approach is the only one to allow closed-form solutions without having to constrain the deterministic part of the process of the factor: how important this apparently minor point actually is will be fully appreciated after the section on the Longstaff and Schwartz model, and after the final conclusions.

2.5.3 Longstaff and Schwartz: Model Implications and Empirical Findings

The Principal Component Analysis presented in the introductory section indicated that the yield curve dynamics could be very satisfactorily explained by invoking as few as three orthogonal factors, i.e. the average level of the yield curve, its slope, and its curvature. These findings indicated that two-factor approaches should plausibly consider the slope of the yield curve as the second factor. Dybvig (1988) challenged this view by arguing that the level and the slope might well explain 95 per cent of the variance of rates or bond prices; however, if one is interested in the pricing of contingent claims, it might very well be that such an additive second factor has a negligible effect on the value of most options. If this second factor were instead taken to be the variance of the first principal component it could have a small effect on bond prices (virtually none at short maturities), but a significant effect on bond option pricing.

This is the view implicitly taken by Longstaff and Schwartz (1992) (LS in the following) in their two-factor equilibrium model. They derive it by considering a (very) stylized version of the economy, in which interest rates are obtained endogenously, rather than received from the empirical yield curve. In their model agents are faced with the choice between investing or consuming *the* single good produced in the economy. There is a single stochastic constant-return-to-scale technology (i.e. a single production process: identical companies in which investors can purchase shares). If $C(t)$ represents consumption at time t, the goal of the representative agent is to maximize, subject to budget constraints, his/her additive preferences of the form

$$E_t \left[\int_t^\infty \exp(-\rho s) \ln(C(s)) \, ds \right] \tag{1}$$

Consumption at time s is "discounted" to present the time t by a utility-discounting rate ρ, which present-values the "pleasure" of future consumption $C(s)$. $E_t[]$ is the conditional expectation operator, i.e. investors maximize their expectation, subject to information available up to time t, of the discounted future consumption. Consumption or reinvestment decisions have to be made subject to budget constraints that, given the assumptions above, have the form

$$dW = W \, dQ/Q - C \, dt \tag{2}$$

i.e. the infinitesimal change in wealth, W, over time dt is due to consumption $(-C \, dt)$ and returns from the production process (dQ/Q), scaled by the wealth invested in it (whence the constant-return-to-scale technology assumption).

The returns on physical investment (the only good produced by the economy) are in turn assumed to be described by a stochastic differential equation of the form

$$dQ/Q = (\mu X + \theta Y) \, dt + \sigma \sqrt{Y} \, dZ_1 \tag{3}$$

where dZ_1 is the increment of a Brownian motion, μ, θ and σ are constants, and X and Y are two state variables (economic factors) chosen in such a way that X is the component of the expected returns unrelated to production uncertainty (i.e. to dZ_1), and Y is the factor correlated with dQ. Both X and Y are Wiener processes described by stochastic differential equations

$$dX = (a - bX)\,dt + c\sqrt{X}\,dZ_2 \qquad (4)$$

$$dY = (d - eY)\,dt + f\sqrt{Y}\,dZ_3 \qquad (5)$$

Given the assumptions made, there is no correlation either between dZ_1 and dZ_2, or between dZ_2 and dZ_3.

If one accepts that the optimal consumption, given the assumption above, is ρW (see Cox, Ingersoll and Ross (1985) for a proof), direct substitution of equation (4) and of the optimal consumption in the budget constraint equation (3), gives for wealth the stochastic differential equation

$$dW = (\mu X + \theta Y - \rho)W\,dt + \sigma W\sqrt{Y}\,dZ_1 \qquad (6)$$

Having obtained the Wiener process followed by the wealth of the representative investor, two results from Cox, Ingersoll and Ross (1985) can be drawn upon to obtain the partial differential equation obeyed by any contingent claim H:

$$H_{xx}(x/2) + H_{yy}(y/2) + (\gamma - \delta x)H_x + (\eta - (\xi + \lambda)y)H - rH = H_\tau \qquad (7)$$

where $x = X/c^2$, $y = Y/f^2$, $\gamma = a/c$, $\delta = b$, $\eta = d/f^2$, r is the instantaneous riskless rate and the market price of risk has been endogenously derived to be proportional to y, rather than exogenously assumed to have a certain functional form.

The set of equations and assumptions described above gives a general equilibrium model for the economy as a whole. Contingent claims are priced in this framework as components of the economy, and their prices are therefore *equilibrium* (rather than "just" no-arbitrage) prices. Whilst this added feature of the LS model is certainly intellectually interesting, it should be kept in mind that their claim of providing a general equilibrium model is only valid within the context of the very stylized economy they assume.

A link between the unobservable quantities X and Y and more directly observable financial quantities can be obtained by remembering that, given the assumed logarithmic form of the utility of wealth function, the instantaneous interest rate is simply equal to the expected return from the production process (dQ/Q) minus the variance of the production returns (notice the similarity with the drift of stock returns in a Black and Scholes world, given by the riskless rate plus a compensation proportional to the standard deviation of the stock returns). Given the definition above, the instantaneous rate is therefore equal to

$$r = \alpha x + \beta y \qquad (8)$$

with $\alpha = \mu c^2$ and $\beta = (\theta - \sigma^2)f^2$. Since the stochastic differential equations for x and y are known, Ito's lemma can be applied to obtain the variance of r:

$$V = \alpha^2 x + \beta^2 y \qquad (9)$$

Finally, the Wiener processes for r and V can be obtained from equations (9) and (10) by using Ito's lemma, giving

$$dr = [\alpha\gamma + \beta\eta - r(\beta\delta - \alpha\xi)/(\beta - \alpha) - V(\xi - \delta)/(\beta - \alpha)]\,dt + \sigma_{r2}\,dZ_2 + \sigma_{r3}\,dZ_3 \qquad (10)$$

$$dV = [\alpha^2\gamma + \beta^2\eta - r\alpha\beta(\beta\delta - \alpha\xi)/(\beta - \alpha) - V(\beta\xi - \alpha\delta)/(\beta - \alpha)]\,dt$$
$$+ \sigma_{V2}\,dZ_2 + \sigma_{V3}\,dZ_3 \tag{11}$$

with

$$\sigma_{r2} = \alpha\sqrt{[(\beta r - V)/(\alpha(\beta - \alpha))]}$$
$$\sigma_{r3} = \beta\sqrt{[(-\alpha r + V)/(\beta(\beta - \alpha))]}$$
$$\sigma_{V2} = \alpha\sigma_{r2}$$
$$\sigma_{V3} = \beta\sigma_{r3} \tag{12}$$

Despite the fact that there are no cross-terms (i.e. $[dZ_2\,dZ_3]$) in the products of equations (11) and (12) (due to the assumptions made about the factors X and Y), there exists a non-zero correlation between r and V, which can be easily computed to be

$$\rho_{rV} = E[dr\,dV]/\sigma_r\sigma_V = \alpha^3 x + \beta^3 y/\sqrt{\alpha^2 x + \beta^2 y}\sqrt{\alpha^4 x + \beta^4 y}$$
$$= \alpha^3 x + \beta^3 y/\sqrt{V}\sqrt{\alpha^4 x + \beta^4 y} \tag{13}$$

Therefore, *in the LS model the value of the short rate volatility V is not uniquely determined by the level of the short rate.*

From the results obtained, it is easy to obtain the (unconditional) variances and expectations of r and V in terms of the parameters α, β, γ, δ, η and ξ:

$$E[r] = \alpha\gamma/\delta + \beta\eta/\xi \tag{14'}$$
$$\text{Var}[r] = \alpha\gamma/(2\delta^2) + \beta\eta/(2\xi^2) \tag{14''}$$
$$E[V] = \alpha^2\gamma/\delta + \beta^2\eta/\xi \tag{14'''}$$
$$\text{Var}[V] = \alpha^4\gamma/(2\delta^2) + \beta^4\eta/(2\xi^2) \tag{14''''}$$

respectively. The crucial importance of these relationships for model calibration will be shown in the following.

As for the joint distribution of the short rate and the variance, it can be shown that, given the absence of correlation between X and Y, it is given by the product of two independent non-central chi-squared distributions.

It is very interesting to examine the one-dimensional distribution $Q(r, t; r_0, V_0)$ resulting from integrating the two-dimensional distribution $q(r, V, t; r_0, V_0)$ over all the possible values of V:

$$\int_{\alpha r}^{\beta r} q(r, V, t; r_0, V_0)\,dV = Q(r, t; r_0, V_0) \tag{15}$$

The result of this integration is shown in Figure 2.10 for several values of t. With t increasing from 0.3 years to one year and to two years one can readily observe a delocalization of the initial value for the short rate of 8.00 per cent. The spreading of the distribution, however, does not increase at the same rate over time, and the rate distribution obtained for five years is virtually indistinguishable from the ten-year distribution. This feature should be contrasted with the type of log-normal distribution assumed, for instance,

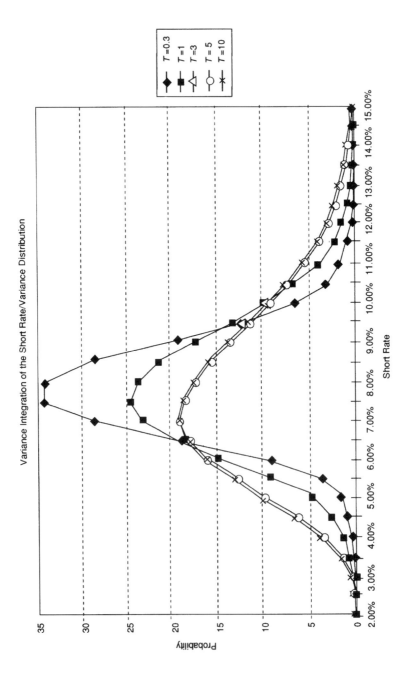

Figure 2.10 Volatility integration of the two-dimensional distribution $q(r, V, t)$ for values of t increasing from three months to ten years. Short rates on the x-axis. Notice how the distribution does not spread out significantly after the first five years

by the BDT model. In similar models, the burden of avoiding rates becoming too dispersed is taken up by imposing a time-dependent (decaying) volatility for the short rate. This *ad hoc* modification is not necessary with the LS model, which obtains more naturally and consistently the same result by virtue of the mean-reverting nature of its rate distribution.

Since any security traded in the LS economy must satisfy the PDE (7), this equation will have to be satisfied, in particular, by a discount bond. When the appropriate boundary condition $P(r, V, T) = 1$ is imposed, and a separation of variables approach is followed, the resulting expression for the value of a discount bond τ years before expiry turns out to be given by

$$P(r, V, \tau) = A^2 \gamma(\tau) B^2 \eta(\tau) e^{(\kappa\tau + C(\tau)r + D(\tau)V)} \tag{16}$$

with

$$A(\tau) = 2\varphi/[(\delta + \varphi)(e^{\varphi\tau} - 1) + 2\varphi]$$

$$B(\tau) = 2\psi/[(\nu + \psi)(e^{\psi\tau} - 1) + 2\psi]$$

$$C(\tau) = [\alpha\varphi(e^{\psi\tau} - 1)B(\tau) - \beta\psi(e^{\varphi\tau} - 1)A(\tau)]/[\varphi\psi(\beta - \alpha)]$$

$$D(\tau) = [-\varphi(e^{\psi\tau} - 1)B(\tau) + \psi(e^{\varphi\tau} - 1)A(\tau)]/[\varphi\psi(\beta - \alpha)]$$

$$\nu = \lambda + \xi$$

$$\varphi = \sqrt{(2\alpha + \delta^2)}$$

$$\psi = \sqrt{(2\beta + \nu^2)}$$

$$\kappa = \gamma(\delta + \varphi) + \eta(\nu + \psi)$$

As noted above, the market price of risk does not appear by itself, but only in combination with the parameter ξ. An infinity of values λ and ξ can therefore give rise to an identical fit to a given yield curve. Only if one supplemented information obtained from bond prices with information about the "real" (as opposed to risk-adjusted) dynamics of the state variables, would it be possible to estimate, within the context of the model, the market price of risk. Therefore, in order to fit a given yield curve, Longstaff and Schwartz (1994) have proposed the following two similar procedures. In both approaches: (i) a statistical analysis of the time series of the short rate and of the variance of the short rate is first carried out; and (ii) from the constraint that x and y should be greater than zero, one then obtains the condition that

$$\alpha < V/r < \beta \tag{17}$$

and one can therefore choose

$$\alpha = \min[V/r] \tag{18}$$

$$\beta = \max[V/r] \tag{19}$$

where the minimum and maximum are taken over the observed time series; (iii) from the simple system of non-linear equations (14) one can then determine the remaining four parameters. Up to this point the two procedures are identical. As for the evaluation of the further parameter ν related to the market price of risk two strategies can then be followed: (iv) (a) solve analytically with these six parameters and a *guess* value for ν the PDE with the boundary conditions appropriate to discount bonds, compare the model values thus obtained with a market-obtained discount function, and vary the value of v until the sum of squared deviations is minimized; or (iv) (b) take the first maturity of interest, t_1, solve the PDE above with the boundary condition pertaining to a zero discount bond maturing at time t_1 with a trial value for $v(t_1)$, thereby obtaining a model price for the discount bond, $P_{mod}(v(t_1))$; vary this trial value $v(t_1)$ until an *exact* match is obtained between the model and the market value; move on to the next maturity, and use the obtained value $v(t_1)$ for the numerical integration from time 0 to time t_1, and a trial value $v(t_2)$ for the period between t_1 and t_2; vary $v(t_2)$ until a match is obtained between observed and model prices. The procedure can be continued until all discount bonds are correctly priced.

It is important to notice that the first strategy is much simpler, since the model discount function can be obtained analytically, as long as v is constant; however, if this approach is employed one cannot in general recover the observed discount function exactly. On the other hand, the second approach recovers the prices of zero coupon bonds by construction, but is rather laborious due to the need to integrate the PDE (7) numerically. These proposed procedures are far from unique: the LS model allows for a combination of the approaches which are often described as "fundamental" (or historical) and "applied" (or implied), by determining some of the model parameters on the basis of historical data, and the remaining in order to fit whatever market quantity one might desire. If one were to take the purely "historical" estimation route, only v would remain free to be fitted. At the other extreme as many as six parameters and two state variables could be seen as degrees of freedom, giving rise to a strongly non-linear optimization problem. Finding an unambiguous absolute minimum can be very difficult, and, therefore, a lot of care should be exercised in choosing how many and which parameters should be optimized, and which should be determined from historical statistical series. To illustrate this point, I have performed a test of the ability of the LS model to price correctly the UK gilt market and the swap markets of the UK, the USA and Germany by best-fitting the six parameters and the two state variables (assumed to be not directly observable). The quality of the fit to the yield curves turned out in general to be very good, as shown in Figure 2.11, even for the case of a very "difficult" yield curve shape.

In the course of this minimization, none of the mathematically unacceptable regions were even encountered in the pre-September 1992 (Black Wednesday) period, despite the fact that no explicit constraint to this effect was put in place. Overall, the variations over time of the coefficients did not seem to be as "wild" as in the analysis of the CIR model, at least in the two sub-periods before and after September 1992. (Strictly speaking, of course, *any* variation of these coefficients, should, from the theoretical point of view, invalidate the model altogether.) After September 1992 (Black Wednesday) all the UK coefficients change radically, which is, after all, not surprising, since the UK yield curve changed drastically both in level and in shape. Needless to say, such a sudden change was in no way compatible with the rate dynamics implied by the model, and should therefore be seen as a "change of universe".

In the procedure described above the short rate was taken to be a completely free parameter in the optimization, and, therefore, the fact that it assumes values very close to the observed short rates is encouraging. On the other hand, since the coefficients were fitted to the market yield curve, and the quality of the fit was always good, the short rate is not really a "free" parameter, since it must, for any reasonable and well-behaved

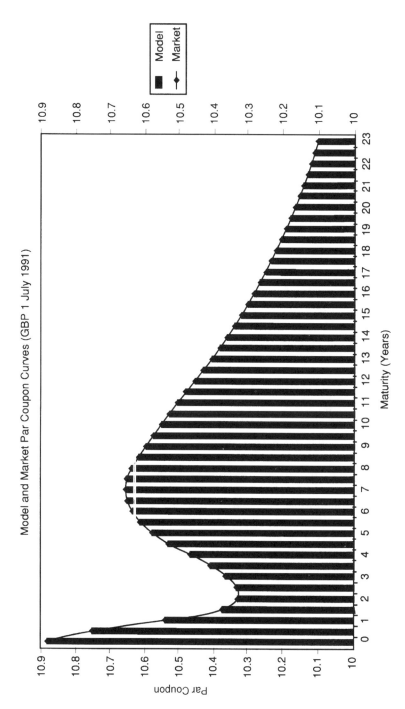

Figure 2.11 Fit of LS model rates (black dots) to market yield curve (bars) for a UK gilt curve of particularly difficult shape (maturities out to 22.5 years on the x-axis)

model, be very similar to the shortest fitted yields. The same considerations apply to the long yields: their closeness to observed values is, at the same time, both encouraging and, to some extent, ensured by the optimization procedure.

It is very interesting to calculate the degree of correlation between the two driving factors, i.e. the short rate and its variance: this correlation, for all the coefficients obtained, is always very high, sometimes as high as 99 per cent. If it were exactly unity, the model would collapse to a one-factor model. Yet, these very high correlations imply the de-correlations between rates of different maturities of very plausible magnitude. Due to this high degree of correlation between r and V, periods of high short rates are associated with periods of high rate volatility which is, to some extent, a plausible and desirable feature. What is less plausible and desirable, however, is that variance and rates move in step with the closeness implied by the obtained correlations. This feature becomes very important for option hedging. Given the excellent fit to market yield curves obtained by estimating cross-sectionally the model parameters, it is in fact natural to check the realism of the implied yield curve dynamics. To explore this feature the sensitivity of the yield curve to the short rate and the variance can be obtained by differentiating equation (16) with respect to these two state variables using the optimized parameters from the market yield curve for a given day. The "experienced" changes in the short rate and variance over two consecutive days can then be taken to be given by the differences of the respective quantities as obtained after the optimization procedure for the two days. With this information at hand, one can then predict the change in the price of a discount bond of maturity τ, as

$$\Delta F(r, V, \tau) = F(r, V, \tau)[C(\tau)\Delta r + D(\tau)\Delta V] \tag{20}$$

By considering the experienced changes in the discount functions over consecutive days the comparison can then be carried out between model predictions and "reality". Figures 2.12 and 2.13 show the results of some of these tests. For the coefficients obtained using the implied procedure, despite some fortuitously suggestive results, the agreement is in general rather poor, often worse than for the simpler BDT model. The reason for this can be traced to the sensitivity of a discount bond price to the variance of the short rate. This sensitivity is in fact large (roughly as large as the sensitivity to the short rate), but, given the very high degree of correlation between the short rate and its variance, a large experienced change in the former almost necessarily entails a large change in the latter; under these circumstances, the variance contribution to the yield change bears very little resemblance to real life contributions, and can therefore be totally unreliable. In short, the second factor, at least as distilled by the optimization procedure described above, fails convincingly to account for the observed yield variations. The hedging implications of these findings are of course very important: in practical situations one will try to match the sensitivity to the underlying factors of a given instrument with the corresponding sensitivities of two other instruments, judiciously chosen. If the sensitivity to one of the factors is a number of very dubious reliability, the reasonableness and effectiveness of the hedging procedure becomes very questionable. It is also important to point out that the high correlation feature is not specific to the "implied" estimation procedure.

Apart from these calibration issues, in order to bring into play market information from instruments dependent on the volatility of the short rate (such as cap prices), or the degree of correlation between rates of different maturities (such as swaptions), the procedure is not as straightforward as for the discount function. The cap volatility curve could for

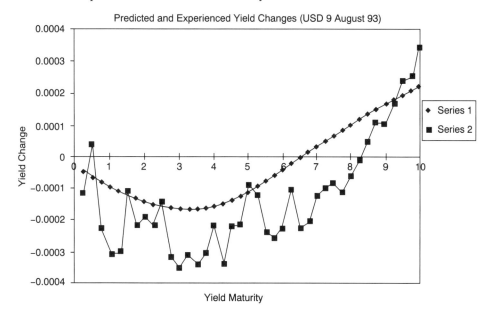

Figure 2.12 An example of a very good prediction (black squares) for a complex pattern of yield changes (USD curve 9th August 1993, maturities out to ten years on the *x*-axis). No one-factor model could reproduce such a complex pattern

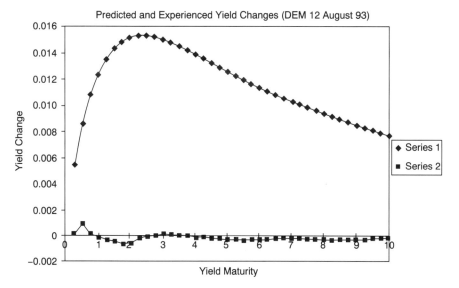

Figure 2.13 An example of a very poor prediction (black squares) for a relatively simple pattern of yield changes (DEM curve 12th August 1993, maturities out to ten years on the *x*-axis). No reasonable one-factor model could produce such big errors for the market yield changes of this particular example

instance be fitted by means of the following procedure: given a set of parameters (α, β, γ, δ, η, ξ and v), however determined, construct a finite difference grid with the terminal pay-off of the cap, and evolve it backwards in time along the three-dimensional (two "space" (r and V) and one time co-ordinate) lattice until time zero is reached; at this time, a two-dimensional array of today's cap values is obtained; for a given (observable) value of $r(0)$ this will collapse to a single vector of cap prices. One can then pick, or interpolate, the volatility V value that gives the correct cap market value. As described, the procedure is suggestively similar to obtaining an "implied volatility" in a Black and Scholes approach.

The problem, however, is that the discount function which describes the model yield curve to be fitted to the market values is a function of the six parameters *and* of the two state variables. The two procedures described above cannot, therefore, be applied independently. The free parameters will specify a yield curve for a given choice of r and V. No "separation of variables" is possible, as it is, implicitly, in the BDT case. The problem is, of course, not insoluble: the degrees of freedom to fit zero coupon bond prices *and* cap volatilities *and* a lot more are all there; what is hard to find, and to my knowledge has not been determined yet, is a procedure to fit both functions in a relatively straightforward way.

The discussion so far has shown that the LS model is very rich and powerful. Ultimately, the success of the model will depend on a successful strategy for the calibration of its many degrees of freedom. Whether fitting all the available market data is desirable is, of course, a different question, whose answer ultimately depends on the confidence the user is prepared to put in a particular model, and on the judgement of the extent to which specific markets (e.g. swaptions) are sufficiently "perfect" (e.g. liquid and/or devoid of institutional frictions) to justify the enforcement of the assumptions that generate the no-arbitrage conditions. Should the user blindly fit a model to these quantities? What should be questioned, the model or the market prices? Is the model indicating trading opportunities?

2.5.4 The HJM Approach

Section 2.3.4 showed that, if the chosen numeraire is the money market account, all assets grow at the riskless rate (equation (5), Section 2.3.4), and forward rates are not martingales but display the drift given by the first term on the right-hand side of equations (7) and (8) of Section 2.3.4, for the discrete and continuous-time case, respectively.

These two equations can be derived within the framework of the Heath, Jarrow and Morton (1992) approach, which can therefore be more aptly described as a no-arbitrage condition rather than a specific model. Reasoning similar to the argument that leads from equations (6) to (8) of Section 2.3.4, in fact, requires that, for a log-normal bond price process, the discrete forward rates from time T_1 to time T_2 as seen from the time-t yield curve, $f(t, T_1, T_2)$, should be given by

$$df(t, T_1, T_2) = 1/(2(T_2 - T_1))[v(t, T_2)^2 - v(t, T_1)^2] \, dt$$
$$+ 1/(T_2 - T_1)[v(t, T_1) - v(t, T_2)] \, dz(t) \qquad (1)$$

where $v(t, T)$ is the time-t volatility of a bond of maturity T (see Carverhill (1993) for the equivalence between the price-based and forward-based formulations). Since this equation simply imposes a relationship between the drifts and volatilities of forward rates, and the price volatility functions of discount bond prices, there is no such thing as *the* HJM model; rather there exist a whole class of models, each characterized by a specific functional form for the volatility functions. It is worthwhile commenting on the complexity and richness of this volatility input. The starting point of any implementation of the HJM approach is the observed yield curve, as described by the collection of discount bonds given at time 0, $P(0, T)$. The link between discount bond prices and instantaneous forward rates $f(0, T)$ (defined as the limit of $f(t, T_1, T_2)$ as T_1 tends to T_2, and denoted, for simplicity, $f(0, T)$) is given by

$$P(0, T) = \exp\left[-\int_0^T f(0, s)\,\mathrm{d}s\right] \tag{2}$$

$$f(0, T) = -\partial[\ln P(0, T)]/\partial T \tag{2'}$$

Either the discount bonds or the forward rates can therefore be taken as equivalent building blocks; in either case the approach recovers by construction any given market yield curve. For the valuation of an option depending on n discrete forward rates, $(f(0, t_i, t_i + \tau), i = 1, \ldots, n)$, these will have to be evolved from time 0 to the option expiry. Equations (7) and (8) of Section 2.3.4 show that the values of $2n$ discount bond volatility functions $(v(0, t_i), v(0, t_i + \tau), i = 1, \ldots, n)$ are needed at time 0. Once each forward rate has been evolved over a time step Δt, the $2n$ volatilities at time Δt of discount bonds of maturity $t_i - \Delta t, t_i + \tau - \Delta t$ will be required to evolve the forward rates over one further step. In principle, unless some strong volatility constraints are imposed, this approach would leave the user with the task of specifying the price volatilities of discount bonds of continuously changing maturities at each point in the evolution of the forward rates. For practical implementations, the need to specify a functional form for the functions $v(.)$ is therefore clear, and to each particular choice there will correspond *a* particular HJM model. A first and absolutely necessary condition on the function $v(t, \tau)$, in order to prevent infinite drifts, is that $v(t, t) \equiv 0\,\forall t$, simply reflecting the certainty of the redemption at par of any discount bond.

A second restriction on the possible functional forms is to impose that the process for the short rate should be Markovian. If this is the case, in fact, HW (Hull and White (1993), see also Carverhill (1992)) prove that the function $v(t, T)$ must be of the form

$$v(t, T) = x(t)[y(T) - y(t)] \tag{3}$$

A further assumption on the volatility functions which, as seen, could in principle depend *both* on calendar time *and* on residual maturity is that of time stationarity, i.e. the requirement that the volatility of the discount bond should depend only on the residual time to maturity, and not on calendar time t. When both these two latter constraints are simultaneously imposed, it is not difficult to prove that the function $v(., .)$ must have the following functional form

$$v(t, T) = [k(1 - \mathrm{e}^{-a(T-t)})]/a \tag{4}$$

whose limit as a tends to zero (i.e. in the absence of mean reversion) is simply

$$v(t, T) = k(T - t) \tag{4'}$$

Inserting (4') in equation (2) of Section 2.5.2 with $B(t, s) = T - s$, and $\sigma(0, T) = kT$, and taking the limit as a tends to zero clearly shows that this particular choice for the volatility function simply gives the continuous-time limit of the HL model, and that the volatilities of spot rates of all maturities, $R(0, T) = -\ln[P(0, T)]/T$, are exactly the same; under this model, therefore, *the whole yield curve can only move strictly in parallel*.

It is interesting to notice that, for choice (4'), the condition of no-arbitrage between bonds is certainly satisfied (by the very construction of the forward rate processes); there still exists the possibility of arbitrage, however, between bonds and the money market account, since rates attain negative values with strictly positive probability in finite time under (4'). This no-arbitrage violation, of course, is no worse than what is found in the HL or extended-Vasicek approaches.

The requirement to make the process for the short rate Markovian (see also the discussion after equation (5) below) is clearly very restrictive, but has the vast computational advantage that any Markov process can always be mapped into a *recombining* lattice, whose number of nodes grows linearly with the number of time steps.

Apart from this special case, an "up" move of all the forwards followed by a "down" move will not, in general, recover the original yield curve. In other words, the accompanying computational tree does not recombine. This feature constitutes the most severe technical drawback connected with the general HJM approach, and it has often forced upon practitioners the use of Monte Carlo techniques. Non-recombining trees have also been proposed, on the basis of the argument that it is the final number of states sampled, rather than the number of time steps, which determines the accuracy of the numerical integration. It has been argued that as few as ten or 12 time steps could give a sufficient sampling for pricing applications, but, in the absence of much published material on the matter, it is difficult to see how a five-year cap with quarterly resets (let alone an option thereon) could be priced using this technique.

Confining oneself to MC approaches, given the choice of numeraire one must be able to discount, prior to the averaging, each pay-off using the value of the money market account obtained in the course of each individual realization. To obtain this quantity one must have access to the value of the short rate at each point in time along the path. The stochastic process for the latter can be shown to be given, for one-factor models, by

$$dr(t) = [\partial f(0, t)/\partial t]\, dt + \left\{ \int_0^t v(\tau, t)\partial^2 v(\tau, t)/\partial t^2 + (\partial v(\tau, t)/\partial t)^2 \right\} dt$$

$$+ [\partial v(\tau, t)/\partial t|_{\tau=t}]\, dz(t) + \left\{ \int \partial^2 v(\tau, t)/\partial t^2\, dz(\tau) \right\} dt \qquad (5)$$

The interpretation of the terms is very interesting: the first clearly reflects the slope of the yield curve as seen from time zero; the third shows that the instantaneous standard deviation of the short rate equals the slope of the price volatility function at the origin, as the running time approaches the maturity; the second term depends on the history of the volatility function up to time t; finally, the fourth depends on the history both of $\sigma(., .)$ and of the Brownian process $z(t)$. From this analysis one can easily see that the process for the short rate is certainly non-Markovian if $v(\tau, t)$ depends on stochastic variables at times earlier than t (see Carverhill (1992)). Furthermore, even if $v(\tau, t)$ only depends on calendar time and time to maturity, the short rate process will still be non-Markovian unless the integrand in the fourth term is identically equal to zero.

For the special choices of the volatility functions mentioned above the short rate processes become

$$dr(t) = \{\partial f(0, t)/\partial t + k^2/(2a)[1 - \exp[-2at]] - ar + af(0, t)\}\, dt + k\, dz \qquad (6)$$

and

$$dr(t) = \{\partial f(0, t)/\partial t + k^2 t\}\, dt + k\, dz \qquad (6')$$

for $a \to 0$ limit. Needless to say, for these choices of the analytic form of the volatility functions, the calibration procedure will not, in general, yield an exact match to the market cap prices.

In the framework of the MC approach, a large number of quantities must therefore be evolved at each time step: as many forwards as caplets in a cap, each in an up and a down state if one needs derivatives, plus the short rate, in the up and down state as well if sensitivity to the discounting is desired; at each reset, one forward, and its accompanying statistics, can be shed, one at a time until the last reset, at which point only the short rate has to be evolved until the option pay-off time. This rather daunting computational task should be compared with a BDT-like tree construction. On the other hand, an option at time t on a bond maturing at time T only requires evolution of the relevant quantities out to option expiry time, thereby saving the wasteful building of the tree out to bond maturity for traditional lattice approaches.

The comparative advantage of the HJM approach is, however, best seen in the case of two-factor models. To begin with, the computational slow-down of Monte Carlo techniques with increasing number of dimensions is less than the speed reduction of finite-difference-based approaches. Furthermore, the analysis carried out in Section 2.3.4 which gives the drift and variance for the forward rates, can be translated almost by inspection into a multi-factor formalism (only the process for the short rate becomes somewhat involved). In addition, the principal component analysis reported in Section 2.2 provides a direct indication of the factors (level and slope) that could be taken to drive the yield curve dynamics. Finally, with appropriate scaling, the loadings (weights) which result from the principal component analysis provide a direct route towards the historical estimation of the volatility functions of the driving factors. Whilst this approach is conceptually straightforward, and bound to make the volatility inputs not only reasonably robust, but also of direct financial appeal (e.g. volatility of the level and of the spread), it will share the shortcomings of historical approaches, in that it will not recover exactly market option prices. The alternative, as usual, is to embrace an "implied" procedure, perhaps after imposing functional constraints on the inputs which embody the gist, if not the numerical output, of the principal component analysis. In this case, however, the calibration to market prices can become very time consuming, especially given the fact that the noise in the price estimates makes the evaluation of the derivatives with respect to the model parameters (needed for Newton–Raphson-like procedures) very arduous.

It is therefore indubitable that the HJM approach has great financial and intellectual appeal, not to mention a certain undeniable elegance; it also fair to say that, at the present stage of computer technology, its practical implementation for actual pricing and risk management applications is at the very boundaries of feasibility.

2.6 CONCLUSIONS OR "HOW TO CHOOSE THE BEST MODEL"

Several different approaches to the pricing of interest rate-dependent options have been reviewed in the preceding sections. The survey has been, by necessity, incomplete, but a few general thoughts should have emerged from the discussion. A distinction was first of all drawn between analytic and algorithmic models, which goes well beyond the greater ease of computation of the former. Starting with analytic approaches, it was shown that the general approach has been to describe the dynamics of the underlying factor(s) by assigning to the drift and variance components of their stochastic processes an explicit functional form in terms of the state variable(s) and of the model parameters. The PDE obtainable from these processes was also shown to contain, in addition to the state variables and the model parameters, the market price of risk. This fact has profound implications for model calibration. It is indeed true, in fact, that statistically and financially well-defined quantities, such as reversion speeds or reversion levels, can be estimated in a conceptually straightforward way. At least some of these quantities, however, only enter the PDE in conjunction with the non-directly observable market price of risk. Two different routes have therefore been followed by researchers and practitioners: the first has been to estimate the financially "observable" quantities pertaining to the factor dynamics (e.g. reversion speeds and reversion levels) from a *time-series* analysis of "real-world" data. Using the estimates thus obtained, *cross-sectional* estimates of the market price of risk can then be carried out via a best fit to the market instruments that price the risk (e.g. bonds). In general, if analytic tractability is to be retained, strong constraints have to imposed on the market price of risk (for the LS model, for instance, it has to be a constant over time). The result of this procedure is that, in general, the pricing of underlying instruments (bonds) implied by the model is not identical to their market values. The severity of the mis-pricing by and large depends on the shape of the yield curve, and will have a different impact for different pricing applications. Earlier models, however, such as Vasicek or CIR, were very seriously deficient in their ability to reproduce any but the simplest yield curve shapes, thus rendering them of little practical use, for instance, for the doubly inflected UK term structure of the early 1990s (see Figure 2.12).

The second approach with analytic models has been to estimate both the parameters in their combinations with the market price of risk and the state variables when not directly observable via a cross-sectional best fit to bond prices. Even with a constant market price of risk this approach has proven capable of recovering, at least for two-factor models such as the LS, complex yield curve shapes with great accuracy. As pointed out in Section 2.5.3, however, the curvature of the yield curve depends both on the expectation of future rates *and* of future volatilities. By an overall best-fit procedure there is therefore no guarantee that, for an imperfectly specified model (and all realistic models by necessity are), the correct (or even a reasonable) apportioning will be found by the minimization procedure of the rate and volatility contribution to the yield curve curvature. To give a concrete example, a model like the CIR, which assumes constant reversion speed and reversion level, can only attempt to account for a humped yield curve with long yields below the current short rate by a very heavy loading on the volatility contribution to the curvature, whilst a more "natural" description of the yield curve shape would plausibly invoke a time-dependent level of reversion.

If cross-sectionally implemented in this fashion, sophisticated two-factor models can therefore be more of a bane than a blessing: as shown in Section 2.5.3, an excellent fit to a given yield curve can in fact give the illusion of a "good" parametrization, whilst in reality a spurious loading can be implying dangerously incorrect sensitivities to the state variables (see Figure 2.12).

A third option is, of course, possible, i.e. to use time series to estimate the financially observable parameters, and to allow for a general time-dependent functional form for the market price of risk, so as to ensure (by construction) perfect fit to the yield curve, whilst retaining, at the same time, control on the financially more transparent quantities. Analytic tractability, however, is in this case lost and, despite the apparently *a priori* specification of the factors' dynamics, the market price of risk effectively becomes a handy *deus ex machina*, not only "fine tuning" possible imperfections in the statistical estimation of the parameters, but effectively picking up the slack of any model mis-specification. If so implemented, the approach becomes virtually indistinguishable, both conceptually and numerically, from a lattice methodology such as BDT, where the drift is algorithmically constructed so as to price in an arbitrage-free way an exogenous term structure.

At this point, the deciding factor becomes one of numerical efficiency, and, especially for two-factor models, the FD schemes necessary to solve the resulting PDEs do not present significant advantages with respect to n-nomial lattices, or, for that matter, skilful MC implementations.

This brings the discussion naturally to the second (i.e. algorithmic) approach. In view of the above, the high degree of control on the inputs and the capability of recovering exactly a given yield curve have obvious appeal. The numerical burden, however, tends to be severe even for one-factor models. This is particularly true for third-generation discontinuous pay-off (knock-out) options, where the fineness of the index sampling is all important for reliable pricing. But also for continuous pay-off options the hedging requirements can exact a very heavy computational toll. The distinction must in fact be made between in- and outside-model hedging. In the first approach, once the tree has been constructed, the security price is discounted backwards along the tree together with the price of a chosen hedging instrument. By analysing the up and down values one or two time steps before the root (and possibly adjusting for the small theta effect), it has been shown that it is straightforward enough to obtain the desired sensitivities to the driving factor (typically the short rate), and hence the hedge ratio. This approach, however, places a heavy burden on the shoulders of the model itself, since it cannot give any indication about the suitability of the hedging instrument: after all, in the context of a one-factor model in which all rates are instantaneously perfectly correlated, one could hedge a 30-year bond option with an overnight deposit. No sensible user would place such confidence on any of the currently available models. The approach is therefore commonly followed to shock the yield curve by an *exogenously* chosen perturbation of, for instance, forward rates, to rebuild the tree, and to reprice the security accordingly. Taking the difference between the security prices with the different yield curves gives an estimate of the desired sensitivity. Needless to say, this approach is in general conceptually inconsistent with the model used for pricing, since the latter will implicitly assign a virtually zero probability to the imposed shock. It is, however, much less dependent on the implied yield dynamics of a given model, which, as amply shown in the preceding section, is far from being satisfactorily described by any of the available models. As a consequence, the latter is the approach preferred by practitioners, and recommended by many academics.

As pointed out in the introduction, the increased market popularity of products strongly dependent on the imperfect correlation between rates is making the need for a two-factor approach more and more acutely felt: not only are spread-type options becoming increasingly common, but indexed or knock-out instruments (where the principal is determined by an index rate different from the rate determining the pay-off) have also met with great interest. The computational burden can therefore be quite demanding even for one-factor models, especially if discontinuous pay-off options are to be valued. As for algorithmic two-factor models the desiderata are a rather tall order: the joint dynamics of the state variables must, of course, be arbitrage free; the inputs should afford a direct financial interpretation (e.g. they could be volatilities of and correlation between observable financial quantities); the calibration procedure should be not only reasonably fast, but also robust; the lattice should recombine if one wants to avoid falling back on minor variations on the MC theme; once built by forward induction, the lattice structure should be storable by keeping at most $O(n^2)$ parameters (e.g. transition probabilities); the sampling of the state variables should be fine enough to allow realistic pricing and hedging of barrier options.

All the existing two-factor models fall short in some respect of some (or most) of these requirements, which explains why, at the present time, they are often used more as qualitative research tools than as actual pricing methodologies. It is in this latter direction, I believe, that the most challenging and exciting developments of interest rate option pricing will take place in the near future.

2.7 REFERENCES

Ames, W.F. (1977) *Numerical Methods for Partial Differential Equations*. New York: Academic Press.

Black, F. (1976) "The pricing of commodity contracts". *Journal of Financial Economics*, **3**, 167–79.

Black, F., Derman, E. and Toy, W. (1990) "A one-factor model of interest rates and its application to Treasury bond options". *Financial Analysts Journal*, 33–9.

Black, F. and Scholes, M. (1973) "The pricing of options and corporate liabilities". *Journal of Political Economics*, **81**, 637–53.

Boyle, P.P. (1977) "Options: a Monte Carlo approach". *Journal of Financial Economics*, **4**, 323–8.

Brennan, M.J. and Schwartz, E.S. (1982) "An equilibrium model of bond pricing and a test of market efficiency". *Journal of Financial and Quantitative Analysis*, **17**, 301–29.

Brown, H.B. and Schaefer, M.S. (1991) "The term structure of real interest rates and the Cox, Ingersoll and Ross model". Unpublished working paper, London Business School, May.

Brown, S.J. and Dybvig, P.H. (1986) "The empirical implications of the Cox, Ingersoll, Ross theory of the term structure of interest rates". *Journal of Finance*, **41**, 617–29.

Carverhill, A. (1992) "A binomial procedure for term structure options; when is the short rate Markovian?". Working paper, Hong Kong University of Science and Technology, Clear Water Bay, HK, January.

Carverhill, A. (1993) "A simplified exposition of the Heath, Jarrow and Morton model". Working paper, Department of Finance, University of Science and Technology, Clear Water Bay, HK 4 October.

Carverhill, A. (1994) "A note on the models of Hull and White for pricing options on the term structure". Working paper, Department of Finance, University of Science and Technology, Clear Water Bay, HK, July.

Chatfield, C. and Collins, A.J. (1989) *Introduction to multivariate analysis*. London: Chapman and Hall.

Cheng, S.T. (1991) "On the feasibility of arbitrage-based option pricing when stochastic bond price processes are involved". *Journal of Economic Theory*, **53**, 185–98.

Clewlow, L. and Carverhill, A. (1994) "Quicker on the curves". *Risk*, vol. 7, no. 5.

Cox, J.C., Ingersoll, J.E. and Ross, S.A. (1985a) "A theory of the term structure of interest rates". *Econometrica*, **53**, 385.

Cox, J.C., Ingersoll, J.E. and Ross, S.A. (1985b) "An intertemporal general equilibrium model of asset prices". *Econometrica*, **53**, 363.

Dybvig, P.H. (1988) "Bond and bond option pricing based on the current term structure". Working paper, Washington University in St. Louis.

Gourlay, A.R. and McKee, S. (1977) "The construction of Hopscotch methods for parabolic and elliptic equations in two space dimensions with a mixed derivative". *Journal of Computing and Applied Mathematics*, **3**, 201–6.

Gustavsson, T. (1992) "No-arbitrage pricing and the term structure of interest rates". Working paper, Department of Economics, Uppsala University, Economic Studies, **2**.

Harrison, J.M. and Kreps, D. (1979) "Martingales and arbitrage in multiperiod securities markets". *Journal of Economic Theory*, **20**, 381–408.

Harrison, J.M. and Pliska, S. (1981) "Martingales and stochastic integrals in the theory of continuous trading". *Stochastic Processes and their Applications*, **11**, 215–60.

Heath, D., Jarrow, R.A. and Morton, A. (1987) "Bond pricing and the term structure of interest rates: a new methodology". Working paper, Cornell University.

Heath, D., Jarrow, R.A. and Morton, A. (1989) "Bond pricing and the term structure of interest rates: a new methodology". Working paper (revised edition), Cornell University.

Ho, T.S.Y. and Lee, S.-B. (1986) "Term structure movements and pricing interest rate contingent claims". *Journal of Finance*, **41**, 1011–28.

Hull, J. and White, A. (1988) "The use of control variate technique in option pricing". *Journal of Financial and Quantitative Analysis*, **23**, 237–51.

Hull, J. and White, A. (1990a) "Pricing interest-rate derivative securities". *Review of Financial Studies*, **3**, 573–92.

Hull, J. and White, A. (1990b) "Valuing derivative securities using the explicit finite differences method". *Journal of Financial and Quantitative Analysis*, **25**, 87–100.

Hull, J. and White, A. (1993a)"Bond option pricing based on a model for the evolution of bond prices". *Advances in Futures and Options Research*, **6**, 1.

Hull, J. and White, A. (1993b) "Efficient procedures for valuing European and American path-dependent options". *Journal of Derivatives*, Fall issue, 21–31.

Hull, J. and White, A. (1994) "Numerical procedures for implementing term structure models I: single factor models". *Journal of Derivatives*, Fall issue, 7, 16.

Jamshidian, F. (1990) "Bond and option evaluation in the Gaussian interest rate model". Working paper, Financial Strategies Group, Merryll Lynch Capital Markets, World Financial Centre, NY, USA.

Jamshidian, F. (1991) "Forward induction and construction of yield curve diffusion models". Working paper, Financial Strategies Group, Merryll Lynch Capital Markets, World Financial Centre, NY, USA.

Longstaff, F.A. and Schwartz, E.S. (1992a) "Interest rate volatility and the term structure: a two-factor general equilibrium model". *Journal of Finance* **XLVII**, 1259–82.

Longstaff, F.A. and Schwartz, E.S. (1992b) "A two-factor interest rate model and contingent claim valuation". *Journal of Fixed Income* **3**, 16–23.

Merton, R.C. (1973) "Theory of rational option pricing". *Bell Journal of Economics and Management Science*, **4**, 141–83.

Nelson, D.B. and Ramswamy, K. (1990) "Simple binomial approximations in financial models". *Review of Financial Studies*, **3**, 393–430.

Press, W.H., Flannery, B.P., Teukolsy, S.A. and Vettering, W.T. (1990) *Numerical Recipes in C*, 2nd edition, Cambridge, Cambridge University Press.

Rebonato, R. (1996) *Interest-Rate Option Models*, Chichester, John Wiley and Sons.

Vasicek, O. (1977) "An equilibrium characterization of the term structure". *Journal of Financial Economics*, **5**, 177–88.

Wilson, T. (1994) "Debunking the myths". *Risk*, **7**, April, 67–73, and references therein.

3

Exotic Options I

EDMOND LEVY

3.1 INTRODUCTION

This is the first of two chapters covering non-standard derivative contracts provided by a relatively small but growing number of financial institutions. "Exotic" option is now common terminology for an option offering a variation from the standard pay-offs of the European or American call and put options. Broadly, these are contracts whose performances are designed to be aligned more closely to the underlying exposure needs of those seeking to hedge against, or those speculating on, future market conditions. Variations on the standard option can be traced back twenty years or more; however, it is only in the last seven years that we have seen the surge of interest in non-standard derivatives resulting in significant transaction flows. Some are one-off structures designed to meet a client's specific need, but many are recognized financial instruments in their own right. At the time of writing exotic options represent about 5–10 per cent of the total derivatives market and is the fastest growing area in the derivatives business.

Classifying such variations from the conventional option contract is not a straightforward task but we can identify three general lines of development. First, the introduction of path-dependency explicitly in the pay-off. This says that the contract not only depends on what the underlying asset price is on the expiration date but also on how it got there (e.g. Asian options, lookbacks and barrier options). The pay-off of an American-style option also depends on where the asset price is at a point in time which can trigger early exercise; however, in exotic options there is an explicit expression of how *ex ante* the path taken by the asset price will affect the option's pay-off. Second, some exotic contracts have pay-offs that depend on choices made by the holder at points in time prior to the expiration date (e.g. compound options and shout options). Finally, there are those exotic options that are a function of more than one asset price (e.g. quantos and basket options).

This chapter will look at Asian options, binary (or digital) and contingent premium options, and a variety of currency-protected options including currency basket options. Some of the technical detail in the development of pricing formulae has been relegated to appendices to facilitate the presentation.

The Handbook of Risk Management and Analysis. Edited by Carol Alexander
© 1996 John Wiley & Sons Ltd

3.2 ASIAN OPTIONS

Asian options are now an established contract in the armoury of hedging instruments. The Asian option is an example of an option whose pay-off depends on the path of asset prices over a prespecified time horizon. Usually the pay-off of this instrument is a function of the arithmetic average of prices taken at various points in time and hence "average options" is also a frequently used term to describe them. However, other forms of averaging are possible, for example the geometric average.

Two types of Asian options are widely offered — the average rate (or price) option (ARO) and the average strike (or floating average) option (ASO). The average rate option is the more familiar of the two and the more popular in terms of volume of transactions. Briefly, the ARO pays off at maturity the difference (if positive) between the average of prices recorded over a prespecified time interval and a specified strike price. Here the expiry date is normally the same date as the last recording date determining the average. The ASO will pay the difference (if positive) between the asset price on the expiry date and the average of asset prices recorded over a specified time interval. In these structures it is fairly common for the user to specify an expiry date to be later than the last recording date in the average. Usually the two parties to the Asian contract will agree on a reputable source for recording the market price for the underlying asset for each date in the averaging period.

3.2.1 Definition and Uses

At this point it would help to introduce some notation. Let $S(t)$ denote the spot (or cash) price at time t. Suppose the average is defined over the time interval $[t_1, t_N]$ and at points (not necessarily equidistant) on this interval t_i for $i = 1, \ldots, N$. We will denote $A(t)$ as the "running average" to date, and is defined for any timepoint t, $t_m \leq t < t_{m+1}$, by

$$A(t) = \frac{1}{m} \sum_{i=1}^{m} S(t_i)$$

for a corresponding integer $1 \leq m \leq N$, and $A(t) = 0$ for $t < t_1$. Thus $A(t_N)$ represents the simple arithmetic average of N prices. The ARO is characterized by the pay-off function at time t_N given by $\text{Max}[A(t_N) - K, 0]$ for a call option, or $\text{Max}[K - A(t_N), 0]$ for a put option. The parameter K denotes the specified strike price of the ARO. The ASO is defined as having pay-off at time T of $\text{Max}[S(T) - A(t_N), 0]$ for a call and $\text{Max}[A(t_N) - S(T), 0]$ for a put where $T (\geq t_N)$ is the expiry date of the ASO.

There are various reasons as to why AROs have become so popular. First, a company's exposure to future price movements is sometimes naturally expressed as exposure to an average of prices in the future. For example, in the absence of a fixed price agreement, the total annual costs of a company will be sensitive to the prices of raw materials used in production over the coming year. However, although a company will have some estimate of its total requirement, it is unlikely that it will know the size and timing of all purchases. More likely, the company will estimate that such costs will be spread evenly (or perhaps with some seasonality) over the year. Such an exposure is better described as a future series of cash flow and total cost will therefore depend on the average (or weighted average) of raw material prices over the year. An ARO call on the price will compensate the company for the difference between the average of prices and a specified strike. Second, averaging is useful as a means to reduce the sensitivity of an option's expiration value to the underlying asset price on the expiration date. Abnormal price movements on the expiration date, arising perhaps from a lack of depth in the market, can lead to distortion of the expiration value of an option. To avoid such effects, some option contracts are expressed as an ARO in which the averaging period is specified as (say) the last ten business days of the option's horizon. A third reason for using AROs is that accounting standards may require translation of foreign currency assets or liabilities at an average of exchange rates over the accounting period. Again an ARO is an obvious choice to reduce the harmful effect that a turbulent currency market might have on a company's balance sheet.

To understand the mechanics of the ARO better let us consider an example of a Japanese exporter to the US who, concerned with an appreciation of yen versus the US dollar, is seeking to hedge the yen value of expected US dollar receipts. Suppose we are at the end of December and the exporter is planning to establish a hedge for his US dollar exposure for the forthcoming year starting in January of next year. He estimates sales receipts to total 12 million dollars which will be spread evenly each month over the coming year. In the past the exporter always sold his US dollar receipts at month-ends. Suppose the current exchange rate is 90.00 yen to the US dollar and the forward value of yen for the end of December next year is 86.90. Our exporter targets a budget exchange rate of 87.00. To cover his exposure he could purchase a strip of 12 European options with expirations every month-end starting the following January. Each option gives the exporter the right to sell (or put) a million US dollars and buy yen at a strike of 87.00. The average premium due on these 12 options might be 2.58 yen per US dollar giving a total premium of 30,960,000 yen for 12 million US dollars cover.

Alternatively the exporter could enter into an ARO put contract. The terms of the ARO contract will specify that the average will be calculated from 12 recordings of the yen per US dollar exchange rate for the last business day of each month from January to December. An agreed source for these recordings (such as the published exchange rate fixing of a central bank or reputable supervisory body) is also specified. Settlement of the contract will be made by comparing the average of fixings with the strike of 87.00. If the average is lower than 87.00 then the exporter will be paid a cash settlement amount in yen of this difference multiplied by 12 million. If on the other hand the average is higher than 87.00 then the settlement amount is zero. Using the same market parameters which determined the premiums for the strip of European put options, the premium for the ARO is 2.11 yen per US dollar or 25,320,000 yen per 12 million US dollars.

In this example, the ARO was 0.47 yen per US dollar cheaper than the strip of European options. In general, the ARO will always be cheaper than the strip. The explanation for this is that there may be occasions when the average is "out-of-the-money" but some of the recordings were "in-the-money". In these instances the ARO will terminate worthless but some of the European options will be exercised. Hence the strip of European options offers a broader exercise criterion and will yield a pay-off which is the same or more than the corresponding ARO. Another way to put this is to note that in general a portfolio of put options on underlying assets is worth more than the option to put the portfolio of such assets.

The difference is directly related to the degree of correlation between the asset prices making up the portfolio. Analogous to basket options (see Section 3.4.3 below), the closer the correlations are to unity the more likely it is that if one option in the portfolio pays off then so will the others (with the same degree of in-the-moneyness). Consequently, if the averaging period is short relative to the option horizon (for instance the last ten days of a 12-month option horizon) we should expect the price of the ARO to be close to the price of a European option of identical strike and expiry date. Notice also that the ARO is a cash-settled agreement. Hence exercise is automatic once all the fixings are determined and their average found to be in-the-money relative to the specified strike. As there is no exchange of currency amounts the exporter has total freedom as to how much of, when and to whom he sells his US dollar receipts.

In this and subsequent examples we consider the US dollar/Japanese yen exchange rate. Suppose the current spot exchange rate is 90.00 yen per dollar, the dollar interest rate is 6 per cent, yen interest rate is 2.5 per cent and annualized volatility for the exchange rate is 13 per cent. Figure 3.1 compares the premium of a US dollar ARO call with that of the strip of European calls at various strikes. In the figure it is assumed that the current date is the end of December and the ARO has fixings every month-end for 12 months starting in January next year. In addition, the ARO is compared to the European call option with expiration end of December next year. In the figure we see clearly that at each strike the relationship ARO < strip < European holds.

The ASO, although less popular, has several uses. Suppose an institution wants to launch a 12-month bond issue whose redemption value is linked to at-the-money (spot) options (puts or calls) on some underlying stock market index. At the indication stage prior to launch it could specify that the strike would be determined by reference to the closing price for the underlying index in (say) a week's time. However, if the institution wanted to avoid the possibility of investors being exposed to market conditions on that particular day (perhaps important economic figures are due to be published around that time) it could alternatively specify the strike to be the average of closing prices for the following two weeks. This alternative specification links the redemption value to an ASO. A second use for the ASO is when a target, that is required to be met, is set based on the average of prices over the coming period but hedges for this period have to be established

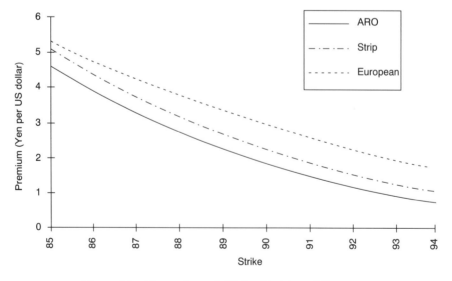

Figure 3.1 Comparison of ARO with strip and European

in advance. If the hedges are placed at the end of the period then there is a mismatch between the target and the hedging vehicle. In this instance an ASO paying the difference between the average over the period and the end-of-period price remedies the mismatch. A similar reason for using ASOs may arise, for example, when a company regularly converts domestic currency receipts from sales in order to pay costs in foreign currency at quarterly intervals. Here the ASO call on the foreign price of a unit of domestic currency will compensate for any difference between the average exchange rate over the quarter and the exchange rate achieved when the foreign currency cost is valued in domestic terms.

When the averaging period is close to the expiry date of the ASO then the premium is close to zero. On the other hand if the averaging period is close to the current date

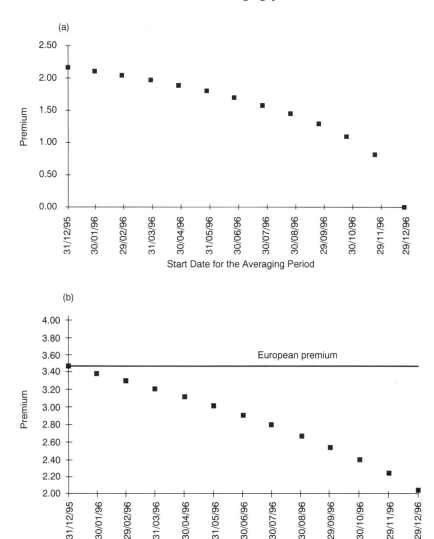

Figure 3.2 (a) Premium for average strike call options, (b) Premium for average strike call options

then the premium for the ASO is close to an at-the-money European option of the same maturity. In Figures 3.2(a) and 3.2(b) we demonstrate these features. In both figures the option horizon is 12 months and the average is determined by 12 points spread evenly over $(t_N - t_1)$. In Figure 3.2(a) the ASO is valued with $t_N = T$ and $(t_N - t_1)$ ranging from zero to 12 months. In Figure 3.2(b), the ASO is valued once more but with $t_1 = 0$ and $(t_N - t_1)$ again ranging from zero to 12 months.

3.2.2 Valuation Approaches

In both AROs and ASOs the terminal value is determined by the average of a history of prices. Option valuation usually assumes asset returns to be normally distributed or, equivalently, that asset prices themselves are log-normally distributed. Because the product of log-normal prices is itself log-normal, the valuation of Asian options determined by a *geometric* average of prices is a relatively simple matter (see Appendix 1). However, the distribution of the *sum* of log-normal components has no explicit representation and complicates the determination of a solution for the (arithmetic) Asian option. In this section we will review various methods that have been proposed for valuing such Asian options.

Define r as the domestic (continuously compounding) interest rate and y the continuous yield on the asset. If the asset is an exchange rate and S is in units of domestic currency per foreign currency, then y is the (continuous) foreign interest rate (denoted r_f in Chapter 4). It is assumed that r and y are constant over the life of the option. In option-pricing, the spot price process assumed is the familiar geometric diffusion

$$dS = \mu S \, dt + \sigma S \, dz \tag{1}$$

where dz is a Wiener process (that is, it is distributed as normal with mean zero and unit variance or $N(0, 1)$ for short), and μ and σ are, respectively, the constant drift and volatility parameters. (As indicated in Appendices 1 and 2, a deterministic term structure for interest rates, yields and volatilities can be incorporated into the analysis without too much trouble.) The pay-off on Asian options is based on the future path of spot prices as described by equation (1). Under equation (1) we can express $S(t_i)$ in terms of $S(t_{i-1})$ as:

$$S(t_i) = S(t_{i-1})e^{(\mu - (1/2)\sigma^2)(t_i - t_{i-1}) + \sigma\sqrt{t_i - t_{i-1}}Y_i} \tag{2}$$

where Y_i is $N(0, 1)$. For $t_i > 0$, $\ln S(t_i)$ is thus normally distributed as $N[\ln S(0) + (\mu - \frac{1}{2}\sigma^2)t_i, \sigma^2 t_i]$.

A popular approach to valuing options is to adopt the risk-neutral transformation of Cox and Ross (1979). This enables us to characterize the solution to the Asian option as:

$$\text{ARO}_C[S(0), K, t] = e^{-rT}E^* \text{Max}[A(t_N) - K, 0] \tag{3}$$

for the ARO call and

$$\text{ASO}_C[S(0), K, t] = e^{-rT}E^* \text{Max}[S(T) - A(t_N), 0] \tag{4}$$

for the ASO call, where E^* is the expectation operator conditional on $[A(t), S(t)]$ at current time $t = 0$ under the risk-adjusted density function. This means we can treat the process for $S(t)$ now as described by the diffusion (1) with μ replaced by $(r - y)$. Suppose we denote $P[A(t_N) = \omega]$, the conditional density function for $A(t_N)$, by $f^*(\omega)$, then the expectation term in equation (3) can be written as:

$$E^* \mathrm{Max}[A(t_N) - K, 0] = \int_K^\infty [A(t_N) - K] f^*(\omega) \, d\omega \qquad (5)$$

For the ASO call we need the joint density of $A(t_N)$ and $S(T)$, $P[S(T) = \xi, A(t_N) = \omega]$. Suppose we denote this by $\gamma^*(\xi, \omega)$, then the expectation term in equation (4) can be written as:

$$E^* \mathrm{Max}[S(T) - A(t_N), 0] = \int_0^\infty \int_\omega^\infty [S(T) - A(t_N)] \gamma^*(\xi, \omega) \, d\xi \, d\omega$$

Because the functions $f^*(\omega)$ and $\gamma^*(\xi, \omega)$ are non-standard, to evaluate these integrals most have resorted to numerical procedures or approximation methods.

Of the various numerical procedures advocated, only the Monte Carlo approach will be discussed below. Interested readers should also be aware of Carverhill and Clewlow (1990) (who adopt a Fourier transform approach to evaluate the convolution of density functions) and the extended binomial tree approach of Hull and White (1993). Geman and Yor (1992, 1993) and Geman and Eydeland (1995) have produced some interesting results using Bessel processes. The approximation methods centre on the log-normal distribution making use of the fact that the moments $E^*[A(t_N)^j]$ (for any integer $j > 0$) can be calculated.

(i) Monte Carlo

Monte Carlo is a numerical procedure widely used in option valuation as well as other fields. (See, for example, Hammersley and Handscomb (1964), Rubinstein (1981) and for an application to option valuation see Boyle (1977).) Briefly, the procedure requires one to generate simulations of the price process and hence calculate simulations of the option pay-off. Repeating this procedure several times produces a distribution of option values. The discounted value of the average of these values is an estimate of the value of the option.

In the case of the Asian option the Monte Carlo technique can be easily employed (as demonstrated by Kemna and Vorst (1990) in the case of the ARO). Return to expression (2) and substitute $\mu = r - y$. If we draw outcomes of Y_i (for $i = 1, \ldots, N$) from the standard normal distribution then a sequence of $S(t_i)(i = 1, \ldots, N)$ can be constructed. For the ARO, the pay-off $\mathrm{Max}[A(t_N) - K, 0]$ must be calculated. Repeat this procedure several times and average all such calculations. Finally taking the present value of this average will produce an estimate for equation (3). To find an estimate for the ASO we should generate an additional random outcome Y_T and calculate $S(T)$ from

$$S(T) = S(t_N) e^{(r - y - (1/2)\sigma^2)(T - t_N) + \sigma \sqrt{T - t_N} Y_T}$$

and hence calculate the pay-off $\mathrm{Max}[S(T) - A(t_N), 0]$.

The strength of the paper by Kemna and Vorst is to recognize the high degree of correlation that exists between the (arithmetic) Asian options and their geometric counterparts. As the solution to the geometric versions of the ARO and ASO are known (see Appendix 1) they can be used as control variates for improving the accuracy of the Monte Carlo estimates. That is, for every sequence of Y_i's, as well as calculating the value for the Asian option (A_M), calculate also the value for the geometric average version (G_M). If the true value for the geometric version is denoted by G, a better estimate for the Asian option is $A^* = A_M + G - G_M$.

(ii) Log-normal approximations

An alternative approach is to approximate the density functions $f^*(\omega)$ and $\gamma^*(\xi, \omega)$. There are several studies supporting the choice of a log-normal density function as a good approximation. Several authors have independently derived similar approximation methods based on this view (for example, Ruttiens (1990), Vorst (1990), Levy (1990, 1992), Ritchken et al. (1990) and Turnbull and Wakeman (1991)). If $\ln A(t_N)$ is distributed as $N(\alpha, v^2)$ then for the ARO we evaluate equation (5) to give:

$$e^{-rT} E^* \text{Max}[A(t_N) - K, 0] = e^{\alpha + (1/2)v^2 - rT} N(x_1) - e^{-rT} K N(x_2) \tag{6}$$

where $N(\cdot)$ is the standard normal distribution function, $x_1 = (\alpha - \ln K + v^2)/v$ and $x_2 = x_1 - v$. For the ASO we assume that the covariance of $\ln A(t_N)$ and $\ln S(T)$ is $\rho v \sigma \sqrt{T}$ and make use of a generalization of the exchange of asset option solution in Margrabe (1978) (see Section 3.4.2 below):

$$e^{-rT} E^* \text{Max}[S(T) - A(t_N), 0] = S(t) e^{-yT} N(y_1) - e^{\alpha + (1/2)v^2 - rT} N(y_2) \tag{7}$$

where $y_1 = [\ln S(t) + (r - y)T - \alpha - \frac{1}{2}v^2 + \frac{1}{2}\Sigma^2]/\Sigma$, $y_2 = y_1 - \Sigma$ and $\Sigma^2 = v^2 + \sigma^2 T - 2\rho v \sigma \sqrt{T}$. The question remains how to determine α, v and ρ.

Suppose we treat $A(t_N)$ as distributed according to the corresponding geometric average $G(t_N) = [S(t_1) \cdot S(t_2) \ldots S(t_N)]^{1/N}$. Thus the parameters α and v become, respectively, the mean and standard deviation of $\ln G(t_N)$. This essentially gives the ARO formula presented in Ruttiens (1990). However, it can be shown that $G(t_N) \le A(t_N)$ and so the central tendency of the distribution is biased downwards. As a result, with this choice of parameters, the formula for the ARO will undervalue call options. To counter this bias, Vorst (1990) suggests correcting the strike price of the option by this difference so that K is replaced by $K^* = K + E^*[G(t_N)] - E^*[A(t_N)]$.

An alternative and more accurate approach is to correct for both the mean and variance directly by observing that if $\ln A(t_N)$ is $N(\alpha, v^2)$, then from the moment generating function of a normal distribution, $E^*[A(t_N)] = \exp(\alpha + \frac{1}{2}v^2)$ and $E^*[A(t_N^2)] = \exp(2\alpha + 2v^2)$ (see, for example, Hogg and Craig (1970, p. 105)). As both $E^*[A(t_N)]$ and $E^*[A(t_N)^2]$ can be calculated (see Appendix 2), we can determine α and v to be consistent with the mean *and* variance of $A(t_N)$. That is, solve the above equations to give:

$$\alpha = 2 \ln E^*[A(t_N)] - \frac{1}{2} \ln E^*[A(t_N)^2] \tag{8a}$$

$$v = \sqrt{\ln E^*[A(t_N)^2] - 2 \ln E^*[A(t_N)]} \tag{8b}$$

The papers of Levy (1990, 1992) and Ritchken et al. (1990) employ this technique and demonstrate that with α and v chosen in this way, equation (6) provides a good approximation for the ARO. For the ASO, in order to use equation (7), we first need to determine ρ. Levy (1992) suggests we assume a joint bivariate log-normal distribution for $A(t_N)$ and $S(T)$ and evaluate ρ using the following equation:

$$\rho v \sigma \sqrt{T} = \ln E^*[A(t_N)S(T)] - [\alpha + \ln S(t) + (r - y - \frac{1}{2}\sigma^2)T] - \frac{1}{2}(v^2 + \sigma^2 T)$$

Although the mean and variance for $A(t_N)$ are perfectly captured, there will inevitably be differences between the skewness and kurtosis implied by the log-normal fit and those for $A(t_N)$. These differences will become increasingly more apparent as we move to higher levels of volatility (above 20 per cent or so) and/or longer option structures. A method, implemented by Turnbull and Wakeman (1991), to adjust for these effects, is to expand the distribution for $A(t_N)$ around the log-normal. Let $a(\omega)$ be the log-normal distribution, then it can be shown that we can expand $f^*(\omega)$ as:

$$f^*(\omega) = a(\omega) + E_1 \frac{\partial a(\omega)}{\partial \omega} + E_2 \frac{\partial^2 a(\omega)}{\partial \omega^2} + E_3 \frac{\partial^3 a(\omega)}{\partial \omega^3} + \cdots \qquad (9)$$

where E_i are terms involving the difference between cumulants (or semi-invariants) implied by the log-normal fit and the true cumulants for $A(t_N)$. For example, E_1 is the difference between the mean of $A(t_N)$ as implied by $a(\omega)$ and the true mean of $A(t_N)$, and E_2 is the difference between the variances. If we substitute equation (9) into equation (5) and evaluate the integral, equation (6) becomes augmented by further terms having $E_i (i = 1, 2, \ldots)$ as coefficients. When α and v are chosen as equation (8), the first two terms are zero (by design), but $E_i (i = 3, 4, \ldots)$ are non-zero. Turnbull and Wakeman take this expansion to E_4 and so correct for differences in skewness and kurtosis.

Levy and Turnbull (1993) show that the log-normal approximation can be further improved by choosing α and v to fit higher moments for $A(t_N)$ but inaccuracies remain at high volatility levels. In a follow-up to this article, Curran (1993) shows that much better results can be obtained by using the risk-neutral distribution of the geometric average, $a(g) = P[G(t_N) = g]$, and evaluating the integral:

$$\int_{K^*}^{\infty} [E^*[A(t_N)|G(t_N)] - K]a(g)\,dg$$

where K^* is found so that $E^*[A(t_N)|G(t_N) = K^*] = K$. Curran shows that this procedure provides estimates for the ARO which are accurate over a wider range of volatilities.

3.2.3 Risk Management of Asian Options

The pay-off of both the ARO and ASO will depend on the progression of the spot price for the underlying asset over the option life. The pricing formulae allow us to measure the instantaneous sensitivity of either option price to the current spot price. Hence, as for European options, at any timepoint we can construct the delta hedge by buying or selling an appropriate amount of the underlying asset in the spot market. The delta hedge is then adjusted dynamically throughout the option's life in line with the progress of the spot price.

As more fixings are recorded more of the average is known and the less is the sensitivity of $A(t_N)$ to the current spot price. In the case of the ARO, this means that both its delta and gamma (the sensitivity of delta to the spot price) diminishes to zero in a discrete fashion. That is, at the moment each fixing is recorded a portion of the outstanding delta hedge will need to be unwound. In Figure 3.3 the delta profile for three ARO calls are compared.

Whether the ARO finishes in-the-money, at-the-money or out-of-the-money, its delta steps to zero. This "delta jump" phenomenon is typical in ARO risk management and is more apparent when N is small relative to the averaging period. A key risk to the trader

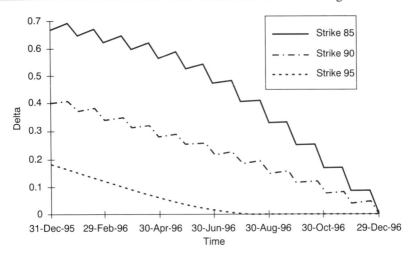

Figure 3.3 Delta profile of ARO calls

here is that he must be able to unwind his residual delta position at a price no worse than the recorded fixing. This risk is analogous to settling European options for cash by calculating its intrinsic value by reference to a predetermined fixing source.

In general, an option trader will aim to minimize the need to rebalance the hedge portfolio by looking for a more stable hedging rule requiring fewer adjustments. For the ARO, a typical strategy would be to choose a European option position that offsets the gamma and volatility exposure. A rule of thumb is to choose a European option with similar strike price to the ARO but with expiration $(t_N - t_1)/3$, that is one-third of the averaging period of the ARO. A more robust hedge would involve a portfolio of European options with similar strikes and expiration dates spread over the averaging period. The rationale behind this is that buying the equivalent strip of European options would cost more than the premium received on the ARO and over-hedges a short ARO position. Alternatively, a weighted strip of European options would minimize the necessary outlay in constructing an initial hedge but maintain gamma and volatility cover. The weights may be chosen by examining the sensitivity of the ARO to changes in (say) $\sigma\sqrt{t_i}$. However, what is suitable initially may require rebalancing at a later date in the light of the progress of recorded fixings. If the expected average remains close to the strike price of the ARO, the trader will have to increase his option cover.

Whereas the delta and gamma of AROs diminish to zero, those for the ASO will converge or (more properly) step to that of the European option with identical expiration date and strike equal to the average. At first, there is likely to be a strong positive correlation between the average and the terminal spot price. However, this correlation will step to zero as more fixings are recorded. Once more delta hedging is possible and, similar to the ARO, this leaves the trader exposed to being able to transact cash hedges at the recorded fixings. If gamma and volatility exposure is a concern then a natural hedging strategy is to regularly purchase at-the-money (spot) options with expiration time T throughout the averaging period. Again, how much is purchased will depend on the progress of the fixings. More importantly, in the case of the ASO the trader is vulnerable to the evolution in implied volatility for these options to a much greater degree than that for hedging AROs. Hence an alternative strategy in constructing an initial hedge is to enter into calendar spreads by buying volatility cover for time T and shorting volatility over the averaging period.

3.3 BINARY AND CONTINGENT PREMIUM OPTIONS

Binary options are also known as bet or digital options. These give the holder the right to receive a prespecified currency amount should the underlying asset price be beyond a specified level (strike) at a point in time (the expiry date). Typically the price of a binary option is quoted per unit of currency. Occasionally they are quoted as a gearing ratio; multiplier paid per unit invested. In practice a reference source, such as a central bank fixing, is agreed to determine the asset price on the expiration date. If this level is above the current asset price then the option is sometimes termed a binary call option. Likewise if the level is below the current asset price then it is termed a binary put option.

Figure 3.4 depicts the price of binary call and put options which pay one dollar for various strikes around the current asset price. In the figure the asset price is assumed to be 100 dollars with annualized volatility (σ) of 15 per cent, its yield (y) is zero, the domestic (continuously compounded) interest rate (r) is 6 per cent, and the term to expiry is three months. Analogous to conventional options, deep-in-the-money call options are those whose exercise and hence pay-out is almost certain. Thus the binary option price will converge to the present value of one dollar payable in three months' time. At the other extreme, where exercise is unlikely, the binary option price will converge to zero.

A contingent premium option is a conventional European option in which the holder pays nothing up front but agrees to pay a prespecified premium at expiry only if the option is in-the-money. These have also been termed pay-later options. Although exercise of the option may be optional, the holder must pay the requisite premium regardless of how deep-in-the-money the option happens to be. Consequently it is possible that, on the expiry date, the holder pays more in premium than he receives in intrinsic value. As

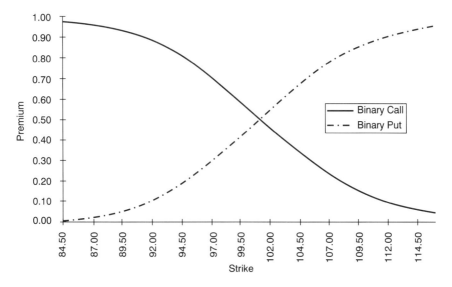

Figure 3.4 Premium for binary options

payment is due only if the option is in-the-money, this payment will always be greater than (and often a multiple of) the premium due on the equivalent European option. Similar to binary options, the terms require a reference source to determine the asset price on the expiry date and hence if payment is due.

Figure 3.5 compares the premiums due on contingent premium options and European options at various strikes. In the figure, the current asset price is 100, $r = 5$ per cent, $y = 0$ per cent, $\sigma = 15$ per cent and term to expiry is 12 months. In Figure 3.6 the expiration value of the contingent premium option at various asset prices is compared to that of the conventional European option. In the figure the strike price for both options is 100.

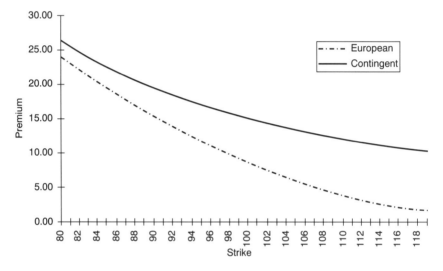

Figure 3.5   Comparison between contingent premium and European call options

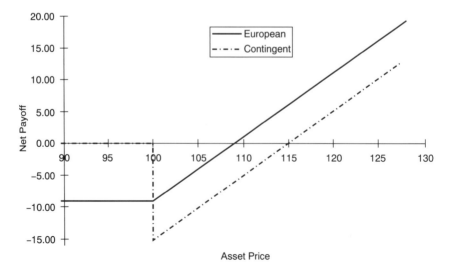

Figure 3.6   Net expiration value of contingent premium and European options

3.3.1 Examples and Uses

Many structures embed one or more binary options. Indeed, the purchase of a contingent premium option can be decomposed into a purchase of a European option and simultaneous sale of a binary option. To see this, look at the pay-off that the contingent premium (call) option offers to the holder:

$$S(T) - K - c \quad \begin{cases} \text{if } S(T) > K \\ 0 \quad\quad \text{otherwise} \end{cases}$$

where $S(T)$ is the asset price at expiry and c is the prespecified premium due on the option. Thus the pay-off is precisely the sum of the pay-off of a European option and sale of a binary call option with strike K and payout c. As the contingent premium option requires no payment up front, c is found so that the binary option here has present value equal to the premium of the European option.

A range-binary option is one where the holder receives a specified currency amount only if the asset price trades at expiry between a lower and upper bound which defines the range. This option can be thought of as a purchase of a binary call (put) option with strike at the lower (upper) bound and sale of a binary call (put) with strike at the upper (lower) bound.

An accrual (sometimes "corridor" or "fairway") option gives the holder the right to receive a prespecified currency amount on expiry for each day the asset price trades within a specified range. The period during which the asset price is monitored to determine payout is often termed the "accrual period". It is easy to see that an accrual option is a portfolio of range-binary options. The portfolio has a range-binary option for each day defining the accrual period. The "maximum payout" is the currency amount paid if the asset price is traded within the range each day in the accrual period. Hence an accrual option will pay the following settlement amount:

$$\text{Settlement} = \frac{\text{Number of accrual days}}{\text{Total days in accrual period}} \times \text{Maximum pay-out}$$

Another use for binary options is in the construction of contingent forward contracts. A contingent forward contract is a forward contract to purchase or sell the underlying asset at an agreed price contingent on the asset price being beyond a specified level on a future date (the expiry date). Suppose the agreed forward price is F and the specified level is B. Typically a contingent forward contract to buy (sell) the asset has B less (greater) than F. In this way there is no commitment to trade if the asset is trading at a price more favourable than B on the expiry date. The structure of this agreement is the purchase of a European call (put) option with strike B and sale of a binary option with strike B and pay-out $F - B$ ($B - F$).

3.3.2 Valuation and Hedging

The articles of Rubinstein and Reiner (1991) and Turnbull (1992) provide a good discussion on the valuation of binary options and contingent premium options. To value binary options and hence all of the structures mentioned in Section 3.3.1 consider first the European call option. Its value under the geometric diffusion process discussed in Section 3.2.2 is given by the celebrated Black–Scholes formula:

$$C = e^{-rT} E^* \text{Max}[S(T) - K, 0] = e^{-yT} SN(x_1) - e^{-rT} KN(x_2) \tag{10}$$

where $x_1 = [\ln(S/K) + (r - y + \frac{1}{2}\sigma^2 T]/\sigma\sqrt{T}$ and $x_2 = x_1 - \sigma\sqrt{T}$. If the asset price is above the strike (K) at expiry then a call option is exercised and the holder pays K units of domestic currency and takes delivery of one unit of the asset. Hence the coefficient of K in equation (10) can be interpreted as the present value of a unit of domestic currency times the (risk-neutral) probability of the asset price being above K at expiry. The pay-off of a binary call option is 1 if $S(T) > K$ and zero otherwise so that its present value can be stated as $C_b = e^{-rT}P(S(T) > K)$ and, from equation (10), $C_b = e^{-rT}N(x_2)$. Similarly, for a binary put option, $P_b = e^{-rT}N(-x_2)$. Noting that $N(-x_2) = 1 - N(x_2)$ we have $C_b + P_b = e^{-rT}$, which is the put–call parity condition for binary options.

To value contingent premium call options, we first need to find a value for the expression $e^{-rT}E^* \text{Max}[S(T) - K - c, 0]$. Let $K^* = K + c$, then equation (10) with K set to K^* is the value for this expression. As contingent premium options are offered at zero premium, solve for c so that $e^{-rT}E^* \text{Max}[S(T) - K - c, 0] = 0$. That is,

$$c = [e^{(r-y)T}SN(x_1) - KN(x_2)]/N(x_2)$$

or e^{rT} (premium of option)$/N(x_2)$. From this discussion we can write down immediately the contingent premium variation for any option, European or other, as the forward value of the option premium divided by the probability of the asset price being at or beyond the strike at expiry. The mark-to-market value of the contingent premium call option (V_c) with agreed payment c is then given by:

$$V_c = (\text{current value of underlying option}) - cC_b(K)$$

that is, a position which is long a European call with strike K and short c binary call options with strike K.

Positions in binary options can be expressed as delta-equivalent positions in the underlying asset. For example, suppose the current asset price is 99.7, $r = 5$ per cent, $y = 0$ per cent, $\sigma = 5$ per cent and term to expiry is three days. A binary call option paying 10 units of domestic currency with strike 100 has value 2.8 and delta 0.75. If the asset price moves to 100.1 its value now is 6.2. Consider the performance of the hedge. At price 99.7 the delta of the binary was 0.75 and so a short position in the binary option requires a hedge of long 7.5 units of the asset. At price 100.1 the loss on the binary position is 3.4 and the profit on the hedge is 3.0. Things are somewhat worse with one day to expiry. At 99.7 the binary is worth 1.4 with delta 0.84 and at price 100.1 the binary is worth 8.4 (5.3 more) with the delta hedge generating a profit of 3.4.

Figure 3.7 shows the delta of the binary option for three days and one day to expiry over a range of asset prices. The reason for the poor performance of delta-hedging is the degree by which delta changes as the underlying asset price moves. We know from European options that the poor performance of a hedge strategy of rebalancing delta hedges at discrete time intervals is directly related to the gamma in the option. Figure 3.8 shows the gamma of the binary option with three days to expiry compared to that of a European option with strike 100. The absolute value of gamma for the binary is greater than that of the European option over most values of the region of asset prices.

A gamma-based hedge for binary options would involve using European options. Consider a portfolio of long a European call with strike K_1 and short a European call with strike $K_2 > K_1$ (having identical expiration to that of the binary option). This has

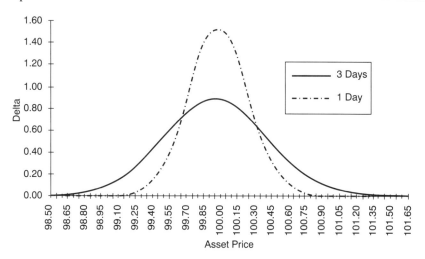

Figure 3.7   Delta of binary options

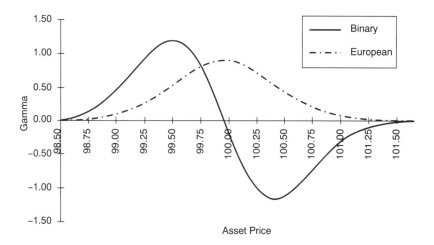

Figure 3.8   Gamma profile for binary and European options

pay-off at expiry given by:

$$
\left.
\begin{array}{c}
K_2 - K_1 \\
S(T) - K_1 \\
0
\end{array}
\right\}
\begin{array}{l}
\text{if } S(T) \geq K_2 \\
\text{if } K_1 \leq S(T) < K_2 \\
\text{if } S(T) < K_1
\end{array}
$$

A purchase of $1/(K_2 - K_1)$ in this portfolio yields one unit of domestic currency on expiry if $S(T) > K_2$. Hence if both K_1 and K_2 are chosen to be close to K then we have an approximation to the binary call with strike K. Indeed if K_1 and K_2 are equidistant around K then as we reduce $(K_1 - K_2)$ the value of the portfolio converges to that of the binary call. To see this, observe that the partial derivative of the European call option with respect to its strike is precisely the value of a binary call with same strike and time to expiry. This suggests we choose K_1 and K_2 to be close to K and their absolute difference consistent with risk tolerance. For example, to hedge a short position in a binary call, both K_1 and $(K_1 + K_2)/2$ are often chosen to be less than or equal to K. Of course as $(K_1 - K_2)$ reduces so the face amount on the call spread strategy will increase. Hence many institutions will constrain the choice of K_1 and K_2 to be consistent with risk limits on European option trading positions.

3.4 CURRENCY PROTECTED OPTIONS

Contracts on foreign assets often entail a degree of foreign exchange risk which may be unwanted. That is, although the foreign asset price might move favourably such gains could be lost when translated to domestic currency terms. What is needed is the ability to participate in the foreign asset market but with a measure of control on the foreign exchange risk that follows. To answer this, many financial institutions have developed a range of forward and option contracts for investors with differing mixtures of preferences to the foreign asset market exposure and to that of the foreign currency risk. In this section several variations are presented together with their respective pricing formula. The section concludes with a discussion of currency basket options.

3.4.1 Cross-Market Contracts

Forward and option contracts that are cross-market based have been discussed in Derman, Karasinski and Wecker (1990), Wei (1991) and Reiner (1992). Depending on the nature of the contract, such contracts may be settled as an exchange of cash for delivery of the foreign asset or by an agreed net cash settlement amount. Throughout this section the following notation is used:

T = the number of years to expiry (the delivery date)
S = the current price of the foreign asset (in units of foreign currency)
$S(T)$ = the price of the foreign asset at T
S^* = the fixed price agreed for the foreign asset in foreign currency units
X = the current exchange rate (units of domestic currency per unit of foreign currency)
$X(T)$ = the exchange rate at T
X^* = the fixed exchange rate guaranteed
r = the domestic risk-free interest rate (continuously compounded)
q = the foreign risk-free interest rate (continuously compounded)
y = the dividend yield on the foreign index (continuously compounded)
σ = the annualized volatility of S
v = the annualized volatility of X
ρ = the instantaneous correlation between movements in S and X

The cross-market contract that is offered will be specified to best meet the investor's outlook and risk preferences. For example, an investor who believes that a foreign equity index will rally and is unconcerned about the foreign exchange risk might desire a contract that pays out:

$$F_1 = X(T)[S(T) - S^*]$$

This is a forward contract to purchase the foreign index at S^* translated at the ruling exchange rate at the expiry date. If a degree of protection is needed in the event the index falls, then a more suitable contract is:

$$C_1 = X(T) \operatorname{Max}[S(T) - S^*, 0]$$

This is a call option on $S(T)$ with strike S^* and with pay-off translated to domestic currency at $X(T)$.

If, on the other hand, the investor requires protection on the rate at which his holdings are translated to domestic terms, then the following contracts may be more suitable:

$$F_2 = X^*[S(T) - S^*]$$
$$C_2 = X^* \operatorname{Max}[S(T) - S^*, 0]$$

The first, F_2, is a forward contract whose value at expiry in foreign currency terms is as before but this is now translated to domestic terms at a predetermined exchange rate X^*. The option variation C_2 is usually termed a *quanto* call option on the index and sometimes referred to as a *guaranteed exchange rate* contract. The holder of this option receives an option pay-off on $S(T)$ as though it were a domestic asset with price X^*S. The interest differential between the domestic and foreign currencies, $(r - q)$, is an important feature determining the relative value of a quanto option to its European counterpart. When the domestic interest rate is high compared to that of the currency of the asset, then the quanto call option will be cheaper than the option on the asset in foreign terms.

Both F_1 and F_2 will have positive value if the index at expiry is above S^*. Consider, however, the following contracts:

$$F_3 = X(T)S(T) - S^*X^*$$
$$C_3 = \operatorname{Max}[X(T)S(T) - S^*X^*, 0]$$

The first, F_3, is a forward contract to take delivery of the foreign asset at S^*X^*, that is at a fixed domestic price. The second is an option to buy the foreign asset at a known strike price in domestic terms. The performance of both contracts will depend *jointly* on $S(T)$ and $X(T)$. The variable $X(T)S(T)$ is the domestic value of the foreign asset at T and either F_3 or C_3 might therefore represent a natural hedge against an open (short) position in the foreign asset when marked-to-market in domestic terms.

Other variations of the cross-market product might be synthetic assets which offer full exposure to the foreign asset but protects the translation exchange rate:

$$F_4 = S(T)[X(T) - X^*]$$
$$C_4 = S(T) \operatorname{Max}[X(T) - X^*, 0]$$

The contract F_4 represents a long position in the foreign asset for delivery at expiry but paid for in domestic terms at a predetermined exchange rate. Hence all movements in the domestic value of the foreign asset due solely to fluctuations in the exchange rate are avoided. The option variation is sometimes called the *equity-linked foreign exchange* contract. This is a currency option whose face amount is linked to the value of a foreign asset. It provides unlimited exposure to the foreign asset but attaches a foreign exchange option to the translation risk with strike X^*.

Finally, a complex mixture is a contract that allows the investor exposure to the foreign asset value when converted to domestic currency at a guaranteed exchange rate yet allows the investor to pay for the asset at a predetermined foreign price:

$$F_5 = S(T)X^* - X(T)S^*$$

$$C_5 = \text{Max}[S(T)X^* - X(T)S^*, 0]$$

3.4.2 Valuation of Cross-Market Contracts

The valuation of these contracts will depend, in part, on the manner in which the exchange rate and asset price enters the pay-off. For example, the pay-offs in the first case, F_1 and C_1, are just the value of forward and option contracts on $S(T)$ in foreign currency terms converted to domestic terms at the ruling exchange rate. Hence, immediately we should value these by taking the current foreign value of these contracts and converting to domestic terms at the current exchange rate. In the third case, $S(T)$ and $X(T)$ are traded assets and so we can treat the product $S(T)X(T)$ as also traded with forward value consistent with those of $S(T)$ and $X(T)$. In the second case, however, although we know today the conversion rate X^*, $S(T)X^*$ is not a traded security. We need a framework that is consistent with the way forward and option contracts on $S(T)$ and $X(T)$ are valued and which is arbitrage free.

To value these contracts, we will assume the following usual stochastic processes:

$$dS = \mu S\,dt + \sigma S\,dz$$

$$dX = \eta X\,dt + \nu X\,dw$$

where dz and dw are Wiener processes with $E(dz\,dw) = \rho$. All the above cross-market contracts have their values derived from S and X. Thus, in principle, the risks in these securities can be hedged by trading in S and X. Appendix 3 argues that we can value cross-market products as though the returns on the foreign asset S and the exchange rate X satisfy $\mu = (q - y - \rho\sigma\nu)$ and $\eta = (r - q)$, respectively. If we were measuring values in foreign currency terms the risk-neutral expected return on S would be $(q - y)$, but in domestic terms the yield on the foreign asset must be increased by $\rho\sigma\nu$. A common adjustment, therefore, is to define a new yield $y^* = [y + (r - q) + \rho\sigma\nu]$ and treat the new "domestic" asset SX^* as having return $(r - y^*)$. Another way to observe this is to note that, given the assumed processes, Ito's lemma gives

$$d(SX) = (\mu + \eta + \rho\sigma\nu)SX\,dt + \sigma SX\,dz + \nu SX\,dw$$

and hence the expected return on SX is $(\mu + \eta + \rho\sigma\nu)$. Arbitrage ensures that the forward exchange rate earns a rate of return of $(r - q)$ and also that the rate of return on SX is $(r - y)$. Hence it follows that $\eta = (r - q)$ and so, for $(\mu + \eta + \rho\sigma\nu) = (r - y)$ to hold, we require $\mu = (q - y - \rho\sigma\nu)$.

Armed with the risk-neutral returns, we can proceed to value the cross-market instruments as $e^{-rT}E^*(F_i)$ and $e^{-rT}E^*(C_i)$ for each i. The expectations needed are given as follows:

$$E^*[X(T)S(T)] = XSe^{(r-y)T}$$

$$E^*[X(T)S^*] = XS^*e^{(r-q)T}$$

$$E^*[X^*S(T)] = X^*Se^{(q-y-\rho\sigma\nu)T}$$

$$\text{and} \quad E^*[X^*S^*] = X^*S^*$$

Hence $e^{-rT}E^*(F_i)$ are evaluated as:

$$e^{-rT}E^*(F_1) = e^{-rT}[XSe^{(r-y)T} - XS^*e^{(r-q)T}]$$

$$e^{-rT}E^*(F_2) = e^{-rT}[X^*Se^{(q-y-\rho\sigma v)T} - X^*S^*]$$

$$e^{-rT}E^*(F_3) = e^{-rT}[XSe^{(r-y)T} - X^*S^*]$$

$$e^{-rT}E^*(F_4) = e^{-rT}[XSe^{(r-y)T} - X^*Se^{(q-y-\rho\sigma v)T}]$$

$$\text{and} \quad e^{-rT}E^*(F_5) = e^{-rT}[X^*Se^{(q-y-\rho\sigma v)T} - XS^*e^{(r-q)T}]$$

To determine the forward price (f_i) for each cross-market forward, solve for S^* (X^* in the case of F_4) in each of the previous expressions to give net present value of zero:

$$f_1 = Se^{(q-y)T}$$

$$f_2 = Se^{(q-y-\rho\sigma v)T}$$

$$f_3 = (X/X^*)Se^{(r-y)T}$$

$$f_4 = Xe^{(r-q+\rho\sigma v)T}$$

$$\text{and} \quad f_5 = (X^*/X)Se^{(2q-r-y-\rho\sigma v)T}$$

To value the cross-market options we use the generalization of Margrabe (1978). Let S_1 and S_2 be the domestic prices of two assets and let $C(T)$ have pay-off $\text{Max}(S_2 - S_1, 0)$ at T, then the current value of C is given by:

$$C = e^{-rT}[E^*(S_2)N(x) - E^*(S_1)N(x - \Sigma\sqrt{T})]$$

where $x = \{\ln[E^*(S_2)/E^*(S_1)] + \frac{1}{2}\Sigma^2 T\}/\Sigma\sqrt{T}$ and Σ^2 is the instantaneous variance of $(dS_2/S_2)/(dS_1/S_1)$. All of the cross-market options above can be viewed as a variation of the exchange of asset option. The risk-neutral expectations have already been derived and hence all that is needed to apply this formula are the appropriate expressions for Σ_i^2 (i denoting one of the five cross-market variations).

In the first case, note that the covariance of $d(XS)/(XS)$ and dX/X is $(v^2 + \rho\sigma v)$ and so $\Sigma_1^2 = (\sigma^2 + v^2 + \rho\sigma v) + v^2 - 2(v^2 + \rho\sigma v) = \sigma^2$. The other expressions are: $\Sigma_2^2 = \sigma^2$, $\Sigma_3^2 = (\sigma^2 + v^2 + \rho\sigma v)$, $\Sigma_4^2 = v^2$ and $\Sigma_5^2 = (\sigma^2 + v^2 - \rho\sigma v)$. Thus, for example, the value of the quanto call option, C_2, is:

$$C_2 = e^{-rT}[X^*Se^{(q-y-\rho\sigma v)T}N(x) - X^*S^*N(x - \sigma\sqrt{T})]$$

with $x = [\ln(S/S^*) + (q - y - \rho\sigma v)T + \frac{1}{2}\sigma^2 T]/\sigma\sqrt{T}$. Likewise, the equity-linked foreign exchange contract, C_4, is given as:

$$C_4 = e^{-rT}[XSe^{(r-y)T}N(x) - X^*Se^{(q-y-\rho\sigma v)T}N(x - v\sqrt{T})]$$

where, $x = [\ln(X/X^*) + (r - q + \rho\sigma v)T + \frac{1}{2}v^2 T/v\sqrt{T}$. To complete this discussion, note that to value the corresponding put options we may repeat the above but swap S_1 and S_2 or, equivalently, use put-call parity and express these as $P_i = C_i - e^{-rT}E^*(F_i)$ for each $i = 1, \ldots, 5$.

The construction of the cash hedge portfolio is discussed in Appendix 3 in general terms. The argument there follows the spirit of Black and Scholes (1976) to derive the relevant partial differential equation which these contracts must satisfy. In hedging the pay-off on cross-market options, delta-hedging alone is inefficient leaving the portfolio exposed to gamma risk. Hedge portfolios for these products are more likely to contain traded options on the asset and/or options on the exchange rate. A short position in any of the cross-market options is a position which is short the asset volatility or short currency option volatility or short both. However, the correlation term enters with a different sign depending on which variation is being managed. A general rule is to hedge the partial gammas using options on the asset and/or currency options. The net partial delta positions can be offset using cash positions. The correct amount of options will depend on the sign and magnitude of the correlation term. It is only efficient to consider each individual gamma in isolation when the correlation term is absent from the valuation formula or negligible in magnitude. In general one could do better by imposing an estimate of the correlation term and examining the local variation in the hedge portfolio to joint movements in S and X.

Finally, a word of caution. As noted in Reiner (1992), even though we are dealing with a two-asset problem, all the cross-market option formulae could be interpreted as the standard Black–Scholes formula but with modified parameters dependent on the nature of the contract. Indeed the generalized exchange of asset formula could also be given a Black–Scholes interpretation. This follows because the assumed processes imply that in each instance $(dS_2/S_2)/(dS_1/S_1)$ is log-normally distributed. Thus once the appropriate risk-neutral expected return and volatility terms are determined, the problem reduces to that of a single asset process. It is true that the appropriate volatility term is immediately seen from the composite nature of the contract pay-off. That is, the Σ term is just σ for contracts C_1 and C_2 as the "optionality" of these contracts is on the foreign asset. Likewise C_4 is essentially a foreign exchange option so that v is the appropriate volatility term. It is also clear that in contracts C_3 and C_5 both volatility terms must enter together with the covariance term $\rho\sigma v$ (positively for C_3 and negatively for C_5). What is not so obvious are the appropriate "interest rate" terms. To ensure that these are specified correctly, a two-asset frame of reference should be adopted which forces us to consider the appropriate risk-neutral drift terms.

3.4.3 Currency Basket Options

It is rare for companies to be exposed to a single foreign currency and hence a single exchange rate. It is more likely that companies will be exporting to, or sourcing raw materials from, several countries. Likewise, fund managers are unlikely to restrict the diversification of their portfolio to investments within a single currency market. The currency basket option was designed to hedge multi-currency risk with a single instrument. Rather than cover the currency risk with a portfolio of options, the basket option offers the ability to own an option on the portfolio.

The make-up of the basket is tailored to meet the requirements of the purchaser in terms of the range of currencies to be included, the respective currency amounts and the domestic currency value of this basket. For example, a UK company may be exporting to the US and Germany. Suppose this exposure is estimated to require the sale of 4 million US dollars and 6 million Deutschmarks, then the appropriate basket option is defined as the right to: sell USD 4 million, sell DM 6 million and receive a fixed amount of sterling.

The fixed sterling amount plays the part of the strike price of the option. Exercise of the option on the expiry date would depend on whether the transactions yield a better net sterling figure if they were carried out under the option rather than in the spot market. The alternative would be to buy sterling call options against the dollar and Deutschmark. Analogous to the discussion above for Asian options, in purchasing a basket option over the portfolio of individual options the opportunity to exercise some or all is forgone. Hence, the premium for the basket option should never be greater than the total premium outlay on the portfolio of individual options.

To value a basket option, one could treat the value of the basket as having a log-normal distribution and adopt the conventional Black–Scholes valuation model (allowing for risk-neutral returns). The volatility of the basket could be based on estimates from historic data together with a view of its performance over the option horizon. Alternatively, information implied from the option market on the individual exchange rates and cross-exchange rates could be used. The pricing methodology most institutions use is one where the risk inherent in the exotic instrument is identified and, where possible, valued by observing the prices of instruments traded which share a common element of this risk. This is precisely because these instruments are likely to form the foundation for the hedge. This principle is embodied in the following pricing methodology (see also Gentle (1992) and Huynh (1994)).

Define the pay-off of the basket option at time T as:

$$B(T) = \text{Max} \left[\sum_{i=1}^{N} A_i X_i(T) - A, 0 \right]$$

where A_i is the foreign currency i amount in the basket of N currency amounts, $X_i(T)$ is the domestic value of one unit of foreign currency i, A is the domestic currency value of the basket to be protected. This can be re-expressed as

$$B(T) = V \text{Max} \left[\sum_{i=1}^{N} w_i X_i(T) - k, 0 \right]$$

where $V = \Sigma_i A_i F_i$, F_i is the current forward exchange rate for X_i with delivery T, $w_i = A_i/V$, and $k = A/V$. We make the usual following assumptions for the stochastic process governing the exchange rates X_i:

$$dX_i = \mu_i X_i \, dt + \sigma_i X_i \, dz_i$$

where μ_i and σ_i are constant and dz_i are Weiner processes with $E(dz_i \, dz_j) = \rho_{ij}$. Define the value of the normalized basket at expiry by $P = \Sigma_i w_i X_i(T)$, then we need to develop a distribution for P which is consistent with those for $X_i(T)$ and risk-neutrality.

Similar to the discussion of valuation ideas behind Asian options in Section 3.2.2 above, we can determine a log-normal approximation for P. The first two risk-neutral moments for P are:

$$E^*(P) = \sum_{i=1}^{N} w_i e^{\mu_i + (1/2)\sigma_i^2} = \sum_{i=1}^{N} w_i F_i = 1$$

by construction, and

$$E^*(P^2) = \sum_{i=1}^{N}\sum_{j=1}^{N} w_i w_j E^*[X_i(T)X_j(T)]$$

Using

$$E^*[X_i(T)X_j(T)] = e^{[\mu_i+\mu_j+(1/2)(\sigma_i^2+\sigma_j^2+2\rho_{ij}\sigma_i\sigma_j)]T} = F_i F_j e^{\rho_{ij}\sigma_i\sigma_j T}$$

we have

$$E^*(P^2) = \sum_{i=1}^{N}\sum_{j=1}^{N} w_i w_j \cdot F_i F_j e^{\rho_{ij}\sigma_i\sigma_j T}$$

Hence a log-normal fit for P is to assume $\ln P$ is normally distributed $N(\alpha, \nu^2)$ where $\alpha = -\frac{1}{2}\ln E^*(P^2)$ and $\nu^2 = \ln E^*(P^2)$. The cross-correlations ρ_{ij} can be inferred from the volatility of the corresponding cross-exchange rate (σ_{ij}) as $\rho_{ij} = (\sigma_i^2 + \sigma_j^2 - \sigma_{ij}^2)/(2\sigma_i\sigma_j)$.

As an example, consider a two-currency basket (US dollars and yen) against sterling. Suppose the basket option is defined as the right to receive USD 14.8 million and JPY 1,450 million and pay a fixed amount of sterling in six months' time. Suppose interest rates are 6 per cent, 2 per cent and 8 per cent for dollars, yen and sterling, respectively, and the current exchange rates are USD 1.5000 and JPY 150.00 to the pound. The six-month forwards are then USD 1.4851 and JPY 145.57 giving an "at-the-money" sterling value for the basket of GBP 19.93 million. If volatilities were σ(GBP/USD) = 9 per cent and σ(GBP/JPY) = 13 per cent with correlation 0.23 (i.e. a USD/JPY volatility of 14 per cent) then the basket option premium is 3.40 per cent on GBP 19.93 million. The individual at-the-money forward option premiums to call dollars and yen are, respectively, 2.44 per cent and 3.52 per cent of the sterling face amount. Hence the basket option would cost GBP 470,000 and the premiums for the individual options would amount to GBP 594,000. Hence the basket option represents about 79 per cent of the cost of the portfolio of options. Figure 3.9 shows how this proportion varies with the correlation between the two exchange rates and with differing degrees of in-the-moneyness (measured relative to

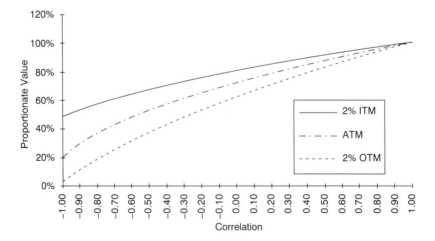

Figure 3.9 Relative value of basket option to portfolio of European options

the forward price). The figure shows that as correlation approaches unity and the option strike moves further in-the-money the saving in premium outlay on the basket option diminishes.

Finally, the standard techniques to hedging options apply to basket options. Traders will both delta- and gamma-manage their positions by trading in the cash and option markets. In the example above, a position long the basket option is one that benefits as volatilities of the X_i's increase but loses value as the correlation between the X_i's increases. The correlation position can be offset by trading options in the relevant cross-exchange rate. In general, the number of currency pair positions in the hedge can be reduced by analysing the statistical make-up of the variance of the basket using principal components or factor analysis.

3.5 APPENDIX 1

In this appendix the geometric ARO and ASO are derived. The geometric average is given by $G(t_N) = [S(t_1) \cdot S(t_2) \ldots S(t_N)]^{1/N}$. Thus $\ln G(t_N) = (1/N)\Sigma_i \ln S(t_i)$. As each $\ln S(t_i)$ is distributed $N(\mu_i, \sigma_i^2)$ then $\ln G(t_N)$ is also distributed as normal $N(\mu_G, \sigma_G^2)$. Hence the ARO call and ASO call are, respectively, given by:

$$e^{-rT} E^* \text{Max}[G(t_N) - K, 0] = e^{\mu_G + (1/2)\sigma_G^2 - rT} N(x_1) - e^{-rT} K N(x_2)$$

where $x_1 = (\mu_G - \ln K + \sigma_G^2)/v$ and $x_2 = x_1 - \sigma_G$, and

$$e^{-rT} E^* \text{Max}[S(T) - G(t_N), 0] = S(t)e^{-yT} N(y_1) - e^{\mu_G + (1/2)\sigma_G^2 - rT} N(y_2)$$

where $y_1 = [\ln S(t) + (r - y)T - \mu_G - \frac{1}{2}\sigma_G^2 + \frac{1}{2}\Sigma^2]/\Sigma$, $y_2 = y_1 - \Sigma$, $\Sigma^2 = \sigma_G^2 + \sigma^2 T - 2\rho_G\sigma_G\sigma_T$ and $\rho_G\sigma_G\sigma_T$ is the covariance between $\ln G(t_N)$ and $\ln S(T)$. The ARO put and ASO put are, respectively, given by:

$$e^{-rT} E^* \text{Max}[K - G(t_N), 0] = e^{-rT} K N(-x_2) - e^{\mu_G + (1/2)\sigma_G^2 - rT} N(-x_1)$$

and

$$e^{-rT} E^* \text{Max}[G(t_N) - S(T), 0] = e^{\mu_G + (1/2)\sigma_G^2 - rT} N(-y_2) - S(t)e^{-yT} N(-y_1)$$

It remains only to derive μ_G, σ_G and $\rho_G\sigma_G\sigma_T$.
The mean of $\ln G(t_N)$ is immediately

$$\mu_G = \frac{1}{N} \sum_{i=1}^{N} \mu_i$$

For constant r, y and σ this can be re-expressed as:

$$\mu_G = \ln S(t) + \frac{1}{N} \sum_{i=1}^{N} (r - y - \frac{1}{2}\sigma^2)t_i$$

and for equidistant fixing intervals from t_1, $t_i = t_1 + (i-1)(T-t_1)/(N-1)(i = 1, \ldots, N)$, we have

$$\mu_G = \ln S(t) + \left(r - y - \frac{1}{2}\sigma^2\right)\left(\frac{T - t_1}{2} + t_1\right)$$

The variance of $\ln G(t_N)$ is given by

$$\sigma^2_G = \frac{1}{N^2}\left[\sum_{i=1}^{N}\sigma^2_i + 2\sum_{i=1}^{N-1}\sum_{j=i+1}^{N}\rho_{ij}\sigma_i\sigma_j\right]$$

where $\rho_{ij} = \sigma_i/\sigma_j$ is the correlation between $\ln S(t_i)$ and $\ln S(t_j)$ for $i \leq j$. Hence

$$\sigma^2_G = \frac{1}{N^2}\left[\sum_{i=1}^{N}\sigma^2_i + 2\sum_{i=1}^{N-1}(N - i)\sigma^2_i\right]$$

when $\sigma^2_i = \sigma^2 t_i$ we have

$$\sigma^2_G = \sigma^2\frac{1}{N^2}\left[\sum_{i=1}^{N}t_i + 2\sum_{i=1}^{N-1}(N - i)t_i\right]$$

and for $t_i = t_1 + (i - 1)(T - t_1)/(N - 1)$

$$\sigma^2_G = \sigma^2\left[\frac{(T - t_1)(2N - 1)}{6N} + t_1\right]$$

As $N \to \infty$ $\sigma^2_G = \sigma^2[(T - t_1)/3 + t_1]$. Finally, the covariance term $\rho_G\sigma_G\sigma_T$ is given by

$$\rho_G\sigma_G\sigma_T = \text{Cov}\left(\frac{1}{N}\sum_{i=1}^{N}\ln S(t_i), \ln S(T)\right)$$

$$= \frac{1}{N}\sum_{i=1}^{N}\sigma^2_i$$

For $\sigma^2_i = \sigma^2 t_i$ we have $\rho_G\sigma_G\sigma_T = (\sigma^2/N)\Sigma_i t_i$ and for $t_i = t_1 + (i - 1)(T - t_1)/(N - 1)$

$$\rho_G\sigma_G\sigma_T = \sigma^2\frac{(T + t_1)}{2}$$

3.6 APPENDIX 2

Although the distribution of $A(t_N)$ is non-standard, closed-form solutions can be readily found for the moments of $A(t_N)$. Indeed Turnbull and Wakeman (1991) describe an efficient algorithm for finding all such moments. Here we provide expressions for the first two moments.

Given that $\ln S(t_i)$ is distributed as $N(\mu_i, \sigma^2_i)$, it follows that the first moment for $A(t_N)$ is given by:

$$A(t_N) = \frac{1}{N}\sum_{i=1}^{N}e^{\mu_i + (1/2)\sigma^2_i} = \frac{1}{N}\sum_{i=1}^{N}F_i$$

where F_i denotes the forward price of $S(t_i)$. For constant interest rates and volatility we have

$$E^*[A(t_N)] = \frac{S(t)}{N} \sum_{i=1}^{N} e^{(r-y)t_i}$$

and for $t_i = t_1 + (i-1)(T-t_1)/(N-1)$

$$E^*[A(t_N)] = \frac{S(t)}{N} e^{gt_1} \cdot \frac{1 - e^{ghN}}{1 - e^{gh}}$$

where $h = (T-t_1)/(N-1)$ and $g = (r-y)$. As the frequency of recordings increases, we have in the limit as $N \to \infty$

$$E^*[A(t_N)] = S(t)e^{gt_1} \cdot \frac{e^{g(T-t_1)} - 1}{g(T-t_1)}$$

The second moment for $A(t_N)$ is given by

$$E^*[A(t_N)^2] = \frac{1}{N^2} \sum_{i=1}^{N} \sum_{j=1}^{N} E^*[S(t_i)S(t_j)]$$

or

$$E^*[A(t_N)^2] = \frac{1}{N^2} \left\{ \sum_{i=1}^{N} E^*[S(t_i)^2] + 2 \sum_{i=1}^{N-1} \sum_{j=i+1}^{N} E^*[S(t_i)S(t_j)] \right\}$$

Noting that $E^*[S(t_i)S(t_j)] = F_i F_j e^{\sigma_i^2}$ for $i \leq j$,

$$E^*[A(t_N)^2] = \frac{1}{N^2} \left[\sum_{i=1}^{N} F_i^2 e^{\sigma_i^2} + 2 \sum_{i=1}^{N-1} \sum_{j=i+1}^{N} F_i F_j e^{\sigma_i^2} \right]$$

For constant interest rates and volatility, we have

$$E^*[A(t_N)^2] = \frac{S(t)^2}{N^2} \left[\sum_{i=1}^{N} e^{(2g+\sigma^2)t_i} + 2 \sum_{i=1}^{N-1} e^{(g+\sigma^2)t_i} \sum_{j=i+1}^{N} e^{gt_j} \right]$$

and for $t_i = t_1 + (i-1)h$

$$E^*[A(t_N)] = \frac{S(t)^2 e^{(2g+\sigma^2)t_1}}{N^2} \cdot \left\{ \frac{1 - e^{(2g+\sigma^2)hN}}{1 - e^{(2g+\sigma^2)h}} + \frac{2}{1 - e^{(g+\sigma^2)h}} \right.$$

$$\left. \left[\frac{1 - e^{ghN}}{1 - e^{gh}} - \frac{1 - e^{(2g+\sigma^2)hN}}{1 - e^{(2g+\sigma^2)h}} \right] \right\}$$

Finally as $N \to \infty$ we have

$$E^*[A(t_N)] = \frac{2S(t)^2 e^{(2g+\sigma^2)t_1}}{(g+\sigma^2)(T-t_1)^2} \cdot \left[\frac{1 - e^{g(T-t_1)}}{g} - \frac{1 - e^{(2g+\sigma^2)(T-t_1)}}{(2g+\sigma^2)} \right]$$

3.7 APPENDIX 3

Consider a cross-market contract $C(t, S, X)$, valued in domestic terms, whose pay-off at T depends on S and X. Given the stochastic processes assumed for S and X in Section 3.4.2, Ito's lemma states that dC satisfies:

$$dC = (C_t + \mu SC_S + \eta XC_X + \tfrac{1}{2}\sigma^2 S^2 C_{SS} + \tfrac{1}{2}v^2 X^2 C_{XX} + \rho\sigma vSXC_{SX})\,dt + \sigma SC_S\,dz + vXC_X\,dw$$

Suppose we have a position which is short one unit of C. The hedged portfolio, P, is constructed by buying h_S units of S and h_X units of X so that P has value in domestic terms:

$$P = h_X X + h_S SX - C$$

and $dP = h_X\,dX + h_S\,d(SX) - dC$. Applying Ito's lemma and collecting terms gives

$$dP = \phi\,dt + (h_X X + h_S S - XC_X)v\,dw + (h_S X - C_S)S\sigma\,dz$$

where $\phi = h_s(\mu + \eta + \rho\sigma v)SX + h_X\eta X - \lambda$ and $\lambda = C_t + \mu SC_S + \eta XC_X + \tfrac{1}{2}\sigma^2 S^2 C_{SS} + \tfrac{1}{2}v^2 X^2 C_{XX} + \rho\sigma vSXC_{SX}$.

To ensure dP is riskless, choose h_S and h_X so that the coefficients in dP for dz and dw are zero, thus:

$$h_S = (1/X)C_S$$
$$h_X = C_X - (S/X)C_S$$

The portfolio also earns the dividend yield on holdings of S and the foreign interest rate on that of X, so that

$$dP = [\phi + ySC_S + q(XC_X - SC_S)]\,dt$$

However, if P is riskless, to avoid arbitrage we require $dP = rP\,dt$. That is

$$\phi + ySC_S + q(XC_X - SC_S) = r(h_X X + h_S SX - C)$$
$$= rC_X X - rC$$

or

$$rC = C_t + (q - y - \rho\sigma v)SC_S + (r - q)XC_X + \tfrac{1}{2}\sigma^2 S^2 C_{SS} + \tfrac{1}{2}v^2 X^2 C_{XX} + \rho\sigma vSXC_{SX}$$

This is the partial differential equation (PDE) that must be satisfied by all cross-market securities $C(t, S, X)$ (together with their boundary conditions). As with single-asset securities, as time progresses, holdings of S and X must be adjusted to keep the portfolio riskless. In general, for the stochastic processes assumed, the Feynman–Kac theorem (see Karatzas and Shreve (1991)) tell us that the function $C(t, S, X)$ defined by the relation $C(t, S_t, X_t) = e^{-r(T-t)}E_t[C(T, S_T, X_T)]$ solves

$$rC = C_t + \mu SC_S + \eta XC_X + \tfrac{1}{2}\sigma^2 S^2 C_{SS} + \tfrac{1}{2}v^2 X^2 C_{XX} + \rho\sigma vSXC_{SX}$$

Hence by choosing $\mu = q - y - \rho\sigma v$ and $\eta = r - q$ we can solve our PDE for $C(t, S, X)$ using $e^{-r(T-t)}E_t[C(T, S_T, X_T)]$.

3.8 REFERENCES

Black, F. and Scholes, M.S. (1973) "The pricing of options and corporate liabilities". *Journal of Political Economy*, May/June, **81**, 637–54.

Boyle, P.P. (1977) "Options: A Monte Carlo approach". *Journal of Financial Economics*, May, **4**, 323–38.

Carverhill, A.P. and Clewlow, L.S. (1990) "Flexible convolution". *Risk*, April, **3**, 25–9.

Cox, J.C. and Ross, S.A. (1976) "The valuation of options for alternative stochastic processes". *Journal of Financial Economics*, September, **3**, 145–66.

Curran, M. (1992) "Beyond average intelligence". *Risk*, November, **5**, 60.

Derman, E., Karasinski, P. and Wecker, J.S. (1990) "Understanding guaranteed exchange-rate contracts in foreign stock investments". Quantitative Strategies Research Notes, Goldman Sachs, June.

Geman, H. and Eydeland, A. (1995) "Domino effect". *Risk*, April, **8**, 65–7.

Geman, H. and Yor, M. (1992a) "Quelques relations entre processus de Bessel, options asiatiques, et fonctions confluentes hypergéométriques". Comptes Renus Academie Sciences Series 1, 471–4.

Geman, H. and Yor, M. (1992b) "Bessel processes, Asian options and perpetuities". *Mathematical Finance*, **3**, 349–75.

Gentle, D. (1993) "Basket weaving". *Risk*, June, **6**, 51–2.

Hammersley, J.M. and Handscomb D.C. (1964) *Monte Carlo Simulation*. London: Methuen.

Hogg, R.V. and Craig, A.T. (1970) *Introduction to Mathematical Statistics*. 3rd Edition, London: Collier Macmillan.

Huynh, C.B., (1994) "Back to Baskets". *Risk*, May, **7**, 59–61.

Karatzas, I.K. and Shreve, S.E. (1991) *Brownian Motion and Stochastic Calculus*. Graduate Texts in Mathematics 113, Springer-Verlag, 2nd Edition.

Kemna, A.G.Z. and Vorst, A.C.F. (1990) "A pricing method for options based on average asset values". *Journal of Banking and Finance*, March, **14**, 113–29.

Levy, E. (1990) "Asian arithmetic". *Risk*, May, **3**, 7–8.

Levy, E. (1992) "Pricing European average rate currency options". *Journal of International Money and Finance*, **11**, 474–91.

Levy, E. and Turnbull, S.M. (1992) "Average intelligence". *Risk*, February, **5**, 53–9.

Margrabe, W. (1978) "The value of an option to exchange one asset for another". *Journal of Finance*, March, **33**, 177–86.

Reiner, E. (1992) "Quanto mechanics". *Risk*, March, **5**, 59–63.

Ritchken, P., Sankarasubramanian, L. and Vijh, A.M. (1990) "The valuation of path dependent contracts on the average". Unpublished manuscript, School of Business Administration, University of Southern California, September.

Rubinstein, M. and Reiner, E. (1991) "Unscrambling the binary code". *Risk*, October, **4**, 75–83.

Rubinstein, R.Y. (1981) *Simulation and the Monte Carlo Method*. New York: Wiley.

Ruttiens, A. (1990) "Classical replica". *Risk*, February, **3**, 33–6.

Turnbull, S.M. (1992) "The price is right". *Risk*, April, **4**, 56–7.

Turnbull, S.M. and Wakeman, L.M. (1991) "A quick algorithm for pricing European average options". *Journal of Financial and Quantitative Analysis*, September, **26**, 377–89.

Vorst, T. (1990) "Analytic boundaries and approximations of the prices and hedge ratios of average exchange rate options". Unpublished manuscript, Econometric Institute, Erasmus University Rotterdam, February.

Wei, Z. (1991) "Pricing forward contracts and options on foreign assets". Faculty of Management working paper, University of Toronto, May.

4

Exotic Options II

BRYAN THOMAS

This chapter will be oriented towards currency options, reflecting the majority of my options experience. But most of the ideas and many of the formulae can be adapted to other markets.

4.1 BARRIER OPTIONS

4.1.1 Definitions and Examples of Single Barrier Options

Single barrier options are path-dependent. Their value at maturity depends not only on the value of the underlying asset at maturity but also on the traded prices of the asset between inception and expiry. The type of path dependency for barrier options is relatively simple. If the underlying asset ever reaches the barrier during the life of the option, one rule is used to calculate the value at expiry; if the barrier is never reached, another rule applies. Barrier options come in two classes: out and in. Those of the "out" class lapse upon reaching the barrier, and may not be exercised. If the barrier is never reached, they are then equivalent at expiry to a European option of the same type, strike and size. These are generally called knock-out options in preference to the alternative term drop-out options, which seems to be falling out of favour. To enhance the descriptiveness or, in legal terms, to specify which direction spot must move to hit the barrier, knock-out options can be called either down & out options, or up & out options.

This type of option was traded in the unregulated OTC equity options market in the US prior to 1975, primarily for credit reasons associated with margin rules on equity purchases. Other financial contracts that predate the development of the analytical model contained embedded knock-out options. Once the model was written that described these moribund or relatively rare contracts, the product was introduced into a wide range of markets. In the currency market, barrier options became extremely popular in Japan in the latter part of the "asset bubble" in the late 1980s. Selling currency options was more prevalent than buying options in Japan. This may have been partially due to the accounting treatment that counted any premiums paid as an immediate cost, and any premiums received as profit. To the extent that "Japan plc" had developed a consensus about what range the JPY would be trading in they could profitably sell options. This was observable in terms of options trades and also in intraday changes in implied volatility, which traded lower in Tokyo time due to the excess of supply and tended to rebound once Tokyo closed. This practice generally worked well, but on occasion events in the rest of the world caused the JPY to diverge from the target zone. Astute option writers noticed that this usually happened after a favourable movement, rather than immediately after they sold the option, which created a very favourable environment for the banks that began marketing knock-out options. Knock-out option premiums can never be worth more than the underlying European option whose pay-off dominates that of the knock-out option, as the maximum return is the same, but it can be worth less if it knocks out and the European option ends up back in-the-money. Despite this lower premium, the risk was also lower, particularly the risk that had previously most bothered those option writers. In addition, the possibility of the option knocking out meant that another option could be written sooner, so over a year, the total premium received could be higher. A trader at a bank selling to a Japanese investor early in this period reported that, out of the first 30 knock-out options that investor sold, 28 knocked out, often within the first week. As these were a new product at the time, the bank offering them got a good margin and, hedging them prudently, made quite acceptable profits — though nowhere near what the seller made. Naturally, customers were anxious to be sure they were getting good prices, so they encouraged other banks to develop the capability to offer these products, who in turn marketed them to other clients, always increasing the familiarity with the knock-out options. Eventually the market made some unanticipated moves, the ensuing foreign exchange losses became harder to offset with equity or property profits after the "bubble" burst, and the one-sided nature of the business began to balance out.

The purchase of knock-out options is a strategy that is particularly well suited for proprietary traders or investors having a directional view. They are cheaper than European options, allowing a larger position to be taken risking the same premium. They have a higher delta, so an initial favourable move has a greater positive impact on the option price. They have lower theta and vega, meaning that the position is less effected by the passage of time or an unfavourable volatility move. Hedgers have also found them appealing. With users from both sectors, they are now reported to be the most popular exotic currency option, accounting for over 10 per cent of all currency option trades (by volume) between banks and their clients.

Barrier options of the "in" class must hit the barrier in order to be able to be exercised at expiry. They are generally called knock-in options, or occasionally drop-in options. When more detail is required, the terms used are down & in and up & in options. A position consisting of an "in" barrier option and an "out" barrier option of the same type, maturity, strike and amount is perfectly equivalent to a European option. Either spot hits the barrier, and the "in" option becomes European, or spot does not hit the barrier, allowing the "out" option to be exercised, if desired, at maturity. This relationship is used in almost every pricing model. Knock-out options are traded more frequently than knock-in options, but at the analytic level, the knock-in option is a more fundamental product, so the price of a knock-out option is calculated as the price of a European option less the knock-in.

Thus far we have spoken of whether barriers are "up" or "down" and "out" or "in", but options are also puts or calls. Thus, there are eight permutations; those where spot

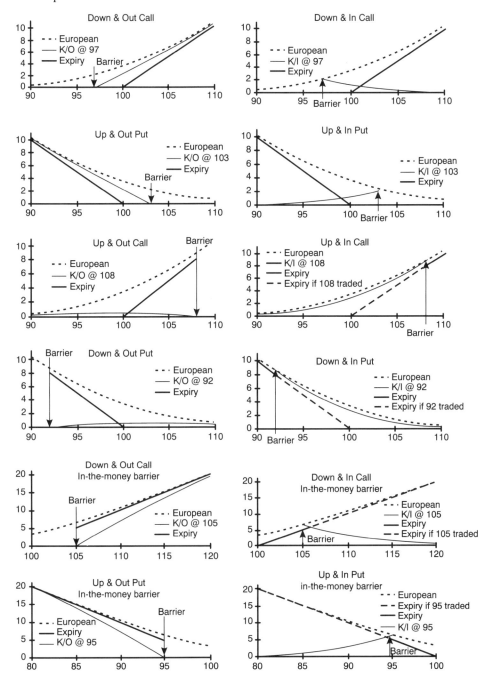

Figure 4.1 Option premiums as a function of spot, with $K = 100$, $r = r_f = 6$ per cent, volatility $= 12$ per cent and $T = 6$ months

must be heading in the in-the-money direction to trigger the barrier are called "reverse". Reverse barrier options must always have their barriers in-the-money, meaning that when spot gets to the barrier, the option is in-the-money. If a reverse knock-out's barrier were out-of-the-money, then it could never be worth anything, as it must have already been knocked out if it were in-the-money at expiry. If a reverse knock-in's barrier were out-of-the-money then it would have the same value as a European option, as it must have already knocked in if it were in-the-money at expiry. The eight types are:

	Normal		Reverse	
	Knock-outs	Knock-ins	Knock-outs	Knock-ins
Calls:	Down & Out Calls	Down & In Calls	Up & Out Calls	Up & In Calls
Puts:	Up & Out Puts	Up & In Puts	Down & Out Puts	Down & In Puts

Of course, if we are considering European or American currency options, every call is a put and vice versa. For a USD/DEM option, a DEM call is a USD put. This applies to barrier options as well. A down & out call on DEM is an up & out put on USD. (Although this terminology is not always agreed between participants, as some prefer to speak of whether the spot rate is going up or down, rather than defining up as the direction that moves a call into-the-money. The presence or absence of the term "reverse", meaning the barrier is reached by spot moving (further) into the money, for a given strike and barrier, is sufficient to remove any possibility of ambiguity.)

For normal barrier options, it is sometimes possible for the barrier to be in-the-money or at-the-money (strike equal to the barrier). If the option is in-the-money, the barrier may be between spot and strike, at the strike, or out-of-the-money. If a normal barrier option is out-of-the-money when dealt, then the barrier must be further out-of-the-money. The risk management characteristics of normal barrier options depend significantly on whether the barrier is out-of-, at-, or in-the-money. Normal barrier options with in-the-money barriers present many of the same risk management challenges as reverse barrier options.

4.1.2 An Analytical Model of Single Barrier Options

A "brute-force" approach to modelling a knock-in option might take an approach like: the integral from now to expiry of the value of a European option with maturity $(T - t)$ and spot = barrier, times the probability of first reaching the barrier at that time, dt. Since the price of a European option itself is an integral, and the function for first passage time isn't simple either, it could be difficult to turn this into a neat analytical formula. Fortunately we are spared all that, thanks to a simple observation illustrated with the following example:

Example 1   Let us consider a GBP call (USD put) struck at 1.5606 K/I @ 1.5300 (that knocks in at 1.5300). For such an option to be worth anything, spot must trade down to 1.5300, then subsequently rise so as to end up above 1.5606 at expiry. The Black–Scholes assumptions do not have belief in trends included. Should spot get to 1.5300 (and we ignore the drift due to interest rate differentials) the market is just as likely to go down to 1.5000 (1.53 divided by 103 per cent) as up to 1.5606 (1.53 times 103 per cent). This is called the reflection principle. For every path leading to the barrier, there are two equiprobable paths leading away from it, one that ends up above and one that ends up below. It is hard to figure out directly the probability of touching the barrier and ending up above 1.5606, but it is easy to figure out the probability of touching the barrier and ending up below 1.50. One cannot end up below 1.50 without having passed the barrier, so the problem thus simplifies into what is the chance of ending up below 1.50, which is contained in the model for a European put. Adjustments must be made for the effect of drift, and the fact that geometric movements from the barrier will mean that the mapping of equiprobable points will be different amounts in-the-money, but the value of the 1.5606 GBP call K/I @ 1.53 is directly related to the value of a European 1.5000 GBP put.

The analytic model is:

$$\Phi Se^{-r_f T}(H/S)^{2\lambda}N[\Psi y] - \Phi Ke^{-rT}(H/S)^{2\lambda-2}N[\Psi(y - \sigma\sqrt{T})] \tag{1}$$

where:

$$y = \frac{\ln[H^2/(SK)]}{\sigma\sqrt{T}} + \lambda\sigma\sqrt{T} \qquad \lambda = \frac{r - r_f + \sigma^2/2}{\sigma^2}$$

$\Phi = \{1$ if call; -1 if put$\}$, $\Psi = \{1$ if down barrier; -1 if up barrier$\}$, $H =$ barrier, $S =$ spot, $K =$ strike, $T =$ time to expiry in years, $\sigma =$ annualized volatility, $r =$ domestic rate*, $r_f =$ foreign rate* (*both are continuously compounded interest rates) and N is the normal distribution function.

If r equals r_f then λ is one-half, and the above terms become much simpler. A bit of algebra shows the formula if a down & in call becomes equivalent to an amount K/H of a European put with strike H^2/K. The same formula also applies to up & in puts and European calls. When the interest rate differential isn't zero it is possible to derive a more complicated expression for the hedge strike and amount. Unfortunately, it is of limited application, as every day the rate differential becomes less important, so the hedge strike and amount are constantly shifting.

Another interpretation of the formula is that the first term is the value of receiving S, if a call, or the cost of paying S, if a put, conditional upon the market having made the required movement (to the barrier then in-the-money) in a risk neutral framework. The second term is the cost of paying K, if a call, or receiving K, if a put, conditional upon exercise. This same observation can be applied to a European option pricing formula. Although the two probabilities are equal (in the real world) as one doesn't happen without the other, the normal distributions are not evaluated at the same points. This reflects the fact that if the option is worth exercising, S will have an expected value different than its current forward. The way the mathematics works out is elegantly expressed as a change in the risk neutral probability rather than as some other factor to be multiplied by S.

The above models are for normal barriers where the strike is out-of-the-money or at-the-money, for which there is no intrinsic value at the barrier. For non-trivial reverse knock-ins and normal knock-ins where the barrier is in-the-money there is intrinsic value at the barrier. Therefore, if the option should approach the barrier when expiry was near, there would be a large jump in price when the barrier was reached. This makes the equivalence to an option of the other type impossible, as option prices are not discontinuous. There the models for these options are more complicated, but are still analytic models. These were first published in a September 1991 *Risk Magazine* article, "Breaking down the barriers" by Marc Rubenstein and Eric Reiner. Excluding rebates, which will be considered later, they derived four terms that can be variously combined to produce the formulae for all of the possible configurations of single barrier options. One was a European option formula, and another was the "normal" knock-in formula where the barrier is out-of-the-money, like equation (1) above.

Using the interpretation of the option formula as (expected) values multiplied by risk neutral probabilities, an intuitive description of their derivation would be that they determine what pay-offs can occur in what ranges on each type of option, and solve the appropriate integrals. Let us first consider a down & in call option where the barrier is higher than the strike. (The initial spot must be higher than either, else it would have already knocked in!) We can split the pay-off at maturity into two partitions, those where it touches the barrier and ends up between the strike and the barrier, and those where it touches the barrier and ends up above it. The first part can be evaluated as a difference between a European option and some kind of quasi-European option that could be exercised only if it were above the barrier at expiry. The formula for such a "conditional" option is obtained by replacing the strike by the barrier inside the normal probabilities, but leaving the strike untouched outside. This can be seen as an application of the intuitive expected value times risk neutral probability idea. Once a formula exists, it is probable that someone will try to market a product based on it, in the never-ending quest to project a "state-of-the-art" image, or on the assumption that there is a bigger margin in products not already being marketed by the competition. As plenty of firms already have a good understanding of these models and some of them have "rocket scientists" busily trying to come up with something new, it would be surprising if such conditional options hadn't already been marketed. However, they are identical to a portfolio of two other products: a European call option with the strike set at the barrier of the "conditional" option and a binary (digital) option that pays out the difference between the "conditional" strike and the barrier above the barrier.

Using the reflection principle, the second part has many characteristics like a normal knock-in option. Consider the paths that reach the barrier and end up below, which are of course equiprobable (adjusting for drift) with the paths that reach the barrier and end up above, in which we are interested. But, instead of having to move from S to H then H to K, the moment spot gets to the barrier it is already in-the-money, so the H^2/SK in the normal probability is replaced by just H/S. The formulae for the terms are:

$$\Phi S e^{-r_f T} N[\Phi d_1] - \Phi K e^{-rT} N[\Phi(d_1 - \sigma\sqrt{T})] \qquad \text{(2) European option}$$

$$\Phi S e^{-r_f T} N[\Phi d_3] - \Phi K e^{-rT} N[\Phi(d_3 - \sigma\sqrt{T})] \qquad \text{(3) "Conditional" option}$$

$$\Phi S e^{-r_f T} (H/S)^{2\lambda} N[\Psi y_1] - \Phi K e^{-rT} (H/S)^{2\lambda-2} N[\Psi(y_1 - \sigma\sqrt{T})] \qquad (4)$$

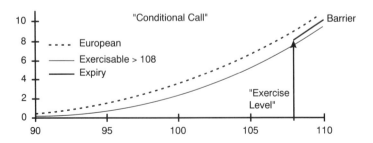

Figure 4.2 A "conditional option, an illustration of equation (3)

where:

$$d_1 = \frac{\ln[S/K]}{\sigma\sqrt{T}} + \lambda\sigma\sqrt{T} \qquad d_3 = \frac{\ln[S/H]}{\sigma\sqrt{T}} + \lambda\sigma\sqrt{T} \qquad y_1 = \frac{\ln[H/S]}{\sigma\sqrt{T}} + \lambda\sigma\sqrt{T}$$

Putting these terms together allows the creation of the analytic models for all of the varieties of single barrier options (see Table 4.1).

Table 4.1

Barrier Option	Barrier vs. Strike	Equation	Φ, Ψ
Knock-in	Out-of-the-money	(1)	$1,1 =$ Down & In Call
			$-1, -1 =$ Up & In Put
Knock-in	In-the-money	$(2) - (3) + (4)$	$1,1 =$ Down & In Call
			$-1, -1 =$ Up & In Put
Reverse knock-in		$(3) + (4) - (1)$	$1, -1 =$ Up & In Call
			$-1, 1 =$ Down & In Put
Knock-out	Out-of-the-money	$(2) - (1)$	$1,1 =$ Down & Out Call
			$-1, -1 =$ Up & Out Put
Knock-out	In-the-money	$(3) - (4)$	$1,1 =$ Down & Out Call
			$-1, -1 =$ Up & Out Put
Reverse knock-out		$(2) - (3) - (4) + (1)$	$1, -1 =$ Up & Out Call
			$-1, 1 =$ Down & Out Put

4.1.3 Alternative Modelling Methods

The Black–Scholes assumptions used in deriving the analytical models are somewhat more stressed by the application to barrier options than they are by European-style options. For example, a price jump during the life of a European option could be compensated for by a quiet period later on. But a price jump across a knock-out barrier has more dramatic results, and no chance for later calm to offset those effects. The interest rate or asset yield may not be constant, implying forwards that are closer to or further away from the barrier than the constant rate or yield assumption would imply. Implied volatilities may have a definite skew or smile curve which traders have adapted to in European option markets, but they are unsure how to apply their experience to barrier options. For these and other reasons, various alternative modelling methods have been tried.

The prime candidates for modelling any exotic option are:

- Binomial or trinomial trees
- Monte Carlo simulations
- Construction of a portfolio of European options to duplicate the exotic option
- Numerical methods/analytic approximations

Price lattices like binomial or trinomial trees have a disadvantage for computing accurate prices for barrier options. With a number of iterations that would provide a perfectly acceptable price for an American-style option, the price between the node just inside the barrier and the node just outside is quite wide. This means that, given a strike price, volatility, maturity and number iterations, a fairly wide range of different barriers would produce exactly the same price, in contrast to the results of the analytical model and intuition. Arbitrarily increasing the number of iterations is not an effective way of overcoming this problem, as the results do not converge monotonically to the desired result.

However, by carefully selecting the number of iterations so that the barrier is just barely beyond a node, a result near the analytic result can be achieved.

It isn't worth implementing a lattice to replicate the analytic result. The purpose is usually to introduce a feature that cannot be properly reflected in the closed form solution. If the forward curve is non-linear, which would be caused by a sloping yield curve in one of the markets, then the different interest rates at each iteration could be reflected, improving the quality of the assessment of the probability of the barrier being reached. If the desire was to evaluate the impact of the volatility term structure or the volatility smile curve, then a trinomial lattice would be required.

In an article entitled "Pricing and hedging with volatility smiles", that appeared in *Risk Magazine* (January 1994), Bruno DuPire described how, using the prices of European options for a whole range of strikes and maturities, one could derive the instantaneous volatility for any future time and spot level within that range. That set of derived future spot-dependent volatilities could be used either to populate a trinomial lattice or in a Monte Carlo simulation for the purpose of pricing a barrier option. (The variance reduction techniques, described in the previous chapter, antithetic and control variate, should be used in implementing an efficient Monte Carlo simulation.)

Using Bruno DuPire's idea, it is possible to recalculate all of the future instantaneous volatilities if the implied volatility of one of the European option volatilities is slightly perturbed (0.01 per cent). A particular barrier could be repriced, allowing the calculation of the sensitivity of the premium of the barrier option to that European option, which can be used to determine how much of that European option to include in the hedge. If the process is repeated for all of the European options used as inputs in the derivation of the future instantaneous volatilities, then the option portion of the hedge portfolio could be derived. (This doesn't determine the spot/forward hedge required, which must be found by other means, such as looking inside the lattice. Changing the initial spot slightly and repricing the option is not the right way to proceed, as a change in spot implies a change in volatilities as well.) Obviously, the resulting hedge portfolio will consist of the options chosen as original inputs. In markets where liquidity is concentrated on standard strikes and maturities, as with exchange traded options, this is helpful. However, for OTC currency options, more work needs to be done to make sure of selecting the right options as inputs.

Bruno DuPire's idea is quite interesting in that it allows the different volatilities of different strikes (the smile curve) to be taken into account when pricing and hedging, and allows for changes in volatility, albeit in a deterministic fashion. (The price, and therefore implied volatility, of any European option may be calculated for any future time and spot level.) Whilst this is an improvement on the Black–Scholes assumptions, and should help explain many of the observed short-term shifts in volatility associated with short-term spot movements, being deterministic, it doesn't fully seem to reflect the full range of changes that can occur to volatility. The level of spot has a profound and significant impact on volatility levels, but it is not the only influence. It could be sufficient to explain the behaviour of volatility when a currency devalues, but would not be powerful in explaining the shifts that occur when some major political change impacts volatility levels, such as what happened to USD/JPY volatility when the LDP lost power in 1993. To model stochastic volatility properly, a two factor (at least) model would be required. The work Bruno DuPire has done should be used as a new starting point, as previous attempts at modelling using stochastic volatility only managed to explain about half of the observed volatility differences between strikes.

4.1.4 Risk Management of Single Barrier Options

(i) Pricing

Unless the counterparty (customer or other dealer) specifically requests a strategy, it is market practice to quote both bid and offer for the requested option and amount. The price could be "live", meaning not referring to a particular spot market price and only valid for the brief time it takes to respond (or even less if the quoter says "Change!"). When quoting a "live" price, the option dealer is exposed to unfavourable changes in the spot market, as it might move at the same time the option is dealt. Accordingly, "live" prices may be somewhat wider to this risk, and are not made immediately prior to scheduled releases of economic data. Most barrier option dealing by dealers with their clients is on the basis of "live" prices.

Alternatively, the price could be quoted on a specific spot reference level, which would be approximately the market when the quote was requested. The dealer would calculate the delta and propose bid and ask prices for the option, based on his also transacting the delta hedge with the counterparty. This makes the market more efficient, as the barrier option bid–ask spread can be shrunk by the delta times the spot market bid–ask spread. Another benefit is that this allows the seeker of the quote the flexibility of comparison shopping. Three banks can be queried, and the responses, even if not simultaneous, will be comparable, and the best can be selected. If the seeker of the quote is in a hurry to transact the option before spot has a chance to move, he can set his spot hedge first, and then search for the best option price. Unlike the OTC market for European-style currency options, the prices are not quoted in volatility terms (like 9.5 per cent to 9.8 per cent), because this could result in either inverted quotes (the bid being higher than the offer) on some barrier options or an inability to actually quote the desired price. (Sometimes the maximum or minimum of the function of premium of a barrier option for its volatility can occur near market volatilities. Considering the other risks in managing the option, the dealer might want to add or subtract a margin to that extremum, which could only be achieved by using a complex number component in the volatility. As this degree of complexity is unwelcome, it is simpler to use price spreads.)

Besides reflecting all of the market parameters required to price a European option, the price of a barrier option should reflect the expected cost of hedging. The analytical model ignores transaction costs, but the real world doesn't. An estimation of the particular transaction costs of a barrier option should be focused on the barrier event:

- how likely is the barrier to be reached?
- is the required action at the barrier a stop loss or take profit order? and
- the expected size of the order at the barrier

As options with out-of-the-money barriers have less sensitivity to volatility than the underlying European option, and the size of the order at the barrier decreases with the passage of time, the width of the bid–ask spread can be similar to or slightly wider than the underlying European option. As buying a knock-out option would generate an easy-to-manage take profit order, the bid is usually close to the theoretical level that would be obtained by using the same inputs as pricing the underlying European option using the market parameters appropriate for the bid side. The offer side may be found by adding a spread, thus using the "extra" spread to protect against the risk of the stop loss order.

The size of the order that must be executed at the barrier increases for barrier options, whether "reverse" or "normal" with in-the-money barriers. Because of this increasing risk, they usually have a bid–ask spread that is two to three times wider than the underlying European option. For barriers that are very far in-the-money, and with little time remaining, the spread can be even wider.

Table 4.2

Option Type (Barrier)	Delta	Gamma	Vega	Theta	Rho
European	0–100	positive	positive	negative	$\sim$ delta$^*T$
K/Out (OTM)	higher	lower	lower	lower	lower
K/In (OTM)	negative	lower	lower	lower	lower
K/Out (ATM)	$\sim$ 100	$\sim$ 0	$\sim$ 0	0– $\sim$ S/N fwd pts	0– $\sim$ delta$^*T$
K/In (ATM)	negative	$\sim$ same	$\sim$ same	negative	variable
K/Out (ITM)	>100	negative	negative	positive	0– $\sim$ delta$^*T$
K/In (ITM)	negative	higher	higher	more negative	variable
Reverse K/Out	lower or –	lower or –	lower or –	less negative or +	variable
Reverse K/In	0–higher	0–higher	0–higher	0–more negative	variable

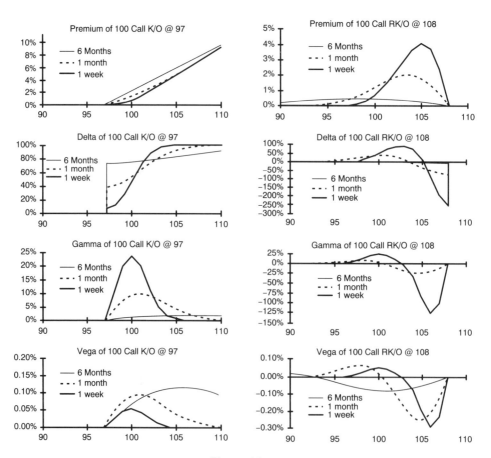

Figure 4.3

(ii) Derivatives

Table 4.2 may serve as a synthesis of several sets of graphs. The barrier option derivatives are compared to the underlying European option when possible.

The experienced option trader is very familiar with matching derivatives to hedge a complicated options position, although he knows he will have to start paying attention to positions by strike as they approach expiry. The same process can be applied to barrier option positions, although it is more important to note how the derivatives shift with spot movement and time to be able to pick a hedge whose derivatives will continue to provide a good match for the barrier options under changing market conditions and some passage of time. If the volume of OTC dealing far outweighs the barrier positions, and the opportunities provided by continuous dealing in those markets mean that it is trivial to adjust the position, then matching local derivatives is sufficient.

(iii) Hedging

As described in the analytical model section, a normal knock-in option has a strong equivalence to a European option of the other type (put vs. call). Hedging down & in calls with European puts and hedging up & in puts with European calls is therefore quite tempting. The strategy works perfectly if the barrier is never reached, but what is important is how well this works when the spot gets to the barrier, which is covered in the next section.

Hedging knock-outs can be broken down into covering the European component, and using the European hedge for the knock-in part. This is not the most common method. As normal knock-outs have less gamma than European options, there is a stronger tendency to rely on delta hedging. To the extent that the vega risk is unwanted, a partial hedge using the underlying European option can be used. The vega position will shift as spot moves nearer to or farther away from the barrier. Most currency options markets have a smile curve (the implied volatilities for different strikes with the same maturity) that is neither flat nor symmetric. Typically, if spot moves towards the side that has the higher volatilities, market volatilities will increase, at least temporarily. Being short a knock-out with only a delta hedge creates a short vega position which decreases when the market moves towards the barrier. If the barrier is on the same side as the part of the smile curve with the higher volatility, then such moves would benefit the delta hedged knock-out position, increasing the willingness of market-makers to be content with just delta hedging.

Another hedging technique is the use of static hedges, constructed with European options that match reasonably well the current and future values of a barrier option in a wide range of spot and volatilities, up to the point where the barrier is reached. This eliminates the necessity to continually rebalance the hedge. As the delta gaps when the option knocks-in or knocks-out, the static hedge must be "costlessly unwound" at that point. If a spot hedge is executed at the barrier level, then this is approximately achievable, if one ignores bid–ask spreads and the effect of any volatility smile curve. The static hedge for a normal knock-in option, like a down & in call or a up & in put, for which the barrier is out-of-the-money, can be derived from the pricing formula. It is straightforward if the rates for each currency are identical. The static hedge for a down & in call is a put, and for an up & in put is a call. The strike of the static hedge is H^2/SK, and the amount required is K/H. When the rates aren't identical, the calculation is more difficult and less useful, as the passage of time will change the hedge strike and amount. If the barrier is never reached,

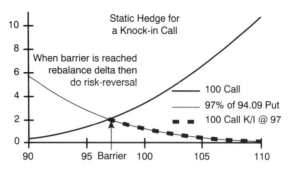

Figure 4.4

this option finishes out of the money, so the hedge would have worked perfectly. More importantly, if one assumes that the volatility smile is always flat, and the interest rates are always identical, then whenever the barrier is reached, the value of the static hedge will match the cost required to buy the European option that the knock-in option has become.

As a knock-out option can be considered as a portfolio of a long European option and a short knock-in option, the static hedge for a normal knock-out option with an out-of-the-money barrier is simply long the underlying European option and short the static hedge for the knock-in option.

Static hedges for barrier options with in-the-money barriers are less common. In fact the solution may be considered more difficult to manage than the original problem. The problem is replicating the way the intrinsic value gaps at the barrier. Although the premium as a function of spot is continuous prior to the moment of expiry, the fact that it gets ever steeper near the barrier as expiry approaches makes it difficult to find a simple static hedge. Consider the case of an up & out call, a 1.50 USD call/DEM put RKO @ 1.60, so spot USD/DEM was somewhere below 1.60. If, close to expiry, spot is near the strike, then the option will behave rather like a European-style 1.50 USD call, because the barrier is unlikely to be reached. Therefore, the 1.50 USD call is a good candidate for inclusion in the static hedge. If only one other option is sought to complete the hedge, the choice is dependent upon time to maturity. Since the up & out call begins to decrease in value as spot approaches the barrier, the sale of some option is indicated. Using an iterative process and least-squared-errors decision rule to find the strike and amount of the option to be sold, assuming 10 per cent volatility, DEM interest rates of 5.5 per cent and USD interest rates of 6 per cent, the results were:

Days remaining	30	15	7	3
Strike	1.5675	1.5780	1.5850	1.5900
Amount	2.615	3.8	5.545	8.32

Of course, any of these would still require an order to be executed at the barrier, and the hedging options "costlessly" unwound. Although any one of these hedges is a good "gamma" hedge on the day it is set, over a wide range of prices, the fit worsens with the passage of time. Therefore, it is necessary to use more than two options in the static hedge.

Assuming that the barrier is far enough in-the-money so the underlying European option would have little time value at that point, then the best static hedge using three options includes the underlying European option and a large spread, the short leg just before the barrier with the long leg equidistant on the other side of the barrier. The amount of the

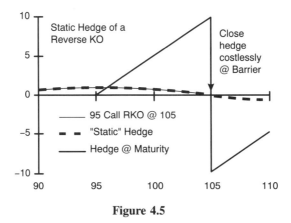

Figure 4.5

spread required is twice the intrinsic value drop at barrier divided by the width between the spread strikes. The closer the spread strikes are to the barrier, and therefore the larger the size of the spread, the better the static hedge matches the reverse knock-out option. Such a large, tight spread by itself is the static hedge for a binary option. Thus, if there were, contrary to current market conditions, a liquid market in binary options, the static hedge would be long the underlying European, and short a binary option struck at the barrier with a pay-off of twice the drop in intrinsic value at the barrier. It has to be twice as large because prior to expiry a binary option is worth half of its pay-off when spot is at the strike (assuming equal interest rates and ignoring the present value effect). Thus the ever steepening decline to barrier is well matched by the binary option.

Should the barrier be not so remote from the strike of a reverse knock-out option, then a fourth option would have to be added to the static hedge, to offset the time value of the underlying European option at the barrier. Changing the size of the binary-like portion of the static hedge is not sufficient, as the time value to be offset must decline as expiry approaches. Instead, an option of similar type, well out-of-the-money, should be sold. To offset the time value, it should have the same kind of relation to the underlying strike as the hedge option for a normal knock-in option, i.e. hedge strike $= H^2/K$, and size $= S/H$ if the interest rates are equal.

(iv) Barrier Events

The analytic model assumes that the hedge is costlessly exited at the barrier, which is easier said than done. The risk of not achieving this can be mitigated by a variety of means. Even before a barrier option is traded, it is important to establish unambiguous legal terms covering the barrier event. Who is responsible for monitoring the market and what are their duties? Most dealers' terms specify that they determine whether or not an option has reached the barrier. This seems to work with clients, but is perhaps a hindrance to interbank dealing. The concept of a partial barrier event is included in some banks' terms, if they are working a take profit order, to manage a sold knock-in or purchased knock-out, but if they only manage to execute part of the order at the barrier, then they would declare that it had only partially knocked-in or knocked-out. For stop loss orders, a partial fill usually means that the rest must be done at a worse price, so barrier events that create stop loss orders do not give rise to partial barrier events. There is an inherent contradiction between the views that could be taken between two dealers having opposite positions in the same barrier option. There have been some attempts to co-ordinate the execution of the two orders, but this is not yet become market standard practice.

When a dealer sells a normal knock-out option with an out-of-the-money barrier to a hedger, they often try to solicit a take profit order in the spot market at the barrier from the client. This can be in the client's interest, because, should the option get far enough out-of-the-money to reach the barrier, then they can usually set a forward hedge at better terms than initially available, even counting the cost of the premium. Some dealers have been known to offer an incentive if the client agrees to make this order irrevocable for the life of the option, usually by lowering the cost of the option by a pip. It is worthwhile for the dealer to do this, as the easy-to-manage take profit order for the size of the option will more than offset the risky stop loss order for the size of the delta. It is also in the client's interest to do this, if he is a hedger, as he will be protected against the possibility of a violent move occurring that would hit the barrier when they are not watching the market, thereby removing their hedge and then rebounding to levels where a hedge is required. As their order would have been filled at the barrier, they could instead use it as the basis to set a favourable forward hedge for their commercial exposure. Such a procedure for the use of knock-out options for hedging can be demonstrated to be less risky than using European options. Given competitive prices, the expected return from each strategy is equal, but at the point the barrier is reached, the hedger using a European option should sell it and replace it with a forward hedge, as he now has substantial gain on his commercial position that is only minimally hedged by the option which is now well out-of-the-money. The amount he will receive by selling the European option depends on the time it takes to reach that level, and what volatility is at that time. Why should the hedger spend extra for the European option at inception, when the reward for that incremental expenditure is the risky value potentially received when the option is resold?

For in-the-money barriers giving rise to stop loss orders, as the delta near the barrier rises as expiry approaches, it can be a good idea to avoid Monday expiries. A gap across the barrier could be caused by some weekend event. Although these are rare, they have happened; remember the Plaza Accord and the Russian coup. If this should happen just prior to expiry when the delta is highest, it could be very expensive. If you are not happy with the gap risk, maybe your client isn't happy with the prospect of the option knocking-out so close to expiry. Give him a call and see if he wants to square up his position.

If that doesn't work, consider dealing in other barrier options with the same (or a nearby) barrier, that will mitigate the size of the order you will have to place. Purchasing an overnight option struck at the barrier in the amount of the stop loss order can protect you, but at a probable high cost.

Concerns of gaps across the barrier aside, using a simple delta neutral hedging strategy relying only on the spot market has an advantage over the more complex hedging strategies using options if the market gets to the barrier, as the transaction costs of unwinding the hedge will be lower.

4.1.5 Barrier Options Combinations

(i) Ladder Options and Step Options

These are spot market level based discrete versions of lookback and lookforward options that can be created as combinations of barrier options. The holder of an option that goes into-the-money prior to expiry has a decision to make: should he sell it to lock in a profit enhanced by the remaining time value or continue to hold it anticipating further gains, but risking both the original premium and the profit? Another choice is to sell the option and buy another one at-the-money, but this involves paying for significant time value. There is an alternative using barrier options, which, for a slightly higher initial premium, allows a profit to be locked in and additional profit potential as well. These are called ladder options or either step-up calls or step-down puts depending upon their type.

Example (2)   Assume spot USD/JPY is at 100. You could buy a one-rung 100 USD step-up call that would lock-in a value of 5 JPY per USD if the spot market reached 105. It can be synthesized as follows:

1.   Purchase a 100 USD call/JPY put European-style

2.   Sell a 100 USD put/JPY call knock-in at 105

3.   Purchase a 105 USD put/JPY call knock-in at 105

All of these trades would be for equal USD amounts and the same expiry. If spot doesn't get to 105 during the life of option, 2 and 3 don't knock-in so only 1, the 100 USD call, matters, in this case having a maximum value of 4.99 JPY, as expected. If spot reaches 105, then the other two options knock-in. 1 and 2 form a synthetic forward purchase at 100. This risky position is protected by 3, the 105 put. If spot at expiry is below 105, then it will be exercised yielding the 5 JPY locked-in profit vs. the synthetic forward purchase. If spot at expiry is above 105, then the holder will let the 105 USD put lapse, and a larger profit can be realized by selling the USD in the spot market.

   The USD put with the strike at the barrier, 3, is obviously more expensive than an option five big figures out-of-the-money with the same barrier and expiry. Thus, this strategy is more expensive than just the purchase of the European option. However, as it provides a second chance it can be much more valuable. It is usually cheaper than selling the European option and then buying an at-the-money option to remain in a position to profit from further favourable movement. It is much cheaper than the purchase of a lookforward option, which will be described later.

   The key to realizing the value lies in selecting the level where the profit locks in. Such considerations are beyond the scope of this chapter, but a technician who thought a particular support or resistance level would be tested might favour the purchase of a ladder option with the level set just inside the chart point. If the chart point holds, then he has locked in some return. If it is broken, then he probably expects that there will be a rapid and significant move. The ladder option would allow him to exploit this opportunity.

   It is possible to add additional rungs or steps. Suppose that it was also desired that a total profit of 10 JPY per USD were to be locked in at 110. The synthesis would be:

4.   Sell a 105 USD put/JPY call knock-in at 110

5.   Purchase a 110 USD put/JPY call knock-in at 110

If 110 is never reached, neither 4 nor 5 has knocked-in. If 110 does trade, then 4 offsets 3, and 5 allows the desired 10 JPY per USD to be locked in. As many rungs can be added as is desired. If there are an infinite number of rungs, each one pip apart, then this is equivalent to a lookforward option, which puts an upper bound on the price of a ladder option. By adjusting the strikes of the knock-in options, different variations can be created, such as an option that locks in half of the intrinsic value.

Implicit in the choice of purchasing an at-the-money option is the realization, in the buyer's market view, that spot has a chance of moving out-of-the-money, otherwise they would have chosen to deal in the spot market, and save the premium. Step-down calls and step-up puts are products designed to provide additional profit potential should such an adverse market move occur. If the market moves far enough against the option, the strike can improve. To synthesize the purchase of a step-down call or a step-up put, buy a knock-out option with a barrier at the level to which the strike is to improve, and a knock-in option with both strike and barrier at that level. If the common barrier is not reached within the life of the option, the knock-out option will be exercisable and the knock-in option will not, so the synthesized product will have the original, unimproved strike. If the barrier is reached, the knock-out option lapses, and the knock-in option with the better strike will be activated.

Step-down calls and step-up puts can have more than one step. As an example, the synthesis of a step-down USD call vs. JPY put with a strike of 100, with steps at 95 and 90, is accomplished as shown in the following example:

Example (3)   Assume spot is above 95 at inception.

1.   Purchase a 100 USD call/JPY put: knock-out @ 95
2.   Purchase a 95 USD call/JPY put: knock-out @ 90
3.   Sell a 95 USD call/JPY put: knock-out @ 95
4.   Purchase a 90 USD call/JPY put: knock-in @ 90

If spot stays above 95, then options 2 and 3 offset each other at expiry, and option 4 is never activated, leaving only option 1, the 100 call, as desired. If 95 trades, but not 90, options 1 and 3 will lapse, and option 4 still hasn't activated, leaving option 3, the 95 call, as required. If spot trades all the way down to 90, then options 1, 2, and 3 have all lapsed, and option 4, the 90 call, has finally been activated, thereby achieving the second step.

This can be extended to as many steps as desired, always by splitting the knock-in option into a long European option and a short knock-out option, and then replacing that European option with a knock-out option whose barrier is at the next step, and a knock-in option with strike and barrier at that step. Each additional step will add to the price of the package, but, if the steps are one pip apart and there are a sufficient number of them, a step-down call is identical to a lookback call, or a step-up put approaches a lookback put. Thus the premium of a lookback option is an upper limit to the price of these products.

As the components of any kind of step options have different strike prices, it is important to make clear which currency amount should remain fixed for all the options. For ladder options, where the pay-off can be a locked-in amount of one currency, the buyer would usually prefer this to be in his home currency if it is one of the pair. Thus a JPY based investor would usually prefer to do equal USD amounts, leaving the pay-off in JPY. A USD based investor would usually prefer to equal JPY amounts, to achieve a USD pay-off. For this reason, for step options, there is a difference between a USD call vs. JPY, which would have equal USD amounts, and a JPY put vs. USD, which would have equal JPY amounts, with strike and step(s) identical. Locking in a JPY pay-off on a

USD bullish/JPY bearish strategy is less expensive than locking in a USD pay-off, as the JPY is less valuable in the region where this pay-off occurs. Therefore a step-up USD call is less expensive than a step-down JPY put.

The equivalence that exists for European, American and barrier options, that a put on one currency is the same as a call on the other, breaks down for all kinds of step and ladder options. It is usually easiest to look at the prices of the component options to see which is more expensive. What is important is to recognize that there is a difference, and not let the point get confused between trader, salesperson and client.

(ii) Barrier–European Combinations

There are many popular strategies involving European options that can be adapted to use barrier options in one or both legs. Four will be discussed here: risk reversals, synthetic forwards, spreads, and strangles.

Risk reversals are the purchase of an out-of-the-money option of one type (put or call), and the sale of an out-of-the-money option of the other type, with the same currency pair, maturity and amount. The most popular version is as a zero premium strategy, where the premium of the option sold offsets the premium of the option purchased. When sold to a hedger with an underlying exposure, this is called variously a cylinder, collar, or Range Forward™, and it creates a risk reward profile like a spread. As it offers some profit potential, limited risk and no out-of-pocket cost, it is probably the most frequently used option hedge. Either the put or the call or both can be replaced with a barrier option. As there are four types of barrier calls, and four types of puts, the inclusion of barrier options means that there are now 25 kinds of risk reversals. We won't examine all of them, only the two most popular.

The strike of the purchased option in a zero premium cylinder determines the risk, and its premium determines the upside potential. Using a normal knock-out option in place of the purchased option allows either more protection or more upside potential, or a combination thereof. If the details of the sold option are left unchanged, that premium can finance a nearer strike on the purchased option, thereby providing a more favourable level of cover if the market moves directly against the underlying position. If the strike of the barrier option is left the same as that of the European option it replaces, then its lower premium permits the option sold to finance it to have a more remote strike, increasing the amount by which a favourable spot movement could benefit the underlying position. The variable we have not yet considered is where to set the knock-out level. In a European cylinder, the hedger may select the strike of the option sold at a level at the limit of what they optimistically expect, if the market is favourable. In this way, the option they are selling is one that they consider will be worthless at expiry. If they wish to extend that view to the choice of barrier, they would set the barrier at the strike of the sold option (or just beyond). There is a risk that spot will reach the barrier, causing the protection to disappear, and then move in the other direction, causing greater losses than if it had moved unfavourably from inception. Hedgers who follow technical advice will therefore set the barrier beyond an important level which, if broken, is forecasted to signal the start of a trend. No matter what the hedger's philosophy, once the barrier is reached, it is obligatory to re-examine the hedge, as its characteristics have irrevocably changed.

The other popular variation on a cylinder is replacing the sold option with a reverse knock-in option. Reverse knock-in options have lower premiums than European options, but only slightly if the barrier is not remote. If the strike of the purchased option is not

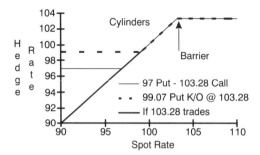

Figure 4.6

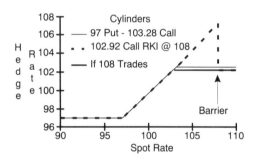

Figure 4.7

adjusted, then the strike of the reverse knock-in option must be closer. This doesn't matter until spot reaches the barrier, which will be further away than the European option's strike would have been. Thus, if the hedger is only modestly constructive, which is usually the case for those using cylinders, they gain more profit potential, provided spot doesn't reach the barrier, which is not a high probability in their market view. This strategy has an advantage over the use of a knock-out option to replace the purchased option in that there is never a situation where the hedger is exposed to unlimited risk.

Hedgers using European options rarely use synthetic forwards, as the standard ones are easier. However, barrier options introduce possibilities not available in the O/R (outright) forward FX market. It is possible to create a knock-out synthetic forward at a level better than the forward. The usual scenario is a hedger has "missed" the market, leaving a position unhedged in the expectation of a favourable move, but the market has not co-operated. They now seek to get a better result than the current O/R forward, and are willing to accept some risk to achieve it. The risk is that the market moves further in the same direction, reaching the barrier and knocking out the synthetic forward, thereby leaving the hedger unhedged at a less favourable spot level than when he initiated the hedge.

A synthetic forward purchase is the purchase of a call financed by the sale of a put with the same strike, maturity and amount. A knock-out synthetic forward purchase at a strike better than the forward is achieved by the sale of a knock-out call struck out-of-the-money and the purchase of a reverse knock-out put at the same strike. A process of iteration is required to find the joint level of the barriers for a given strike level. Reverse knock-out options are quite cheap if the barrier isn't too remote, so this can allow for the barrier to be a seemingly safe distance from spot. During the life of the option, if spot never gets to the barrier, then one of the options in the synthetic forward will be exercised, allowing the hedger to unwind his position at a better level than originally available.

Spreads are the purchase of one option and the sale of another of the same type and amount (differing amounts are called ratio spreads). If they have different strikes, but the same expiry, they are called vertical spreads. If they have the same strike, but different expiries, they are called calendar spreads. If both strike and expiry are different, it is a diagonal spread. Buying a vertical spread (the option sold being the one that is less valuable) is a popular way of having the advantages of a long option position but at a lower cost, achieved by accepting a cap on the potential pay-off. The cost can be further reduced by making both options knock-out options. The barriers could be set at the same level, usually at or beyond the purchased option's strike. As it is not too expensive to adjust slightly one of the barriers, it can be tempting for a technically based trader to set the barrier of the sold option just inside some important technical level, and the purchased option's barrier just beyond. If the barrier should hold, then the buyer could benefit from the unlimited profit potential of his long option, uncapped as the sold option had lapsed, all for a price less than a European spread.

Traders expecting a period of range trading consider selling strangles (sale of a put and a call of the same amount and maturity), with the strikes set at the edges of the range. Normally the options sold are out-of-the-money, with the put struck at the bottom of the range and the call struck at the top. However, except for credit and finance considerations, it would make no difference if both options were in-the-money, the premium received would be higher but the pay-off at maturity would be higher as well. Using the in-the-money version, reverse knock-in options can be substituted for both European options. "I expect it will be within the range at expiry" is the view required to expect maximum profit in a European strangle. If the seller's view of the range validity is stronger, i.e. "I expect it will stay within the range until expiry", then he might be willing to set the barriers of each option at the strike of the other. If the barriers are near, then the initial premium is almost as large as the in-the-money European strangle, but if spot trades at neither barrier then there is no pay-off to the buyer, in contrast to the European version where the minimum pay-off is the difference between the strikes. Thus the profit potential to the seller is substantially larger. Larger profit potential occurs only at the acceptance of greater risk. Outside of the range the pay-off to the buyer is the same as the European version, but the initial premium is lower. Even if it is inside the range at expiry, should both barriers be reached during the life of the strangle, then the pay-off will be as large as the European version.

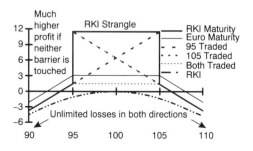

Figure 4.8

4.1.6 Rebates

A rebate is a payment that is received by the buyer of a barrier option if they are not in a position to be able to exercise it. For knock-out options with rebates, if the market trades at the barrier, the buyer will receive a payment, either immediately or when the option would have expired. Rebates on knock-in options are payable if the option never knocks in, which can only be determined with certainty at maturity, therefore the rebate is potentially payable only at that time. Rebates were a part of the early history of knock-out options, speculators buying shares on margin who sold down & out calls against their position, so if they were forced by a margin call to sell the shares they wouldn't be exposed any longer to a rebound in the share price. In order to get the buyer to accept the knock-out feature, it was necessary to offer them a rebate.

Rebates have now acquired a life of their own. As one could buy a barrier option with a rebate, and sell the same barrier option without a rebate, it is possible to create a "naked" rebate. These are usually called one-touch binary options (or one-touch digital options), as they have a pay-off like a binary option, but don't need to finish in-the-money, but merely need to touch the barrier. They are also known as American binary options, as they will exercise it whenever it gets in-the-money. Some market practitioners use the term digital instead of binary. As there is a higher probability of being in-the-money at some time during the life of an option than being in-the-money at maturity, one touch binary options are clearly more expensive than the binary options discussed in the previous chapter.

A rebate payable at maturity can be synthesized by a knock-in "box" spread, all having the same barrier. A box spread is a put spread and a call spread, each using the same pair of strikes. With European options it creates the equivalent of a money market deposit; wherever the market ends up, the return is always the same. By making all of them knock-in or reverse knock-in options all triggered by the same barrier, that fixed payment at maturity is triggered if the barrier is reached. An analytical formula for rebates is provided in Mark Rubenstein and Eric Reiner's *Risk Magazine* article, "Breaking down the barriers", September 1991.

(i) Money-Back Options

A money-back option is a knock-out option with a rebate equal to the initial premium. These are usually normal knock-out options, in which case they cost more than European options. The biggest difficulty in selling options is the premium, and much of the success of the more popular exotic options, such as average rate options and barrier options, can be credited to potential to achieve the same return (under certain circumstances), at a lower premium. The high cost of money-back options has made them relatively rare. To determine the premium to charge for money-back options, divide the premium of the knock-out option without the rebate by (one minus the rebate premium as a portion of the rebate).

Money-back options made with reverse knock-outs are cheaper than European options (provided the intrinsic value at the barrier is larger than premium/rebate). These are not very common yet, but seem to have good potential, as the main disadvantage of buying reverse knock-outs (getting nothing if the market goes too far in-the-money) is mitigated by the return of the premium.

(ii) Exploding Options

Exploding options are reverse knock-out options with a rebate equal to the intrinsic value at the barrier. They can be likened to European options vertical spreads, buying one option and selling another option with the same maturity and for the same amount, but at a strike that is (further) out-of-the-money. Vertical spreads are a popular strategy, but the disadvantage is that if the market gets to the strike of the sold option prior to maturity, the maximum profit is not yet realizable, due to the time value of that option. If the position isn't squared up, in hopes that further favourable movement or simply no movement will permit making the full profit on the spread, a reversal could wipe out the initial gain. An exploding option locks in (if the rebate is paid at maturity), or pays immediately, the maximum profit should the barrier be reached. Obviously, this is a higher probability than being above that level at maturity, so exploding options are more expensive than the equivalent spread. They have found a usefulness in warrant issues, which need to offer a liquidity substitute. Traditionally warrants were American style, allowing the holder to have a choice other than reselling them should they want to realize a profit prior to expiry. This raises the costs of the agent, making their fees higher, etc. If a warrant has an exploding feature, the buyer knows if the market has a good move in his favour, his profit will be locked in or paid immediately, so he need not worry about exercising early.

(iii) One-Touch Contingent Premium Options

A variation on the contingent options discussed in the previous chapter are one-touch contingent premium options. These are the purchase of a European option financed by the sale of a one-touch binary option. As a one-touch binary is more expensive than a plain binary option, the contingent premium, if triggered, is lower. Obviously, there is no reason why the European option strike must also be the barrier that triggers the rebate. There is a whole range of choices, but an interesting one to consider is where the contingent premium is the same as an "at maturity" contingent premium option. The buyer then can take a view as to whether the risk is higher of ending up in-the-money or having touched the necessarily more remote barrier.

4.1.7 Discontinuous Barriers

Most markets close for the weekend, and some event could make the first price on Monday not very close to the last price on Friday, so every barrier option could be considered to have a discontinuous barrier. Sometimes this is made explicit in the terms, usually due to liquidity considerations or to assure verifiability that the barrier was reached. A "fixing" barrier option can only knock in or out if the market level, taken from a specified source at a particular time each day, is at or through the barrier. Market movements in between these times do not trigger the barrier event.

A "fixing" knock-in option is less likely to become a European option than an otherwise identical continuous knock-in, therefore the "fixing" knock-in will have a lower premium. These can be modelled by an approximation where the analytic model is used with a more remote barrier, using a binomial lattice with a number of iterations that is a multiple of the number of days by a Monte Carlo simulation.

Other variations have included options where the barrier only applied during a portion of the life of the option, such as only during the first half, and a barrier that changes as a predetermined function of time. If the barrier is an exponential function of time, there is an analytic solution extant.

4.1.8 Double Barrier Options

A double barrier option has two barriers, one above and one below the current spot market. Reaching either barrier triggers the appropriate action: activation for double barrier knock-ins or disactivation for double barrier knock-outs. If the option is initially out-of-the-money, one of the barriers must be in-the-money, otherwise it is a trivial product, equivalent to a European option for a knock-in, or worthless for a knock-out. If the option is in-the-money at inception, the barrier in the same direction as the strike price could be either in- or out-of-the-money.

The usual equivalence, a knock-out option plus a knock-in option equals a European option, applies to double barriers, so the price of the double barrier knock-out can be found by subtraction. The price of a double barrier knock-in option must be higher than either of the single knock-in options having the same strike and maturity, with its barrier the same as one of the two barriers of the double barrier option, as it is more likely to knock in. The price of a double barrier knock-in option must be lower than the sum of those two single barrier options, as a widely swinging spot market could trigger both, producing a higher pay-off than the double barrier option.

If the barriers are not remote, double barrier knock-in options are even closer to European option prices than reverse knock-in options, and double barrier knock-out options have very low premiums. Thus the more popular strategies involve buying double barrier knock-outs or selling double barrier knock-ins. Buying in-the-money double barrier knock-outs when both barriers are in-the-money can result in a very high potential pay-off compared to the premium spent, although the likelihood of getting any pay-out is quite low. From the dealer's perspective, managing these options is similar to managing a reverse knock-out, except that the chance of hitting the barrier is increased. Accordingly, wider spreads around the theoretical price are observed, especially since fewer participants are active in this product.

4.1.9 Second Market Barriers

Second market barriers, or "outside" barrier options, have a barrier that is triggered by a movement in another market more than the one in which the optional transaction may take place. In common with the currency protected options described in the previous chapter, the premiums of these options are additionally dependent on the parameters of the barrier market and the correlation between the barrier market and the underlying market. These are described in the *Risk Magazine* article (September 1991) by Mark Rubenstein and Eric Reiner, which also includes an analytic model. These would more normally appeal to investors managing multicurrency portfolios, than to commercial transaction hedgers.

4.2 COMPOUND OPTIONS

4.2.1 Definition and Examples

A compound option is an option on an option. As there are two types of options, calls and puts, there are four types of compound options: calls on calls, calls on puts, puts on calls and puts on puts. The underlying option has an amount, strike price and expiry. The compound option also has a strike price and expiry. The compound option's strike price is the premium paid to buy the underlying option. The compound expiry is the date and

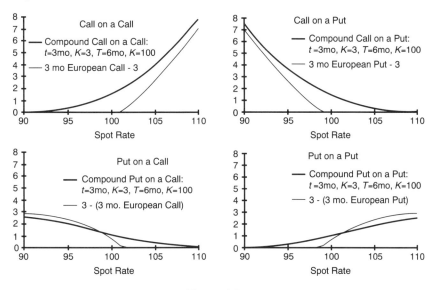

Figure 4.9

time by which buyers must decide whether or not to exercise the compound option. It must be no later than the underlying expiry. Most compound options are European-style options on European-style options. Calls on options are much more common than puts on options. In that case, even if it was an American-style option on a European-style underlying option, there would be no incentive to exercise early. Why pay the same amount earlier for something that cannot be used until much later?

4.2.2 Geske's Model

After people began comparing the results of the Black–Scholes formula with observed equity options prices, they noted that the implied volatilities of at-the-money options when applied to out-of-the-money options always understated the market prices. A variety of explanations have been put forward, including Jump–Diffusion Processes and Stochastic Volatility. Also, equity in most firms should behave like an option, as the shareholders have limited liability. If the value of a firm's assets is subject to a random process that happens frequently enough, then the value of those assets at some future time will be log-normally distributed. Most firms have debt, which we will assume can be repaid at face value at any time. Thus the shareholders collectively have a "call" on the assets of the firm where the "strike price" is the cost of redeeming the debt. Professor Robert Geske of the Anderson Graduate School of Management at UCLA published a model "The valuation of compound options" (1979) for equity options on the basis of the hypothesis that the equity behaved like an option. This model has made it much easier for participants in a whole range of markets to do compound options, giving him well-deserved recognition. However, as an actual tool for pricing equity options, it is not generally used. A company can have a great deal of influence on the riskiness of its assets, and subject to lending covenants a range of flexibility in its gearing as well. Thus the shareholders could try to maximize the value of their "option" by increasing the volatility or changing the "strike price". This would make it difficult to estimate volatility. However, this behaviour is rare because the shareholding of companies on which equity options are listed is generally widely split, and the management has a relatively small percentage ownership. Management's interest in keeping lucrative jobs frequently overrides their oft-stated objective of maximizing shareholder value, unless their bonus scheme was particularly adapted to co-ordinating their incentives. For increasing the value of the option by increasing the volatility also increases the chance that the "option" will end up out-of-the-money. In this case, out-of-the-money means in the hands of the creditors, which could mean that most of the senior management are out of a job. The exception to this management self-interest dressed up as "prudent management" was the LBO era, where the takeover specialists tried to maximize the value of the option inherently written by purchasers of corporate debt and bank lenders. As these option writers (bondholders) had been used to dealing with previously security oriented managements, they had probably priced the option using too low a volatility (too low a credit spread, or too flexible covenants).

Geske's model used all the same assumptions as the Black–Scholes model: constant volatility, constant interest rates, no dividend on the asset, no transaction costs, etc. Various later work has shown how to relax some of these assumptions in the case of a European option. The volatility need not be constant so long as the average is known. Changing interest rates impact the discounting and the forward price of the asset. The discounting problem can be overcome by using the continuously compounded rate equivalent to the yield of a zero coupon bond maturing at the expiry of the option. The changing rate's impact on the forward price can be corrected for by using the volatility of the forward asset price. (This is made easier if there is a listed futures contract.) A yield on the asset is handled by a change in the drift term. John C. Hull's book, *Options, Futures, and Other Derivative Securities* (1993), shows a compound option model incorporating a yield on the asset.

The particular questions that need to be answered when using a model are: how can the market rates be reflected as inputs to the model? With regard to compound options, given a term structure of rates, of asset yields and of volatility, exactly how can all this be reflected in the model? Certain fairly logical adjustments can be made to the compound option model to allow the three term structures their proper impact upon the final price. This has been implemented in several proprietary exotic option systems and at least one that is commercially available. The rate, yield and volatility in terms associated with the time to expiry of the compound option (T_1) should be the market parameters of that shorter maturity. The rate, yield and volatility in terms associated with the time to expiry of the underlying option (T_2) should be the market parameters of that longer maturity.

The rate, yield and volatility in terms associated with the time between the expiries of the compound option and the underlying option should be the forward–forward market parameters implied between those dates. It is easy to calculate forward–forward rates for continuously compounded rates:

$$_1r_2 = (r_2T_2 - r_1T_1)/(T_2 - T_1) \tag{5}$$

Forward–forward volatilities are less commonly discussed, but they are needed to determine S^*, the level where the market would have to be to make one indifferent between exercising or letting the compound option expire. Volatility is just an annualized standard deviation. Standard deviation squared is variance, and variances are additive. Therefore, the forward–forward volatility is:

$$_1\sigma_2 = \sqrt{(\sigma_2^2 T_2 - \sigma_1^2 T_1)/(T_2 - T_1)} \tag{6}$$

For example, if one-month implied volatility were 10 per cent and two-month implied volatility were 11 per cent, then the forward–forward volatility for one month against two months would be about 11.92 per cent. S^* clearly needs to be found by an iterative process, such as the Newton–Raphson method, which converges quickly thanks partly to the well-behaved nature of the option price as a function of the asset price.

The correlation term in the bivariate normal distribution was modelled as the square root of T_1/T_2, referring to the correlation between the possible asset prices at time of the compound option expiry and the possible final asset prices at the expiry of the underlying option, which is correct if volatility is constant. If there was a period of high expected volatility followed by a period of low volatility, then there would be a higher correlation between the asset prices at those times. Consider purchasing a compound option on a Tuesday, with compound expiry on Friday ($T_1 = 3$ days) and underlying expiry on Monday ($T_2 = 6$ days). If there is no G-7 meeting or other potentially market moving event scheduled for that weekend, then the correlation between Friday's and Monday's possible asset prices should be more like 87 per cent ($\sqrt{0.75}$) than 71 per cent ($\sqrt{0.5}$).

Alternatively, if one contemplated purchasing a compound option on Friday, with compound expiry Monday ($T_1 = 3$ days) and underlying expiry on Thursday ($T_2 = 6$ days), then the correlation could be just 50 per cent ($\sqrt{0.25}$). Other effects besides weekends and holidays can impact, such as the timing of economic releases. Fortunately, these are all reflected in the term structure of volatility. Therefore, the correlation term should be written as $\sigma_1/\sigma_2\sqrt{T_1/T_2}$. If $\sigma_1 = \sigma_2$ then the correlation term collapses back to the way it appears in Geske's paper.

Taking into account the above means of incorporating the information contained in the term structures, the model becomes, when generalized for all four types of compound options:

$$
\Phi\Psi Se^{-r_{f2}T_2}N_2[\Phi\Psi a, \Psi d_1; \Phi\sigma_1/\sigma_2\sqrt{T_1/T_2}]
$$
$$
- \Phi\Psi Ke^{-r_2T_2}N_2[\Phi\Psi(a - \sigma_1\sqrt{T_1})\Psi(d_1 - \sigma_1\sqrt{T_2})\Phi\sigma_1/\sigma_2\sqrt{T_1/T_2}]
$$
$$
- \Phi ke^{-r_1T_1}N[\Phi\Psi(a - \sigma_1\sqrt{T_1})]
\tag{7}
$$

where $\Phi = \{1$ if compound call; -1 if compound put$\}$, $\Psi = \{1$ if underlying call; -1 if underlying put$\}$, S = asset price, K = underlying strike price, k = compound strike price, S^* = asset price on T_1 that makes the underlying option exactly worth k, $N[x]$ = probability of cumulative normal less than x, $N_2[x, y, \rho]$ = probability of bivariate cumulative normal less than x and y for correlation ρ

$$
a = \frac{\ln(S/S^*) + (r_1 - r_{f1} + \sigma_1^2/2)T_1}{\sigma_1\sqrt{T_1}}
$$

$$
d_1 = \frac{\ln(S/K) + (r_2 - r_{f2} + \sigma_2^2/2)T_2}{\sigma_2\sqrt{T_2}}
$$

For a means of calculating N_2, see Divgi (1979).

The formula can be interpreted in an intuitive fashion, provided the view is taken from a "risk neutral" world. Take, for example, the case of a compound call on a call. The first term is the value of receiving the asset S at maturity, provided that the compound option was worth exercising ($S_1 > S^*$) and the option ended up in-the-money ($S_2 > K$).

The second term is the cost of paying the premium K at maturity provided again that the compound option was worth exercising and the option ended up in-the-money. The third term is the cost of paying the compound premium k provided that the compound option was just worth exercising. This works because the only random process applies to S. To the extent that one could master the difficulties of calculating cumulative probabilities of a trivariate normal, it could be possible to extend this process to create a model for an option on a compound option, the next step on the road to instalment options, which we will consider later.

When considering options on shares, commodities or bonds, it is clear which is the asset and which is the unit of account. However, for currency options, both are assets and both are units of account. For vanilla options (European- and American-style exercise), there is no practical difference between a DEM call for which one delivers USD to exercise the option and a USD put for which one receives DEM. The Garman–Kollhagen model (European) or Cox–Ross model (American) calculates the premium in USD for a DEM call or in DEM for a USD put. But the premium is paid up front, so, if desired, it can be converted to the other currency at the spot rate. But for compound options, care must be taken, not with the initial premium, but with the compound strike (k). A simple conversion at the outright forward rate for that maturity does not suffice. Take an example of a call on a GBP call (USD put) having a compound strike of 4.5 US cents per GBP. If the forward rate was 1.50, then a certain future cash flow of 4.5 cents could be converted into 3p. However, it is not certain that the compound option will be exercised. If the pound is strong, the holder of the compound option will exercise and pay the 4.5 cents, at a time when that would be worth less than 3p. If the pound weakened, the option would not be exercised. If the compound option seller had sold forward the USD to protect against the phenomena described above, there would be a cost to unwind that hedge. In this example, the USD compound strike is inherently lower than its forward equivalent in GBP. Therefore, the premium for a compound call on a GBP call with a USD compound strike must be higher than a call on the same underlying option with a GBP compound strike of equivalent size.

This difference is straightforward to model. Simply remember the origins of the model. If the compound strike is not in the profit currency (USD for cable or DEM for USD/DEM) but instead is in the "asset", it is necessary to invert the inputs to the model, using one over the spot rate, switching r and r_f. The inverse of volatility is itself. This difference means that there are actually eight kinds of compound options.

4.2.3 Risk Management

Specific Option Hedges

It is tempting for those used to hedging European options to create an analogy to the delta hedging process with which they are already familiar, whereby the underlying option fulfils a role analogous to the spot hedge. Because of the non-linearity of the underlying option price, this is not usually sufficient in the region where there is still some uncertainty whether the compound option will be exercised or not. Clearly, if the underlying option is nearly worthless, then no option hedge is required for a compound call. If the underlying option is much more valuable than the compound strike, then a 100 per cent option hedge will do nicely. In between, however, this doesn't work as well. Any hedge in the underlying option that matches the vega will require a spot hedge to match the net delta.

Given that one option is not a complete hedge, let us consider also whether there are any others that might prove useful in constructing a good hedge, one where the derivatives have a good initial match, and won't rapidly diverge. The compound expiry is normally between the inception date and the expiry date. If it were the same as the day the compound option was purchased, then it would be identical to the underlying option, but with the premium divided into two arbitrary parts. The buyer wouldn't have bought the compound option unless he planned to exercise it. A 100 per cent hedge in the underlying option is a viable but overcautious strategy for the seller of a compound call.

The other extreme case would be a compound option whose expiry was the same as the underlying expiry. Again, the compound becomes identical to a European option. The pay-off for such a compound call on a call would be $(S - K - k)$ which is clearly equivalent to a European call with strike $K + k$. A call on a put where $T_1 = T_2$ is the same as a European put with strike $K - k$. Since paying later is better than paying earlier, and more choice is better than less choice, compound calls become more valuable as T_1 increases for a given T_2. Thus a European option with a strike shifted by k but otherwise identical to the underlying option is a strategy that dominates the pay-off of the compound option. This is less expensive than a 100 per cent hedge in the underlying. In a very illiquid market, it provides a ceiling price above which one should not pay for a compound option.

Another European option to consider is one with an expiry the same as the compound expiry, and with a strike price equal to S^*. An amount of this option equal to the delta of the underlying option when $S = S^*$ and expiry equal to $T_2 - T_1$ provides a very good gamma and theta hedge around the critical point where the compound option is near its strike at expiry. At spot levels further in-the-money, the value of the compound option exceeds the value of this hedge, as the delta of the compound option increases towards 100 per cent of the full amount, whilst the S^* delta weighted hedge is already limited to a 100 per cent delta on a smaller amount. It is easy to see that this strategy provides a floor price to a compound call. The addition of small additional option positions at various strikes so as to track the increasing delta as the underlying option goes further in-the-money can provide an even closer hedge over a wider range of spot prices at compound expiry.

Such a strategy will be destabilized by changes in interest rates or volatility. Any such change will change S^*, creating strike risk. If the volatility shifted enough, S^* might shift by one or two big figures. If spot trends away from S^* then this won't matter, but if it ends up near, this could prove expensive, depending on the way spot moves on the last day.

4.2.4 Extensions

(i) Instalment Options

Instalment options have a schedule of payments which must all be made to have the right to exercise the option at expiry. The buyer can elect to abandon the instalment option prior to any scheduled payment, by giving notice to the seller, and have no future obligation. The economic incentive to abandon the option is created when a "new" instalment option with the same underlying option can be arranged with lower payments than the one about to be abandoned. If the buyer's hedging requirements or market view had changed, then he would prefer to sell the option rather than to abandon it. If he was still interested in the option, yet it was uneconomic not to let it lapse, it is probable that the seller would be quite interested in offering a cheaper instalment schedule, as he would already have the hedge in place.

Like hire purchase, the instalment payments are usually evenly spaced and of equal size. This requires that the pricing model be used in an iterative fashion, starting out with an estimate of the instalment size, setting all instalments except the first one to that amount, and solving for the first payment. If this payment is higher than the other instalments, a higher instalment must be tried, and the process repeated until a figure within an accepted tolerance is achieved. Then any derivatives required for hedging would be calculated. To price an instalment option where the schedule is already specified is easier; there will be some initial payment, which would be lower or higher than the rest of the instalments depending on how the market had changed since the first trade.

When it comes to modelling an instalment option, the most frequent choice is a binomial lattice, though for a low number of instalments an analytic model, requiring numeric integration methods to calculate the multivariate normal probabilities, could be used. The number of iterations would have to be chosen so as to allow an accurate representation of the spacing of the instalments, with sufficient steps between each instalment to have a good approximation of a log-normal distribution. This can raise the total number of iterations quite high, making the model run more slowly than most of the other options in the book. However, as instalment options are a relatively low volume product, this shouldn't seriously affect overall system performance. The nodes between instalments are identical to the intermediate nodes found in a binomial model for a European option. The value of such a node is the discounted probability weighted average of the value of the nodes reached if the market rises or falls. The value of a node where an instalment is due is:

$$\text{Node}_{i,j} = \text{Max}(0, e^{-rT/N}(\text{Prob(up)}\ \text{Node}_{i+1,j} + (1 - \text{Prob(up)})\ \text{Node}_{i+1,j+1} - \text{Instalment}))$$

If the lattice is carried all the way out to expiry, the values of the terminal nodes are $\text{Max}(0, \Psi(S - K))$. It is possible to save some iterations if the terminal nodes are set at the last instalment and an analytic model is used to calculate the value of the underlying European option finally purchasable at those nodes, which have a value of $\text{Max}(0, \text{European Premium} - \text{Instalment})$. Or Geske's compound option model could be used at the penultimate instalment, possibly further speeding up the computation. It is possible to build binomial trees that reflect the term structure of rates, which is worth doing if there is a steep (or steeply inverted) yield curve.

Instalment options can be combined with bonds to create interesting structures. The instalment dates can be set to match the coupon payments and dates. This could be used to create a currency linked bond that, if the investor were no longer interested in the potential appreciation from the option component (probably because the market had moved in the opposite direction from that required to get any capital gain), then he could elect to begin receiving coupons, and forgo the possibility of a redemption value higher than par.

There is a close relative of instalment options, called pay-as-you-go options. There is a schedule of instalments, but instead of a single underlying option, there is a series of options. Usually the expiry date of each option (except the last one) is also an instalment date. If the buyer decides not to pay an instalment, he forgoes the rest of the options remaining in the series. These first appeared as pay-as-you-go caps, a series of interest rate options having the same strike, providing cover against higher rates. The idea has been applied to foreign exchange to cover the needs of exporters or importers having regular currency flows to manage.

(ii) Chooser Options

A straddle is the purchase of a call and a put, both having the same strike and expiry. At maturity only one will be in-the-money, so the holder will choose to exercise that one. Because they are always worth something at maturity, straddles have high initial premiums. Much of the development of exotic options can be traced to the quest to lower premiums, without lowering the option's utility to some buyers. Chooser options are like straddles, in that the buyer has a choice of having a put or a call, but he must make the choice on a specified date prior to expiry of the underlying. The buyer's self-interest will lead him to choose whichever option is more valuable. If, because of his directional view on the market, he prefers to own the other option, he can sell the expensive one and buy the cheaper one (or if his credit lines permit, do a forward trade to create a synthetic option of the type he wants). Clearly, there is some possibility that the option he chooses will end up out-of-the-money, which means the potential maturity value can be less than a straddle. As it can never be worth more, the chooser must therefore be less expensive than the straddle. Another way to see this is to consider the values on the "choose date" (the date the buyer must choose between the put and the call). On that date the straddle must be more valuable than the more expensive of its two parts. Chooser options are also called "as-you-like-it" options.

Chooser options are most frequently employed when some upcoming event (election, central bank meeting, economic statistic) is expected to have a trendsetting effect on the market, but in an unknown direction. The choose date is selected for immediately after the event, when the outcome will be known. The expiry is set to some later date, allowing time for the market to have moved. A look at historical charts can give an indication of how long previous trends have persisted before a significant reversal. If the event by itself would move the market greatly, then a straddle to the choose date would be a more rewarding strategy. In this age of instantaneous communications, with most markets being subject to continuous professional analysis and significant amounts of capital searching for any market anomaly to achieve a higher return, it is hard to see how such trends could persist. It would either take some less direct linkage for which the effect happens over an extended period of time, or an inertia to the market, perhaps caused by central bank intervention, which will eventually be overcome by market pressures.

From a modelling perspective it is easier to consider that a chooser is a combination strategy, consisting of two products. The holder of a chooser can consider himself long a call to the expiry date, and that he also has an option which allows him to exchange that call for a put. This exchange option is like a compound option (a call on a put), except that the compound strike is a call option rather than a cash payment. If the put has different characteristics than the call, it can be modelled using the same approach as Geske. (UBS extended this idea further by issuing "Presidential Warrants" in 1992 where the choose date was set slightly after the November presidential elections. Warrants are merely transferable certificates representing ownership of options listed on an exchange. At the choose date, the holder of the warrant could pay a premium to receive either a put or a call on a stock market index. Thus it was an option on a chooser. As the compound expiry and the choose date were the same, the model required for pricing was kept simpler than if there were two different dates. As a marketing idea, the product was very appealing. That summer, the stock market was perceived to be worried about the possibility of a Clinton victory, and the polls were showing a tight race developing. However, the outcome wasn't the one that was most favourable to using a chooser. By the time the election neared, the result was known, and the market had already discounted the effect.)

However, for the special but very common case of the put and call having the same strike and expiry, there is a much easier way of hedging, and therefore pricing, a chooser. The seller of the chooser can be considered to have delivered a call to the buyer, and remains under the obligation to exchange that call for a put on the choose date, if the buyer so chooses. If the underlying market goes up, the buyer will not want to make the exchange, and will keep the call. Therefore, the seller should have bought the call as part of his hedge.

If the market goes down, the buyer will choose to exchange the call for the put. The buyer will be buying a call and selling a put, with the same strike and expiry. This is equivalent to buying the underlying outright forward at the strike price on the delivery date! So, when the market declines by the choose date, the seller finds himself buying the outright forward. Thus the seller has implicitly sold a put expiring on the choose date, with delivery that is later than the customary two business days, two business days after the expiry instead. Such an option can be priced on correctly implemented foreign currency option pricing software, such as is found in most banks; as two business days can vary due to weekends and holidays the European option model can handle different periods between exercise and expiry. As these kinds of options do not trade interbank (although they do have a fair equivalent in the serial options on currency futures, i.e. July or August option expiries on the September futures contract), it is necessary to determine the best available hedge. Three elements define the required put option: expiry, strike and amount. We already have determined that the expiry should be the choose date. Whether the holder of the chooser will pick the put or the call will be determined by which is more valuable. The more valuable one will be the one that is in-the-money. Thus if the outright forward is above the strike on the chooser, then the call is more valuable, so the holder will keep the call, and the implicit put expiring on the choose date will not be exercised. If that forward is below the strike, then he will choose the put, thereby exercising the implicit put. The crossover point is when the forward equals the strike. What spot rate would cause that? The interest rates on each currency are known (and temporarily assumed to be stable). Thus the usual forward vs. deposit arbitrage formula can be used to calculate the strike price of the choose date put. Using continuously compounded rates:

$$K_c = K e^{((r_f - r)T - (r_{fc} - r_c)T_c)} \tag{8}$$

where the subscript c refers to that variable on the choose date.

When the holder decides to choose the put, the seller will exercise the OTC put and have to roll the spot position out to the forward date with a swap (buying and selling the put currency, selling and buying the call currency). As the market practice is to do all swaps with the near leg at the spot rate, there will be a positive cash flow at the spot date (as the option was in-the-money, else it would not have been exercised). There will also be a negative cash flow at the forward date. The positive cash flow must be invested to offset the future negative cash flow. Continuing to rely on our constant interest rate assumptions, we conclude that the amount of the choose date put must be equal to the present value of the size of the chooser option, thereby completing our hedge. Since there will be no future profits or losses, the cost of the hedge portfolio is the price of the chooser.

The same logic could have been used, starting with the underlying put and a choose date call, but the price works out the same, thanks to put-call parity. The difference between the two hedging methods is the rhos, or interest rate exposures. If the chooser is hedged with an expiry call and a choose date put, there is some probability that the put will be chosen requiring the seller to borrow the put currency and lend the call currency. Should the interest rates of the put currency rise, or the call currency decline, there would be a loss. However, if the chooser was hedged with an expiry put and choose date call, the same rate shifts would result in a profit. Therefore, the initial rhos can be reduced by using a portion of each hedging method. If the strike price were at-the-money forward, then the appropriate hedge would be a straddle to the expiry date in half the size of the chooser, and a straddle to the choose date of the present value of half the size of the chooser.

Dynamically, the hedge will require some adjustment to maintain low rhos when spot moves. If spot declines, the likelihood of the put being chosen increases, therefore a forward–forward FX position should be taken to anticipate the probable requirement to roll forward the amount of the choose date put that may be exercised. This could also be managed by trading FRAs in each currency, interest rate futures, FXAs, or by adjusting the options position. A change in rates changes the strike price and the amount of the option required at the choose date. This "should" be hedged by trading options, but for small changes, it is more practical to do a spot trade.

Provided the rate changes and spot changes happen at different times there is no problem, the position adjustments required to keep the risk limited are costless. However, if both markets move at the same time, there will be profits or losses. For example, if a rise in the interest rate of a currency made it more attractive, so the spot rate rose, the put on that currency would be less likely to be exercised, so some of the hedges locking in borrowing costs in that currency could be unwound at more favourable rates, producing a profit. In this example, a positive correlation between spot and the "leading" currency interest rates is a source of profits. Of course, the effect on changing the option's strike and amount also needs to be considered for a complete view, but if the choose date is relatively close and the forward is close to the strike, a small shift in the spot rate can cause a big shift in the rhos. An appreciation of this effect on a particular position can be gained through simulation analysis, by observing the P/L changes caused by a matrix of spot and interest rate movements. A rate increase is not always good for a currency. Frequently, if a currency is perceived to be "under attack", any currency weakness is accompanied by an increase in interest rates, as the market anticipates the possibility that the central bank will decide to raise rates to defend the currency.

Observing that correlation affects the hedge performance results in two action points. The pricing, and therefore the model, should be changed to incorporate the correlation. Also, the correlation risk should be measured and managed. There are few direct means of trading correlation, but many products that also produce correlation risk. These should be viewed as an ensemble, with an eye to finding some other product that can produce offsetting correlation risks. This particular type of correlation, spot vs. interest rate (or interest rate differentials), can also be observed in American-style FX options, diff swaps, and interest rate options that are quanted into another currency. As to improving the model, the usual response is, given that choosers are relatively low volume products, it is sufficient to widen out the price to cover the risk. Some banks are reported to have developed models that explicitly factor in a correlation, but these are proprietary, and besides correlation is notoriously unstable, making the value of the effort unclear.

A variation on chooser options, where the seller chooses on the intermediate date whether the buyer has a put or a call, has been modelled, but I haven't heard of any trades. The structure would mostly appeal to sellers, but premium would be lower than either the put or the call.

4.3 LOOKBACK OPTIONS

4.3.1 Definition and Examples

Barrier options existed before the analytical model. The compound option model was developed to model an existing feature, the effect of leverage. In the lore of finance, lookback options turned this relationship around. The model was developed first, and not for any commercial purpose. Trading in lookback options was sparked by the existence of the model. It was a model looking for a market, like an answer looking for a question. Actually, the product was frequently discussed, but not in the usual forums. Who hasn't heard a trader say, "I should have …", or "I could have …", usually followed by "I would have …". The model for a lookback option puts a price on a wish, of a very limited sort.

A lookback call (put) option gives the buyer the right to buy (sell) at the expiry date a fixed amount of the call (put) currency at the lower (higher) of the strike price or the lowest (highest) spot rate that traded during the life of the option. Only if the spot market, at the moment of expiry, is at its extremum low, for a call, or extreme high, for a put, will it not be optimal to exercise. A lookback option is never out-of-the-money. Even if the strike were set out-of-the-money, the instant it was traded, the right to buy or sell would update to the current spot level and become at-the-money. Most lookback options are initially at-the-money, but one that has a recorded low or high that is better than the current spot is exactly equivalent to a new one with that extremum as its strike. Lookback options are therefore described as having strikes that improve, and it is typical that the new strike, if updated, is communicated to buyer by the seller in a timely fashion, to allow any questions to be resolved when the memory of the events is still fresh.

There is a related product, lookforward options, which are cash settled for a value determined as the maximum of zero and, for a call (put), the profit due from buying (selling) a fixed amount of the call (put) currency at the strike price and selling (buying) it at the highest (lowest) spot rate that traded during the life of the option. If the strike price is, as is most common, the initial spot rate, making the lookforward option at-the-money, the option would be exercised unless spot moved out-of-the-money immediately, and stayed there. A more favourable strike price would create an in-the-money lookforward option. Unlike lookback options, it is possible to have an out-of-the-money lookforward option, where the spot market would have to move some distance before there would be any value in the settlement formula. An existing lookback option carries with it some history, not just the strike, but the most favourable settlement rate to date.

There are some parity relationships between lookback and lookforward options. The purchase of a lookback straddle, struck ATM, will have a pay-off of the range that that currency pair trades in during the life of the option, as the lookback call gives the right to buy at the low and the lookback put gives the right to sell at the high. The purchase of a lookforward straddle, struck ATM, also produces the same pay-off, as the lookforward put gives the right to buy at the low and sell at the strike, whilst the lookforward call gives the right to buy at the strike and sell at the high. The purchase and sale at the strike is offset, leaving a profit equal to the range identical to the lookback straddle.

It is possible to synthesize an ATM or an ITM lookforward option with an ATM lookback option of the other type and a synthetic forward trade at the strike. An ATM lookback put gives the right to sell at the high. The purchase of a European call and sale of a European put struck at spot produces an unconditional forward purchase at the strike, which is the inception spot rate. Thus, this portfolio is perfectly equivalent to a lookforward call. Synthesizing an OTM lookforward option from a lookback option is slightly trickier; the lookback option has to be ITM, with the same strike as the lookforward, so that if spot fails to improve the strike, the lookback option merely offsets the synthetic forward, producing the pay-off of an option that stayed out-of-the-money, zero.

Lookback and lookforward options are almost always worth something at expiry, therefore they must have high premiums, obviously higher than European options, as the pay-off will be at least as high, usually higher. This makes them very difficult to sell. The most popular exotic options, barrier and average rate options are cheaper than European options. There is also a psychological reason for their unpopularity. Most professionals in finance are better paid than average, presumably to reward them for their knowledge of the markets. How can such a person justify the paying of an extra high premium for a lookback option that automatically assures his firm of the best price? Where is the value of his market judgement? For whatever reason, lookback and lookforward options are relatively rarely used for hedging, but some have been built into structures marketed for smaller investors.

4.3.2 An Analytical Model

Goldman, Sosin and Gatto (1979) derived an analytical model for a European lookback call option using the Black–Scholes assumptions. The formula contains the price of the European option with the lookback option's current strike and what has been described as a "strike bonus" option, that reflects the value of the improvement in the strike and any value at maturity between the final strike and the closer of the original strike or the final spot price. Using the same notation as previously used in this chapter, the formula for a "strike bonus" option can be written as follows:

$$\frac{\Phi \sigma^2}{2\delta} \left(K e^{-rT} (S/K)^{2\lambda} N \left(\Phi \left(-d_1 + \frac{2\delta\sqrt{T}}{\sigma} \right) \right) - S e^{-r_f T} N(-\Phi d_1) \right) \qquad (9)$$

where $\delta = r - r_f$.

Whenever spot sets a new relevant extreme, the lookback parameters change. The European option component has a new strike, as does the strike bonus. Mark Garman has pointed out that such formulae are difficult to implement if the foreign and domestic rates should be equal, as there would be a zero in the denominator. However, the price is a continuous function of either interest rate, so the price of a lookback option at a zero rate differential is the limit as the rate differential approaches zero.

From general appearances, the formula for a call looks like a certain amount of hybrid between a knock-in put and a European put, as it has a discounted strike multiplied by a factor similar to one appearing in a knock-in option, times a risk neutral probability minus discounted spot times a risk neutral probability. This makes sense as spot must decline to make the strike bonus portion of a lookback call have a value.

4.3.3 Alternative Models

Due to the similarity between lookback options and structures of barrier options, the same methods have been applied to deal with the same weaknesses in the assumptions. The implementation of any binomial method was thought to be computationally difficult prior to Simon Babbs' or Eric Reiner's work.

4.3.4 Risk Management

(i) Derivatives

The delta of an ATM lookback option, which includes any time that it is setting a new maximum, is equal to its premium. This also applies to puts. If the initial premium is paid in the foreign currency, no delta hedge is required at inception. Once the market begins to diverge from the strike, the delta begins to get closer to that of the underlying European option. In spite of this change, the delta is a continuous function of spot, although the gamma is not. The high price of a lookback option is a product of the potential movement, both down and up. Therefore lookback options have high vegas. Theta will also be high, as the volatility requires time to act.

(ii) Options Hedges

The most frequently mentioned means of hedging a short lookback option is to buy an ATM straddle and roll it to the new strike whenever a new extreme in the spot market improves the lookback's strike. Consider a lookback call: if the spot market never sets a new low, the purchased European call will cover the pay-off. If spot moves down first, the cost of buying a new ATM straddle will be covered by the sale of the previous one, as the put has become more valuable. Eventually, when the low for the whole period had occurred, the call at that strike would cover the full lookback pay-off.

The previous paragraph, like Black–Scholes, ignores transaction costs. In the real world, the straddle strike would only be adjusted when the strike had changed enough to make it worthwhile. The risk of following this strategy is that a sudden drop and immediate rebound would count in improving the strike of the lookback, but would not allow for enough time to adjust the hedge. As this is the opposite kind of gap risk than usually worries barrier option dealers, managing the usually smaller lookback book in conjunction with the barrier book can mitigate the larger risk.

4.3.5 Extensions

(i) Discontinuous Lookbacks

The disadvantage of the high cost of lookback options can be mitigated by limiting the times when the lookback feature is in operation. The liquidity of the underlying market or the need for an independently verifiable measure of the extreme sometimes leads to lookback options that are based on periodic samples, like daily fixings. These variations can be priced using the method described in Simon Babbs' article on binomial pricing of lookback options, which contains an astute method of keeping the tree from becoming too bushy.

A discontinuous lookforward with a relatively low number of fixings is referred to as a "cliquet" or ratchet option. These have been built into multi-year retail equity index products, where the final return is dependent on the appreciation from inception to the highest yearly close. The simplest version of a ratchet option would be one where the cash settlement was based on the better of the spot price at one intermediate date (the ratchet date) and at maturity. This can be viewed as a purchase of an option expiring on the ratchet date, but where the pay-off was deferred until the actual maturity and the purchase of a forward start option, where the strike will be set on the ratchet date at the then current spot market, or the original spot whichever is worse, and expiring at the actual maturity. If the final spot was not as favourable as the intermediate spot, then the forward start option could finish out-of-the-money, and the sole pay-off would be from the European option with the deferred pay-off. If the final spot were more favourable, then the pay-off of the two options would combine to produce the payment for the full movement since inception. The forward start options usually modelled do not have any restriction on the level at which their strike can be set, so this simile may be tricky to implement, but it does show the inter-relatedness of various species of exotic options.

(ii) American Lookbacks

Even though lookback options give the right to deal at an extreme, they aren't necessarily worth their maximum value at maturity. For example, if a lookback call is 10 per cent above its minimum one week prior to expiry, spot could easily decline somewhat by expiry without getting anywhere near the minimum. Selling the lookback option or hedging by selling a European option or dealing in the spot market are all suitable ways of locking in a profit. Eric Reiner has suggested a numerical method of calculating a price for an American-style lookback option, should the buyer not be satisfied with the above methods of realizing a value prior to maturity.

(iii) Shout Options

We have discussed various means of providing lookforward-like features at lesser premiums by discretizing the sampling for the favourable extreme. Ladder options sample at preset levels only, ratchet options sample at preset times. A shout option gives the buyer the right, at one moment of his choosing during the life of the option, to set the then current spot level as the sample point (see Thomas (1993) which describes how to adapt a binomial lattice to model this product).

4.4 EVEN MORE EXOTIC OPTIONS

For a while it seemed that whatever a "rocket scientist" could invent would be sold. Options with formula based pay-offs, like power options or options linking the prices of two unrelated markets seemed about to proliferate. The reaction to publicized losses from derivative products seems to have changed the focus away from novelty for its own sake. Instead the recent thrust seems to be packaging a series of the products described above. This can cut down the exposure to an unfortunate conjunction of the expiry date and an unfavourable market move, although the maximum return is effectively limited as well. These create a different challenge for the modeller, system developer and risk manager, as each trade can involve dozens or maybe even hundreds of component trades. These need to be handled en masse, lest the costs of processing outweigh the potential profits.

4.5 REFERENCES

DuPire, B. (1994) "Pricing and hedging with volatility smiles". *Risk Magazine*, January.

Dvigi, D.R. (1979) "Calculation of univariate and bivariate normal probability functions". *Annals of Statistics*, **7**, no. 4, 903–10.

Geske, R. (1979) "The valuation of compound options". *Journal of Financial Economics*, **7**, 63–81.

Goldman, M.B., Sosin, H.B. and Gatto, M.A. (1979) "Path dependent options: Buy at the low, sell at the high". *Journal of Finance*, December, **34**, 1111–27.

Hull, J.C. (1993) *Options, Futures, and Other Derivative Securities*. 2nd Edition, Prentice Hall International Editions, 417–18.

Rubenstein, M. and Reiner, E. (1991) "Breaking down the barriers". *Risk Magazine*, September.

Thomas, B. (1993) "Something to shout about". *Risk Magazine*, May.

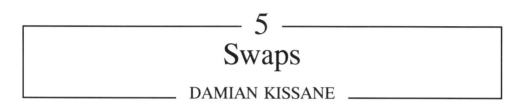

5
Swaps
DAMIAN KISSANE

5.1 INTRODUCTION

This chapter provides the reader with an introduction to interest rate and currency swaps and their uses, discusses interest rate swaps as an extension of an FRA and then outlines the various uses of interest rate and currency swaps. The principles underlying zero coupon pricing are outlined and applied to the pricing of a simple structured transaction — Libor in arrears. The uses of swaps are outlined and the merits of a number of more complex swap structures which have achieved notoriety rather than popularity are discussed.

5.2 CASH MARKET TRANSACTIONS AND THE ORIGINS OF DERIVATIVES

The starting point for all derivatives is an understanding of cash markets and the need to hedge interest rate and currency exposures in the future. When we refer to the cash markets we mean:

- Cash deposits and advances in the case of the interest rate markets
- Spot foreign exchange ("FX") in the case of the foreign exchange markets

In the interbank cash markets we express everything in terms of Libor which can have a maturity from overnight to 12 months and beyond, generally with interest calculated from two days forward (sterling being an exception which starts on the same day). In the interbank FX markets we quote the exchange rate between two currencies for settlement in two days' time. In all cases these transactions involve the movement of cash equivalent to the principal amount of the transaction at the outset, for example placing money on deposit for six months or the spot exchange of Swiss francs for US dollars.

If we wish to value cash flows in the future we can use cash interbank rates. Thus the right to receive USD 100 in six months' time can be valued by creating an equal and opposite cash flow in six months' time equivalent to USD 100.

The Handbook of Risk Management and Analysis. Edited by Carol Alexander

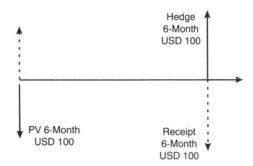

Figure 5.1   Hedged cash flows

This equal and opposite cash flow can be created by borrowing money today such that the principal and interest will exactly offset the receipt of USD 100 in six months' time — a perfect hedge. The money borrowed today equivalent to USD 100 discounted back at Libor is the present value of that future cash flow, i.e. the right to receive USD 100. Hedging involves creating equal and opposite cash flows to offset future assets and liabilities thereby creating a present value for each cash flow in the future.

The recent international debate on the dangers of derivatives tends to overlook their functions and origins. Derivatives exist and thrive because of their advantages over cash markets. Cash markets have bid–offer spreads, e.g. the Libid to Libor spread of 0.125 per cent. If we attempt to use the interbank cash markets to fix the cost of borrowing or investing in the future, the cost becomes prohibitive because as we move further out in time the effective bid–offer spread between Libor and Libid at which we can transact hedges widens markedly. The bid–offer spread of the cash market instruments does not change but the bid–offer spread of the hedges does. This will be explained in more detail below. Intuitively, as bankers we might expect that the bid–offer spreads in the cash markets should widen over time reflecting the higher risks of doing business. Fortunately they do not. Remaining fixed at 0.125 per cent is sufficient to make hedging using interbank cash markets unattractive and the further out in time the exposures we are seeking to hedge, the more expensive the hedge.

The graphs in Figure 5.2 show how the spread between the forward borrowing and investing rates widens very quickly over time in a moderately positive yield curve. The curves graph the arbitrage-free cost of borrowing or investing for a three-month period at various dates in the future starting from 19th November 1995. The forward Libor–Libid rates are derived from the spot cash market rates on 19th November 1995. Within one year the difference between three-month Libor and Libid starting on 19th November 1996 is in excess of 1 per cent.

The simplest interest rate derivative, the forward rate agreement (discussed below) was developed to overcome the above problems of widening bid–offer spreads. It is essentially an agreement between two parties to fix a Libor rate in the future. It is confined within the so-called arbitrage boundaries above where a fixed borrowing rate could be achieved in the future using the cash markets. Its advantage over cash market hedges is that it requires no settlement of cash until the end of the contract period. As a result it has less credit risk and a lower allocation of bank capital which provides an environment

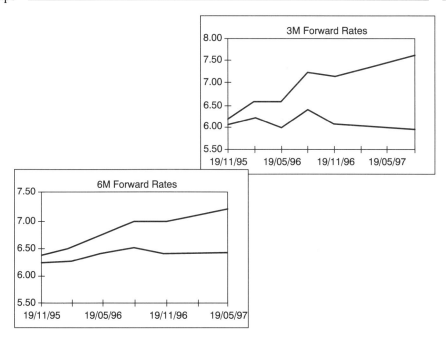

Figure 5.2   Cash market arbitrage forward rates

for a very liquid contract to develop with many buyers and sellers and a more narrow bid–offer spread.

Other derivatives, for example options, or the contracts evidencing those derivative agreements, may allow settlement of the calculated gain or loss on the contract (netting) rather than an exchange of the underlying principal amount. Therefore, they may have smaller credit exposures for the counterparts. Note that the risks are the same from hedging with derivatives as if the parties were hedging in the cash markets. The exposures may be smaller because there is no exchange of underlying principal amounts. An exception we will encounter below is the currency swap because it involves a full exchange of the principal amount of each currency at the maturity of the contract.

Derivatives exist because the need to manage risk is so universal that instruments with narrower bid–offer spreads and therefore more liquidity have arisen. Those instruments are derivatives. Rather like the old saying — if they did not exist we would have to invent them. Derivatives are a natural extension of cash markets and the universal need to manage future cash flows efficiently.

It should hopefully also be obvious from the above discussion that derivative prices are determined by supply and demand characteristics within boundaries which can be defined by the cash markets, so-called arbitrage boundaries, where the cash market can replicate the derivative transaction. Even at these boundaries, however, derivatives may offer a competitive edge because they do not involve exchanges of the underlying principal amounts. Further, derivatives will appear more or less attractive relative to cash markets at different times according to supply and demand factors within the derivative markets themselves. We will look in detail below at the basic derivative instruments.

5.3 FORWARD RATE AGREEMENTS

The forward rate agreement is a single interest period derivative. It is effectively a futures contract tailored to meet the exact requirements of the user. Thus an investment manager looking to fix the reinvestment rate on a cash inflow in three months' time could hedge using cash markets as discussed above but this would be prohibitively expensive. Alternatively he could sell Eurodollar futures to hedge that reinvestment risk. However, the futures contract would be unlikely to match his cash position exactly as to size or timing and would only hedge exactly a further three-month investment horizon. Additionally, the contract would have to be executed on a futures exchange with the consequent requirements for margining, etc. A forward rate agreement (an "FRA") can be tailored to match the exact cash flows of the anticipated reinvestment.

It is a simple bilateral agreement with a bank to pay $(-)$ or receive $(+)$ the difference between an agreed fixed rate (the FRA rate) and Libor in the future calculated for a fixed interest period. As an example, an investor wishing to lock in a future reinvestment rate could contract at a rate of 4.00 per cent with the bank and would receive the difference between 4.00 per cent and Libor, if Libor was below 4.00 per cent, and pay the difference if Libor was above 4.00 per cent. Settlement is calculated at the beginning of the agreed interest period by discounting back the difference between the previously contracted FRA rate and the then prevailing Libor. Remember, in a cash transaction, Libor is calculated at the beginning of the period but settlement, i.e. actual payment of monies, occurs at the end of the interest period. The net effect is that the investor locks in a future reinvestment rate of 4.00 per cent under all interest rate scenarios.

Consider the example, on 7th June 1995, of an investor seeking to lock in a US dollar reinvestment rate on 7th September 1995 for 90 days. He is quoted an FRA rate of 3.64/3.60 per cent. The company can lock in a Libor rate of 3.60 per cent if it wishes to protect itself from Libor falling or 3.64 per cent if it is concerned about interest rates rising. This excludes any margin relative to Libor for borrowing or depositing money with the bank. The contract only refers to the underlying index, here three-month Libor. On 5th September 1995 the FRA is settled for the value of 7th September thus:

$$(1) \text{ FRA settles} = \frac{(\text{FRA rate} - 3 \text{ month Libor}) \times \text{Number of days in period}}{36,000^* \times \left[1 + \left(3 \text{ month Libor} \times \frac{\text{Number of days in period}}{36,000}\right)\right]}$$

The FRA purchaser agrees to pay or receive the difference between a three-monthly rate of 3.60 per cent and the actual three month Libor rate for the 90-day period, 7th September to 6th December 1995.

If Libor on Tuesday 5th September 1995 is 4.00 per cent, the payment due to settle the FRA on 7th September 1995 is a payment by the investor to the bank of:

$$(2) \text{ FRA settles} = \frac{((3.60 - 4.00) \times 90)}{36,000 \times \left[1 + \frac{(4.00 \times 90)}{36,000}\right]}$$

$$= -0.09901 \text{ per cent, i.e. USD 990.10 per USD 1 million}$$

* 365 in the case of sterling.

If Libor on Tuesday 5th September 1995 is 3.00 per cent, the settlement is payment on 7th September 1995 by the bank to the investor of:

$$(3) \text{ FRA settles} = \frac{((3.60 - 3.00) \times 90)}{36,000 \times \left[1 + \dfrac{(3.00 \times 90)}{36,000}\right]}$$

$$= 0.14888 \text{ per cent, i.e. USD 1,488 per USD 1 million}$$

In order to match the exact cash flows of the investor's underlying investment position and thereby lock in an exact rate of 3.60 per cent, the investor must borrow the cash payment (2) or invest the positive settlement amount (3) at Libor for 90 days so as to match the cash flows on the underlying investment, i.e. the investor expects the following investment interest receipts on 6th December 1995:

$$= 3.60 \times \frac{90}{36,000},$$

$$= 0.90 \text{ per cent, i.e. USD 9,000 per USD 1 million}$$

If, however, Libor on Tuesday 5th September 1995 is 3.00 per cent, the investor receives from the deposit with the bank at its maturity:

$$= 3.00 \times \frac{90}{36,000},$$

$$= 0.75 \text{ per cent, i.e. USD 7,500 per USD 1 million}$$

a shortfall of 0.15 per cent from the desired interest receipts. However, the FRA generates a receipt of 0.14888 per cent, i.e. USD 1,488 per USD 1 million on 7th September which reinvested at the prevailing Libo rate gives:

$$= 0.1488 \times \left(1 + \left[3.00 \times \frac{90}{36,000}\right]\right),$$

$$= 0.15 \text{ per cent, i.e. USD 1,500 per USD 1 million, combined with the interest}$$
receipt of USD 7,500 gives:

$$0.75 + 0.15 = 0.90 \text{ per cent}$$

$$= 3.60 \text{ per cent per annum}$$

If Libor on Tuesday 5th September 1995 is 4.00 per cent, the investor receives from the deposit with the bank at its maturity:

$$= 4.00 \times \frac{90}{36,000},$$

$$= 1.00 \text{ per cent, i.e. USD 10,000 per USD 1 million}$$

However, the investor has to make a payment of 0.09901 per cent, i.e. USD 990.10 per USD 1 million to the bank on 7th September 1995. This has to be borrowed at Libor for ninety days:

$$= -0.09901 \times \left(1 + \left[4.00 \times \frac{90}{36,000}\right]\right),$$

$$= -0.10 \text{ per cent, i.e. USD 1,000 per USD 1 million}$$

$$1.00 - 0.10 = 0.90 \text{ per cent}$$

$$= 3.60 \text{ per cent per annum}$$

Under all scenarios the investor achieves a reinvestment rate of 3.60 per cent for the 90 day period. However, if the investor cannot invest or borrow at Libor then the FRA will not exactly match the cash flows of the underlying investment proposition. As an alternative, if the FRA is settled at the end of the investment period instead of at the beginning, then this risk borrowing/investment would be removed and the investor would have a perfect hedge.

FRAs are expressed in terms of giving or receiving the fixed rate vs. Libor and are quoted numerically, for example:

- the three-month rate starting in three months' time is the 3/6
- the three-month rate starting in six months' time is the 6/9
- the six-month rate starting in three months' time is the 3/9

Alternative nomenclature for the 3/6 can be "3s, 6s", "3s against 6s", 3-6, 3.6, or 3 × 6. FRAs are used:

- To hedge single period cash flows in the not too distant future
- As an alternative to futures

Futures have the advantages of high volume, no practical credit risk and market transparency, whilst FRAs offer the user the advantages of no margining requirements because it is a bilateral contract and also has the ability to tailor the FRA to meet the user's exact requirements as to size, maturity, strike, etc.

The FRA defines market forward rates of interest from current cash and swap curves which themselves are determined by supply and demand factors about the future. The drawback with FRAs is that the FRA rate is different for each maturity in the future, i.e. the 3/6 FRA is not the same as the 6/9 FRA. However, when we seek to manage our interest rate risks, particularly in a large corporate environment, we desire cash flows which are regular over time, i.e. a constant fixed rate until the maturity of our borrowing or investment horizon. Unlike the interest rate swap, the FRA as a product does not offer that flexibility.

5.4 INTEREST RATE SWAPS

An interest rate swap in its most common form is an agreement to exchange a fixed rate (the "swap rate") for a series of floating or variable rate payments, most typically Libor, which vary over time. The fixed rate payments are generally paid annually (exceptions are sterling and yen, semi-annual) whilst the floating rate payments are invariably paid six monthly, linked to six-month Libor.

The interest rate swap is in essence a strip of FRAs with the same fixed interest rate and the settlement of the interest amount at the end of each interest period rather than at the beginning. Swaps, unlike FRAs, generally do not net settle the difference between the agreed fixed FRA rate and the floating or variable rate Libor as in the above

Table 5.1 Interest rate swap example: 7 per cent
fixed vs six-month Libor

	Floating Rate Payer (A)	Fixed Rate Receiver (B)
18/10/95		
18/04/96	(USD 6m Libor)	
18/10/96	(USD 6m Libor)	USD 7.00
18/04/97	(USD 6m Libor)	
18/10/97	(USD 6m Libor)	USD 7.00

FRA examples. The parties make full payments to one another of the fixed and floating amounts on each interest payment date as they fall due although netting of payments is allowable. In this respect it is no more than a contract for the exchange of one series of cash flows for another series of cash flows on terms which are set at the outset of the transaction.

The cash flows can be paid according to any agreed schedule: monthly, quarterly, semi-annually, annually, etc., based on an agreed principal amount or even varying schedules of amounts through time (accreting, amortizing and roller coaster swaps). The exchanges of cash flows need not occur on the same dates and can be referenced to short-term interest rates other than Libor, for example the domestic commercial paper borrowing rate in the US or the base rate in the UK.

Table 5.1 outlines the cash flows on a conventional swap from the point of view of one party who has contracted to receive two equal payments of 7.00 per cent over the next two years in exchange for agreeing to pay four semi-annual payments of six-month Libor at the end of each six-month period over the next two years. Both sides of the swap have the same principal amount.

5.4.1 Swap Terminology

When we talk about swaps we tend to use a certain amount of jargon. In Table 5.1 we would refer variously to the:

- *Floating Rate Payer* (A) who can also be called the Fixed Rate Receiver (B)
- *Swap Counterpart* In the table the Fixed Rate Payer whose position is not shown
- *Notional Amount* or Principal Amount of the swap (USD 100.00)
- *Fixed Rate* of 7.00 per cent (Ann, 30/360)
- *Floating Rate* six-month USD Libor plus or minus any agreed margin
- *Maturity Date* of two years
- *Start Date* or effective date from which interest is calculated
- *Value Date* upon which the two sides of the swap are valued as being equivalent after any initial upfront payments/adjustments
- *Initial Floating Rate* setting, i.e. the first Libor if it is already known, for example with an immediate or spot start swap

5.4.2 Swap Rates

Each bank will quote its own swap rate to exchange fixed cash flows for floating in each maturity along the curve, typically out to ten years. The market swap rates quoted on brokers' screens at any point in time are derived from the best prices of the participants in the swap market. As an example, in a three-year maturity, BT&T Asset Management may be on the bid, i.e. the highest payer of the fixed rate in the market, but bank A will be on the offer, i.e. the most aggressive receiver of fixed. For example, three-year maturity,

Bank A quotes	7.00–7.10 per cent
BT & T quotes	7.05–7.15 per cent
Market swap rate is	7.05–7.10 per cent

Unlike the foreign exchange market participants do not quote, as a rule, two-way prices. They are either "on the bid" or "on the offer". One conclusion from this is that a swap desk will itself be more or less aggressive against the market at different times.

Additionally like spot and forward foreign exchange markets, the market does not separately or accurately price credit. Credit is rationed not priced. This is a very interesting aspect of the swap market. It is a criticism of derivatives and a potential advantage to many of the users. It suggests that the swap market can create marketing opportunities for credit arbitrage for corporates or banks within and between markets and currencies.

5.4.3 Analysing Swaps

A simple way to look at an interest rate swap is to consider it as holding a long or short position in a fixed rate bond with an equivalent short (long) position in a floating rate note which pays interest linked to six-month Libor. Alternatively the floating cash flows can be thought of as a variable rate term loan or deposit. The net present value of the two sides of the transaction should be equivalent at the outset.

In Table 5.2 a swap to receive fixed for two years at 7.00 per cent vs. payment of floating six-month Libor is equivalent to borrowing floating for two years and investing those borrowed funds in a fixed rate investment yielding 7.00 per cent. Because the principal payments on the bond and the FRN at the beginning and the end of the investment period are identical, they cancel each other out. This representation of an interest rate swap as the combination of a bond and FRN provides a mechanism for valuing swaps. Summarizing, in an interest rate swap only the interest payments are exchanged, thus a commonly used term to describe derivatives is "contract for differences". We will look at some other types of swaps below before we discuss their pricing and uses.

Table 5.2 Interest rate swaps and bond/FRN positions: interest rate swaps are similar to long FRN and short bond positions 7 per cent fixed rate bond vs. six-month Libor FRN

	Floating Rate Note	Fixed Rate Bond
18/10/95	100.00	(100.00)
18/04/96	(6m Libor)	
18/10/96	(6m Libor)	7.00
18/04/97	(6m Libor)	
18/10/97	(100.00 + 6m Libor)	100.00 + 7.00

5.4.4 Basis Swap

A basis swap is a series of payments which vary over time according to some agreed calculation basis for an alternative series of payments which vary over time according to a different method of calculation or different schedule of payment — "floating/floating" or "basis" swap.

Table 5.3 Interest rate basis swap: US dollar basis swap six-month Libor vs. 12-month Libor

	USD Floating Rate Payments	USD Floating Rate Receipts
18/10/95		
18/04/96	(6m Libor)	
18/10/96	(6m Libor)	12m Libor
18/04/97	(6m Libor)	
18/10/97	(6m Libor)	12m Libor

5.4.5 Currency Swap

Exchange of a series of cash flows in one currency for a series of cash flows in a different currency.

Table 5.4 Currency swap example: 7 per cent in Deutschmarks vs. six-month US dollar Libor

	USD Floating Rate Payments (A)	DM Fixed Rate Receipts
18/10/95	100.00	(DM 170.00)
18/04/96	(6m Libor)	
18/10/96	(6m Libor)	DM 11.90
18/04/97	(6m Libor)	
18/10/97	(6m Libor + 100.00)	DM 11.90 + DM 170.00

A currency swap will also embrace the exchange of floating rate cash flows in one currency for floating rate cash flows in a different currency — a "cross currency basis swap".

Because the initial and final amounts to be exchanged will not be the same throughout the life of the swap in terms of each other, i.e. DM 170.00 will not always be equivalent to USD 100.00 they do not cancel out at maturity as in the case of the interest rate swap. At the outset both sides of the swap will be equivalent. This may necessitate an initial payment between the counterparts. In order to ensure the value of the swap to both counterparts is the same at the end as at the beginning, there is a final exchange of the original principal on each side of the swap at maturity, i.e. USD 100.00 for DM 170.00. In practice the typical swap will include an "initial" exchange and a "final" re-exchange of currency.

A currency swap can also be viewed as the combination of two simultaneous borrowing and lending transactions. In the above example the swapper borrows USD 100.00 from the swap counterpart. He pays the swap counterpart interest up to and including maturity and at maturity repays the swap counterpart USD 100.00. The swapper at the outset simultaneously lends the Deutschmark equivalent to USD 100.00 (DM 170.00) at that date to the swap counterpart and receives from the swap counterpart fixed interest of 7.00 per cent per annum in Deutschmarks up to and including maturity when he receives the DM 170.00.

5.5 SWAP PRICING AND HEDGING

If we can analyse interest rate swaps as the combination of a long position in a bond and an equivalent short position in an FRN then we can value swaps. In order to value the two sides of the swap we need to be able to value the unknown Libor cash flows and a stream of fixed cash flows. We know at the outset that the two sides are equivalent.

We can calculate the present value of the Libor cash flows if we analyse them as a floating rate note. We know that if our marginal cost of funding or investing is Libor — a fundamental assumption of international banking — the present value of a floating rate note which pays six-month Libor until maturity based on a face value of 100 per cent is that face value of 100 per cent i.e.

Table 5.5 Present value of a six-month Libor bearing FRN

	Floating Rate Payer
18/10/95	100.00
18/04/96	(6m Libor)
18/10/96	(6m Libor)
18/04/97	(6m Libor)
18/10/97	(100.00 + 6m Libor)

The present value of all the cash flows of the FRN is the sum of each cash flow multiplied by its appropriate discount factor DF_0, DF_1, DF_2, DF_3, etc. We obtain the discount factors from the current par swap rates at each point along the curve. We can use this approach to value the Libor side, excluding any margin, of the interest rate swap. Rearranging the floating side of the swap is equivalent to:

Table 5.6 Present value of a six month Libor bearing FRN until Maturity

	Floating Rate Payer
18/10/95	$100.00 \times DF_0$
18/04/96	
18/10/96	
18/04/97	
18/10/97	$(100.00) \times DF_4$

We know at the outset of the swap that the present value of the floating cash flows must be equivalent to the present value of the fixed cash flows and some simple rearrangement provides us with:

Table 5.7 Interest rate swap valuation example: 7 per cent fixed vs. six-month Libor

18/10/95	$100.00 \times DF_0$
18/04/96	
18/10/96	$(7.00) \times DF_2$
18/04/97	
18/10/97	$(107.00) \times DF_4$

Both sides of the swap must be equal in value at the outset. If one side is more valuable than the other then the net present value of cash flows will not be zero and in order to induce the swap counterpart into the swap an initial payment will be required or an adjustment to the margin above or below Libor paid or received on the floating side of the swap. Given the above approach to viewing cash flows on the swap we can value any swap and we do not need to know what Libor will be in the future.

It is not appropriate to use the par swap rates obtained straight from the yield curve itself. As an example consider valuing the following fixed cash flows:

Table 5.8 Fixed cash flows

	Cash Flow
Year 1	USD 100
Year 2	−USD 300
Year 3	USD 100
Year 4	USD 150

Using the following yield curve:

Table 5.9 Yield curve (per cent per annum)

	Yield Curve
Year 1	6
Year 2	7
Year 3	8
Year 4	9

We would normally discount the cash flows at the interest rate corresponding to the furthest maturity — the yield to maturity or internal rate of return approach — using a constant interest rate R, assuming that at all points in time we can borrow or reinvest at that interest rate R. Discounting at a constant rate of 9 per cent per annum gives a net present value of USD 22.721 for the cash flows.

In order to be certain about the value we assign to our cash flows we need to be able to hedge those cash flows until maturity using the current par yield curve and secure a net present value of USD 22.721.

Table 5.10 Present value of cash flows

	Yield Curve	Disc Factor	Present Value
Year 1	6	0.9174	USD 91.743
Year 2	7	0.8417	−USD 252.504
Year 3	8	0.7722	USD 77.218
Year 4	9	0.7084	USD 106.264
		Sum	USD 22.721

If we hedge the cash flows using swaps we can make the assumption that we can borrow or lend at Libor at all times, in which case a positive receipt of USD 150.00 in four years' time can be hedged by creating an equal and opposite cash flow of USD 150.00 in four years' time. We can create a negative cash outflow in four years' time by borrowing an amount of money today, P, at Libor such that the total we have to repay at maturity in four years' time is equivalent to USD 150.00.

Table 5.11 Hedging a four-year cash flow

	Cash Flow	Yield Curve	4-year Hedge	Net Cash Flow
Year 0			137.615	
Year 1	USD 100	6	−12.385	87.615
Year 2	−USD 300	7	−12.385	−312.385
Year 3	USD 100	8	−12.385	87.615
Year 4	USD 150	9	−150.00	

	Yield Curve	Net Cash Flow	3-year Hedge	Net Cash Flows
Year 0			81.125	
Year 1	6	87.615	−6.490	81.125
Year 2	7	−312.385	−6.490	−318.875
Year 3	8	87.615	−87.615	
Year 4	9			

	Yield Curve	Net Cash Flows	2-year Hedge	Net Cash Flows
Year 0			−298.014	
Year 1	6	81.125	20.861	101.986
Year 2	7	−318.875	318.875	
Year 3	8			
Year 4	9			

What we observe is that the present value of all the cash flows hedged using the four-year par swap rate of 9.00 per cent is USD 16.938, not USD 22.721. The correct value for our cash flows is derived from the cost of their exact hedge, so that we have no resultant interest rate exposure. Therefore, the internal rate of return approach to valuing cash flows is not appropriate for accurate valuation and hedging. In practice we need to discount each cash flow at a discount rate appropriate to its own particular maturity and not a single interest rate for all cash flows in the future no matter when they occur, as implied by the internal rate of return approach to cash flow valuation.

This can be thought of more simply by observing the par swap rates themselves. If you enter into a one-year swap you will secure a return of 6.00 per cent for one year. If you lock into a two-year swap you can secure a return of 7.00 per cent in year one and 7.00 per cent in year two. If, however, you are prepared to receive 6.00 per cent for one year then the difference between 7.00 per cent and 6.00 per cent must relate to the fact that you have secured a two-year rate or you have given up the opportunity value on your investment for two years. If you were to receive no intervening coupon on your investment at the end of year one, you would demand as a minimum an additional 1.00 per cent at maturity in order to induce you to give up your money for two years. We need to derive a set of discount factors which are applicable to each individual cash flow as it occurs: zero coupon discount factors.

We can calculate the appropriate zero coupon discount factors starting from year one:

$$1 \text{ year} \quad \frac{1}{\left(1 + \dfrac{6.00}{100}\right)} \qquad\qquad = 0.9434$$

$$2 \text{ year} \quad \frac{100 - (7.00 \times 0.9434)}{(100 + 7.00)} \qquad\qquad = 0.8729$$

$$3 \text{ year} \quad \frac{100 - (8.00 \times 0.9434) - (8.00 \times 0.8729)}{(100 + 8.00)} \qquad\qquad = 0.7914$$

$$4 \text{ year} \quad \frac{100 - (9.00 \times 0.9434) - (9.00 \times 0.8729) - (9.00 \times 0.7914)}{(100 + 9.00)} = 0.7021$$

etc.

If we use these discount factors to value our cash flows we derive a new net present value.

Table 5.12 Cash flow valuation using zero coupon discount factors

	Yield Curve	Net Cash Flows	1-year Hedge	Sum
Year 0			96.213	16.938
Year 1	6	101.986	−101.986	
Year 2	7			
Year 3	8			
Year 4	9			

which is identical to the valuation derived using our hedges.

The zero coupon approach to swap valuation is now generally accepted as the most appropriate method for valuing cash flows. It is extremely powerful, particularly as it can provide an accurate valuation of even the most irregular series of cash flows which can be fully hedged at inception thereby giving accurate mark-to-market valuations for fixed and variable cash flows in the future. A swap book will apply the above methodology to value any series of cash flows in order to arrive at a valuation where the two sides of the swap have an equivalent present value.

As a proof of the approach we should be able to value a four-year swap, fixed vs. floating, where the fixed swap rate is the four-year par swap rate and the two sides should be equivalent, i.e. the present value of the fixed cash flows should be equal to the present value of the Libor cash flows. We should also be able to hedge that swap to prove that the two sides are equal in value.

Table 5.13 Hedging a four-year par swap cash flow

	Swap Cash Flow
Year 0	−USD 100
Year 1	USD 9
Year 2	USD 9
Year 3	USD 9
Year 4	USD 109

5.6 SOME CONCLUSIONS ON SWAPS

What can we say about FRAs and swaps as a generalized summary? First, FRA rates are confined to cash market boundaries which we can quickly calculate. A strip of FRAs with settlement at the end of each period is no more than an interest rate swap. Therefore there must be an arbitrage relationship between swap rates and cash market rates. A currency swap, for example a fixed–fixed currency swap, can be broken down into a series of foreign exchange forwards and FRAs. What the interest rate and currency swap provide is a convenient packaging appropriate to the way in which companies borrow or invest money over time.

5.7 USES OF SWAPS

Swaps effectively link the capital markets of all major currencies. They enable counterparts, as we have seen above, to value and make direct comparisons between cash flows in the same and in different currencies. In this section we will look at the practical applications of swaps in investment management, namely:

- Asset and liability management
- Investment or borrowing arbitrage
- Tailored financial packages (structured financing)

5.7.1 Asset and Liability Management

The most common use of interest and currency rate swaps is for asset and liability management purposes. A company, "Triple Apple", with a floating rate obligation, for example from a loan upon which it is currently paying a floating rate of interest at Libor plus a margin, can consider fixing the cost of that financing via an interest rate swap in order to protect itself against the adverse exposure from further interest rate rises.

Triple Apple has a three-year facility with its bank (funding bank) to borrow at six-month Libor plus 0.25 per cent per annum (s/a, A/360). Triple Apple is concerned that interest rates are set to rise over the next few years and would now like to fix the future cost of its borrowing. The swap market currently quotes 8.00/7.90 per cent (Ann, A/360).

Interest Rate Swap

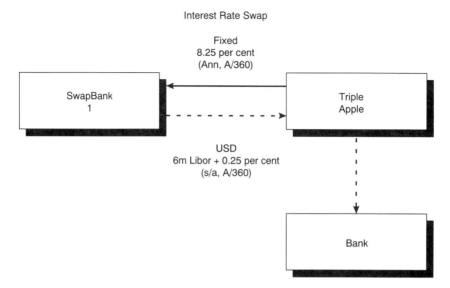

Figure 5.3 Interest rate swap diagram

It is prepared to "receive" a fixed rate of 8.00 per cent each year, "receive fixed", vs. payment of six-month Libor. At the same time it will "pay fixed" at 7.90 per cent for three years vs. receipt of six-month Libor. The difference between the two rates is the swap market's bid–offer spread expressed as an annual yield difference. Triple Apple enters into a swap to pay fixed at 8.00 per cent for three years vs. receipt of six-month Libor (see Figure 5.3).

In the above example Triple Apple locks in a cost of funds of 8.25 per cent (Ann, A/360). Note that in the figure the swap will receive a higher rate of 8.25 per cent in return for paying Triple Apple 0.25 per cent above Libor in order to match Triple Apple's exact cash flow obligations on its financing which are semi-annual. In practice the exact rate may not be quite 8.25 per cent (Ann, A/360) but it will be extremely close.

(i) Asset Management

"Liquid Investments plc" currently invests short term in money market instruments with maturities of not more than six months. Liquid is concerned that interest rates in six months' time will be lower and wishes to protect itself from that event. Twelve-month interest rates are currently higher than six-month rates but Liquid is constrained to invest principal amounts in assets with maturities of less than six-months. Through an interest rate swap Liquid can lock in the prevailing higher 12-month Libor without extending the maturity of its investments beyond six months. For example:

Six-Month Libor	8.75 per cent (s/a, A/360)
Twelve-Month Libor	9.00 per cent (Ann, A/360)

In the above example Liquid Investments locks in a return of 9.00 per cent (Ann, A/360) independent of the direction of interest rates. Liquid deposits its money for six months at a time rolling the deposit over at the end of the first six-month period.

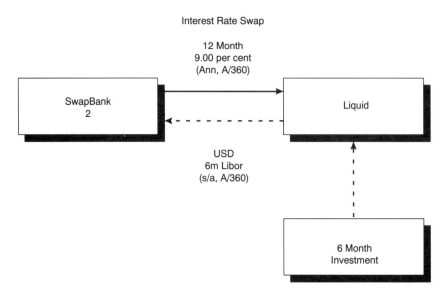

Figure 5.4 Interest rate swap example diagram

5.7.2 Investment or Borrowing Arbitrage

Investment or borrowing arbitrage exists where assets or liabilities can be swapped from one interest basis in a currency, for example a fixed rate annual bond, to another basis in the same or a different currency, for example floating rate in order to create a more attractive cost of borrowing or investment opportunity than available from borrowing or investing directly.

(i) Borrowing Arbitrage: Bond Issuer Arbitrage

The most common example of borrowing arbitrage is that available to issuers in the Eurobond market who are able to issue fixed rate Eurobonds and swap the liability of those bonds to floating rate liabilities at more attractive rates than could be obtained domestically from bank lines of credit or accessing the floating rate note market direct.

Consider the example of a company issuing a fixed rate bond at an all-in cost of 10.00 per cent per annum. The swap market is willing to pay an annual fixed rate of 10.00 per cent (30/360) to match the coupon on the bond and in return receive six-month Libor less 0.25 per cent per annum (s/a, A/360). The company, if it were to access the floating rate market or to borrow floating normally, will have to pay a margin above six-month Libor, for example 0.15 per cent. Thus a saving is created in the order of 0.40 per cent (s/a, A/360) in this example (see Figure 5.5).

In the above example the quoted market swap rate is 10.25 per cent vs. six-month Libor.

(ii) Investment Arbitrage

In investment arbitrage the investor is often a bank with a variable rate (Libor based) funding source. By paying away via a swap an unwanted fixed income stream, received

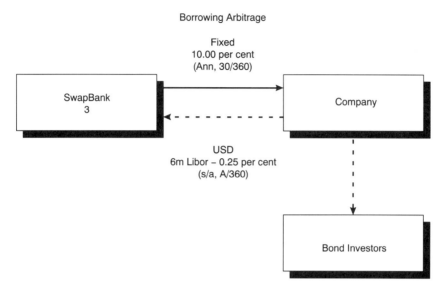

Figure 5.5 Borrowing arbitrage

for example from a fixed rate bond investment, the bank secures a yield at a spread above Libor, akin to the return on bank loans with which it is familiar.

From the perspective of the investors, the banks, this "asset swap" structure is attractive because it offers a floating rate investment to replace assets lost through the general disintermediation process which has occurred from the international growth in issuance of short-term paper facilities by top quality credits and has led to a shortage of traditional banking assets and a suppressing of spreads in the last seven to eight years.

Historically, the largest volume of this paper has been low coupon ex-warrant paper, either bank guaranteed or non-guaranteed. However, straight bond issues regularly come to market. The most common form of this structure is the fixed rate bond repackaged as a floating rate instrument.

As an example, the swap market is willing to receive an annual fixed rate of 10.00 per cent (Ann, 30/360) exactly matched to the coupon on the bond and in return pay six-month Libor plus 0.25 per cent per annum (s/a, A/360). If the bank were to lend the bond issuer funds directly it would expect to earn a margin above six-month Libor of, say, 0.15 per cent (s/a, A/360). The asset swap provides an improvement of 0.10 per cent (s/a, A/360) (see Figure 5.6).

In the above example the quoted market swap rate is 9.75 per cent vs. six-month Libor.

The one effect of repackaging from a trading perspective is to severely reduce the liquidity of an issue. This is particularly severe when an otherwise apparently unrepack-ageable issue has had an unsuccessful initial syndication, or the lead manager has used the technique to clear away some unwanted bonds of his underwriting.

(iii) Price Constraints of Borrowings and Investment Arbitrage

The two examples above point to some constraints imposed upon bond prices by the swap market. Consider the yield curve defined by the outstanding issues of a particular borrower (see Figure 5.7).

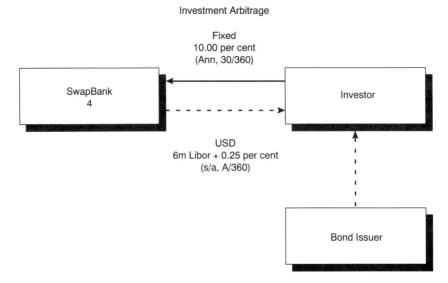

Figure 5.6 Investment arbitrage

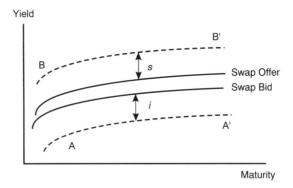

Figure 5.7 Swap/bond arbitrage example

The figure sets out the two arbitrage extremes imposed on the yield at which a particular issuer's paper may trade relative to the interbank swap curve. Suppose the borrower concerned desires a three-year issue cost after swap of Libor less 0.25 per cent (s/a, A/360) and suppose also that investors will buy the same borrower's three-year paper in repackaged form at Libor plus 0.20 per cent (s/a, A/360). This defines a yield range of 0.45 per cent (in reality a little larger because of swap bid–offer spreads) beyond which the yield of the bond may not stray.

If, for example, the bond yield falls below this range, defined by curve AA', a new issue is likely because the company can issue bonds and swap them to floating rate costs of funds more attractive than their stated target. The new supply of paper will force yields up into the range. If the yield rises beyond this range, defined by curve BB', the bonds will be bought and repackaged as asset swaps offering over Libor plus 0.25 per cent per annum.

These relationships provide some useful pointers to the interaction of bond and swap markets. However, the problem is of course made more complex when bonds are capable of being repackaged into several different currencies.

5.8 TAILORED FINANCIAL PACKAGES

Tailored financial packages are constructed in a whole variety of different forms to suit borrowers' and investors' demands. A common example is embedding forward interest rate or foreign exchange contracts or equity options on indices such as the FTSE 100, the CAC 40 in France or the DAX in Germany into the swap, or alternatively the forward prices of commodities such as gold or oil into structures aimed at satisfying specific investor requirements. These structures which include so-called "90:10" funds or "money back" structures use swaps extensively to produce the desired pay-off profiles for investors.

The different types of structures can be categorized under two broad headings:

- Future or forward linked structures
- Option linked structures

Future or forward linked structures require the investor to hold a forward position in the underlying index at a level fixed at the outset thereby creating an exposure to upward and downward movements in the index. Option structures can be used to generate one directional investment positions and more complex financial packages involving spreads, straddles, strangles or involve complex options such as averages, vanishes, knock-ins, triggers, lookbacks, lookforwards, digitals and currency protected structures; so-called quantos or diffs. We will look at one example of a structured swap in the next section.

A basic tailored financial package swap structure is the simple Libor linked note. A Libor linked note provides the investor with a simple performance play on the level of Libor at the maturity of the note:

Instrument:	Euro medium term note
Total size:	USD 10 million
Start date:	10th June 1996
Maturity date:	10th June 1997
Price:	100 per cent
Coupon:	7.00 per cent paid annually in arrears
Redemption:	100 per cent + leverage × Z (subject to a minimum of 0 per cent)
Formula for Z:	

$$\frac{\text{Strike rate} - \text{1-year Libor at maturity} \times (\text{Actual days}/360)}{1 + \text{1-year Libor at maturity}/100 \times (\text{Actual days}/(360))}$$

Leverage:	Six times
Strike rate:	5.75 per cent

Libor setting: 1-year Libor rate will be set two London business days before
the maturity date according to Telerate page 3750

In the above example the redemption of the note is linked to the level of 12-month Libor
at maturity.

Table 5.14 Table of redemption prices and
annual yield for Libor linked note

Libor (%)	Redemption (%)	Yield (%)
4.50	107.27	14.27
4.75	105.80	12.80
5.00	104.34	11.34
5.25	102.89	9.89
5.50	101.44	8.44
5.75	100.00	7.00
6.00	98.57	5.57
6.25	97.14	4.14
6.50	95.72	2.72
6.75	94.31	1.31
7.00	92.90	−0.10

The note is constructed through the combination of a one-year USD 10 million face
value floating rate note paying interest six monthly, issued at its face value, representing
the issuer's obligations on the financing provided. A one-year interest rate swap to
exchange the issuer's six-monthly Libor payments for one single interest payment at
maturity is also based on USD 10 million and a USD 60 million 12/24 FRA.

5.9 USING ZERO COUPON PRICING TO VALUE
A SIMPLE SWAP STRUCTURE

The Libor in arrears structure first appeared in the mid 1980s as a simple structure which
allowed borrowers to take advantage of expectations of falling interest rates. Borrowers
normally borrow with interest calculated in advance and settled at the end of each interest
period. In a Libor in arrears swap the borrower pays at the end of each interest period the
interest amount which is calculated by reference to the Libor rate at that time not at the
beginning of the original interest period. Thus the rate for calculation purposes is always
the rate at the end of the interest period (see Table 5.15).

Table 5.15 Libor in arrears swap

	Borrower Receives	Borrower Pays
Year 0		
Year 1/2	6m Libor$_1$	6m Libor$_2$
Year 1	6m Libor$_2$	6m Libor$_3$
Year 1 1/2	6m Libor$_3$	6m Libor$_4$
Year 2	6m Libor$_4$	6m Libor$_5$

Table 5.16 Valuation of Libor in arrears swap

			Libor in Arrears		
Date	Par Swap Rates	Discount Factors	Normal FRAs	Arrears FRAs	Difference (%)
11/11/95		1.00000			
11/11/96	6.5625	0.93826	6.5625	7.3411	0.779
11/11/97	6.9375	0.87409	7.3411	8.1546	0.813
11/11/98	7.3125	0.80819	8.1546	9.0143	0.860
11/11/99	7.6875	0.74136	9.0143		
		Present Value of Difference (%)			2.136
		Annual Equivalent (%)			0.815

We can use our zero coupon approach to calculate quickly the value of this swap. Let us consider an example of a three-year annual Libor in arrears structure. The borrower in the swap expects to receive the normal stream of Libor payments which he can use to offset his underlying cost of borrowing. He, in return, contracts to pay the arrears calculated Libor payments on the same settlement dates as the underlying borrowing. The obligation to pay the Libor stream can be hedged via an interest rate swap or more conveniently via a strip of FRAs, 12/24, 24/36, etc. The arrears side of the swap locks in these same rates but as if each is paid one period early (see Table 5.16). The structure can be valued as two strips of FRAs.

In order to induce the borrower to enter into the above Libor in arrears swap he would need to pay to the swap counterpart not Libor flat but Libor in arrears less 0.815 per cent per annum — a significant reduction. Herein lies the interest in the Libor in arrears structure. If the borrower believes that interest rates are unlikely to rise over the life of the swap or alternatively that they may rise but not to the levels implied by the forward curve, i.e. up to 8.15 per cent by year three, the structure makes economic sense to the borrower. In simple marketing terms if he believes that Libor will not rise by more than 0.815 per cent per annum he will profit from the structure overall and he will secure the full value of an outcome which he does not expect.

It is immediately apparent that a rational borrower would not execute a Libor in arrears structure without some view on the direction and timing of interest rates. It is less obvious that this is equally true of the decision to execute any interest rate swap. The forward rates derived from the current yield curve are our best approximation, with a small adjustment, to the market's best expectation of interest rates in the future and the decision to enter into a swap for a borrower to pay fixed is ultimately the decision to lock into those implied forward rates.

PART 2
Risk Measurement

A Survey of Risk Measurement Theory and Practice

STAN BECKERS

6.1 INTRODUCTION

Financial risk quantification, analysis and control have evolved dramatically over the last decades. The old approach may be illustrated by the advice from the American comic Will Rogers (1879–1935): "Buy a stock. If it goes up, sell it. If it doesn't go up, don't buy it." In the old days, individual positions were evaluated separately on their own merits and risk was defined as negative return. Significant advances in academic theory have had a major impact on practical risk measurement. Applications such as risk diversification, portfolio construction and hedging are no longer the esoteric domain of the academic ivory tower but are now widely applied by every bank, market-maker, investment management organization and pension fund.

In this chapter, we will briefly sketch the major academic developments that are generally considered as milestones in our thinking about risk: the principle of risk diversification, beta as an exponent of the single index model and multiple factor models. This gradual progression reflects an increasingly richer description and quantification of the risk dimension.

As the academic treatment of risk became multidimensional and more "realistic", the resulting interplay between academic and real world led to ever broader applications. In particular, the idea that risk is a relative rather than absolute concept highlighted the need to identify and clearly specify the neutral or benchmark position. We will show that benchmarking is therefore an essential prerequisite for a systematic and structured approach to risk control.

Finally, we will briefly dwell upon the added complexity of risk in internationally diversified portfolios or books. In particular, it is not *a priori* clear what repercussions the growing international economic integration has on the risk profile of "global" positions. The international economic fabric is generally assumed to change rather slowly. Structural change would therefore be hard to detect. The same cannot be said, however, for the

The Handbook of Risk Management and Analysis. Edited by Carol Alexander
© 1996 John Wiley & Sons Ltd

associated currency regimes. We will therefore also look into the complexities of currency risk management as a special case of international portfolio diversification.

Before we dive into the intricacies of exchange rate risk, we need to return to the roots of all modern risk analysis.

6.2 THE BASICS

6.2.1 Markowitz and the Principle of Diversification

There is no doubt that all modern forms of risk quantification find their origins in the seminal work of Harry Markowitz (1959): *Portfolio Selection: Efficient Diversification of Investments*. Although the idea of not putting all your eggs in one basket was certainly not new, Markowitz was the first to formalize and apply it to financial instruments. He started from the assumption that each portfolio construction decision can be structured in function of the expected mean and standard deviation of the portfolio return.[1] His main insights can be summarized as follows:

- Whereas the portfolio return is a simple weighted average of the individual asset returns, the portfolio risk will typically be less than the weighted average of the individual asset risks

- The portfolio risk will be lower, the lower the correlations between the constituent asset returns (the famous diversification principle)

- Therefore the risk of each asset can be thought of as consisting of two components: some of its risk can be made to disappear through a judicious combination of this asset with other assets (the diversifiable risk). The other part will always have to be borne by an investor.

Portfolio selection was reduced to the choice of maximizing the return whilst at the same time minimizing the risk. An investor who is driven by this mean-standard deviation criterion would make a rational choice that could be formalized in a quadratic programming problem.

As a result of this problem formulation, the correlation between different financial instruments came to the fore as the crucial characteristic that defines the optimal portfolio profile. It also helped establish the notion that an instrument cannot be evaluated in isolation: its attractiveness will largely depend on its contribution towards the overall portfolio return and standard deviation.

Risk characterization and quantification using Markowitz's approach presupposes a knowledge of the "full covariance matrix", e.g. an exact measure of means, standard deviations and correlations of all assets under consideration. The practical estimation of this covariance matrix is not straightforward since the standard deviations and correlations need to be estimated on the basis of historic time series using daily, weekly or monthly observations. The length of the observation history to be used is partially determined by the number of assets in the matrix: to ensure that the covariance matrix is well behaved (semi-positive definite), the number of observations has to (significantly) exceed the number of assets.

For example, a covariance matrix of 30 different assets will have 435 different entries. Estimating these covariances using 12 observations would result in a matrix with rank 66.

Intuitively, this is equivalent to saying that 66 out of the 435 entries contain information whereas the remaining 369 estimates would be pure noise.

In addition, at least 200 observations are typically needed to reduce the standard error of the correlation coefficients to reasonable proportions.[2] Although the standard error of the estimates can be reduced by increasing the number of observations, this will also amplify the risk of incompletely capturing a structural change in the relationships. Using long time series, there is a significant danger that fundamental changes in the interrelationships will be lost in the large number of observations. Luckily, the structural behaviour of some asset categories (such as equity markets) will only change slowly relative to each other. In other cases, such as exchange rates for instance, violent and significant structural shifts are commonplace.[3] These structural changes will be picked up slowly using the historical covariance matrix, thereby reducing the practical relevance of the "full covariance" approach.

In sum, the practical implementation of the full covariance approach to risk estimation as developed by Markowitz runs into severe implementation problems when large numbers of assets are involved and especially when returns are not jointly stationary. This observation naturally leads us to the question of modelling the risk (variances and correlations) as a function of the underlying asset characteristics. An important step in this direction was the Capital Asset Pricing Model (CAPM).

6.2.2 Sharpe and the Distinction Between Systematic and Residual Risk

Markowitz's book revolutionized economic thinking, particularly a little known aspect of it — financial economics. Indeed, until then most academic work had concentrated on corporate finance and financial statement analysis. Structured portfolio selection opened new opportunities for quantitatively oriented financial economists.

(i) The Capital Asset Pricing Model

The next leap forward was achieved by the work of Sharpe (1964), Lintner (1965) and Mossin (1966). They extended the portfolio diversification principle of Markowitz by introducing the (simplifying) assumption of homogeneous expectations: if all interested parties agree on the expected returns, standard deviations and correlations of the available investment alternatives, they will effectively be facing the same opportunity set. Assuming that they behave rationally as defined by the Markowitz portfolio selection rule, they will all end up choosing the same portfolio.

The formalization of this analysis led to the Capital Asset Pricing Model that would dominate academic thinking for the next decades. It is important to note that the model is a normative equilibrium model: it prescribes how the world should behave if all investors are rational and markets are efficient.[4] Under these circumstances only the non-diversifiable risk of an asset would be rewarded. (Why would one expect to be compensated for needlessly carrying diversifiable risk?) Formally:

$$E(R_j) = R_f + \beta_j[E(R_M) - (R_f)] \tag{1}$$

where $E(R_j)$ = expected return on asset (portfolio) j, β_j = Covariance(R_j, R_M)/Variance(R_M), $E(R_M)$ = expected return on the capitalization weighted portfolio of all assets and R_f = risk-free return.

It is not surprising that the Capital Asset Pricing Model was not enthusiastically received by the financial community. It effectively says that 99 per cent of all financial analysts, investment managers, brokers and market-makers are wasting their time and have no socially redeeming value. Indeed, if the world would behave exactly as prescribed by the Capital Asset Pricing Model:

- Then all investors would hold the same portfolio (i.e. the market portfolio), which — by definition — is perfectly diversified

- The only thing one would ever need to know about an asset would be its beta with respect to the market portfolio (since the beta fully determines its expected return)

Luckily financial practitioners don't have to feel guilty about their scepticism because the Capital Asset Pricing Model is very hard to validate empirically: it is set in terms of expected returns which are not directly observable and the "market portfolio", which contains all assets (not restricted to those traded in financial markets), is impossible to quantify (Roll (1977)).

(ii) Single Factor Models of Risk

The major value of the Capital Asset Pricing Model must therefore not be sought in its formalization of the (normative) return generating equation, but mainly in the fact that it helped structure the risk quantification and decomposition. Early attempts to empirically validate the Capital Asset Pricing Model relied upon time series regressions of the following form:

$$R_{jt} - R_{ft} = \alpha_j + \beta_j(I_{mt} - R_{ft}) + \varepsilon_{jt} \qquad (2)$$

where R_{jt} = return to asset j in period t, R_{ft} = risk free rate in period t, I_{mt} = return to market index m in period t, α_j = non-index related return to asset j, β_j = beta of asset j with respect to index I and ε_{jt} = residual return of asset j in period t.

If *ex post* realized returns over long periods accurately reflect *ex ante* expectations and if index I_m completely captures the market portfolio, then the regression test would be a direct test of the CAPM. (According to the theory one would then expect $\alpha_j = 0$.) It is now generally accepted that both of these conditions never hold and that therefore the CAPM cannot be empirically (in)validated.

The above equation, however, is much more interesting because it helps segment the return on an asset in an index related component and a return that is residual to the index. This segmentation does not require any financial theory and can be performed with respect to any index. It has significant repercussions for the risk decomposition of an asset:

- The risk equivalent of equation (2) is

$$\sigma_j^2 = \beta_j^2\sigma_I^2 + \sigma_\varepsilon^2 \qquad (3)$$

where σ_ε^2 = Variance of ε_{jt}. In words, the total risk of an asset (portfolio) can be divided into two orthogonal components that can be visualized as shown in Figure 6.1. Note that by construction the residual return will always be independent of the index related return.

- The crucial risk measure of an asset (portfolio) is the beta of that asset (portfolio) where beta is defined as Covariance (r_j, r_I)/Variance (r_I) and r_j and r_I are the excess return on asset (portfolio) j and the index respectively.[5] This beta is related to the

Figure 6.1

hedge ratio that determines the number of index futures contracts that need to be sold to eliminate the index related risk from the portfolio[6].

Using old capital markets terminology the beta as measured by (2) is nothing more than a quantification of the extent to which a stock is cyclical (high beta) or defensive (low beta) with respect to the prevalent index. In sum, although the single index model (2) finds its origins in the early attempts to test the Capital Asset Pricing Model, it has now taken on a life of its own as a convenient way to segment the risk of an asset into index related and residual risk. Since the Single Index Model is not based on any financial theory, it does not presuppose whether a_j should be zero or not.

The practical implementation of the risk segmentation (3) is flawed by the simplifying assumptions underlying (2):

- The correlation between the different assets arises from a common source, i.e. the index. No other sources of communality (correlation) are recognized.
- The measure of communality (beta) is assumed to be stationary through time. Relatively long time series are needed to obtain accurate estimates of beta. At best regression (2) will have an R^2 of 35 per cent for individual equities[7].
- The residual risk σ_ε^2 is assumed to be entirely company specific and would diversify very quickly. There is no correlation between the company specific returns.

As a result, the main use of the single index model (2) is typically concentrated in hedging away the benchmark related risk in portfolios or books using index-based futures or derivatives. Very few organizations or academics would "model" asset risk based on one explanatory variable. On the contrary, it is now generally recognized that risk is multidimensional and needs to be explained using a multitude of characteristics or attributes. This has naturally led to Multiple Factor Models.

6.3 MULTIPLE FACTOR MODELS

Although the empirical evidence substantiating the multidimensional nature of risk goes back to the late 1960s,[8] its standing was significantly enhanced through the development of the Arbitrage Pricing Theory (Ross (1976)). The Arbitrage Pricing Theory can be thought of as a generalization of the Capital Asset Pricing Model. Using a somewhat less restrictive set of assumptions (mainly doing away with the need for investors to make decisions on the basis of mean and standard deviation), the theory infers that there may be a multitude of risk premia associated with an individual asset.[9] Unfortunately the theory does not tell us how many risk factors could be at play. *A fortiori* it cannot identify the exact nature of these risk factors.

The multifactor Arbitrage Pricing Theory can be formulated as follows:

$$E(R_j) = R_f + \beta_{1j}[E(F_1) - R_f] + \beta_{2j}[E(F_2) - R_f] + \beta_{3j}[E(F_3) - R_f] + \beta_{4j}[E(F_4) - R_f] + \cdots \tag{4}$$

where $E(R_j)$ = expected return on asset (portfolio) j, β_{ij} = sensitivity of asset j to risk factor i, R_f = risk-free return and $E(F_i) - R_f$ = expected risk premium associated with factor i.

The Arbitrage Pricing Theory (as the Capital Asset Pricing Model) is a normative equilibrium theory. If indeed, on average, assets would behave as prescribed by the theory, we would observe

$$R_{jt} - R_{ft} = \alpha_j + \beta_{1j}(F_{1t} - R_{ft}) + \beta_{2j}(F_{2t} - R_{ft}) + \beta_{3j}(F_{3t} - R_{ft}) + \beta_{4j}(F_{4t} - R_{ft}) + \cdots + \varepsilon_{jt} \tag{5}$$

where R_{jt} = return to asset j in period t, R_{ft} = risk-free rate in period t, F_{it} = risk premium associated with factor i in period t, α_j = non-factor related return to asset j, β_{ij} = sensitivity of asset j with respect to risk factor i and ε_{jt} = residual return of asset j in period t.

Since α_j should be zero (no free lunch), the stylized matrix notation of equation (5) can be written as:

$$\mathbf{R_t} = \mathbf{B f_t} + \mathbf{E_t} \tag{6}$$

where $\mathbf{R_t}$ = vector of individual asset excess returns (over the risk-free rate) for period t, $\mathbf{B}$ = matrix of asset exposures to the different risk factors, $\mathbf{f_t}$ = vector of factor risk premia (in excess over the risk-free rate) for period t and $\mathbf{E_t}$ = vector of individual asset residual returns for period t with corresponding risks.

$$\mathbf{V} = \mathbf{B'FB} + \mathbf{\Omega} \tag{7}$$

where $\mathbf{V}$ = covariance matrix of asset returns $\mathbf{R_t}$, $\mathbf{F}$ = covariance matrix of factor risk premia $\mathbf{f_t}$ and $\mathbf{\Omega}$ = (diagonal) matrix of asset residual risks $\mathbf{E_t}$.

Close inspection of equation (7) reveals that in fact the original Markowitz "full covariance" matrix is broken up into factor related risks and residual risks. The notion of a multitude of risk factors driving asset returns is now widely accepted. Unfortunately the identification of these risk factors remains an empirical exercise about which there is no consensus. Broadly speaking three approaches can be used to identify these factors. They can be classified by which components of (6) are presupposed to be known: fundamental factor models assume the $\mathbf{B}$ as given and estimate the $\mathbf{f_t}$. Macroeconomics models on the other hand take the $\mathbf{f_t}$ as given and estimate the $\mathbf{B}$. Statistical models try simultaneously to estimate $\mathbf{B}$ and $\mathbf{f_t}$. In the following paragraphs we will briefly discuss each of these alternatives.

6.3.1 Fundamental Factor Models

Fundamental factor models try to fill in equation (6) based on the observation of the day-to-day activity of investment managers, brokers and financial analysts. In their pursuit of return, they use a multitude of decision variables. It is therefore reasonable to assume that these decision variables have some relation to the factor sensitivities $\mathbf{B}$. Although it is virtually impossible to draw up a completely exhaustive list of factor exposures $\mathbf{B}$, there is a fairly large consensus on the company or asset characteristics which are assumed to play a role in explaining differential asset returns. Among these are: market capitalization, asset liquidity, price earnings ratio, interest rate sensitivity, stability of earnings growth, dividend yield, exchange rate sensitivity as well as the economic or industrial sectors in which the company operates. The fundamental factor model uses these company or asset attributes as proxies for $\mathbf{B}$. A cross-sectional regression of the type (6) will identify whether for any time period t there was a significant risk premium $\mathbf{f_t}$ associated with some or all of these attributes.

Estimating the cross-sectional regressions (6) over consecutive time periods will yield a history of factor risk premia $\mathbf{f_t}$ which can be used to estimate the factor covariance matrix $\mathbf{F}$. The main advantage of this approach is the fact that it allows for quick adaptations to structural changes in asset characteristics: the effect of an exogenous change in the company's dividend yield or leverage (interest rate sensitivity) will feed through immediately in that company's risk characterization in equation (7). Indeed, given $\mathbf{F}$, the volatility and correlation of any asset (not necessarily market traded) can be derived immediately from its attributes $\mathbf{B}$.

The disadvantage of the fundamental factor approach derives from the fact that it presupposes that an exhaustive set of mutually exclusive company attributes $\mathbf{B}$ can be identified and quantified. If an important attribute is overlooked, the resulting residual variance matrix $\mathbf{\Omega}$ in (7) will not be diagonal, potentially resulting in an underestimation of the real portfolio risk. Since the matrix $\mathbf{\Omega}$ is assumed to be diagonal, all specific return correlations are by definition set to zero. If unidentified common factors are left undetected in the specific return series, the true correlations between the specific returns will be non-zero. These specific risks will therefore not diversify as quickly as assumed by the zero correlation assumption.

Fundamental factor models are probably the most widely used for risk estimation and quantification purposes. Separate models have been estimated for about 20 of the leading stock markets across the world. Table 6.1 summarizes the fundamental company attributes that have been found to be relevant in a representative sample of these markets. Note that some attributes are found to contribute consistently to explaining differential stock returns in all markets (such as market capitalization, price earnings ratio, recent performance), whereas others (such as book value to market value) are unique to a given market.

6.3.2 Macroeconomic Factor Models

Instead of taking the asset sensitivities to the different factors as given, macroeconomic models try to approximate the factor risk premia $\mathbf{f_t}$ through a time series of macroeconomic variables. This approach presupposes that the macroeconomic events which have a pervasive impact on the future cash flows (and therefore present values and returns) of different assets can be identified. Since expected changes are already reflected in current prices, this approach tries to link surprises in major macroeconomic events to individual asset behaviour.

The empirical implementation of this approach has many variants. However, the following set of unexpected changes is typically used as a proxy for the time series $\mathbf{f_t}$: changes in inflation, industrial production, investor confidence[10] and interest rates. Note that each of these variables can be expected to impact the (real) present value of the future cash flow of most assets.

The predefined time series $\mathbf{f_t}$ (e.g. the realized unexpected changes in the above variables) can then be used in a time series estimation of (6) to identify $\mathbf{B}$, the average

Table 6.1 Fundamental factors

	US	Japan	UK	Germany	France	Switzerland
Historic Volatility	X	X	X	X	X	X
Recent Performance (Momentum)	X	X	X	X	X	X
Market Capitalization	X	X	X	X	X	X
Liquidity	X	X	X		X	
Earnings Growth	X	X	X			X
Price/ Earnings	X	X	X	X	X	X
Book Price	X					
Earnings Variability	X		X	X		X
Leverage	X	X	X	X	X	X
Foreign Income	X	X	X	X		
Labour Intensity	X		X	X	X	
Yield	X		X	X	X	X
Interest Rate Sensitivity		X				
+ Industries						

Source: BARRA International.

sensitivity of each asset to these risk premia. Note that this estimation procedure is conceptually very similar to the time series estimation of beta in the single index model (2). It therefore suffers from the same drawback, namely that the estimated factor exposure of an asset will change only slowly through time. Conversely it will take some time before a structural change in the characteristics of an asset will feed through in the estimated **B**.

The macroeconomic model also shares the drawback of the fundamental model in that an accurate estimation of (6) assumes that all pervasive risk premia can be exactly identified and quantified (and that they are more or less mutually exclusive).

A risk analysis using the macroeconomic model would proceed along the same lines as the fundamental factor approach: given **B** and $\mathbf{f_t}$, equation (7) can be used to characterize the risk of any combination of assets.

6.3.3 Statistical Models

Statistical models are most closely associated with the original tests of the Arbitrage Pricing Theory. As the name implies, they rely upon pure statistical analysis of the return series to infer **B** and $\mathbf{f_t}$. The statistical model pleads total ignorance about the nature of the risk premia or factor sensitivities that are at play within a given market.

The statistical model uses the full covariance matrix $\mathbf{V}$ as a starting point and applies a factor analysis or principal components procedure to decompose $\mathbf{V}$. The statistical procedure will typically yield a set of factor exposures $\mathbf{B}$, which can then be used in cross-sectional regression (6) to yield the factor return $\mathbf{f_t}$. The procedure is conceptually similar to the fundamental factor approach, except that the factor exposures are identified using a statistical procedure rather than (subjective) fundamental analysis. The statistical model has the significant advantage that the factor exposures are completely orthogonal in the estimation sample (but not necessarily out of sample). However, the statistical factor exposures (and associated factor returns) have no direct economic interpretation. Further analysis (and subjective judgement) is needed to attach some economic rationale to the statistical constructs.

The methodology also suffers from the fact that the factor exposures will only change slowly through time and will react to structural changes with a long lag. Obviously the matrix $\mathbf{V}$ can be observed over different time intervals, presumably using the history which is deemed to be most relevant for the forecast horizon. Using slightly shorter or longer histories will yield slightly different factor exposures. However, given the number of observations needed to minimize the estimation error of the (co)variances, in $\mathbf{V}$ it is unlikely that the factor exposures will change significantly from one estimation to the next.

6.3.4 A Comparison

Although each of the three methods has its adherents, arguably the fundamental factor model is used most widely for risk forecasting purposes. This is partially due to the fact that it is couched in a language and uses concepts that most financial analysts, brokers, market-makers and investment managers are familiar with. The out-of-sample risk forecasts will — by nature — also react more quickly to structural changes.

A recent article by Connor (1995) compares the explanatory power of the three models as applied to the US equity market and concludes that the statistical and fundamental models significantly outperform the macroeconomic model. The fundamental model also has a slight edge over the statistical model.

It is interesting to note that the risk breakdown as described in (7) (irrespective of the estimation procedure) also allows for the refined estimation of drift in certain components of $\mathbf{F}$ or $\mathbf{\Omega}$. Indeed the GARCH class of estimation procedures can be applied to the time series of asset related factor variances or residual variances.

In general the multiple factor models allow for a refined breakdown of the asset risks and correlations and hereby improve upon forecasting accuracy by separating structural sources of variability from the incidental ones.

6.4 ABSOLUTE vs. RELATIVE RISK

The risk models we discussed in Section 2.1 form the core of all risk measurement and management activities. In fact, the matrices $\mathbf{V}$ and $\mathbf{F}$ can be thought of as the engines that drive all risk quantification. The usage of these models will differ significantly depending on objectives and time frame. In the following paragraphs we will discuss the essential role of the benchmark in all risk control activities. Indeed risk is always a relative concept and it cannot be discussed meaningfully unless the neutral point has been identified. Whereas market-makers and corporate treasurers probably worry most about the absolute value of money at risk, money managers are continually evaluated against their peer group. This leads to two distinct applications of the risk models.

6.4.1 The Role of the Benchmark

Risk quantification is (should be) at the core of all activities for traders, corporate treasurers and market-makers. They worry about how much money they stand to make or lose, given their current positions. They typically have a short time frame that is measured in terms of days or (at most) weeks. Their natural risk measure is therefore the value at risk in their current positions.

This value at risk concept can be quantified using the covariance matrix $\mathbf{V}$ as follows.

Let $\mathbf{P}$ be the vector of (dollar) value positions in the different instruments (i.e. each component P_i is the dollar amount in instrument or asset class i). Note that this vector can contain both positive and negative values. The value at risk (VAR) is then derived from $(\mathbf{P}'\mathbf{V}\mathbf{P})^{1/2}$, after translation into an appropriate confidence interval.

This VAR tells us how much money the aggregate position can make or lose with 66 per cent probability. (Doubling the number will increase the confidence band to 95 per cent.) The time horizon over which this forecast applies depends on the nature of the matrix $\mathbf{V}$. If $\mathbf{V}$ is calibrated within a daily time frame (i.e. it is put together using daily data), then the risk forecast will apply over a one-day horizon.[11] VAR implicitly assumes that putting the aggregate value of all positions on short-term (one day, a week ...) deposit is the neutral or benchmark position. VAR therefore effectively measures how much more money can be made or lost in comparison to a short-term deposit strategy.

Whether the value at risk is acceptable or not depends crucially on the capital backing up the positions. The VAR can be used directly to evaluate whether the minimum solvency requirements are met.

Note that the VAR concept is different from the risk characterization as proposed by the Basle Committee of the Bank for International Settlements and from the European Union Directive (EEC 93/6). These regulatory authorities ignore the impact of the covariance matrix $\mathbf{V}$ and consider the risks in individual positions to be completely additive. This results in more stringent capital requirements than those implied by the value at risk number. Banks and traders are consequently required to be better capitalized than strictly necessary given the real risks being incurred. It is somewhat disappointing that these capital adequacy standards make no allowance for the potential diversification effect of offsetting positions.

Whereas market operators have a short time frame and are mainly concerned about not losing (too much) money, investment managers are working with slightly different objectives. Portfolio managers are typically expected to outperform the market average or their peer group (or both). They will be evaluated over longer time frames (typically on an annual cycle).

In fact the (implicit or explicit) objective of most portfolio managers is to add value relative to a predefined alternative. This alternative is often defined as a market index. Presumably the owner of the funds argues that she does not have to hire a highly paid investment manager to produce the average return as reflected in the market index. Indeed, over the past decade a number of investment managers have specialized in providing nothing more than this "average" index return. These index fund managers typically succeed in very closely mimicking the index return at extremely low costs.[12]

The objective of the portfolio manager is therefore to create a portfolio that is sufficiently different from the index to allow her to outperform it. This leads to a segmentation of the portfolio risk into two components: the risk inherent in the benchmark and the active risk added onto it by the portfolio manager.

It is fair to argue that the benchmark risk is the responsibility of the owner of the funds: she sets the target and requests the manager to outperform the target. Let us assume that a client decides to invest in a Japanese mutual fund and learns from the manager that this fund targets an outperformance of the Nikkei 225 index. If, subsequently, the Japanese equity market crashes resulting in a negative return on the Nikkei 225, the client cannot blame the manager for the resulting losses. In fact a manager can have performed well by losing less money than the benchmark (for example by turning in a return of −10 per cent when the index does −15 per cent). Conversely a manager who achieves a return of 30 per cent when the benchmark has a total return of 35 per cent has nothing to be proud of.

The above example illustrates the segmentation of the risk in institutionally managed portfolios: benchmark related risk is the responsibility of the owner of the funds. The investment manager tries to add value relative to the benchmark by incurring active risk relative to the benchmark. Mathematically this active risk can be expressed as follows:

Let $\mathbf{W_p}$ = vector of portfolio weights (i.e. W_{iP} is the percentage weight of asset i in the portfolio P)

$\quad\mathbf{W_M}$ = vector of index weights (i.e. W_{iM} is the percentage weight of asset i in index M)

then the active variance risk of portfolio P is given by

$$(\mathbf{W_p} - \mathbf{W_M})'\mathbf{V}(\mathbf{W_p} - \mathbf{W_M}) \tag{8}$$

Note that the active risk uses percentage weights to measure the exposure to the risk matrix $\mathbf{V}$. The active risk is a direct function of the extent to which individual assets are weighted differently to their weight in the index (if all $\mathbf{W_p}$ are equal to $\mathbf{W_M}$, the active risk will be zero). The direct implication of this observation is that the neutral (no information) position in an asset is the market weight.

Given that the exposures are expressed in percentage weights, the active risk will be expressed in percentage terms. An active risk of 5 per cent, for instance, would imply that the portfolio has a 66 per cent (95 per cent) chance to obtain a return bounded by the benchmark return plus or minus 5 per cent (10 per cent).

Since the time horizon used to evaluate investment managers usually extends over longer time periods (anywhere from one to three years), the matrix $\mathbf{V}$ will typically be estimated using monthly observations. The resulting risk measures can be annualized by multiplying them by the square root of 12. Active risks are mostly quoted on an annual basis.

6.4.2 The Notion of Tracking Error

The active risk of the portfolio is mostly referred to as the tracking error since it quantifies the extent to which the portfolio can be expected to obtain a differential return from the benchmark. It is a direct quantification of the aggressiveness of the portfolio manager's style: managers who aggressively pursue outperformance of the benchmark will do so by holding assets in wildly different weights $\mathbf{W_p}$ from their benchmark weights $\mathbf{W_M}$. This may result in tracking errors of up to 10 per cent or more. Conservative managers on the other hand may have tracking errors of 2 per cent to 4 per cent. Index fund managers will have tracking errors of less than 0.50 per cent.[13]

An alternative way of looking at the tracking error can be derived from equation (1):

$$E(R_p) - R_f = \beta_p[E(R_M) - R_f] + E(e_p)$$

i.e. the excess return on portfolio p is proportional to the beta of the portfolio with respect to index M. (Note that $E(e_p)$ is zero according to the Capital Asset Pricing Model.)

Therefore the active return of the portfolio over the market index M is

$$[E(R_p) - R_f] - [E(R_M) - R_f] = \beta_p[E(R_M) - R_f] - [E(R_M) - R_f] + E(e_p)$$

and the variance of the active return is given by $(\beta_p - 1)^2\sigma_M^2 + \sigma_\varepsilon^2$. This alternative expression for the tracking error variance (which can be shown to be mathematically equivalent to expression (8)) clearly illustrates the two main sources of potential value added: the tracking error will increase as the portfolio beta will deviate significantly from 1 and as the residual risk of the portfolio increases.

Illustrating this with a practical example, assume that the portfolio has a beta of 0.8 and a residual risk of 5 per cent. If the standard deviation of the market index is 20 per cent, the tracking error will be $\sqrt{[(0.8 - 1)^2 \cdot 400 + 25]} = 6.40$ per cent, implying that the return on this portfolio will, two years out of three, deviate up to 6.4 per cent from the market index return.

The sources of value added (and associated risks) in a portfolio can be broken down into two components: market timing and less than perfect diversification (giving rise to residual risk). In practice very few portfolio managers will aggressively engage in market timing since it is an "all or nothing" strategy. By constructing a portfolio with a beta that is significantly higher (or lower) than 1, the portfolio manager effectively bets on an exceptionally high (low) index risk premium. The market will very quickly prove the manager right or wrong.

Conversely there are thousands of ways of introducing residual risk in the portfolio. The manager can

- overweight or underweight individual stocks relative to their index weights (stock picking)
- over- or underemphasize individual sectors or industries
- take a view with respect to certain types of companies (such as high yield, small capitalization, low price earnings, etc.).

In other words, there are thousands of sources of residual risk in the portfolio. Each investment manager will have her own preferences, giving rise to her own investment style. There are as many styles as there are investment management organizations, although a number of classifications of style have been introduced (such as small capitalization, value, growth, income etc.). Table 6.2 summarizes the most frequently used investment styles, together with the associated tracking errors.

It is also worth mentioning that the tracking error is directly related to the business risk of the investment manager: portfolios with a high tracking error have a higher probability of significantly outperforming (underperforming) the benchmark. Since there is a high correlation between out (under)performance and client (dis)satisfaction, only investment managers with strong convictions can afford to run portfolios with high tracking

Table 6.2

Investment Style	Typical Tracking Error Relative to Cap Weighted Market Index (%)
Market Timer	>10
Small Capitalization	>7
Growth	>5
Value (Income)	>4
Quantitative	>4
Traditional Stock Picker	2–4
Tilted Fund	2
Index Fund	<0.50

errors. The self-preservation instinct of most portfolio managers drives them towards lower (safer) tracking errors: they prefer to make many small bets in a portfolio rather than a few big ones.

Very crudely it can be said that investment management organizations sell tracking error to their clients. It is up to the client to decide how much tracking error she would like to bear and which kinds of tracking error are more likely to give rise to market outperformance. Although there is a bewildering choice of tracking errors and styles on offer, it is a sobering thought that by definition the average reward to all these tracking errors is zero.[14]

Although tracking error can be measured with respect to any benchmark, the point of reference that is most frequently used is the market index. However, as is evident from equation (8), the formula can be applied with respect to any externally defined neutral position. In the extreme, a short-term time deposit could be used as the benchmark in which case (8) reduces to measuring the total volatility of the portfolio (over the appropriate risk-free rate). (The tracking error with respect to the risk-free rate is the total portfolio risk.)

The quantification of the portfolio tracking error only presupposes that a benchmark has been predefined. A portfolio manager will (should) be at a loss as to what to do if the performance benchmark has not been identified *a priori* (choosing W_p if W_M is unknown is virtually impossible). Although this seems a self-evident truth, there are still many portfolio managers who take on mandates without exactly agreeing with the client on the benchmark. Not surprisingly they feel unfairly treated when *ex post* the client pulls a different performance evaluation benchmark out of a hat.[15]

6.4.3 Concluding Remarks

Although value at risk and tracking error both use matrix V as the "driving" force, the accuracy of the risk model plays a more important role in the value at risk calculation. Indeed, the tracking error typically concentrates on a small proportion of the total portfolio risk (the tracking error rarely makes up more than 20 per cent of the portfolio risk). The value at risk calculation on the other hand is a direct function of the total volatility of the aggregate position value.

This does not diminish the importance of accurate risk forecasting for both types of applications. It should be kept in mind that there is no such thing as a risk model that will satisfy all needs: traders and treasurers will be interested in short-term fluctuations and short-term risk whereas portfolio managers' V should satisfy long-term

Table 6.3 A comparison of short-term vs. long-term risk models

Factors	US	UK
Capitalization	X	X
Short-Term Beta		X
Short-Term Volatility	X	X
Short-Term Momentum		
+ Industries	X	X
Typical R^2 (Adj)	0.23	0.22
Typical R^2 (Adj) Long-Term Fundamental Factor Model	0.38	0.35

Source: BARRA International.

needs. These different objectives will also be reflected in the factor decomposition of the different **V**.

Short-term risk models are much more driven by technical factors related to market imbalances (such as liquidity, turnover, bid–ask spread, high–low, open interest, etc.) which help explain differential short-term volatility of different assets. Long-term risk models in turn are more sensitive to the fundamental characteristics of the underlying instruments (such as the vital signals that are reflected in balance sheet and income statements). A factor decomposition of matrix **V** will therefore crucially depend on the forecast time horizon.

Table 6.3 illustrates the "fundamental" factors driving a short-term risk model for the US and UK equity market.

Note that the explanatory power of the short-term risk model is significantly lower than that of a longer-term model. This is due to the prevalence of more idiosyncratic events in day-to-day observations (whereas the impact of these events would be diversified away through time and therefore have less impact on monthly observations). Short-term risk is also much less stable through time given the transient nature of short-term market themes or forces.

However, this does not mean that longer-term risks are immune to structural changes in the underlying relationships. A good risk model will try to adapt as quickly as possible to these changes. This is the theme we turn to next.

6.5 INTERNATIONAL PORTFOLIO DIVERSIFICATION

The benefits of risk diversification derive from the fact that individual positions have less than perfect correlation. Casual empiricism suggests that international capital markets are becoming more integrated, implying that the correlation between markets, sectors and individual instruments is increasing. The question about the extent to which international markets are segmented or integrated has therefore received a fair amount of attention in the financial literature. In the next paragraph we will review some of the insights that have been derived from this research.

6.5.1 Integration vs. Segmentation

There is currently no clear evidence suggesting that the growing international economic integration (European Economic Community, European Free Trade Association, North

American Free Trade Association, GATT, etc.) results in significant increases in correlations. However, it should be pointed out from the outset that economic integration can be perfectly reconciled with low correlations to the extent that different markets or regions are dominated by different types of industrial activity. For example, despite the growing harmonization of monetary, economic and fiscal policies within the European Economic Union, it is perfectly reasonable to observe a continued low correlation between the French equity market (with a relative dominance of oil and consumer goods) and the German market (banks and chemicals).

As long as low correlations are driven by the different industrial fabric, international diversification will continue to yield significant benefits. The situation changes to the extent that countries with a similar economic profile will be less and less impacted by purely domestic (country specific) events and will be influenced more by transnational (global) effects. Under those circumstances, a growing macroeconomic integration will automatically lead to a stronger correlation on the microeconomic level (at least for companies within the same sector). The question we are effectively asking is to what extent the behaviour of individual stocks is explained by purely domestic factors or by transnational variables and whether the transnational variables have been gaining in explanatory power in the recent past.

Several academic studies have investigated this problem (Grinold, Rudd and Stefek (1989), Beckers, Grinold, Rudd and Stefek (1992), Heston and Rouwenhorst (1994)). They invariably come to the conclusion that stock price behaviour is dominated by purely local (domestic) forces. For example, Grinold et al. (1989) find on the basis of a world-wide sample of 2,500 companies, that the nationality (domicile) of a company is much more powerful than a company's industrial classification in explaining differential stock returns. A similar conclusion was arrived at by Beckers et al. (1992) for a sample of 1,400 European stocks: the R^2 for a typical company is 32 per cent using country of domicile as explanatory variable whereas industrial classification only accounts for 21 per cent of the stock variance. Adding the industrial classification as a second explanatory variable to the country of domicile leads to an insignificant increase in R^2. Both studies also conclude that over the decade of the 1980s, the explanatory power of the transnational industry affiliation variable has not increased (i.e. domestic factors appear to be as important and dominant at the end of the 1980s as at the start of the decade). Heston and Rouwenhorst (1994) similarly conclude that over the last 20 years, industrial structure is a weak explanatory variable when analysing cross-sectional return differences. They find that the low correlation between stock markets is almost completely due to country specific events.

The general evidence therefore points in the direction of markets that continue to be driven by purely domestic factors. This is also reflected in the way in which most portfolio managers and market-makers operate: as long as assets will be classified, analysed and researched first and foremost on the basis of their "nationality" and as long as portfolios will be structured in a top-down fashion (choosing country allocation first before filling in the individual country portfolios), we will continue to observe a dominance of domestic over international factors. There may be a slow shift in the direction of a more global view, mostly at the level of financial analysis where increasingly companies within a given sector are compared to each other, irrespective of their domicile. However, so far this globalization of security analysis has had no discernible impact on individual correlations.

Table 6.4 Local currency perspective correlations: Long-term government bonds (monthly observations (1991:01–1995:02))

Belgium	Denmark	France	Germany	Italy	Neth	Spain	Sweden	UK	
—	0.7123	0.6835	0.7050	0.4901	0.7017	0.6179	0.5644	0.6139	Belgium
	—	0.8343	0.7138	0.5791	0.6984	0.7597	0.5466	0.6698	Denmark
		—	0.8804	0.5856	0.8471	0.6855	0.4991	0.7015	France
			—	0.5032	0.9555	0.5648	0.4598	0.6542	Germany
				—	0.4568	0.7328	0.6049	0.4571	Italy
					—	0.5405	0.4761	0.6780	Neth
						—	0.5777	0.5663	Spain
							—	0.4801	Sweden
								—	UK

The above analyses suffer somewhat from the relatively weak power of statistical significance tests of differences in correlation coefficients. Given that most correlation coefficients are based on a fairly limited set of observations, their estimation error will typically be large (see endnote 2). It is therefore difficult to prove statistically that correlation coefficients have indeed increased (or decreased) significantly through time.

A related but equally relevant question regarding market correlations concerns their stability across different market regimes. A recent study (Erb, Harvey and Viskanta (1994)) hints at the possibility that correlations may be the highest in periods when they matter most. There is indeed some evidence that recent crash periods such as October 1987 have simultaneously and uniformly affected almost all markets. The benefits of international diversification were not as strong during these periods as originally thought on the basis of the average historic correlations. It remains, however, very difficult to establish statistically that correlations are different in down from up markets.

So far we have mainly addressed the question of correlation within and across equity markets. Whereas there is little evidence of significant correlation changes through time, the same cannot be said for the fixed income markets. For instance, we can observe a high degree of correlation in term structure movements within the European Monetary System currencies. Table 6.4 summarizes the (local currency) correlations of bonds returns for the major EMS fixed income markets.

Obviously the benefits of diversification are much less strong within the European government bond markets (with an average correlation of 0.63) than in the corresponding equity markets. The (slow) emergence of a single currency will eventually eliminate these benefits completely.

When evaluating cross-country correlations for equity and fixed income markets, it is easiest to discuss these in local (excess) return terms (as we have done so far), otherwise exchange rate and local market effects are mixed together, thereby confusing the picture. In the following paragraph we will discuss exchange rate (or currency) correlations in more detail.

6.5.2 The Problem of Currency Risk

The currency exposure should be looked at as a separate decision variable when evaluating the risk of internationally diversified portfolios or market-maker positions. Taking on a position outside the non-domestic market does not necessitate carrying the associated currency risk. Let us make this point formally.

Looking at the return received from an internationally diversified position, we will use the following notation:

Let r_n = total rate of return on a foreign asset expressed in the investor's numeraire currency

r_x = rate of return due to changes in exchange rates

r_l = total rate of return on an asset as experienced by a local investor

Therefore $1 + r_n = (1 + r_x)(1 + r_l)$

Let r_{fl} = risk-free rate a local investor would receive in her home market

r_c = random rate of return due to changes in exchange rate plus any interest received as a result of an investment in the foreign risk-free rate

In other words $1 + r_c = (1 + r_x)(1 + r_{fl})$
Therefore

$$r_n = (r_x + r_{fl}) + (r_l - r_{fl}) + r_x r_l$$
$$= r_c + (r_l - r_{fl}) + r_x(r_l - r_{fl})$$

The last term of this expression reflects the cross product of exchange rate movements and excess local market returns. It can be shown that this term is typically negligible (see for instance Beckers et al. (1992)), such that the above expression reduces to

$$r_n = r_c + (r_l - r_{fl}) \tag{10}$$

In other words, the rate of return received from a "foreign" position is approximately equal to the currency rate of return plus the "foreign" excess rate of return. The risk equivalent of (10) is

$$\sigma_n^2 = \sigma_c^2 + \sigma_l^2 + 2\sigma_{cl} \tag{11}$$

The risk can therefore be straightforwardly broken down into currency risk, local market risk and the covariance between them. Although currency risk and local market risk are not necessarily independent (they clearly are not in the case of fixed income instruments), they can be treated separately for risk management and control purposes.

Currency risk is probably the most unstationary of all asset categories. Currencies are subject to periods of excessive volatility and the behaviour of different currencies relative to each other may change dramatically through time (think of the on-again off-again love affair of sterling with respect to the European Monetary System). Estimating currency risks and correlations is therefore the most problematic of all risk measurement activity. For example, Tables 6.5 and 6.6 summarize the correlations in exchange rate movements (using the USD as base currency) for 1993 and 1994 using daily data. Compared to 1993, the JPY correlations almost doubled in 1994. Using the 1993 estimates in 1994 would therefore have resulted in some unpleasant surprises.

One way of mitigating the effect of these instabilities is to measure volatilities and correlations using high frequency data over short observation periods. Most currency risk measurement (even for longer-term investment purposes) would use daily data. This data may be exponentially weighted to give more weight to recent observations so as to rapidly capture regime changes. Alternatively, there is no doubt that the ARCH class of volatility

Table 6.5 Dollar based exchange rate return correlation: daily data for 1993

GBP	Yen	DM	SFr	DFl	FFr	
—	0.305	0.782	0.733	0.746	0.741	GBP
	—	0.341	0.356	0.305	0.269	Yen
		—	0.858	0.934	0.873	DM
			—	0.838	0.795	SFr
				—	0.891	DFl
					—	FFr

Table 6.6 Dollar based exchange rate return correlation: daily data for 1994

GBP	Yen	DM	SFr	DFl	FFr	
—	0.430	0.783	0.790	0.788	0.790	GBP
	—	0.573	0.548	0.573	0.574	Yen
		—	0.939	0.994	0.983	DM
			—	0.937	0.929	SFr
				—	0.981	DFl
					—	FFr

estimation procedures has proven much more valuable in currency markets than for any other asset category.

There are plenty of tools available to recombine historical currency returns and deduce better risk forecasts. However, there is not a single procedure that has taken the upper hand in this context. Short-term currency risk (and correlation) forecasting therefore remains somewhat more of an art. The artists have a bewildering toolkit of instruments available. Unfortunately the currency market environment is so unstable that no methodology can be shown to be always superior.

6.5.3 Concluding Remarks

We live in a changing world that is subject to continuous structural change. However, this structural change is harder to prove statistically than originally thought. Except for currency markets, no clear evidence exists which points in the direction of significant drift or regime changes in asset (category) risks and correlations.

Although sophisticated statistical procedures can be used to improve risk forecasting accuracy, it is also widely established that the collective market wisdom is probably a better risk forecaster than any individual (or combined) statistical procedure. These consensus risk forecasts can be derived from the prices of traded options. It is well known that the future volatility of the underlying instrument over the remaining life of the option is the major (and in most cases only unknown) determinant of the value of that option. By observing the market traded price, one can therefore effectively back out the market consensus risk forecast.[16] In a very limited number of cases (such as the option to exchange one instrument for another) it may even be possible to extract the market consensus correlation forecast.

Although the forecasting accuracy of these option implied volatilities is widely recognized, they can only be effectively used for the limited set of instruments on which options are traded. Even then these implied volatilities are extremely valuable to calibrate other (statistical) risk estimation and forecasting procedures.

6.6 CONCLUSION

In this chapter we have tried to give a historical overview of the evolution in risk management and risk measurement. Although the foundations of modern risk measurement were laid by Markowitz almost 40 years ago, his principles and ideas remain as topical as ever. Risk reduction through a judicious spread of money across a wide range of alternatives remains central to all financial practice.

A correct estimation of volatilities and correlations is an essential prerequisite to quantifying accurately the actual risks being run. As a result, a lot of the risk forecasting activity has concentrated on identifying and quantifying the structural causes of risk and correlation. Indeed, it is only through the separation of structural from incidental (spurious) risks that more reliable forecasts can be achieved.

This quest for structural risk models started with identifying "the market" as the main source of communality in stock risks. However, this single-minded approach quickly evolved into a richer description of the structural causes of risk as reflected in multiple factor risk models. These models try to identify an exhaustive set of risk factors that help explain common stock risks and correlations. The application of a multi-factor approach will typically lead to a richer understanding of the nature of the risks being incurred and will also lead to vastly improved risk forecasts.

Once a reliable risk model has been estimated, it can be used to quantify the business risk of brokers, market-makers, corporate treasurers and investment managers. Although each of them will probably use the risk model in a slightly different fashion, they are ultimately all concerned about the extent to which they will be able to live up to (externally defined) expectations. In other words, each of the financial market operators lets her actions be determined by a benchmark. Risk and return will be evaluated relative to this benchmark.

In the case of market-makers, brokers and corporate treasurers, the benchmark would typically be not to lose money or to make more money than what can be achieved through putting money on deposit. This establishes the value at risk concept as an appropriate risk measure since it quantifies the amount of money that can be made or lost over the predetermined time horizon.

Investment managers on the other hand are more concerned about their tracking error with respect to the predefined benchmark (typically a market index). They worry about the extent to which they can out- or underperform this benchmark and sell their clients the tracking error that they think will most likely lead to fame and glory (or at least one of these two).

The calculation of value at risk and tracking error both use the risk model (covariance matrix) as their central engine. This engine needs to be fine-tuned to the needs of the user. In particular the time frame over which risks need to be forecast will have an important impact on the way in which the risk model will be estimated. Although more detailed risk model classification models are possible, an important distinction relates to the forecast time horizon: short-term risk models are typically fundamentally different from long-term models.

When forecasting risks, it is always worrisome to note that the historical information used to estimate the risk model may not necessarily be reflective of the current market conditions and relationships. Historical models will always lag structural changes in the market place. Luckily though there is little statistical evidence of sudden fundamental structural changes in the interrelationships in equity and bond markets. In currency markets on the other hand, non-stationarity of relationships is common and needs to be accommodated in the risk forecasting procedures. Exponential smoothing, ARCH processes and implied volatilities and correlations can somewhat mitigate these problems although currency risk forecasting remains more of an art than a science. Luckily the artists have a vast array of highly sophisticated instruments available to practise their artistry.

This chapter has mainly concentrated on the traditional approach to risk quantification using the concepts of variance and standard deviation. As the usage of derivatives (options, futures and warrants) spreads ever more widely, it becomes increasingly obvious that these standard risk measures are no longer appropriate. No single alternative risk measure has, however, become generally accepted. Although concepts such as semi-variance, downside risk and downside probability are slowly coming to the fore, their usage also depends heavily on a more complete and robust characterization of the higher moments of the return distributions of the underlying instruments. The academic who can match the success of the Markowitz concept of diversification to include asymmetric distributions probably has a prize waiting in Stockholm.

6.7 ENDNOTES

1. Markowitz, even in his early work, clearly recognized the limitations of standard deviations as a potential risk measure. In effect, the use of standard deviation presupposes a symmetric return distribution around the expected return. Although this assumption may be acceptable for common stocks and bonds over relatively short observation intervals, it is clearly violated in the case of options and warrants. In his book Markowitz hints at the potential superiority of other risk measures such as semi-variance, shortfall risk or shortfall probability. He rejects them because of the computational complexity they entail. Whereas improved analytical solutions and vast increases in computing power have mostly remedied these objections, it is fair to say that the majority of the standard risk measurement approaches continue to rely heavily on the basic mean-standard deviation framework.
2. The standard error of a correlation coefficient is proportional to 1 over the square root of the number of observations.
3. The regular realignments of the currencies within the European Monetary System immediately come to mind.
4. Market efficiency is a well-defined concept that refers to the assumption that all relevant information is immediately and accurately reflected in the market prices.
5. Note that we are using beta here to refer to the regression coefficient of the time series regression (2). This beta is distinct from the Capital Asset Pricing Model beta of equation (1). In other words, there are as many betas as there are indices that can be used in regression (2). It is therefore never possible to talk about "the" beta of an asset.
6. Let Y denote the returns to the portfolio and X denote the returns to the hedging instrument over the hedging period. Then the expected return to the hedged position with hedge ratio δ is

$$E = E(Y) + \delta E(X)$$

and the variance of the hedged position is

$$V = V(Y) + \delta^2 V(X) + 2\delta \mathrm{Cov}(X, Y)$$

Choosing δ to maximize $E - rV$, where $r > 0$ denotes the degree of risk aversion, yields the optimal δ to be

$$\hat{\delta} = (E(X) - 2r\mathrm{Cov}(X, Y))/(2rV(X))$$

Now it is usual to assume that the hedge follows a random walk, so $E(X) = 0$ and in this case

$$\hat{\delta} = -\mathrm{Cov}(X, Y)/V(X)$$

is the optimal hedge ratio, which can be obtained as the OLS estimate in the linear regression model

$$Y_t = \alpha + \delta X_t + \varepsilon_t$$

7. These R^2 will differ significantly from country to country. The average R^2 will be about 30 per cent in developed markets such as the US, Japan and the UK. In high volatility environments such as Thailand, Taiwan or Mexico the average R^2 can be as high as 50 per cent or 60 per cent. This is a natural byproduct of the fact that on average it is easier to explain what happens to individual stocks in markets that are subject to market-wide violent price corrections. In other words, the index will explain a higher proportion of the total volatility when that total volatility is high.

8. See, for example, King (1966) and Rosenberg (1974).

9. The term Arbitrage Pricing Theory refers to the main insight that assets that have an identical exposure to the different risk factors should also have an identical expected return. Otherwise there would be obvious riskless arbitrage opportunities.

10. Investor confidence is mostly measured as the yield spread between corporate and government bonds.

11. The calibration involves more than the choice of daily, weekly or monthly observation intervals. Indeed when using a daily time frame, the riskless instrument is a one-day time deposit. The excess returns used to calculate the covariance matrix $\mathbf{V}$ should therefore use the overnight money rate as the risk-free rate. A weekly or monthly risk model would use one-week or one-month rates as the risk-free rate to calculate excess returns.

12. Since index fund managers do not have to engage in investment research, financial analysis or return forecasting, their operating costs are greatly reduced. As a consequence the management fee will be several orders of magnitude lower than the one charged by traditional active managers. The transaction costs incurred by index funds will also be low since they pursue a buy and hold strategy as opposed to the active managers who may turn over significant fractions of the portfolio during the course of the year.

13. Although an index fund in theory should have zero tracking error, it is not always possible to continually hold all assets which are part of the index at exactly their index weight. This may be due to irregular cash flows into or out of the portfolio. Alternatively portfolios trying to duplicate indices consisting of a large number of assets may not always be able to buy all assets in the index. Sampling or optimization procedures are then used to minimize the tracking error.

14. By definition, for every manager who overweights an asset, sector, or industry relative to the market, there must be another one who underweights that asset, sector, industry. Relative to the market average, investment management is a zero sum game: for every investment manager who outperforms the average, there must be another one who underperforms. In this sense the aggregate value added (relative to the market average) of all investment management activity is zero.

15. In these cases the *ex post* benchmark chosen by the client usually happens to be the asset category or market which performed best over the evaluation period.

16. See for instance Latane and Rendleman (1976) and Beckers (1981) for early applications of these ideas.

6.8 REFERENCES

Beckers, C. (1981) "Standard deviations implied in option prices as predictors of future stock price variability". *Journal of Banking and Finance*, **5**, 363–81.

Beckers, C., Grinold R., Rudd A. and Stefek, D. (1992) "The relative importance of common factors across the European equity markets". *Journal of Banking and Finance*, **16**, 14–38.

Bollersev, T. (1986) "Generalized Autoregressive Conditional Heteroskedasticity". *Journal of Econometrics*, **31**, 307–27.

Bollersev, T., Chou, R. and Kroner, K. (1992) "ARCH modelling in finance: A selective review of the theory and empirical evidence with suggestions for future research", in Engle and Rothschild (eds) "ARCH models in finance". *Journal of Econometrics*, **52**, 5–59.

Connor, G. (1995) "The three types of factor models: A comparison of their explanatory power". *Financial Analysts Journal*.

Engle, R. and Bollersev, T. (1986) "Modelling the persistence of conditional variances". *Econometric Review*, **5**, 1–50.

Erb, C.B., Harvey Campbell, R. and Viskanta Tadas, E. (1994) "Forecasting international equity correlations". *Financial Analysts Journal*, November–December, 32–44.

Grinold, R., Rudd, A. and Stefek, D. (1989) "Global factors: Fact or fiction". *Journal of Portfolio Management*, Fall, 79–88.

Heston, S.L. and Rouwenhorst, K.G. (1994) "Does industrial structure explain the benefits of international diversification?". *Journal of Financial Economics*, **36**, 3–27.

King, B. (1966) "Market and industry factors in stock price behavior". *Journal of Business*, January.

Latane, H. and Rendleman, R. (1976) "Standard deviations of stock price ratios implied in option prices". *Journal of Finance*, **31**, 369–81.

Lintner, J. (1965) "The valuation of risk assets and the selection of risky investments in stock portfolios and capital budgets". *Review of Economics and Statistics*, February.

Markowitz, H. (1959) *Portfolio Selection: Efficient Diversification of Investments*. New York: John Wiley and Sons.

Mossin, J. (1966) "Equilibrium in a capital asset market". *Econometrica*, October.

Roll, R. (1977) "A critique of the asset pricing theory's tests: Part I: On past and potential testability of the theory". *Journal of Financial Economics*, **4**.

Rosenberg, B. (1974) "Extra-market components of covariance in security returns". *Journal of Financial and Quantitative Analysis*, **9**, 263–74.

Ross, S. (1976) "The arbitrage theory of capital asset pricing". *Journal of Economic Theory*, **13**, December, 341–60.

Sharpe, W. (1964) "Capital asset prices: A theory of market equilibrium". *Journal of Finance*, September.

7
Calculating Risk Capital
THOMAS C. WILSON*

7.1 INTRODUCTION

One of the most important developments in risk management over the past few years has been the development and implementation of a new class of risk measures which are specifically designed to measure and aggregate diverse risky positions across an entire institution using a common conceptual framework. Although these measures come under any one of many different institution-specific guises (e.g. Bankers Trust's Capital at Risk (CaR), J.P. Morgan's Value at Risk (VaR) and Daily Earnings at Risk (DEaR), other institutions' Dollars at Risk (DaR) and Money at Risk (MaR), etc.), they all have as their foundation a common definition comprising three elements: risk capital is generically defined as the maximum possible loss for a given position or portfolio within a known confidence interval over a specific time horizon.

Slightly confusing for the organization considering implementing these measures is the fact that, although all institutions begin with the same generic definition, the actual calculation methods used by each differ markedly. In fact, it seems that, just as each institution has a unique name for its risk capital, each also has a unique technical implementation. In all fairness, the different technical implementations are based in part on theoretical grounds, in part on systems considerations, and in part on the institutional and strategic context in which the calculations are employed to measure and control risks. But the myriad of different context-specific methods only serves to highlight the need to evaluate carefully the trade-offs between the different methods when deciding which method is best suited to your particular business.

The purpose of this chapter is to give a concise technical overview of some of the most prevalent techniques used for calculating risk capital, clearly starting their (implicit)

* The author is a partner in the Zurich office of McKinsey and Company, specializing in serving financial institutions, and would like to thank many individuals in McKinsey & Company as well as industry professionals in Frankfurt, London, New York and Zurich for providing valuable comments. This work draws substantially on previous work published over the past three years in *Risk Magazine*; thanks are therefore also due to *Risk Magazine* and its publisher, Peter Field, for providing an excellent forum for the exchange of ideas. This chapter corrects an error in a previous article (Wilson (1994b)); any remaining errors remain those of the author. Please direct any comments or questions to: Thomas C. Wilson, McKinsey & Company, Unterwerkstr. 3, 8065 Zurich, Switzerland.

The Handbook of Risk Management and Analysis. Edited by Carol Alexander
© Thomas Wilson, McKinsey & Company, Inc.

assumptions and their relative strengths and weaknesses from a theoretical as well as practical perspective. In order to frame the question in manageable terms, we focus here only on market or price risks as opposed to other risk categories such as credit risk, operational risks, business risks, etc. In addition to providing an overview of existing methods, we also develop a new method for calculating risk capital based on a delta–gamma approximation (or second-order Taylor series expansion of the portfolio value function), which overcomes some, but not all, of the problems inherent in some of the more popular methods. Before we go into the technical details, however, we begin by providing some motivation for looking at risk capital as a measure of risk for financial institutions.

7.2 USES OF RISK CAPITAL

Risk capital is an interesting risk measure for many financial institutions for three important reasons.

7.2.1 Risk Comparability

First, *risk capital can be consistently applied across a wide variety of diverse risky positions and portfolios, allowing the relative importance of each to be directly compared and aggregated.* How, for example, can the interest rate risk of a futures contract be put on comparable terms with the volatility risk of an option? with the foreign exchange risk of a currency swap? How can these diverse market risk positions be aggregated within a trading book? across an institution? Whilst there are a wide variety of standard risk measures available for characterizing the *individual risks* in a trading or derivatives portfolio (e.g. delta, gamma, vega, shifts, rotations, etc.[1]), they provide little guidance when trying to interpret the *relative importance* of each individual risk factor to the portfolio's bottom line or for *aggregating* the different risk categories to a business unit or institution level. The ability to do so correctly allows an institution to gain a deeper understanding into the relative importance of its different risk positions and better gauge its aggregate risk exposure relative to its aggregate risk appetite.

Risk capital accomplishes these objectives by defining a common metric which can be universally applied across all risk positions or portfolios: the maximum possible loss within a known confidence interval over a given holding period. Besides being able to be universally applied, this metric is also expressed in units which are (or should be) meaningful at all levels of management: dollars (or pounds, francs, etc.). It therefore serves as a relevant focal point for discussing risks at all levels within the institution, creating a risk dialogue and culture which is difficult to achieve given the otherwise technical nature of the issues.

7.2.2 Determinant of Capital Adequacy

This leads to the second important reason for calculating risk capital: because risk capital is calculated in currency units and is designed to cover most, but not all, of the losses which might face a trading portfolio, it also has the intuitive interpretation as the *amount of economic or equity capital which must be held to support that particular level of risky business activity.* In fact, the definition of risk capital given above is completely compatible with the role of equity as perceived by many financial institutions: whilst reserves or provisions are held to cover *expected* losses incurred in the normal course of business, equity capital is held to provide a capital cushion against any potential *unexpected* losses. Since an institution cannot be expected to hold capital to cover all unexpected losses with 100 per cent certainty (as this would require, for example, 100 per cent equity financing of all credits, never selling an equity call option, etc.), the level of this capital cushion must be determined within prudent solvency guidelines over a reasonable time horizon needed to identify and resolve problem situations. The same type of logic is often applied to the determination of the optimum level of exchange margining or collateralization in the OTC (over-the-counter) market (see Longin (1994)).

The philosophy that economic risk capital is the relevant measure for determining capital requirements for risk businesses is also being increasingly adopted by both regulators and supervisors. In the regulatory context, the Bank for International Settlement's Subcommittee on Banking Supervision recently released a proposal for market risk capital adequacy (Basle (1995a, 1995b), reviewed in Kupiec and O'Brien (1995a, 1995b)) which would allow banks to use their own internal risk capital calculation models to determine the capital needed to support their trading activities. Of interest is the fact that the class of allowable models is only slightly constrained by the proposal, prescribing only a few parameters and guidelines[2] but *no* specific calculation methodology: each qualifying institution is allowed to use their own proprietary model. In order to qualify, however, institutions must also have in place a sufficiently developed management control organization and policies.

In the supervisory context, the Derivatives Policy Group (DPG), formed at the suggestion of chairman A. Levitt of the Securities Exchange Commission (SEC) in August 1994, also makes similar recommendations regarding the determination of capital adequacy for the unregulated affiliates of SEC-registered broker–dealers and Commodity Futures Exchange Commission (CFEC)-registered futures commission merchants (DPG (1995)). These recommendations, which would allow institutions to determine the amount of capital needed to support their given trading activities based on proprietary models subject to the same 99 per cent confidence interval/ten-day holding period horizon parameters, are also complemented by other recommendations regarding the existence of a well-defined management policy and risk controlling organization. They are also broadly in line with the industry sponsored Group of Thirty (G30) Report's recommendations (G30 (1993)).

Unfortunately, whilst we are seeing convergence in terms of the acceptance of risk capital as the relevant determinant of capital adequacy for trading books *in concept* and even a few of the *relevant parameters* (e.g. 99 per cent confidence interval/ten-day holding period horizon), the actual *calculation rules* are left up to the individual institution by both regulators and supervisors. This is unfortunate as there exist a wide variety of different methods, each presenting the institution with non-trivial trade-offs; many of these different methods, as well as their trade-offs, will be described in detail below.

7.2.3 Performance Measurement

The final important reason for calculating risk capital is to *help management evaluate the performance of business units and strategies on a risk adjusted basis*. Given the interpretation of risk capital as the minimum equity required to support a risky business, it is natural to use this measure when evaluating the relative performance of different businesses by calculating the return on that equity, where equity is defined as *risk*-rather than *regulatory*-capital. In fact, many Risk Adjusted Performance Measures (RAPMs) such as Bankers Trust's Raroc (Risk Adjusted Return on Capital) use the concept of risk capital in just this manner to adjust returns for the amount of risk undertaken by each position or business.[3]

These RAPM measures are used by management to evaluate the relative and absolute performance of different businesses. For example, how does 25 bp on a straight loan compare with 10 bp on an interest rate swap with the same counterparty and maturity? with a different counterparty or maturity? or, how does a net return of USD 150 million on proprietary trading compare with USD 50 million from custodial services? or USD 75 million from derivatives trading? It is well known that evaluating performance relative to *regulatory* capital requirements may lead to the wrong signals being sent to management.[4] What, then, is the relevant measure of capital for a portfolio or business? Risk capital, with its interpretation as the economic capital needed to support a risky business, is becoming the *de facto* standard in helping management to adjust returns for the risks involved.

In summary, risk capital plays three important roles within a modern financial institution: first, it allows diverse risky positions to be directly compared and aggregated; second, it is a measure of the economic or equity capital required to support a given level of risk activities and, as such, is increasingly recognized by regulators for this purpose; and, finally, it helps management to make the returns from diverse risky businesses directly comparable on a risk adjusted basis. Whilst there are a few open issues regarding its calculation, risk capital is proving nonetheless to be a very useful tool for helping management to steer and control diverse risk businesses.

7.3 ISSUES FOR CALCULATING RISK CAPITAL

The problem is that there are a wide variety of different ways to implement the definition of risk capital, each having distinct advantages and disadvantages. In order to get a better feeling for the trade-offs implicit in each of the methods, it is important first to understand the issues surrounding the calculation of risk capital, many of which are currently being discussed at great length in the financial literature.[5] In this context, risk capital can be thought of as comprising two distinct elements (Figure 7.1):

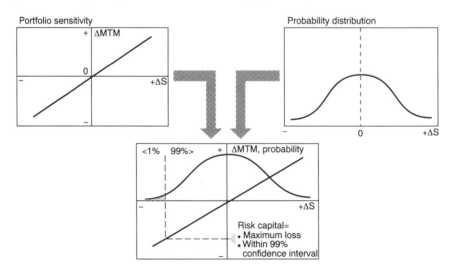

Figure 7.1 Elements of risk capital

- The *sensitivity of a portfolio's market value to changes in market rates*, illustrated in the diagram on the left. The slanted line is a stylized representation of the aggregate change in mark-to-market value of a portfolio as market rates change, with the change in value on the *y*-axis and the change in market rates on the *x*-axis

- The *(joint) probability distribution of changes in market rates over the desired reporting period horizon*, illustrated in the diagram on the right. The stylized curve in the diagram can be thought of as the (marginal) probability density function for changes in the market rate of a given size, with probability on the *y*-axis and the change in market rates on the *x*-axis

When "combined", as is intuitively done in the diagram at the bottom of the figure, the desired definition of risk capital is implemented: the maximum possible loss within a known confidence interval over a predetermined holding period horizon. In practice, however, the calculation of risk capital requires that simplifying assumptions need to be made with regard to one or both of these components, e.g. the portfolio's sensitivity or the joint distribution of market rate innovations. To illustrate this, consider the closed-form RiskMetrics^{TM} Value at Risk (VaR) formula, described and motivated in greater detail in Section 7.5.3:

$$\text{VaR} = \alpha\sqrt{\omega'\sum\omega}\sqrt{\Delta t}$$

where α is defined as the constant that gives the appropriate one-tailed confidence interval for the standardized normal distribution, e.g. $\alpha = 2.33$ for a 99.0 per cent confidence interval, ω is the $N \times 1$ vector of portfolio position weights, Σ is the $N \times N$ annualized covariance matrix of position returns and Δt is the holding period horizon as a fraction of a year. This formula, most often associated with RiskMetrics, comprises two clearly identifiable sets of assumptions: first, a set of assumptions regarding *position sensitivities* embodied in the risk position weights (ω), derived from RiskMetrics mapping technology designed to map specific transactions into risk positions, and second, a set of assumptions and calculation rules regarding the *probability distribution* of market rate innovations embodied in the covariance matrix of position returns (Σ).

The most common critiques of the popular risk capital calculation methods, including RiskMetrics, can therefore be thought of as *critiques of these two component assumptions rather than of the concept itself.*[6] In the rest of this section, we will therefore highlight some of the most important critiques commonly made regarding the price sensitivity and distributional assumptions.

7.3.1 Portfolio Sensitivity Assumptions

The first set of critiques is aimed at the portfolio sensitivity assumptions often made in practice. Broadly speaking, these critiques can be divided into three categories: risk factor coverage, adequacy of local measures and model risks.

(i) Risk Factor Coverage

The first concern is whether or not the local measures used in calculating risk capital recognize *all* of the potential sources of risk which might affect the value of the portfolio. For example, some risk capital calculations ignore the volatility or vega risk of option portfolios for convenience, even though this can be one of the most significant sources of risk for the trading book (especially when the trading strategy and limit structures constrain the book to have no directional price, or delta, risk). Some methods solve this issue by treating the term structure of implied volatilities as another "market price", treating the "vega" as another "delta" or directional price sensitivity, and incorporating it directly into such standard methods as the Asset-Normal/RiskMetrics or Delta-Normal methods (more on this issue later).

More problematic by far is the fact that many calculation rules ignore second-order or gamma effects (e.g. risk capital is often calculated based only on the portfolio's delta or directional price risk), although risk managers and options traders know that higher order terms such as the portfolio's gamma or even cross-gamma terms can be equally important, especially for option portfolios. To illustrate this point, consider the (linear) portfolio sensitivity illustrated in diagram A of Figure 7.2; whilst this line represents exactly the pay-off profile for a straight equity position, the same linear, or delta, representation may be a poor representation for a portfolio containing options. Diagram B of Figure 7.2 represents both an exact call option pay-off profile as well as its delta, or first-order, representation and its delta–gamma, or second-order, representation. It is interesting to note that the approximation error arising from a delta-representation increases with the size of the unexpected market rate innovation (an effect also discussed in JPM (1994–95)); unfortunately, large market events are exactly the events which we are typically concerned about when calculating capital at risk. This approximation error decreases, however, when the delta–gamma, or second-order, representation is used (an observation which motivates the Delta–Gamma method developed later).

Whilst all traders will agree that delta as a risk measure is not sufficient to manage an options book and, in fact, many options books are run with an explicit strategy of being delta-neutral at all times, paradoxically, many of the most popular risk capital techniques (e.g. the Delta-Normal and Asset-Normal/RiskMetrics methods) recognize *only* directional price or delta risks. This is one reason that J.P. Morgan does not recommend that their RiskMetrics technique be applied to portfolios including options.[7]

Along a similar line, many methods ignore potentially important cross-gamma effects.[8] Consider, for the simplest example, an at-the-money foreign currency interest rate forward

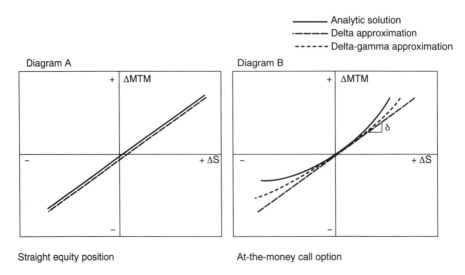

Figure 7.2 Stylized portfolio sensitivity profiles

rate agreement (FRA) where the profit and loss, and therefore risk capital, is reported in the domestic currency. Because this position is at-the-money, it has no foreign currency value and therefore no first-order currency risk.[9] However, if foreign interest rates were to move in an adverse manner, therefore creating a foreign currency loss, their impact could be mitigated or exacerbated by foreign exchange rate movements when translating the loss into your reporting currency. The net impact on risk capital depends on whether foreign interest rates are positively or negatively correlated with exchange rate movements. This cross-rate effect caused by P/L translation may be of substantial importance for all standard, first generation products such as forward rate agreements, straight equity positions, FX forwards, interest rate and currency swaps, etc. Second-order cross-rate effects become even more important for some second-generation correlation products (e.g. choosers, diff swaps or quantos, etc.) which are expressly designed to play a view on correlation risks.

A delta–gamma approximation overcomes many of these problems by capturing the direct- and cross-gamma or convexity risks of the portfolio and incorporating them into the risk capital calculation. In the past, the problem was one of how to incorporate gamma into the risk capital calculation in a simple manner which could be easily implemented. This problem has been resolved with the development of the Delta–Gamma method, described in detail below.

(ii) Local Measures are not Sufficient

Standard local sensitivity measures or "Greeks" such as deltas, gammas and vegas are often used as the basis for representing the portfolio pay-off profile when calculating risk capital. The measures themselves are "local" in the sense that they measure the sensitivity of the portfolio's value to infinitesimal changes in market rates around current rates. These local measures are then often used to construct a Taylor Series Expansion to represent the portfolio pay-off profile in order to greatly simplify the calculations (for details, refer to the description of the Delta–Normal and Delta–Gamma methods described below).

Unfortunately, these representations of the portfolio pay-off profile based on local measures may not be sufficient to fully characterize the portfolio pay-off for large market events. Consider Figure 7.3 which illustrates a stylized pay-off profile for a short-dated, deep-in or out-of-the-money option portfolio. Such portfolios can exhibit large swings in their deltas and gammas, and therefore values, under extreme market movements. Although the delta–gamma method captures the portfolio's convexity or gamma risk for small market movements, it still suffers from the fact that it is based on *local* as opposed to *global* risk measures (as illustrated by the dotted line in the figure), with the approximation error most likely to increase with extreme market rate movements. Thus, using local risk measures alone may be inadequate when calculating capital at risk.

This observation is perhaps more eloquently put by Bob Gumerlock, Swiss Bank Corporation, "When O'Connor set up in London at Big Bang, I built an option risk control system incorporating all the Greek letters — deltas, gammas, vegas, thetas and even some higher order ones as well (the delta of the gamma and the gamma of the vega). And I'll tell you that during the crash it was about as useful as a US theme park on the outskirts of Paris" (Chew (1994b)). As we discuss later, simulation techniques are the only methods available which can capture these non-local risks for complex options portfolios.

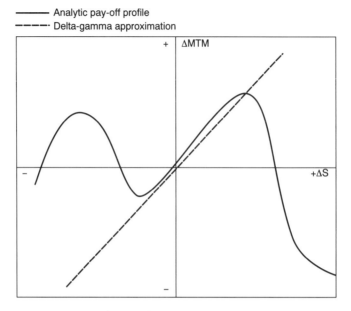

Figure 7.3 "Non-local" risks

(iii) Pricing Model Risk

Many of the derivatives pricing models used to value transactions and calculate their risk profiles are based on some simplifying assumptions about market liquidity or the way that market rates evolve and these assumptions often contradict the spirit of risk capital calculations.

For example, many models assume that markets remain liquid when faced with large price movements, thereby allowing the book to be rebalanced or dynamically hedged on a continuous basis. In fact, many of the models used to price derivatives implicitly assume that a delta hedge, rebalanced continuously, is sufficient to create an exact replicating portfolio, thereby allowing the transaction to be priced based on a "no-arbitrage" argument. In addition to ignoring transaction costs, these models ignore the fact that, when large market movements do occur, they typically take what little market liquidity there is with them and what little liquidity there is left tends to be in one direction only–that of the stampeding herd. This phenomenon arguably was the death knell for the concept of portfolio insurance, which relied on the concept of option replication, when the crash came in 1987. Thus, whilst it might have been theoretically correct to allocate no risk capital at the time to equity portfolios covered by portfolio insurance, the practical realities based on lessons learnt from the 1987 crash are somewhat different.

7.3.2 Distributional Assumptions

In order to calculate the maximum possible loss within a known confidence interval as in Figure 7.1, portfolio sensitivity measures must somehow be combined with a probability measure defining how likely adverse movements actually are. Simplifying assumptions are therefore also often made with regards to the distribution of market rate innovations, generating several standard criticisms in their own right.

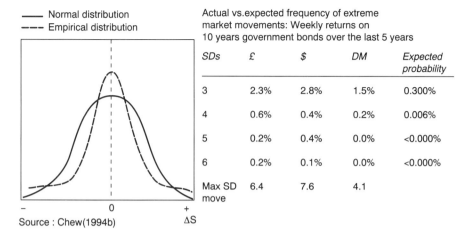

Figure 7.4   Fat tails

(i) Fat Tails

Many calculation methods assume that (proportional) market rate innovations over "small" time horizons are jointly normally distributed with independent realizations. This assumption has direct and controversial implications for the implied probability of extreme events as well as the shape of the distribution itself and its evolution over time.

Several empirical studies[10] have demonstrated that the historical return distributions in a wide variety of markets demonstrate a far higher incidence of very large market rate movements than is predicted by the normal distribution (a statistical property called kurtosis or fat tails) and have a higher peak at the mean than is predicted by the normal distribution (a property called leptokurtosis). These properties are demonstrated in Figure 7.4, with the diagram on the left graphically illustrating the phenomenon and the table on the right showing how dramatic this effect can be in various government bond markets. The table indicates that three standard deviation movements occurred with a frequency of 2.3 per cent of the time (respectively, 2.8 per cent and 1.5 per cent) over the sample period for the ten-year sterling (respectively, dollar and Deutschmark) government bond markets when the normal distribution would predict such events only 0.3 per cent of the time.

The consequence in terms of risk capital calculations is dramatic: although we think that we should be looking at 2- or 3-sigma events based on the assumed normal distribution, we should really be looking at 4- to 6-sigma events based on the empirical distribution. This could lead both to a gross under-allocation of risk capital as well as exacerbate the problem of local measures discussed earlier.

This has led many authors to investigate the properties of other distributions with "fatter tails" than the normal distribution, e.g. the Stable Paretian and Student-t distributions, as well as other price processes such as jump-diffusion and subordinated stochastic processes,[11] in an effort to better model the evolution of market prices.

(ii) Stable and Exploitable Relationships

Most methods of calculating risk capital rely on estimates of the volatilities and correlations of market rate innovations in order to aggregate diverse risky positions. These parameters are estimated based on specific statistical models, many of which require that the parameters be constant over the sample period or, even more trivially, that they exist at all.

The motivation for recognizing correlations is clear: the aggregate risk capital needed for a spread position consisting of a long DM/USD and a short GBP/USD position based on the high historical or implied correlation estimates between the DM/USD and GBP/USD rates may be significantly less than the sum of the risk capital for the two positions when considered in isolation: as the value of one position goes up, the other is likely to go down due to their correlation, implying a lower overall P/L volatility. The problem is that this correlation may be highly unstable, as the ERM crisis of 1992 demonstrated. So, whilst the risk manager might believe that he or she has entered into a relatively riskless spread trade, the amount of risk capital should actually be much higher since the relationship itself, although historically quite stable, might prove to be quite unstable in times of stress. These same qualitative statements can also be made regarding the stability of market rate volatilities.

Many authors are moving towards alternative statistical models to describe and forecast market rate dynamics,[12] such as factor-GARCH and cointegration representations. There have even been attempts to integrate the fact that volatilities and correlations may not be constant into the calculation of risk capital (see, for example, Alexander (1994) and Wilson (1993)), although they will only be mentioned in passing here. It should be noted, however, that many of these attempts are aimed at generating a better forecast for the covariance matrix which will govern next period's returns (see Alexander (1994)), rather than incorporating the correlation and volatility forecast uncertainty itself into the risk capital calculation; the exception is Wilson (1993) who demonstrates that forecast uncertainty may lead to the fat tails phenomenon described earlier.

Nonetheless, similar critiques may be valid for these "next generation" methods — their representation of correlations and volatilities may only be valid in "normal", 2-sigma periods — but what happens in times of stress, e.g. 5-sigma events, when these unobservable parameters also exhibit extreme movements which exceed what the model predicts? Although some of the implications from following such a modelling strategy are desirable, specifically a more accurate estimate of risk capital and a better understanding of market rate dynamics, senior management should not delude itself into thinking that these models are a panacea and become complacent in their implementation: the models merely push the assumptions regarding constant distributional parameters to a lower, more obscure level. Whilst quite useful for calculating risk capital as well as supporting front-office activities, the performance of these models (as with *all* models) must be back-tested continuously against actual market developments.

(iii) Arbitrage Relationships Violated

When implementing risk capital calculations, it is often expedient to ignore certain no-arbitrage conditions in order to make the problem tractable. For example, some institutions simply assume that proportional innovations in the DM/USD, GBP/USD and DM/GBP rates follow a highly correlated, jointly normal process when calculating the risk capital for an exchange rate book, thereby ignoring the triangular no-arbitrage relationship between the three currency pairs. This no-arbitrage relationship dictates that, if the innovations in any two of the three rates are given, the third is uniquely determined; otherwise, a triangular arbitrage between the resulting spot rates would exist. The result from ignoring the no-arbitrage condition is that risk capital may be allocated to cover events which can never occur such as an appreciating DM/USD and a depreciating GBP/USD at the same time as a depreciating DM/GBP rate. Similarly, it is often assumed that interest rates follow an arbitrary geometric Brownian motion process estimated using market data without checking whether or not the implied process is arbitrage free.

(iv) Miscellaneous Distributional Assumptions

Another problem with the assumption of normally distributed market rate innovations is that the normal distribution is symmetric, whereas the empirical distributions tend to be skewed (see JPM (1994–95)), implying that we may have under- or over-allocated risk capital depending on whether we have long or short positions. A more critical issue related to the symmetry of the distribution is that, depending on how the market rate process is discretized, assuming the normality of market rate innovations could imply that interest rates, equity prices or exchange rates may become negative with positive probability[13] for extreme innovations in the assumed geometric Brownian motion process. This is clearly not a desirable property for many market price processes.

Finally, it is often assumed that market rate innovations are independently distributed (see, again, JPM (1994–95)). This contradicts many of the empirical studies and no-arbitrage models which have found, for example, mean reversion in interest rates, the reliability of the forward rate hypothesis or interest rate parity theorem, etc.

(v) Model Risks

Furthermore, most option pricing models are based on assumptions regarding market rate processes which are at odds with price dynamics during stress periods. For example, many models assume that market prices evolve in a continuous fashion, e.g. that they are governed by a diffusion rather than a jump process, and that market rate innovations are symmetrically distributed. As an example of the inadequacy of these assumptions, consider the ERM crisis of 1992 when various European currencies came under speculative attack: it was clear at the time that, if the sterling rate was going to move out of its band, it was going to make a big move and then only in one direction — depreciation. Whilst some market practitioners were rumoured to have models which were capable of coping with such a market rate process, many did not and had to rely on "rule of thumb" adjustments to volatility parameters (see Chew (1992)). These model risks not only had implications for the way that institutions priced transactions during this volatile period, but also for the way that they measured risks and hedged the positions, and therefore for the amount of risk capital needed to support the business.

7.3.3 Parameter Assumptions

The final major source of criticism for standard models is the relative arbitrariness of the key parameters (e.g. confidence interval and reporting period horizon) which determine to a great extent the amount of capital which should be held against any given risky position. Whilst many institutions have chosen an overnight time horizon combined with a 99 per cent confidence interval (see, for example, Chew (1994b), the Group of Thirty Report (1993) and JPM (1994–95)), many others have chosen to set different parameters. For example, Bankers Trust uses a one-year time horizon for all positions (see, again, Chew (1994b)). Still other institutions, such as Barclays de Zoete Wedd, set their time horizons equal to an "orderly liquidation period" on a risk-by-risk basis in order to bring it in line with the individual market's liquidity (see Lawrence and Robinson (1995b)). The actual

Summary

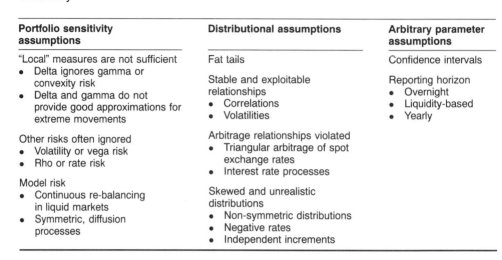

Figure 7.5   Common critiques of capital calculations

liquidation period therefore depends on both the markets considered as well as the size of the position. This assumption has the admirable consequence that positions in illiquid markets will bear more risk capital for the same volatility due to their illiquidity. These assumptions differ from those advocated by the BIS and DPG proposals discussed earlier.

In conclusion, there are several criticisms of the most common risk capital calculation methods (summarized in Figure 7.5). These critiques are directed less at the concept of risk capital itself and more at the underlying assumptions used to technically implement the concept. For example, many methods rely too heavily on local risk measures and specific models when approximating the portfolio pay-off profile, whilst others make assumptions about the process generating market rate innovations which are violated in reality (e.g. fat tails, negative rates, stable or predictable correlations, diffusion processes, etc.).

Although many of the critiques may seem quite problematic, the practitioner should not despair: methods for calculating risk capital are continual evolving and improving as new analytical techniques are being developed and computational algorithms improved, a wide variety of which are discussed in the next section. A word of caution is perhaps in order: as the techniques become more and more complex, their implicit assumptions and pitfalls also tend to become less and less transparent and, worse yet, management tends to become overly complacent with their implementation. Fortunately, the efficacy of the individual techniques is also dependent on the specific risk portfolio or trading strategy as well as the risk management and controlling procedures employed by the institution. In this context, the sentiments of Daniel Mudge, Bankers Trust, are relevant: "I would prefer a C-rated model with weaknesses and have people with experience and intuition to run our risk management than an A-rated model with a C-rated team of people who don't understand the model and are therefore unable to question the numbers that the system churns out" (Chew (1994b)).

Therefore, when choosing between the various popular methods described below, risk managers will always need to make informed trade-offs in terms of computational efficiency, information requirements and theoretical "correctness". The bottom line is that, if the shortcomings of each particular method are well understood and controlled, risk managers are finding that the information which even the simplest calculation methods provide can be invaluable in spite of their limitations.

7.4 DELTA–GAMMA METHOD[14]

In this section, we develop a new methodology for calculating risk capital which recognizes the convexity or gamma risks, including possible second-order, cross-market effects, from an arbitrary portfolio. We accomplish this by using a second-order approximation of the portfolio's value function similar to that illustrated in Figure 7.2. This new method therefore eliminates several of the criticisms described earlier (e.g. it captures the portfolio's direct and cross-market gamma or convexity risks as well as its vega risks), but it does so using local rather than global risk measures. Because it uses local measures, however, this new method has the advantage that it can be calculated using the standard risk measures (e.g. delta, gamma, vega and theta) which are readily available for most portfolios; its main advantages are therefore that its implementation requires significantly less systems integration efforts than other methods and that it can be calculated quickly for portfolios based on aggregate risk measures. Against this must be balanced the fact that it is based on local, rather than global, measures.

Following industry standards, we define risk capital as *the maximum possible loss over a specific time horizon within a given confidence interval*. The solution technique that we develop in this chapter takes a new approach by taking this definition literally. If interpreted literally, the definition can be seen to outline a very concrete and well-defined optimization programme: *solve for the market event which* maximizes *potential losses* subject to the constraint *that the event and all events generating less losses are within a given confidence interval*. We can formulate this problem very generally in the following manner:

$$\text{VAR} = \underset{\{\mathbf{S}\}}{\text{Max}} - \Delta P(\mathbf{S}) = \sum_i [P_i(\mathbf{S}) - P_i(\mathbf{S_0})]$$

$$\text{subject to } F(\mathbf{S}) \leq \varkappa \tag{1}$$

where $\Delta P(\mathbf{S})$ is defined as the change in portfolio value, $P_i(\mathbf{S})$ is the price function for each of the individual transactions, $i = 1 \ldots N$, as a function of market rates, $\mathbf{S}$ is the $M \times 1$ vector of market rates with $\mathbf{S_0}$ being the current market rates, $F(\mathbf{S})$ is defined as the probability that this event *or one of greater negative impact* will actually occur (note that this constraint is very complex unless simplified in some manner) and $\varkappa$ is the confidence level that the risk manager wants to achieve, expressed in per cent (e.g. the maximum loss within a 1 per cent confidence interval). If left in all of its generality, the solution to this problem must be determined by numerical methods, be they Monte Carlo methods or numerical search algorithms.

In practice, however, there are many simplifying assumptions commonly made which give an approximate solution to this very general optimization problem, yielding either closed solutions or simple algorithms (see the analysis of several common methods in the last section of this chapter). First, assumptions are typically made regarding the price functions, $P_i(\mathbf{S})$, which determine the value of position i given the observable market rates, $\mathbf{S}$. Second, assumptions are almost always made regarding the joint distribution of the market rates in the future.

Based on some very standard assumptions about the price functions and market rate distributions, we simplify the optimization problem given in equation (1) and derive three solution techniques for calculating risk capital which are easy to implement in practice, including a closed form solution. The benefits of this new approach are that:

- It captures the portfolio's straight- and cross-gamma risks as well as its vega risk and incorporates them into the calculation of risk capital

- It uses readily available portfolio information (e.g. deltas, gammas, vegas, etc.), requiring less systems integration effort and calculating quickly

- It also calculates the actual values of market rates which imply the worst case scenario. This additional information is of tremendous value for risk managers and controllers as it allows them also to assess which combination of market rates produces the "worst case" scenario for their specific portfolio

The exact closed form solution, developed in detail below, is given in the box which accompanies this chapter; the other two solution techniques are based on numerical techniques. In the remainder of this section, we develop these solutions in greater detail.

(i) Market Rate Assumptions

We begin by making a very standard assumption regarding the innovations to market rates; more specifically, we assume that innovations to market rates are jointly normally distributed with mean zero:[15]

(A1)   Market rate innovations have a joint normal distribution:

$$\Delta \mathbf{S} \sim N\left(0, \, \boldsymbol{\Sigma} \Delta t\right)$$

where $\boldsymbol{\Sigma}$ is the $M \times M$ covariance matrix of market price innovations, Δt is the elapsed time or orderly liquidation period and where we have assumed that the mean vector is zero without loss of generality. From a theoretical point of view, this assumption can be justified for all diffusion processes by using Ito's lemma if the time horizon is sufficiently "short" (refer to Wilson (1992, 1993) for examples and justifications). Assumption (A1) is also consistent with one of the most common assumptions made in practice, that market rates are governed by a joint geometric Brownian motion (GBM) process, described in some detail in Section 7.5.6.

In order to incorporate vega or volatility risk into the analysis in an internally consistent manner, we treat the K-period ahead implicit market volatilities, where $K > 1$, as market rates just like any other market rates, e.g. we assume that innovations in market rate volatilities are also jointly normally distributed. This assumption is consistent with our assumption (A1) if we continue to assume that the square roots of the diagonal elements of $\boldsymbol{\Sigma}$, the covariance matrix governing the realization of *next period's* (e.g. $K = 1$) market rate innovations, are equal to the *one period ahead implicit volatilities* and are *known with certainty* and if we restrict ourselves to calculating risk capital over a *one period holding period horizon*. In this respect, only the K-period ahead implicit volatilities, for $K > 1$, are assumed to be "market prices" which affect next period's P/L and which are jointly normally distributed.

(ii) Price Sensitivity Assumptions

Our assumptions about the price functions are also quite standard, although less transparent. Implicitly, we assume that the standard risk measures which risk managers use every day to manage and control the risk of their portfolios are sufficient to characterize the risk of the portfolio for calculating risk capital. We begin by taking a second-order Taylor Series Expansion of the portfolio's value function around current market rates. We will call this a delta–gamma approximation to contrast it with the first-order expansion used by the Delta-Normal approximation technique described later.

(A2)   Delta–gamma approximation:

$$\Delta P(\mathbf{S}) = \theta \Delta t + \delta' \Delta \mathbf{S} + \Delta \mathbf{S}' \gamma \Delta \mathbf{S}/2 + o(3)$$

$$\Delta P(\mathbf{S}) \approx \theta \Delta t + \delta' \Delta \mathbf{S} + \Delta \mathbf{S}' \gamma \Delta \mathbf{S}/2$$

where θ is the portfolio's theta, or $\partial P(\mathbf{S})/\partial t$; δ, an $M \times 1$ vector, is the portfolio's vector of delta sensitivities to changes in market rates; γ, an $M \times M$ symmetric matrix, is the portfolio's gamma matrix with respect to the various market risk factors; and $o(3)$ is the approximation error term which is of order 3.

More specifically, the portfolio's delta is defined as the first derivative or gradient of the portfolio's value with respect to the vector of market rates, e.g. $\partial P(\mathbf{S})/\partial \mathbf{S}$, which is simply the sum of the individual transaction's deltas, e.g. $\partial P(\mathbf{S})/\partial S_j = \Sigma_{i=1...N} \partial P_i(\mathbf{S})/\partial S_j$, for transactions $i = 1$ to N. Treating interest rates as market rates and redefining the risk measure "rho" for options as a "delta" allows us to capture the interest rate risk or rho of options. Analogously, treating the K-period ahead volatilities (for $K > 1$) as "market rates" and renaming the standard risk measure "vega" as another "delta", allows us to capture volatility risks for options in the same framework.

The gamma matrix is defined as the second derivative, or Hessian, of the portfolio's value function (e.g. $\gamma_{ij} = \partial^2 P(\mathbf{S})/\partial S_i \partial S_j$ for the i,j-element of the matrix), which is also the sum of the individual position's gammas. These gamma terms are more readily recognizable for $i = j$, in which case gamma i is defined as $\partial^2 P(\mathbf{S})/\partial S_i^2$, or the change in delta i for a change in market rate i. We may ignore the cross-product terms of the expansion (e.g. when $i \neq j$) if the individual prices are functions of only one market price or if the cross-product effects are trivial (a potentially dangerous assumption which is often made implicitly by risk managers, see Wilson (1995b)). For other, correlation-dependent products such as diff swaps, choosers, etc., the cross-product terms can be significant and cannot be ignored.

Substituting (A2) into equation (1) and rewriting, we get:

$$\text{VAR} = \underset{\{\Delta \mathbf{S}\}}{\text{Max}} \ -[\delta' \Delta \mathbf{S} + \Delta \mathbf{S}' \gamma \Delta \mathbf{S}/2]$$

$$\text{subject to } \Delta \mathbf{S}' \mathbf{\Sigma}^{-1} \Delta \mathbf{S} \leq \alpha^2 \qquad (2)$$

where we have taken advantage of assumption (A1) to rewrite the constraint in a quadratic form. The $\Delta \mathbf{S}' \mathbf{\Sigma}^{-1} \Delta \mathbf{S}$ term represents the M-dimensional ellipsoid for the jointly normal innovations to market rates and α in equation (2) is the number of standard deviations required to give the appropriate one-tailed confidence interval for $\varkappa$ in equation (1), e.g. $\alpha = 2.33$ for $\varkappa = 1$ per cent. Since market rate events lying outside of this ellipsoid occur with probability less than the desired confidence interval, we can restrict our search for worst case market rate events by looking in the interior and at the boundary of this ellipsoid. If the worst case scenario occurs at an extreme value of this ellipsoid, then this constraint will be binding (e.g. $\Delta S' \Sigma^{-1} \Delta S = \alpha^2$); otherwise, if the worst case scenario occurs when rates do not move "too much", e.g. an interior solution, then the constraint will not be binding (e.g. $\Delta S' \Sigma^{-1} \Delta S < \alpha^2$).[16]

Method 1: Spreadsheet solution. Equation 2 is now a quadratic programming problem (the objective function is quadratic, as is the constraint) and, as such, many numerical methods exist for solving it. One method is to set up the appropriate Lagrangian or Kuhn–Tucker equation and differentiate, where we find that the first-order, Kuhn–Tucker conditions[17] which describe the solution to (2) are as follows:

$$\text{(a)} \quad \left[-\gamma - \lambda \Sigma^{-1} \right] \Delta S = \delta \text{ or } A(\lambda) \Delta S = \delta$$

$$\text{(b)} \quad \Delta S' \Sigma^{-1} \Delta S \leq \alpha^2 \tag{3}$$

$$\text{with (c)} \quad \lambda \left(\Delta S' \Sigma^{-1} \Delta S - \alpha^2 \right) = 0 \text{ and } \lambda \geq 0$$

where λ is the Kuhn–Tucker multiplier associated with the constraint. Equation (3c) states that, if the worst case scenario occurs at an extreme value and the constraint is binding, then the Kuhn–Tucker multiplier must have a value greater than zero; conversely, if the worst case scenario is an interior solution, implying that the constraint is not binding, then the multiplier will have zero value. The Kuhn–Tucker multiplier has a useful interpretation: it measures the marginal amount of additional risk capital which will need to be allocated to the portfolio if the confidence interval (squared), or α^2, is increased.

One method of solving this system of equations is to do a numerical search over $\lambda \geq 0$, inverting the matrix $A(\lambda)$ for each λ to solve for ΔS using equation (3a) and then checking to see whether the constraints (3b) and (3c) are satisfied to some tolerance level. This process can be done using the "solver" function in standard spreadsheets and converges rapidly for small M. Unfortunately, it is time intensive using only the functions in a spreadsheet as the number of risk factors, M, increases since it must invert an M-dimensional matrix with each iteration in order to solve equation (3a) for ΔS. If, however, external routines or procedures are called, the solution time for arbitrarily large matrices can be improved.

Method 2: Faster, numerical solution. The speed can be increased if we diagonalize A and transform the risk factors into independent variables. In this case, equation (3a) implies closed form solutions for ΔS given λ, e.g. $A(\lambda)$ can be inverted analytically. We accomplish this task by using the following theorem from Sheffe (1959) where the notation has been adapted to match our own:

Theorem Let ΔS be an $M \times 1$ vector of normal random variables with joint distribution $\Delta S \sim N(0, \Sigma)$ with Σ non-singular; let γ be any non-singular, symmetric $M \times M$ matrix (symmetry in our case is satisfied by definition). Consider the quadratic form of ΔS defined by $Q = \Delta S' \gamma \Delta S$. Then, by means of a linear transformation, for appropriate matrices T and P, we can define Q^* in the following manner:

$$Q^* = \Delta \mathbf{S}^{*\prime} \boldsymbol{\gamma}^* \Delta \mathbf{S}^*$$

where Q^* is equivalent to $Q = \Delta \mathbf{S}' \boldsymbol{\gamma} \Delta \mathbf{S}$ in distribution and where $\Delta \mathbf{S}^* = \mathbf{T}' \mathbf{P}^{-1} \Delta \mathbf{S}$ and $\Delta \mathbf{S}^*$ are independently distributed normal random variates with unit variance, e.g. $\Delta \mathbf{S}^* \sim N(\mathbf{0}, \mathbf{I})$.

For this transformation, $\mathbf{P}$ is the non-singular Cholesky decomposition of $\boldsymbol{\Sigma}$ defined by $\boldsymbol{\Sigma} = \mathbf{PP}'$, satisfying the equation $\mathbf{P}^{-1} \boldsymbol{\Sigma} \mathbf{P}'^{-1} = \mathbf{I}$, and $\mathbf{T}$ is the orthogonal matrix which satisfies the equation $\mathbf{T}'(\mathbf{P}' \boldsymbol{\gamma} \mathbf{P}) \mathbf{T} = \boldsymbol{\gamma}^*$, where $\boldsymbol{\gamma}^*$ is the diagonal matrix of the eigenvalues of the matrix $\mathbf{P}' \boldsymbol{\gamma} \mathbf{P}$ and $\mathbf{T}$ is the matrix of eigenvectors of $\mathbf{P}' \boldsymbol{\gamma} \mathbf{P}$.

Proof   See Sheffe (1959).

This leads us to the following proposition:

Proposition   Defining $\boldsymbol{\delta}^* = \mathbf{T}' \mathbf{P}' \boldsymbol{\delta}$ and $\Delta \mathbf{S}^* = \mathbf{T}' \mathbf{P}^{-1} \Delta \mathbf{S}$ we can rewrite equation (2) in the following manner:

$$\text{VAR} = \begin{array}{c} \text{Max} \\ \{\Delta \mathbf{S}^*\} \end{array} - [\boldsymbol{\delta}^{*\prime} \Delta \mathbf{S}^* + \Delta \mathbf{S}^{*\prime} \boldsymbol{\gamma}^* \Delta \mathbf{S}^* / 2] \qquad (4)$$

$$\text{subject to } \Delta \mathbf{S}^{*\prime} \Delta \mathbf{S}^* \leq \alpha^2$$

Proof   The equivalence of equations (2) and (4) is straightforward to prove. First, note that $\Delta \mathbf{S}^{*\prime} \boldsymbol{\gamma}^* \Delta \mathbf{S}^*$ is equivalent in distribution to $\Delta \mathbf{S}' \boldsymbol{\gamma} \Delta \mathbf{S}$ under the linear transformation as a consequence of the Theorem stated above or equivalently,

$$\Delta \mathbf{S}^{*\prime} \boldsymbol{\gamma}^* \Delta \mathbf{S}^* = \Delta \mathbf{S}' \mathbf{P}'^{-1} \mathbf{T} \mathbf{T}' \mathbf{P}' \boldsymbol{\gamma} \mathbf{P} \mathbf{T} \mathbf{T}' \mathbf{P}^{-1} \Delta \mathbf{S}$$

$$= \Delta \mathbf{S}' (\mathbf{PP}^{-1})' \boldsymbol{\gamma} (\mathbf{PP}^{-1}) \Delta \mathbf{S}$$

$$= \Delta \mathbf{S}' \boldsymbol{\gamma} \Delta \mathbf{S}$$

Second, note that $\boldsymbol{\delta}^{*\prime} \Delta \mathbf{S}^* = \boldsymbol{\delta}' \Delta \mathbf{S}$ by the following:

$$\boldsymbol{\delta}^{*\prime} \Delta \mathbf{S}^* = \boldsymbol{\delta}' \mathbf{P} \mathbf{T} \mathbf{T}' \mathbf{P}^{-1} \Delta \mathbf{S}$$

$$= \boldsymbol{\delta}' \mathbf{PP}^{-1} \Delta \mathbf{S}$$

$$= \boldsymbol{\delta}' \Delta \mathbf{S}$$

Third, note that $\Delta \mathbf{S}^{*\prime} \Delta \mathbf{S}^* = \Delta \mathbf{S}' \boldsymbol{\Sigma}^{-1} \Delta \mathbf{S}$, as proven below:

$$\Delta \mathbf{S}^{*\prime} \Delta \mathbf{S}^* = \Delta \mathbf{S}' \mathbf{P}'^{-1} \mathbf{T} \mathbf{T}' \mathbf{P}^{-1} \Delta \mathbf{S}$$

$$= \Delta \mathbf{S}' (\mathbf{PP}')^{-1} \Delta \mathbf{S}$$

$$= \Delta \mathbf{S}' \boldsymbol{\Sigma}^{-1} \Delta \mathbf{S}$$

thereby completing the proof.

The first-order conditions for equation (4) can now be rewritten in the following form:

(a) $\quad [-\boldsymbol{\gamma}^* - \lambda\mathbf{I}]\Delta\mathbf{S}^* = \boldsymbol{\delta}^*$ or $\mathbf{A}(\lambda)\Delta\mathbf{S}^* = \boldsymbol{\delta}^*$

(b) $\quad \Delta\mathbf{S}^{*\prime}\Delta\mathbf{S}^* \leq \alpha^2$ $\hspace{5cm}$ (5)

(c) $\quad \lambda(\Delta\mathbf{S}^{*\prime}\Delta\mathbf{S}^* - \alpha^2) = 0$ and $\lambda \geq 0$

where $\mathbf{A}(\lambda)$ is a diagonal matrix, implying that the values of $\Delta\mathbf{S}^*$ which solve (5a) for each λ can be determined analytically. This further implies that the matrix A does not have to be inverted with each iteration of the search and therefore reducing the time it takes to solve for the solution of the system of equations given by (5). More concretely, the solution to (5a) for each ΔS_i^* is given by the following equation:

$$\Delta S_i^* = -\delta_i^*/(\gamma_{ii}^* + \lambda) \hspace{4cm} (6)$$

Nonetheless, the system of equations defined by (5) must still be solved numerically by searching over $\lambda \in [0, \infty)$, calculating the values of $\Delta\mathbf{S}^*$ which solve (6) and then checking the constraints in (5)

The implications for the computation speed are dramatic as the risk factor dimensionality, or M, increases. In order to understand this gain in speed, one must realize that we are essentially trading-off one principle components calculation and one Cholesky decomposition (for $\mathbf{P}$ and $\mathbf{T}$), against having to invert the $\mathbf{A}(\lambda)$ matrix with each iteration of λ. For large M, this up-front calculation of $\mathbf{T}$ and $\mathbf{P}$ can be accomplished more quickly than the matrix inversions for each iteration of λ. Nonetheless, the procedure still requires a numerical search over $\lambda \in [0, \infty)$, verifying the constraints in (5b) and (5c) for each iteration. In addition, there may be multiple solutions to equations (5), some of which may represent local extrema. As such, each solution needs to be checked.

Method 3: Closed form approximation. If we are willing to make one more approximation, however, then we can develop a closed form solution to the problem and avoid this time-intensive numerical search. Let us expand equation (4) and concentrate on only those terms that involve ΔS_i^*, the ith transformed market rate, in the objective function:

$$\delta_i^* \Delta S_i^* + \gamma_{ii}^* \Delta S_i^{*2}/2 \hspace{4cm} (7)$$

Equation (7) measures the contribution of the ith transformed market rate, ΔS_i, which is by construction a standardized, independent unit normal variable, to the change in value of the portfolio. By construction, equation (7) passes through zero and has no cross-product terms due to the transformation. Further, for non-zero γ_{ii}^*, it may have any one of the shapes shown in Figure 7.6.[18]

Since we are ultimately concerned about the behaviour of equation (7) when the ith variable is at its extreme, consider constructing a piece-wise linear function to approximate equation (7). This piece-wise linear function is illustrated in Figure 7.7 and is chosen to have its breakpoint at zero, passing through zero as well as the extreme values of the function when evaluated at the confidence interval that we desire. The formula for this equation is given below:

$$\delta_i^* \Delta S_i^* + \gamma_{ii}^* \Delta S_i^{*2}/2 \approx \phi_i^+ \Delta S_i^* \text{ for } \Delta S_i^* > 0$$

$$\approx \phi_i^- \Delta S_i^* \text{ for } \Delta S_i^* \leq 0 \hspace{2cm} (8)$$

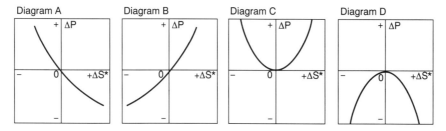

Figure 7.6 Impact of diagonal risk factors

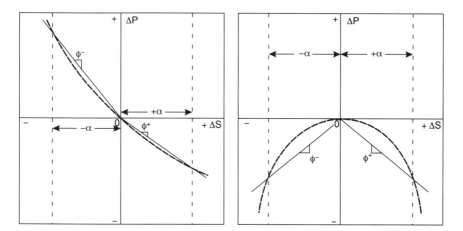

Figure 7.7 Piecewise linear approximation

where $\phi_1^- = (\delta_i^* - \gamma_{ii}^*\alpha/2)$, $\phi_i^+ = (\delta_i^* + \gamma_{ii}^*\alpha/2)$ and α is the number of standard deviations required to achieve the desired confidence interval. Define $\phi_i = \text{Min}[\phi_i^-, \phi_i^+, 0]$. We will interpret ϕ_i as the delta or linear pay-off profile which approximates the actual pay-off profile in the region of the (joint) worst case scenario. Our rationale for doing so is as follows: it is clear that the solution to the optimization programme defined by equation (4) occurs in the region for which equation (7) is best approximated by $\phi_i^*\Delta S_i^*$ for $\phi_i < 0$. Furthermore, inspection of the quadratic constraint in equation (4) indicates that, if $\phi_i^+ > 0$ and $\phi_i^- > 0$ (e.g. the contribution of the ith transformed market rate is always positive as in Figure 7.6c) then the solution is to set $\Delta S_i^* = 0$.[19] These observations are incorporated into the definition of ϕ_i.

Substituting $\phi_i \Delta S_i^*$ for each $\delta_i^*\Delta S_i^* + \gamma_{ii}^*\Delta S_i^{*2}/2$ in equation (4) linearizes the objective function by eliminating the quadratic term. Solving the first-order conditions for this transformed problem, we find that the worst case scenario is defined by the following transformed market rate factors:

$$\Delta S_i^* = -\alpha^*\phi_i \Bigg/ \sqrt{\sum_i \phi_i^2} \qquad (9)$$

Substituting equation (9) into the linearized objective function, we find that we can express the arbitrary portfolio's capital at risk in the following form:

$$\text{VAR}_{\delta\gamma} = \alpha\sigma_{\delta\gamma}\sqrt{\Delta t} \qquad (10)$$

where $\sigma_{\delta\gamma} = \sqrt{\Sigma_i\phi_i{}^2}$ or $\sqrt{\phi'\phi}$. This is the same formula as for the Delta-Normal or Asset-Normal/RiskMetrics method described below, only we have substituted a different volatility parameter which is adjusted to capture the convexity of the portfolio into the calculation rule. Furthermore, given that the actual market rate innovations, e.g. ΔS_{ij} are a linear transformation of the optimal, transformed innovations, e.g. ΔS_i^*, we find that the "worst case" scenario in terms of market rates is the following:

$$S_{\text{worst}} = S_0 + P^{-1}T^{-1}\Delta S^* \tag{11}$$

where ΔS^*, T and P are as defined in the Theorem and in equation (9) above.

There is some intuition behind this calculation method: by using the Theorem, we have effectively made the individual risk factors independent from one another and therefore have isolated their first- and second-order influence on the portfolio's value. By isolating the impact of each individual risk factor, we can then approximate each factor's influence via a piece-wise linear function which is valid only at the extremes where the worst case scenario is likely to occur; since the transformed market rate innovations are independent of one another, we can simply choose the "worst" section of the piece-wise linear approximation and create a linear approximation. Having effectively linearized the portfolio's sensitivities to the transformed risk factors at the extremes, we could then use the properties of the standard normal and the familiar RiskMetrics formula to calculate risk capital.

7.5 OVERVIEW OF ALTERNATIVE METHODS

As mentioned earlier, there is no single "best" method of calculating risk capital. Each of the popular methods reviewed below involves explicit (or implicit) trade-offs between computational efficiency and theoretical accuracy; all are subject to at least one of the critiques outlined earlier. Complicating matters further is the fact that many of the adverse trade-offs can be mitigated through the tailored design of risk management control procedures. This implies that the best method for a particular institution, or even a particular trading book within an institution, depends on the risk characteristics of the portfolio in question, its business strategy and the management and control procedures and organization designed to support its risk management objectives.

In this section, we review many of the most common methods of calculating capital at risk. These methods range from the simple "Building Block" approach preferred by some regulators in lieu of more complex proprietary models to the complex and computationally expensive simulation methods preferred by industry professionals. For each of these methods, we discuss the calculation rules, the implicit assumptions and their applicability. For convenience, we have summarized our analysis in Figure 7.8, including how well each of these methods stands up to the most common criticisms levelled at capital at risk calculation methods.

7.5.1 Regulators' "Building Block" Approach[20]

(i) Calculation Rules

As a matter of practicality, most regulators prior to 1995 had been advocating simple rules or algorithms for the calculation of risk capital. This approach "builds" the capital

Method	Regulator's "Building Block" Approach	Covariance Methods Portfolio Normal	Asset-/Delta-Normal or RiskMetrics Methods	Delta–Gamma Methods	Simulation Methods
Description	General and specific charges with predefined, tabular offsets between selected, bucketed positions	Assume directly that portfolio returns are normally distributed. Using standard formula: $\textbf{VAR} = \alpha \times \sigma_p$	Assume that asset returns are jointly normal, implying linear asset pay-off profiles and normally distributed portfolio returns. Using formula: $\textbf{VAR} = \alpha \times \sigma_p$ $= \alpha \times \sqrt{\delta' \Sigma \delta}$	Assume that market rate innovations are normal but that pay-off profiles approximated by local, second-order terms	Approximates portfolio profit/loss distribution based on simulated rate movements, either historical or model based
Advantages/ disadvantages	+ Simplicity – Overly conservative – No recognition of cross-market correlations, even within risk class – Draconian measures applied to option risks (e.g. gamma, vega)	+ Simplicity + Useful for top-down, business unit capital attribution – Assumes normality of business unit returns, ignoring fat tails, skewness, kurtosis, etc. – Assumes constancy of risk strategy and portfolio characteristics	+ Simplicity — can be calculated using a spreadsheet + Based on Markowitz/ CAPM concepts – Assumes normality of returns; ignoring fat tails, skewness, etc. – Assumes predictable covariances – Assumes linear pay-off profile, not viable for convex products or non-local movements	+ Simplicity + Captures gamma – Assumes normality of returns – Assumes predictable covariances – Does not capture risks of non-local movements	+ Captures local and non-local price movements + Not subject to model risks (historical simulation) – Model risk for empirical simulation – Computer intensive

Figure 7.8 Comparison of selected methods

required to support a trading book out of several "building blocks", the two most important being a charge for specific and general risks. The specific risk charge is "designed to protect against an adverse movement in the price of an individual security owing to factors related to the individual issuer" (BIS (1995a)). The general risk component is designed to capture the risk of loss arising from changes in market rates and is often based on a banding or bucketing of risk positions into homogeneous groups or maturity buckets similar to those for RiskMetrics with inter-band offsets used to recognize correlations between groups rather than using the actual correlations as is done in the Asset-Normal/RiskMetrics approach. The practicality of this approach is underscored by the fact that it is the fall-back solution proposed under the BIS 1995 proposals for institutions which choose not to develop their own internal risk capital models since it is (arguably) less costly to implement in terms of systems and skilled resources than are proprietary models (see BIS (1995a)).

As an example to illustrate the approach, consider the band and bucket structure which the BIS has proposed to cover interest rate risks, illustrated in Figure 7.9 (BIS (1995a)). In addition to a specific risk charge depending on the remaining life of the instrument and the issuer,[21] a general risk charge is also calculated. This general risk charge is calculated by summing four values:

- The net short or long position for the entire trading book
- The "vertical disallowance" calculated using the following rule: first, weight the gross long and short positions with the factors in the table on the left to reflect their interest rate sensitivity, with the weighting determined by the remaining life for fixed rate

Table A: "Vertical Disallowance" Weights

	Coupon of 3 per cent or more	Coupon less than 3 per cent	Risk weight
Zone 1	≤ month	≤ month	0.00%
	1-3 months	1-3 months	0.20%
	3-6 months	3-6 months	0.40%
	6-12 months	6-12 months	0.70%
Zone 2	1-2 years	1-1.9 years	1.25%
	2-3 years	1.9-2.8 years	1.75%
	3-4 years	2.8-3.6 years	2.25%
Zone 3	4-5 years	3.6-4.3 years	2.75%
	5-7 years	4.3-5.7 years	3.25%
	7-10 years	5.7-7.3 years	3.75%
	10-15 years	7.3-9.3 years	4.50%
	15-20 years	9.3-10.6 years	5.25%
	>20 years	10.6-12 years	6.00%
		12-20 years	8.00%
		>20 years	12.50%

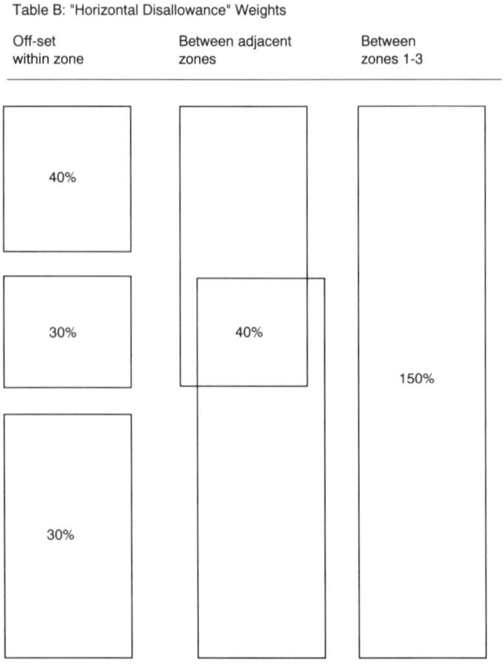

Figure 7.9 Regulators' "Building Block" approach

positions and the time to next interest rate reset for floating rate positions. A charge of 10 per cent is then allocated against the smaller of the gross long and short positions to reflect basis and gap risk (called the "vertical allowance")

- The "horizontal disallowance" calculated by allowing the gross long and short positions to offset one another using the table on the right side of the figure. For example, the "horizontal disallowance" is equal to 40 per cent of the net exposure in zone 1 plus 30 per cent of the net in zones 2 and 3 plus 40 per cent of the net residual between zones 1 and 2 and zones 2 and 3 plus 100 per cent of the residual between zones 1 and 3
- Finally, a charge for option positions to capture convexity and volatility risks. Using the "simplified approach", these charges are calculated in the following manner:
  - For gamma risk, multiply the net negative gammas per maturity band by a weight and by the square of the market value of the underlying
  - For vega risk, the net vega amount per time band calculated using a ±25 per cent proportional shift in volatility

The offset rules designed to capture correlations between changes in position values were defined after empirically simulating the rules against a wide variety of portfolios designed specifically to stress those rules. The rules are only then set once they have been shown not only to cover the worst case market rate development but also to cover the "worst case portfolio" within the band structures. In addition, the offset rules never extend between the most obvious correlated pairs, e.g. net long DM interest rate positions are not allowed to offset net short HFL positions, net short vega is not allowed to offset net long vega in a different maturity band, short gamma is not allowed to offset long gamma, etc., even though the pairs of risks may be highly correlated.

(ii) Assumptions and Implications

The simple bucketing and banding rules may work well for positions with simple structures which can be decomposed, mapped and represented by non-contingent cash flows, e.g. swaps, forwards, futures, etc. All option positions, however, do not naturally lend themselves to being "bucketed" without making heroic assumptions (e.g. bucketing their delta equivalents) and levying draconian surcharges to cover gamma and vega risks.

If the institution relies on the arbitrary bucketing or banding techniques as described, then it may be consistently over-allocating risk capital for three reasons: first, because, as mentioned earlier, the banding or bucketing techniques are essentially designed to cover the *worst possible portfolio* within the band structure in *the worst case market scenario*. This differs subtly from allocating risk capital to cover the worst possible market rate event for the *actual* portfolio of interest. Second, because the arbitrary netting between buckets or bands does not extend between different risk factors, any cross-market hedges using highly correlated instruments will not be recognized. Finally, the proposed methods used to capture gamma and vega risk are relatively draconian by design in an effort to "keep it simple".

(iii) Applicability

Based on our observations, the most likely application of these bucketing techniques is in the regulatory context where it is arguably necessary to develop simple rules so that all financial institutions can implement them in a cost effective manner and so satisfy their regulatory reporting requirements (although this is questionable given the current industry concern over the costs of implementing the CAD guidelines). For the internal management and control of an institution's risk positions, its efficacy is less clear, especially given the availability of other methods which are just as easy to implement (e.g. the Delta-Normal or Delta–Gamma methods), which have synergies with other risk management and trading applications (e.g. the calculation of correlations and volatilities) and which recognize the convexity and correlations between positions.

7.5.2 Portfolio-Normal Methods

(i) Calculation Rules

This method calculates risk capital as a multiple of the standard deviation of the portfolio's or business unit's returns, e.g.:

$$\text{VAR} = \alpha \sigma_p \sqrt{\Delta t}$$

where α is defined as the constant that gives the appropriate one-tailed confidence interval for the standardized normal distribution (e.g. $\alpha = 2.33$ for a 99.0 per cent confidence interval), σ_p is the (annualized) standard deviation of the portfolio/business unit's returns and Δt is the holding period horizon as a fraction of a year.

(ii) Assumptions and Implications

This calculation rule is justified if portfolio or business unit returns are normally distributed, e.g. $\Delta P \sim N(\mu_p, \sigma_p)$, since it is a well-known property of the normal distribution that confidence intervals can be expressed as a multiple of the standard deviation. The normal assumption is valid for a portfolio in one of three situations:

- If the portfolio is comprised of a large number of positions whose limiting distribution is the normal distribution (see below for an example), or

- If the portfolio returns are in fact normal and the portfolio strategy and composition is "constant", implying that the returns are drawn from a distribution with constant mean and variance, or

- If the portfolio is comprised of a set of asset positions, each of which is normally distributed. These assumptions define the Asset-Normal/RiskMetrics assumptions and will therefore be discussed in the next section.

Given these (implicit) assumptions, almost all of the common critiques (e.g. local measures, model risks, fat tails, non-constant parameters, symmetry, etc.) can therefore be applied to this method.

(iii) Applications

As discussed, the Portfolio-Normal method is typically used in one of two contexts. The first involves portfolios comprising a large quantity of identical but independent positions whose limiting distribution is the normal distribution. For example, consider calculating the risk capital of a large, well-diversified portfolio of small consumer credits where we are interested in the amount of the portfolio which might go into default. Since, in the limit, the distribution of the sum of binomial variates converges in probability to the normal distribution, the portfolio's absolute return distribution will approach that of a normal distribution in the limit as the number of credits increases. Since we are justified in assuming a normal distribution in the limit, we might feel comfortable assuming that, for very large portfolios of identical and independent positions, the return distribution is approximately normal. This method is therefore often used to calculate the capital at risk for large, well-diversified portfolios of consumer credits, credit card receivables, or the credit risk of mortgage pools.

The second potential use of the Portfolio-Normal method is to develop a quick and dirty capital at risk capital methodology based on historical profit and loss information *at the business unit level*. For example, consider calculating capital at risk for an equity trading unit by dividing monthly net income over the past three to five years by the market value of its equity holdings. Based on this time series, one could estimate the standard deviation of returns per dollar invested in the equity portfolio; using the formula, this would be used to estimate the risk capital needed to support each dollar worth of open "equity" position. This method assumes that, beyond changes in the volume, the composition or trading strategy of the equity trading book is constant, an obviously unreasonable assumption.

Whilst this application may prove useful in terms of getting a first cut at business unit risk capital for performance measurement purposes, it is not a long- (or even medium-) term solution in terms of risk controlling. Nonetheless, it is quite useful as a starting point for the top-down evaluation of a business unit's risk adjusted performance, especially in the context of a portfolio of businesses (see D. Wilson (1995) and T. Wilson (1992)).

7.5.3 Asset-Normal or RiskMetrics Methods

(i) Calculation Rules

As with the Portfolio-Normal method, this method also calculates risk capital as a multiple of the standard deviation of the portfolio's or business unit's returns, e.g.:

$$\text{VAR} = \alpha \sigma_p \sqrt{\Delta t}$$

where α and Δt are defined as above. The only difference is that the standard deviation of the portfolio returns, σ_p, is calculated using a set of portfolio weights, ω, and the covariance matrix of position returns, Σ, using the formula $\sigma_p = \sqrt{\omega' \Sigma \omega}$.

(ii) Assumptions and Implications

The Asset-Normal method assumes that the $N \times 1$ vector of *position* returns is jointly normal, $N(0, \Sigma)$ where 0 and Σ are the $N \times 1$ vector of expected returns for one unit of position i and the $N \times N$ covariance matrix of returns on position i, respectively[22] Note that we are assuming that the returns on market *positions* (e.g. zero bonds, equity index positions, equity options, etc.) are normally distributed[23] and not that market *rate* innovations (e.g. changes in interest rates, exchange rates, etc.) are normally distributed; this latter assumption is made in the Delta-Normal method described below. Since a portfolio is a weighted sum of its underlying positions and since the sum of normal variates is itself normally distributed, it follows that the expected returns of the portfolio are also normally distributed with mean $\mu_p = \omega' \mu$ and variance $\sigma_p^2 = \omega' \Sigma \omega$.

If the market prices for individual positions are assumed to be governed by a diffusion process similar to the geometric Brownian motion process described earlier, then this assumption can be justified on theoretical grounds but only over infinitesimally short time intervals and for "small" market rate innovations (see Wilson (1992, 1993)); thus, this assumption can be thought of as valid only "locally". Almost all of the common critiques (e.g. linear approximations, local measures, model risks, fat tails, etc.) are therefore valid for this method of calculating capital at risk.

(iii) Applications

The Asset-Normal or RiskMetrics method has a long history of being applied to investment portfolios; in fact, its assumptions (e.g. that position returns are normally distributed and that the variance or standard deviation of portfolio returns is a good measure of risk) are at the heart of the Capital Asset Pricing Model developed by Sharpe (1964) and Lintner (1965) as well as the portfolio optimization techniques of Markovitz (1952) (see footnote 24). As such, investors have been calculating value at risk for a long time without even knowing it every time they considered the standard deviation of returns as a risk measure in the CAPM framework.

In addition, the Asset-Normal assumptions form the basis for RiskMetric's VaR methodologies. At its core, RiskMetrics[24] comprises two basic components: first, a set of techniques to map a wide variety of *products* into standardized risk *positions* (e.g. zero coupon bonds, equity positions and net open exchange rate positions) and, second, advanced techniques applied to the estimation of the covariance matrix (e.g. the handling of missing data, exponential weighted average covariance estimation, etc.). Notwithstanding the extensive maths and theory utilized as well as the tremendously beneficial impact for the industry, it should be noted that RiskMetrics makes basically the same assumptions about position returns (e.g. normally distributed) and position sensitivities (e.g. linear) that Markowitz made in 1952. As such, the advantages and disadvantages of the model have been well understood and documented over the years.

One important problem is that, since position returns are assumed to be normally distributed, the Asset-Normal or RiskMetrics methodologies are not suitable for products with non-symmetric return distributions (e.g. options, etc.). The issue of non-linear pay-offs can only be addressed through other models such as the Delta–Gamma method, simulation techniques or the factor push method.

7.5.4 Delta-Normal Methods

A natural problem with the Asset-Normal/RiskMetrics approach arises when the number of positions (N) is quite large relative to the number (M) of market rates (S) which determine the value of the portfolio. Consider the following examples:

- Suppose we are interested in capturing the volatility risks of options. In order to capture option risks, we would either have to estimate the covariance between each individual option's returns or try to come up with some mapping technique to map an arbitrary option position into standardized risk positions as is done in RiskMetrics for non-contingent cash flows by mapping bonds, FRAs, etc. into a cash flow grid. This would be a very complicated and inaccurate mapping since the price of an option depends on many different factors, including volatility, degree of "moneyness", time to expiration, etc. The easier approach would be to focus on volatility itself as a risk factor and try to characterize how the portfolio's value changes with changes in volatilities rather than try to model the covariance between position returns as is done in the Asset-Normal/RiskMetrics approach

- As a further example, suppose that we have 16 zero coupon maturity bucket grid points per currency which are all highly dependent on the level of interest rates. Rather than estimating the correlations and variances of all 16 positions for a large number of currencies, it might make sense instead to reduce the dimensionality of the problem by focusing on only two or three "risk factors" which capture most of the variation in the level and shape of the term structure. So, instead of modelling the highly correlated returns of 16 individual positions, one would measure the risk of a portfolio under two to three independent interest rate scenarios instead. This reduction in dimensionality can be accomplished through principle components or factor analysis techniques as described in Kaarkki and Reyes (1995) and Wilson (1994a) and implemented in a risk capital framework by understanding the correlation between interest rate shifts and rotations rather than between position values directly.

The ability to reduce the dimensionality of the problem is accomplished by the delta-normal approach because it focuses on *risk factors* instead of *risk positions*. As such, it is a slightly more useful method of calculating risk capital for option portfolios.

(i) Calculation Rule

This method calculates capital at risk as a multiple of the portfolio's standard deviation, e.g.:

$$\text{VAR} = \alpha \sigma_p \sqrt{\Delta t} \tag{1}$$

where α and Δt are as defined above. Here, however, σ_p is calculated using the portfolio's delta sensitivities to market rates as the portfolio weights using the following formula: $\sigma_p = \sqrt{\delta' \Sigma \delta}$, where δ is the $M \times 1$ vector of portfolio sensitivities and Σ is the $M \times M$ market rate covariance matrix.

(ii) Assumptions and Implications

Implicitly, the assumption is made that the portfolio returns are normally distributed. This result follows from making market rate assumptions similar to those made for the Delta–Gamma methods: market rate innovations are assumed to be jointly normally distributed, e.g. $\Delta S \sim N(\mu, \Sigma \Delta t)$, where rates are defined as interest rates, exchange rates, etc., rather than position prices (e.g. zero coupon bonds, etc.) as is the case for the Asset-Normal/RiskMetrics case. This assumption is identical to assumption (A1) made earlier and will therefore not be discussed in detail here.

Given that the market rate innovations are assumed to have a joint normal distribution, the only way that the portfolio returns can also be normally distributed is if all of the price functions are linear in terms of changes in the underlying market prices. This follows directly since a linear combination of normal variables is itself normally distributed. The implicit assumption is that the price functions can be reasonably approximated by a first-order Taylor Series Expansion around the current market prices. We will call this expansion a delta approximation to differentiate it from the second-order, delta–gamma approximation discussed earlier. More concretely:

(A2) Delta approximation:

$$\Delta P = \theta \Delta t + \delta' \Delta \mathbf{S} + o(2)$$

$$\Delta P \approx \theta \Delta t + \delta' \Delta \mathbf{S}$$

where θ is the portfolio's theta, or $\partial P(\mathbf{S})/\partial t$, δ is the portfolio's $M \times 1$ vector of delta sensitivities, or $\partial P(\mathbf{S})/\partial \mathbf{S}$, and $o(2)$ represents the approximation error which is of order 2. Again, this approximation error can be theoretically ignored if market rates are governed by a diffusion process and if time horizons are very "short", see for example Wilson (1992, 1993) for a discussion. Using the properties of the normal distribution, it follows directly that portfolio returns are normally distributed, e.g.:

$$\Delta P \sim N \left(\theta_p, \delta'_p \Sigma \delta_p \Delta t \right)$$

The capital at risk calculation rule given in equation (1) above follows directly where we define $\sigma_p = \sqrt{\delta'_p \Sigma \delta_p}$.

(iii) Applications

As mentioned, this method may be a reasonable one for calculating risk capital if the time horizon is very short, e.g. intraday, and if the products themselves have a relatively linear pay-off profile, or, because it is easy to calculate, if a quick and dirty method is required. Thus, it may be very well suited for measuring and controlling intraday risks of a money market or foreign exchange book with few option positions. Its advantage over the Asset-Normal/RiskMetrics approach is that it can be used to capture volatility risks as well as reduce the dimensionality of the problem significantly. In addition, its calculation also relies on the portfolio's deltas which should be readily available without the need to develop complex mapping techniques.

7.5.5 Empirical Simulation Methods

(i) Calculation Rule

This method, although difficult to implement in a cost effective manner at the transaction level for arbitrary portfolios involving any but the simplest derivatives, is the one most often chosen by regulators to set the optimal parameters for the "Building Block" approach because it is considered more robust and intuitive than other, model-based methods.

The method is based on a three-step simulation technique using historical rate movements and is therefore quite intuitive:

- Take a suitably long historical time series of market rates, $\{\mathbf{S}_t\}_t = -T \ldots 0$, typically three to five years of daily data, where $\mathbf{S}_t$ is the vector of market rates at time t
- Calculate a time series of the change in value of the portfolio of interest over the assumed liquidation period using the actual price functions, $P_i(\mathbf{S}_t)$ (e.g. the Black–Scholes or Garman–Kohlhagen formulae for simple options, zero coupon discount functions for cash flows, etc.), where $P_i(\mathbf{S}_t)$ represents the price of position i given market rates at time t. Alternatively, define and simulate an approximating portfolio pay-off function over this region, perhaps using a local, quadratic function, an N-dimensional cubic spline, a polynomial spline, linear interpolation, etc., based

on portfolio sensitivities evaluated at one-sigma intervals (including crosses) around the initial market rates. This pay-off function approximation step is optional if all of the portfolio's transactions can be accessed and evaluated directly in an efficient manner

- Finally, tabulate the empirical return distribution generated from these historical rates and determine the appropriate risk capital for the portfolio by examining the extreme values of that distribution.

(ii) Assumptions and Implications

This method makes very few assumptions about the market price processes generating the portfolio's returns: it simply assumes that market price innovations in the future are drawn from the same empirical distribution as those market price innovations generated historically; it is, however, dependent on the specific historical context chosen. This implies that the exact time frame used is somewhat critical as it could arbitrarily include or exclude extreme price movements actually observed. For example, a five-year period would capture the bond crash of 1994 but not the stock market crash of 1987, whereas a ten-year period would.

To its benefit, by using the empirical distribution, one avoids many of the problems inherent in explicitly modelling the evolution of market prices, e.g. the fact that market prices tend to have "fatter tails" and be slightly more skewed than predicted by the normal distribution, the fact that correlations and volatilities can vary over time, etc. The main advantage of this method, therefore, is that one does not inadvertently introduce model risk into the calculation of risk capital, except to the extent to which models of the stochastic behaviour of market rates are required to calculate non-observable parameters such as volatilities and correlations.

Also to its benefit is the fact that, if one follows this method exactly, then there are no assumptions made regarding the price functions: one would use the exact price functionals, $P_i(S_t)$, to generate the historical distribution of portfolio returns. This implies that the actual pay-off profile of the portfolio is captured globally, rather than having to rely on local approximations. If an approximating pay-off profile is used, model risk or approximation error is introduced which might be mitigated by the choice of a tighter grid for calculating the approximation.

However, the full simulation method is quite costly, to implement from a systems perspective. First, it requires that *all* of the institution's positions are accessible by the same system in some form or another or, equivalently, that the organization have an institution-wide, transaction-oriented database. This presents certain challenges in itself for institutions which have to integrate a wide variety of legacy systems, or whose operations are geographically dispersed or which innovate new products frequently. Second, it requires that all of these transactions are able to be priced centrally on the back of this transaction database. Again, this may be a difficult task if new product structures are being introduced frequently and there may be a lead time before the new structures are implemented centrally. Third, it requires substantial computing power in order to calculate the empirical return distribution, essentially entailing the marking-to-market of the portfolio every day over the three-to five-year historical period in order to calculate a single risk capital number. It may be the case that such computing capacity is not warranted from a risk control perspective alone, in which case the implementation of the full simulation method must find at least partial justification from the trading or front division as well. Finally, it requires that an adequate historical time series of market rates is constructed. This method may therefore be difficult to apply in emerging markets which have no "history" or when attempting to capture market risk factors which are not directly observable such as rate volatilities and correlations for correlation dependent options.

(iii) Applicability

As mentioned earlier, however, the full simulation method is robust to most of the common criticisms levelled at capital at risk calculations (e.g. local measures, model risk, fatter tails, etc.). It is therefore most useful in the context of portfolios which meet two conditions: first, the computing infrastructure is justified by both the front divisions as well as risk controlling and, second, the products covered are highly complex with pay-off profiles which cannot be easily approximated at the extremes by other, simpler methods.

7.5.6 Monte Carlo Simulation Methods

(i) Calculation Rules

The Monte Carlo simulation method calculates capital at risk by using the three-step procedure outlined in Figure 7.10. Just like the empirical simulation method, except that the simulations are based on specific models for market rate innovations over the holding period rather than on the historical innovations.

(ii) Assumptions and Implications

The evolution of each market risk factor must be explicitly modelled in order to implement this method. Although some complex representations of single and multi-country, arbitrage-free rate dynamics are implemented (e.g. Heath–Jarrow–Morton, Langstaff–Schwartz or other representations for single currency rate environments as well as other multi-currency, multi-asset class representations), they are very complex to implement as they require the estimation of non-observable parameters and significant intellectual and systems infrastructure to make them operational. Due to the complexity of their implementation, these models are most commonly used for calculating risk capital *only if* they are used by the front for the pricing and risk management of complex derivative portfolios.

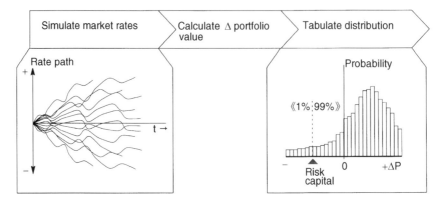

Figure 7.10 Simulation procedure

The most common (and the simplest) Monte Carlo implementation involves the assumption that market rates follow a joint geometric Brownian motion (GBM) process with constant drift and volatility parameters as given below:

$$d\mathbf{p}(t) = \mu(t)\mathbf{p}(t)\,dt + \sigma(t)\mathbf{p}(t)\,d\mathbf{Z}$$

implying the stochastic integral

$$\mathbf{p}(t + \Delta t) = \mathbf{p}(t)\exp\left[\int_{\Delta t}\mu(s)\,ds + \left(\int_{\Delta t}\sigma(s)\,ds\right)\sqrt{\Delta t}\omega\right]$$

where $\mathbf{p}(t)$ is the $N \times 1$ vector of market rates at time t, $\mu(t)$ is the $N \times 1$ vector of instantaneous drift terms at time t (often set so that the process fits the implied forward rates), $\sigma(t)$ is $N \times 1$ vector of instantaneous, annualized volatilities of the process, $d\mathbf{Z}$ is an $N \times 1$ serially independent standard Wiener process with correlation matrix Σ, and $\omega \sim N(\mathbf{0}, \Sigma)$.

In order to implement the Monte Carlo method assuming a GBM process, one would apply the following process:

- First, estimate the relevant parameters of this representation (e.g. σ and Σ) along the following lines (this is described in great detail in many standard textbooks on options such as Hull (1988)):
  - Calculate a new series by taking the first difference of the natural log of the market rate observations
  - Estimate the correlation matrix (Σ) and standard deviations (or the square root of the variances) of these series possibly using a GARCH model (see Alexander (1994))
  - Scale the standard deviations so that they represent annualized values. For example, if data used to estimate the parameters were daily and there are 250 working days in the year, then this standard deviation vector would be scaled by multiplying it by $\sqrt{250/1}$.
- Second, set the drift term as desired (e.g. consistent with the risk neutral price path, to fit the implied forward curve or for zero expected drift)
- Third, simulate the innovations to the $N \times 1$ market rate vector:
  - Typically, this will be done by first generating a random sample of an $N \times 1$ vector of independent, $N(\mathbf{0}, \mathbf{I})$ random variables, $\bar{\omega}$. The next step would be to use the Cholesky decomposition of the covariance matrix, $\Sigma = \mathbf{X}\mathbf{X}'$, to create a new, correlated set of innovations which have the same covariance structure as the market rate innovations, e.g. $\omega = \bar{\omega}\mathbf{X}$, so that $E(\omega\omega') = E(\bar{\omega}\mathbf{X}\mathbf{X}'\bar{\omega}') = \Sigma$ (see JPM (1994–95) for a discussion)
  - These innovations will then be used to calculate additive changes in observable market rates using a discretized version of the market rate model, e.g. $\Delta\mathbf{p}(t) \equiv \mathbf{p}(t + \Delta t) - \mathbf{p}(t) \approx \mathbf{p}(t)\mu\Delta t + \mathbf{p}(t)\sigma(t)\sqrt{\Delta t}\omega$, where $\mu(t)$ may be set equal to zero to achieve a random walk process; alternatively, $\mu(t)$ can be set so that the implied process is consistent with the implied forward curves (see step two defined above)

– In theory, simulating the P&L distribution will provide us with an estimate of the actual distribution, with the estimate converging to the actual as the number of simulations increases to infinity. Since it is impractical to simulate the P&L an infinite number of times, there will always remain some estimation error. For this reason, some type of variance reduction techniques, e.g. antithetic or control variates, quasi-random sequences, etc.,[25] are typically employed to improve the efficiency of the Monte Carlo sampling procedure.

• Finally, revalue the portfolio for each simulation run using either the actual transactions or an approximating pay-off profile as described in Section 7.5.5.

Depending upon which models are chosen, this approach is subject to many of the standard distributional criticisms, e.g. fat tails, symmetric distributions, etc. More disturbing for regulators is the fact that this method introduces model risks for the market rate processes which need to be modelled before being simulated. In addition, some models (e.g. the GBM assumption) do not necessarily restrict the market rate processes to be arbitrage free whereas other models may have the desired arbitrage-free properties. Although some assumptions regarding the price functions may be made, normally the simulated distribution is generated using the actual price functions. If an approximating pay-off profile is used, then approximation errors may be introduced.

This method is therefore as challenging to implement in terms of systems as the empirical simulation method. An additional cost arises, however, in that the institution must also be in a position to estimate the relevant model parameters, thus increasing the skilled resources required.

(iii) Applications

Nonetheless, if the modelling is correctly done, it is one of the most robust methods available in terms of its ability to be applied to many diverse product structures. Furthermore, the skills and systems built up through its implementation may lead the institution to be a stronger player in the derivatives markets, allowing them to better structure solutions for their clients. Because of these points, it is probably not cost effective to implement a Monte Carlo method based solely on a risk measurement mandate: if the institution has already developed Monte Carlo models to price and manage complex structures for their clients, then these can be leveraged in terms of risk assessment. Otherwise, their implementation probably does not make sense on a stand-alone basis except on a simplified basis.

7.5.7 Factor-Push Methodology

(i) Calculation Rule

The Factor-Push Method, often used for calculating the potential credit exposure from derivatives transactions, determines the most disadvantageous direction that market prices can go and then "pushes" the prices in that direction in order to calculate risk capital. The amount by which the individual factors are pushed typically depends on their volatilities but not on their correlations; for example, the DM/USD and HFL/USD rates may each be "pushed" by 2.33 standard deviations if a 99.0 per cent confidence interval is desired, but perhaps in opposite directions even though the rates are themselves very highly correlated. More concretely, the Factor-Push method calculates capital at risk through the following process (see Figure 7.11):

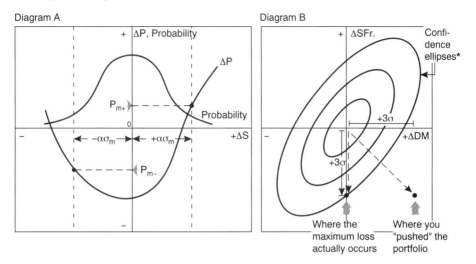

Figure 7.11 Factor-Push method — single dimension

1. For $m = 1 \ldots M$, define P_{m+} equal to the value of the portfolio when evaluated when the mth market price is "pushed" up by α standard deviations (e.g. $S_m = S_{m0} + \alpha\sigma_m$, where α equals the number of standard deviations required to give the desired confidence interval and σ_m is the volatility of the mth market rate innovation), all other market prices being held constant. Define P_{m-} analogously.

2. Define a "worst case" scenario which "pushes" all of the variables in the worst possible direction. This is accomplished by valuing the portfolio using $+ \alpha\sigma_m$ if $P_{m+} < P_{m-}$ and $- \alpha\sigma_m$ otherwise for each of the M market rates.

3. The risk capital for this portfolio is calculated as the difference between this "worst case scenario" and the portfolio's value at current market prices. Alternatively, sometimes the sum of the individual deviations is taken (e.g. take the sum of (Min $[P_{m+}, P_{m-}] - P_0$) over all M).

(ii) Assumptions and Implications

There are several problems with this methodology which are illustrated by the diagrams in Figure 7.11.

- First, it assumes that the maximum possible loss will occur at the extreme values of the price distribution. Consider diagram A of Figure 7.11, which illustrates a position for which the losses occur when rates remain stable, not when they reach their extremes. Because we are pushing each of the market prices by α standard deviations, we are actually pushing the position further into-the-money; for this example, the maximum possible loss is found closer to, rather than farther from, the current market prices

- Second it does not optimally recognize factor sensitivity trade-offs, e.g. it pushes all of the factors by two or three standard deviations, regardless of the portfolio's sensitivity to the individual factors. Consider, for example, diagram B in Figure 7.11 which illustrates this effect for a portfolio which has a small short DM position with relatively low sensitivity to an appreciating DM/USD rate but a very large long

CHF/USD position and therefore high sensitivity to depreciating CHF/USD rate. For this example, the maximum possible loss within a 97.5 per cent confidence interval does not occur when both rates are pushed equally by two standard deviations; this would only be the case if the portfolio was equally as sensitive to both rates. Rather, it occurs when the CHF/USD rate is pushed by more than two standard deviations and the DM/USD rate by less. Intuitively, by pushing the DM/USD rate by the same amount even though it has less of a negative impact on the value of the portfolio, you are wasting valuable probability, probability which could better be used by pushing the CHF/USD rate in a direction that pushes the portfolio even further into the red

- Third, by pushing each rate based on its marginal distribution, it ignores specific properties of their joint distribution. For example,

    - It ignores correlations between the rates. In the example above, based on the high correlation between the DM/USD and CHF/USD exchange rates, both rates are more likely either to appreciate or depreciate rather than go in separate directions (as is illustrated by the diagram)

    - In addition, even if the rates are uncorrelated, pushing each of the rates by two standard deviations based on their marginal distribution actually describes an event which is much less likely to occur given the joint distribution of the exchange rates

The critique that the Factor-Push method does not capture correlation effects can be mitigated to some extent by first using principal components or factor analysis to create independent risk factors with unit variance (see Kaarkki and Reyes (1995) and Wilson (1994a) for a description) which can then be "pushed" independently of one another. Unfortunately, this process ignores (or creates) second-order effects which can be significant. To see this, consider the second-order Taylor series expansion given by (A2) earlier:

(A2)   Delta–gamma approximation:

$$\Delta P(\mathbf{S}) \approx \theta \Delta t + \boldsymbol{\delta}' \Delta \mathbf{S} + \Delta \mathbf{S}' \boldsymbol{\gamma} \Delta \mathbf{S}/2$$

where $\Delta \mathbf{S} \sim N(\mathbf{0}, \boldsymbol{\Sigma})$ with $\boldsymbol{\Sigma}$ non-diagonal. For expositional purposes, assume that $\boldsymbol{\gamma}$ is diagonal implying that, to the extent that there are cross-product effects, they come only through the covariance matrix, $\boldsymbol{\Sigma}$. Next, consider creating a new set of independent risk factors by applying the linear transformation implied by the principle components technique. More specifically, define

$$\Delta \mathbf{S}^* = \mathbf{P}^* \Delta \mathbf{S}$$

where $\mathbf{P}^* = \mathbf{P}\boldsymbol{\Lambda}^{-1/2}$ and $\mathbf{P}$ is the matrix of eigenvectors of $\boldsymbol{\Sigma}$ and $\boldsymbol{\Lambda}$ is the diagonal matrix of eigenvalues of $\boldsymbol{\Sigma}$. Inserting this relationship into (A2) gives the following:

$$\Delta P(\mathbf{S}) \approx \theta \Delta t + \boldsymbol{\delta}^{*'} \Delta \mathbf{S}^* + \Delta \mathbf{S}^{*'} \boldsymbol{\gamma}^* \Delta \mathbf{S}^*/2$$

where $\boldsymbol{\delta}^* = \boldsymbol{\delta}\mathbf{P}^{*-1}$ and $\boldsymbol{\gamma}^* = \mathbf{P}^{*'-1}\boldsymbol{\gamma}\mathbf{P}^{*-1}$. Inspection of $\boldsymbol{\gamma}^*$ reveals that, even if there were no cross-product terms initially (e.g. $\boldsymbol{\gamma}$ was diagonal), cross-product terms will have been introduced after the factorization of the market rate innovations. The only way to eliminate these (second-order) cross-product effects is to use the results of the Theorem given earlier.

(iii) Applications

As mentioned, this method is most often used for evaluating the potential credit exposure arising from derivative transactions, particularly for evaluating in isolation a single swap transaction whose value depends on a single market rate (thereby avoiding the problematic correlation issue); the end products of such an effort typically include potential credit exposure envelopes for standard swap transactions used to replace the BIS haircuts and the ability to "push" a portfolio of single factor, counterparty transactions "on the fly" to aid marketers. This method is preferred because it is easier to implement under an arbitrary netting set definition.

Unfortunately, the rationale for using this method is based more on systems limitations than on measurement accuracy: by implementing this method, the institution potentially sacrifices correlations and interior solutions but gains the ability to calculate counter-party potential exposure in the "front" applications where the transaction data and pricing algorithms reside, implying that less systems integration work and a less comprehensive modelling effort need to be undertaken. As such, this method should be considered an interim solution at best.

7.5.8 Numerical Search Methods (Scenario Analysis)

(i) Calculation Rule

This method, described in Allen (1994), is an attempt to reflect the fact that statistical relationships such as correlations and volatilities, whilst valid during "normal" market periods, are most likely to fall apart with extreme market movements. In an effort to calculate the risk capital needed to support extreme market movements when "normal" correlations may no longer be valid, it ignores statistical relationships entirely through the following process (see Figure 7.12):

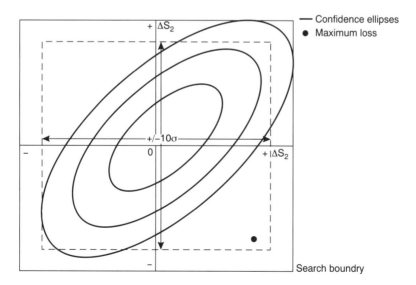

Figure 7.12 Numerical search methods

- First, specify a region in $\mathfrak{R}^N$ within which to search for the worst possible outcome. In this example, we have chosen a two-dimensional rectangle where the length of each side is set arbitrarily equal to a ten standard deviation innovation in the underlying market rates

- Second, use the actual pay-off profile or an approximating pay-off function over this region, perhaps using an N-dimensional cubic spline, a polynomial spline, linear interpolation, etc., based on portfolio sensitivities evaluated at 1-sigma intervals around the initial market rates. As for the simulation techniques, the creation of an approximating pay-off profile is optional if all of the portfolio's transactions can be accessed and evaluated directly

- Third, "search" the pay-off profile over this region for the worst possible event. If a gradient search method is used, then use various initial conditions to ensure that a global rather than a local minimum is achieved

(ii) Assumptions and Implications

This numerical search method makes no assumptions regarding the stochastic process generating return innovations (except, perhaps, with regards to the maximum possible innovations which is a parameter to be set by management, e.g. ten-sigma in the example) in an attempt to capture the absolute maximum risk capital required to cover truly extreme market rate movements when "normal" statistical relationships tend to break down. It therefore also ignores potentially useful information and relationships which might govern markets during more "normal" periods. As such, it is impossible to give the result a confidence interval interpretation. Both of these criticisms are reflected in Figure 7.12 where the solution to the numerical search (represented by the dot) lies clearly outside of the confidence intervals of the joint process (represented by the ellipsoids).

In terms of price sensitivities, it may or may not assume that the portfolio's pay-off function is closely approximated by an approximating function over the relevant search region, depending upon whether transaction data are available or not.

(iii) Applications

This method was developed to answer a specific question: what is absolutely the worst case scenario for the portfolio if absolutely everything goes against the book, ignoring all historical correlations and volatilities? As such, it may be interpreted as an extreme type worst case scenario and therefore provides some useful information. Nonetheless, it needs to be supplemented by other measures of risk capital which are valid as well during more "normal" times in order for it to be made operational and provide the information required by management to run their risk businesses.

7.5.9 Extreme Value Methods

(i) Calculation Rule

A relatively new development, and one which is clearly still in its infancy, is the use of asymptotic extreme value theory to calculate capital at risk. Longin (1994) proposes a method for calculating the optimal margining requirement for futures markets based on the asymptotic extreme value distribution. The question of the optimal margin requirement is directly related to the concept of risk capital given above, e.g. as the amount of capital needed to support a given risky position over some time horizon. Towards this end, Longin uses extreme value theory which gives the exact form for the asymptotic distribution of the minimum of a random variable (in this case, position returns), the form of which is independent of the distribution of daily price changes: different processes of daily price changes imply different parameters (a location parameter, β, a scale parameter, α, and a tail index, τ) but the same (generalized) functional form of the asymptotic extreme value distribution (see equation 5 in Longin (1994)).

(ii) Assumptions and Implications

The functional form of the extreme distribution is relatively robust, covering, for example, serially correlated price changes, innovations which exhibit "fat tails", ARCH processes, and mixtures of jump-diffusion processes. Nonetheless, one is modelling directly the extreme value of the price of a given product or portfolio and estimating the relevant parameters directly rather than using a Logo™ approach to build the portfolio distribution from the joint distribution of the underlying positions.

(iii) Applications

As mentioned, the use of asymptotic extreme value distributions for the calculation of risk capital is still in its infancy. Longin suggests that there are several important extensions in this area before it can be implemented in practice. The first and most important is the extension of the results to a multivariate context in order to capture spread or open positions in correlated markets; the second is the extension of the results to positions such as options which do not have a symmetric pay-off distribution. These extensions, needed in order to make the method usable in practice, may prove to be extremely challenging.

7.6 ENDNOTES

1. See Hull (1988) for a concise description of many of the most important risk measures used in practice.
2. For example a 99 per cent confidence interval, ten-day holding period, minimum of one year of market data, correlation to be captured within but not between risk classes, minimum of six bands for interest rates, ability to capture non-linear options related risks, etc.
3. For a discussion of RAPM methodologies from a practical and theoretical standpoint, see Chew (1994a), D. Wilson (1995) and T. Wilson (1992, 1995a).
4. For example, when evaluating credit risks, there is a bias towards lower rated counterparties if returns are measured relative to regulatory capital since regulatory capital adequacy rules are not sufficiently differentiated by credit risk or rating.
5. See, for example, Alexander (1994), Allen (1994), Chew (1994b), Lawrence et al. (1995a), Longerstaey et al. (1995) and Wilson (1993, 1994b).
6. Although it is certainly correct to ask under what conditions risk capital is a meaningful measure of risk for an individual or in market equilibrium. In addition, some financial institutions question whether or not Expected Maximum Loss (EML) or the probability of ruin would not be better measures of aggregate institution risk. Wilson (1995a) addresses some of these issues.
7. See, again, JPM (1994–95), Lawrence et al. (1995a) and Longerstaey et al. (1995).
8. See Wilson (1995b) for an empirical investigation of the importance of cross-rate effects and Ashraff, Tarczon and Wu (1995) for cross-rate hedging techniques.
9. To see this, consider the explicit formula for the mark-to-market value of this position in terms of your domestic currency:

$$\mathrm{MTM}_t = e_t[\mathrm{d}f(t_1) - (1 + {}_tf_{t_1 \to t_2}{}^*(t_2 - t_1)/360)^* \, \mathrm{d}f(t_2)]$$

where MTM_t is the mark-to-market value at time t, e_t is the spot exchange rate, domestic currency/foreign currency, $df(t)$ are the foreign currency discount factors for a single currency unit to be paid/received at time t, $_tf_{t_1 \to t_2}$ is the forward rate, at t, from t_1 to t_2. Since the FRA is assumed to be concluded at time t and at current market rates, the expression in brackets (e.g. $[df(t_1) - (1 + {_t}f_{t_1 \to t_2}{}^*(t_2 - t_1)/360)^* \, df(t_2)]$) is equal to zero. Taking the partial derivative of the MTM expression with respect to the spot exchange rate gives $\partial \text{MTM}/\partial e_t = [df(t_1) - (1 + {_t}f_{t_1 \to t_2}{}^*(t_2 - t_1)/365)^* \, df(t_2)] = 0$. Thus, this position has no first-order foreign exchange risk. Nonetheless, it does have a second-order foreign exchange risk, represented by the second (cross-rate) derivative $\partial^2 \text{MTM}/\partial e_t \partial r_t = \partial[df(t_1) - (1 + {_t}f_{t_1 \to t_2}{}^*(t_2 - t_1)/365)^* \, df(t_2)]/\partial r_t$.

10. See, for example, Blattburg and Gonedes (1974) and Praetz (1972) for equity prices, Rogalski and Vinso (1978) and Wilson (1993) for foreign exchange rates; see also JPM (1994–5) for a multi-market evaluation.

11. See the references cited in note 10. In addition, it is interesting to note that stochastic volatility models predict a similar "fat tails" phenomenon as is demonstrated by historical price series. See, for example, Wilson (1993).

12. For a very good overview, see Alexander (1994).

13. Consider the standard geometric Brownian motion (GBM) process given by:
    (a) $dp(t) = \mu(t)p(t)\,dt + \sigma(t)p(t)\,dZ$
    with stochastic integral given by:
    (b) $p(t + \Delta t) = p(t)^* \exp\left[\left(\int_{\Delta t} \mu(s)\,ds + \left(\int_{\Delta t} \sigma(s)\,ds\right)\left(\int_{\Delta t} dZ\right)\right]\right.$
    This process is typically discretized using the following approximation:
    (c) $\Delta p(t) = \mu(t)p(t)\Delta t + \sigma(t)p(t)z$
    where z is assumed to be a unit normal variable. Whilst the stochastic integral of (a) given by (b) guarantees strictly positive rates, its equivalent discrete version given by (c) does not.

14. This section corrects an error in an earlier article (Wilson (1994b)) and expands it by explicitly including vega, or volatility risk, and rho, or interest rate risk, for option portfolios.

15. We can replace the assumption that market rate innovations are normally distributed with the assumption that they are distributed as multivariate Student-t random variables with υ degrees of freedom common to each. As discussed, the Student-t distribution seems to fit the empirical data better than the normal distribution as it has fatter tails. The assumption of a common degrees of freedom parameter may be problematic, however. For a more detailed discussion of these points, see Wilson (1993).

16. Roughly speaking, under assumptions (A1) and (A2), interior solutions can only occur if the γ matrix is positive definite and if δ is "sufficiently" small in absolute value, implying that the portfolio pay-off function is represented (roughly) by a quadratic, M-dimensional hyperbole; this would be the equivalent to a long-straddle position in all risk dimensions. In practice, these conditions are rarely met for multi-market portfolios, implying that interior solutions will be rare using this method.

17. See Varian (1984) for a discussion of constrained optimization, Lagrangian and Kuhn–Tucker conditions.

18. For ease of exposition, we have sketched only those hyperbolic cases with $\delta = 0$ (e.g. diagrams C and D). The methods specified below provide reasonable approximations when this is not the case.

19. See previous footnote.

20. The discussion and evaluation of the regulators' "Building Block" approach is not meant to be comprehensive, but only to illustrate the concept and issues. Interested individuals should read the references cited in the section for a more detailed description.

21. For example 0.00 per cent for government issuers; 0.25 per cent (for remaining life less than six months), 1.00 per cent (between six and 24 months) and 1.60 per cent (greater than 24 months) for qualifying issues (essentially, qualifying issues are investment grade issues); and 8 per cent for all other issuers.

22. Note that the assumption of a zero mean return vector can be relaxed easily.

23. Note that we could have assumed that the percentage returns rather than absolute returns on market positions were normally distributed as is done in standard CAPM situations. For short time intervals, these are roughly the same. What is important here is that it is the *position*

(e.g. zero bonds, options, etc.) returns which are roughly normal rather than *market rates* (e.g. interest rates, exchange rates, etc.)
24. The discussion and evaluation of the RiskMetrics techniques in this chapter are not complete. Interested individuals should read JPM (1994, 1995), Longerstaey and Zangari (1995) and Lawrence and Robinson (1995).
25. See Brotherton-Ratcliff (1994) for a discussion.

7.7 REFERENCES

Alexander, C. (1994) "History debunked". *Risk Magazine*, December.
Allen, M. (1994) "Building a role model". *Risk Magazine*, September.
Ashraff, J., Tarczon, J. and Wu, W. (1995) "Safe crossing". *Risk Magazine*, July.
Basle Committee on Banking Supervision (1995a) "An internal model-based approach to market risk capital requirements". April.
Basle Committee on Banking Supervision (1995b) "Planned supplement to the capital accord to incorporate market risks". April.
Blattberg, R. and Gonedes, N. (1974) "A comparison of the stable and Student-t distributions as statistical models for stock prices". *Journal of Business*, April.
Brotherton-Ratcliff, R. (1994) "Monte Carlo motoring". *Risk Magazine*, December.
Chew, L. (1994a) "Conscious efforts". *Risk Magazine*, April.
Chew, L. (1994b) "Shock Therapy". *Risk Magazine*, September.
Cookson, R., Chew, L. (1992) "Things fall apart". *Risk Magazine*, October.
Derivatives Policy Group (1995) Voluntary Oversight of OTC Derivatives.
Group of Thirty (1993) Derivatives: Practices and Principles. Global Derivatives Study Group, Washington DC.
Gumerlock, R. (1993) "Double trouble". *Risk Magazine*, September, vol. 6, no. 9.
Hull, J. (1988) *Options, Futures and other Derivative Securities*. New York: Prentice Hall.
J.P. Morgan (JPM) (1994-95) *RiskMetrics-Technical Documentation*. Releases 1-3, J.P. Morgan.
Kaarkki, J. and Reyes, C. (1994) "Model relationship". *Risk Magazine*, December.
Kupiec, P. and O'Brien, J. (1995a) "Internal affairs". *Risk Magazine*, May.
Kupiec, P. and O'Brien, J. (1995b) "Model alternative". *Risk Magazine*, June.
Lawrence, C. and Robinson, G. "How safe is RiskMetrics?". *Risk Magazine*, January.
Lawrence, C. and Robinson, G. (1995b) "Liquid measures". *Risk Magazine*, July.
Lintner, J. (1965) "The valuation of risk assets and the selection of risk investments in stock portfolios and capital budgets". *Review of Economic Studies*, **47**.
Longin, F. (1994) "Optimal margin level in futures markets: A parametric extreme-based method". IFA working paper 192-94, London Business School.
Longerstaey, J. and Zangari, P. (1995) "A transparent tool". *Risk Magazine*, January.
Markowitz, H. (1952) "Portfolio selection". *Journal of Finance*, **7**.
Praetz, P. (1972) "The distribution of share price changes". *Journal of Business*, **45**, January, 49-55.
Rogalski, R. and Vinso, J. (1978) "Empirical properties of foreign exchange rates". *Journal of International Business Studies*, **9**, Fall, 69-79.
Sharpe, W. (1964) "Capital asset prices: A theory of market equilibrium under conditions of risk". *Journal of Finance*, **19**.
Sheffe. (1959) *Analysis of Variance*.
Varian, H. (1984) *Microeconomic Analysis*. New York: W.W. Norton.
Wilson, D. (1995) "Marriage of ideals". *Risk Magazine*, July.
Wilson, T. (1992) "Raroc remodeled". *Risk Magazine*, September, vol. 5, no. 6.
Wilson, T. (1993) "Infinite wisdom". *Risk Magazine*, June, vol. 6, no. 6.
Wilson, T. (1994a) "Debunking the myths". *Risk Magazine*, April, vol. 7, no. 6.
Wilson, T. (1994b) "Plugging the gap". *Risk Magazine*, November.
Wilson, T. (1995a) "Risk capital and performance measurement: The theoretical underpinnings". Working paper.
Wilson, T. (1995b) "Implementing the delta-gamma method and estimating the importance of second-order cross-rate effects". Working paper.

APPROXIMATE DELTA–GAMMA METHOD

Assume that return innovations are jointly normally distributed with mean zero and non-singular $M \times M$ covariance matrix $\Sigma \Delta t$, e.g. $\Delta S \sim N(0, \Sigma \Delta t)$; define δ as the portfolio's $M \times 1$ delta vector with respect to each of the market rates (e.g. $\partial P/\partial S$) and γ as its (non-singular), symmetric gamma matrix (e.g. $\partial^2 P/\partial S_i \partial S_j$).

Define $\mathbf{P}$ as the non-singular Cholesky decomposition of Σ defined by $\Sigma = \mathbf{PP}'$, satisfying the equation $\mathbf{P}^{-1}\Sigma\mathbf{P}^{-1} = \mathbf{I}$, and, $\mathbf{T}$ as the orthogonal matrix which satisfies the equation $\mathbf{T}'(\mathbf{P}'\gamma\mathbf{P})\mathbf{T} = \gamma^*$, where γ^* is the diagonal matrix of the eigenvalues of the matrix $\mathbf{P}'\gamma\mathbf{P}$ and $\mathbf{T}$ is the matrix of eigenvectors of $\mathbf{P}'\gamma\mathbf{P}$.

Define $\phi = \text{Min}[\phi^-, \phi^+, 0]$, where $\phi^- = (\delta'\mathbf{PTe} - \alpha e'\gamma)$ and $\phi^+ = (\delta'\mathbf{PTe} + \alpha e'\gamma)$, an $M \times 1$ vector, where $\mathbf{e}$ is an $M \times 1$ vector of 1s, α is the number of standard deviations required to give the desired confidence interval for a standardized univariate normal variate, and the Min[] operator is defined element by element for the vector. Finally, define $\sigma_{\delta\gamma} = \sqrt{\phi'\phi}$. Then the capital at risk of the portfolio is approximated by:

    (i) $\text{VAR}_{\delta\gamma} = \alpha\sigma_{\delta\gamma}\sqrt{\Delta t}$

This "worst case scenario" is achieved by setting the market rates equal to the following:

    (ii) $\mathbf{S}_{\text{worst}} = \mathbf{S}_0 + \mathbf{P}^{-1}\mathbf{T}^{-1}\Delta\mathbf{S}$
where
    (iii) $\Delta S_i = -\alpha\phi_i \bigg/ \sqrt{\sum_i \phi_i^2}$

8

Volatility and Correlation Forecasting

CAROL ALEXANDER

8.1 INTRODUCTION

Accurate forecasting of volatility and correlation is the key to successful risk management and analysis. These forecasts lie at the centre of so many financial systems, from the statistical backbone of value at risk modelling to pricing and hedging derivative products. This chapter is concerned with how to construct such forecasts, and how to evaluate their effectiveness: then other chapters in this book describe how to employ measures and forecasts of volatility and correlation in numerous applications.

What is volatility? A standard non-parametric definition is that X is "more volatile" than Y if $P(|X| > c) > P(|Y| > c)$ for all c. So if y_t is a time series it becomes more volatile when $P(|y_{t+1}| > c) > P(|y_t| > c)$ for all c. But when y_t has a stationary normal distribution, this occurs if and only if $\sigma_{t+1} > \sigma_t$ where σ_t denotes the conditional standard deviation of y_t. Hence the use of standard deviation to measure volatility is commonplace, and if standard deviation is measured on daily, weekly or monthly returns, volatility is usually annualized and expressed as a percentage, thus:

$$\text{volatility at time } t = 100\sigma_t\sqrt{A} \text{ per cent} \qquad (1)$$

Prices, rates or yields often have infinite variance — a property of random walks — and volatilities are measured as standard deviations of returns, not of asset prices themselves. Returns are usually stationary time series, in that they have constant finite unconditional means and variances. The finite variance implies that they are tied to the constant mean, a property which is often referred to as mean-reversion. Now, if one takes two associated returns series x_t and y_t — returns on two gilts for example — we expect them to be not only individually stationary but also jointly stationary, because the (unconditional) covariance between them will also be a finite constant. In this case we can calculate their correlation as

$$\text{corr}(x_t, y_t) = \text{cov}(x_t, y_t)/\text{stdev}(x_t)\,\text{stdev}(y_t) \qquad (2)$$

Note that joint stationarity is necessary for the existence of correlation, and that it is the exception rather than the rule. Two arbitrary returns series, such as the USD/Rupee

---

The Handbook of Risk Management and Analysis. Edited by Carol Alexander

exchange rate and a stock in the FTSE 100, will be totally unrelated and are not likely to be jointly stationary, so correlations between these two time series do not exist. Of course, one can calculate a number based on the correlation formulae given in this chapter, but it does not measure unconditional correlation unless the two series are jointly stationary. In such cases "correlation" is found to jump about a lot over time — a sign of non-joint stationarity.

Correlation does not need to be annualized, as does volatility, because it is already in a standardized form: correlation always lies between -1 and $+1$. A negative value means that returns tend to move in opposite directions and a positive value indicates synchronous moves in the same direction. It is important to bear in mind that returns series can be perfectly correlated (value $+1$) even though the prices (or rates or yields) are in fact moving in opposite directions. Correlation really only measures short-term co-movements in returns, and has little to do with any long-term co-movements in prices. For common trend analysis in prices, rates or yields the technique of *cointegration* offers many advantages (Alexander (1994)).

There is one final distinction to make clear in this introductory part of the chapter, and that is the difference between an *estimate* and a *forecast*. In general, historical data is used to estimate volatility or correlation, and the estimate is then used to construct the forecasts. In Section 8.2 the forecast is simply the estimate itself, but in later sections we show how a whole term structure of volatility and correlation forecasts can be calculated from the estimates of the parameters of a single model. The emphasis of this chapter is on forecasting rather than estimating volatility and correlation, and so I have not covered the *stochastic variance* models which have been developed in recent years (see Andersen (1994) and Taylor (1994)). Stochastic variance models such as the Autoregressive in Variance (ARV) model, have proved very efficient at estimating parameters of volatility and correlation diffusion processes in two-factor models, but it is extremely difficult to construct forecasts from them.

The chapter is structured as follows: Section 8.2 looks at moving average volatility and correlation estimation methods: the equally weighted "historic" method and the exponentially weighted moving average method which is currently used in J.P. Morgan's RiskMetrics[TM]. Section 8.3, although the longest section, gives only an overview of the huge literature on GARCH modelling in finance. Section 8.4 reviews implied volatility and correlation forecasts and Section 8.5 shows how to evaluate the effectiveness of different forecasting procedures, and how to apply them to market risk measurement. It also recommends appropriate procedures for value at risk modelling. Section 8.6 concludes with a brief overview of some of the new directions of research into volatility and correlation forecasting.

8.2 MOVING AVERAGE METHODS

A moving average is an average — often an arithmetic average rather than a geometric or harmonic one — taken over a *rolling window* of a fixed number of data points. Thus the average is first calculated on data points $x_1, x_2, \ldots, x_n$, then on data points $x_2, x_3, \ldots, x_{n+1}$ and so on. Each time the window is rolled one point is knocked off behind and another is added at the end, so that the sample size remains fixed. Recording the average in this way creates a new time series which begins at time period n of the original time series.

Moving averages have been a useful tool in financial forecasting for many years. For example, in technical analysis, where they exist under the name of "stochastics", the relationship between moving averages of different lengths can be used as a signal to trade. Traditionally they have also been used in volatility estimation, indeed these methods are still entrenched in standard option pricing models. However, recent advances in time series analysis allow a more critical view of the efficacy of such methods, which will be one of the major themes of this section.

8.2.1 "Historic" Volatility and Correlation

Efficient markets imply asset prices are random walks, but asset returns will be stationary. Returns are therefore taken as inputs to volatility and correlation analysis and we denote by y_t the asset return at time t. The traditional "historic" volatility has a term structure because it has been used to value options of different maturities. Thus we speak of *n-period historic volatility* at time T to denote the quantity $(100\hat{\sigma}_T\sqrt{A})$ per cent where A is the number of observations per year and

$$\hat{\sigma}_T^2 = \sum_{t=T-n}^{t=T-1} y_t^2/n \qquad (3)$$

Thus $\hat{\sigma}_T$ is the unbiased estimate of standard deviation over a sample size n, assuming the mean is zero. Sometimes the non-zero mean standard deviation s_T is used in place of $\hat{\sigma}_T$, where

$$s_T^2 = \sum_{t=T-n}^{t=T-1} (y_t - \overline{y})^2/(n-1) \qquad (4)$$

and $\overline{y} = \Sigma_{t=T-n}^{t=T-1} y_t/n$ is the unbiased estimate of the sample mean (see Section 8.3.1).

"Historic" correlations of maturity n are calculated in an analogous fashion, again either with zero or non-zero mean assumptions. Thus if x_t and y_t are two returns series (possibly in mean-deviation form) which are not only individually stationary but also jointly stationary, then n-period historic correlations may be calculated as

$$r_T = \frac{\sum\limits_{t=T-n}^{t=T-1} x_t y_t}{\sqrt{\sum\limits_{t=T-n}^{t=T-1} x_t^2 \sum\limits_{t=T-n}^{t=T-1} y_t^2}} \qquad (5)$$

This gives a correlation measure for every point in time T of our historic data set, after the initial n observations. Now traditionally, the estimate over the previous n periods has been used as a forecast of volatility or correlation over the subsequent n periods. However, when we examine the time-series properties of historic volatilities and correlations we see that they have some undesirable qualities. These are described below with reference mainly to volatility, although similar comments apply to "historic" correlation.

(i) "Ghost Features"

Figure 8.1 shows 30-day and 60-day historic volatilities of the FTSE 100 index, calculated from daily data between January 1987 and February 1994. The sharp rise in volatility at

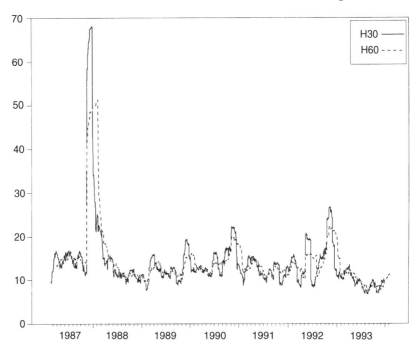

Figure 8.1 Thirty-day and 60-day historic volatilities of the FTSE

the beginning of the period, which coincides with Black Monday, lasts exactly 30 days in the 30-day series and exactly 60 days in the 60-day series. In general, n days after a major market movement there will be a sharp fall in n-period volatility, but since nothing at all happened on that day we call such a movement a "ghost feature".

(ii) All Variation is Due to Sampling Error

Perceived changes in volatility and correlation can have important consequences, so it is essential to understand what is the source of variability in any particular model. In the "historic" model, all variation is due only to differences in samples. A smaller sample size yields a less precise estimate, the larger the sample size the more accurate the estimate. So a short period moving average will be more variable than a longer moving average (and, as expected, the 30-day volatility series in Figure 8.1 is more variable than the 60-day series). Now, whether we are using 30-day or 60-day volatility, and whether we are taking the sample period to be in 1989 or in 1995, we are still estimating the *same thing*: the unconditional volatility of the time series. This is one number, a constant, underlying the whole series. So variation in the n-period historic volatility model, which we perceive as variation over time, is consigned to sampling error alone. There is nothing else in the model that allows for variation! This is a feature of *all* moving average models, of volatility or correlation, since they are estimates of unconditional moments, which are constants.

(iii) The Model Ignores Information Inherent in the Dynamic Ordering of Returns

If you "shuffle" the data within any given n-period window, you will get the same answer (provided of course for correlation the two returns series are shuffled "in pairs").

Hence the "historic" model is taking no account of dynamic properties of returns, such as autocorrelation — it is essentially a "static" model which has been forced into a time-varying framework.

8.2.2 Exponentially Weighted Moving Averages

The "historic" models explained above weight each observation equally, whether it is yesterday's return or the returns from several weeks or months ago. It is this equal weighting that induces the "ghost features", which are clearly a problem. An *exponentially weighted moving average* (EWMA) places more weight on more recent observations, and this has the effect of diminishing the problematic "ghost features". The exponential weighting is done by using a *smoothing constant* λ: the larger the value of λ the more weight is placed on past observations and so the smoother the series becomes. An n-period EWMA of a time series x_t is defined as

$$\frac{x_{t-1} + \lambda x_{t-2} + \lambda^2 x_{t-3} + \cdots + \lambda^{n-1} x_{t-n}}{1 + \lambda + \lambda^2 + \cdots + \lambda^{n-1}} \tag{6}$$

Since the denominator converges to $1/(1 - \lambda)$ as $n \to \infty$, an infinite EWMA may be written

$$(1 - \lambda) \sum_{i=1}^{\infty} \lambda^{i-1} x_{t-i} \tag{7}$$

It is this type of EWMA that is used for volatility and correlation forecasts in RiskMetrics (Third Edition, May 1995). The extensive technical document contains much detail on how their forecasts are constructed.

RiskMetrics forecasts of volatility and correlation over the next day are calculated by taking $\lambda = 0.94$ and using squared returns as the series x_t. The infinite EWMA model is equivalent to an IGARCH model (see Section 8.3.2), although the parameter λ is estimated in a sub-optimal way in RiskMetrics. So the next day forecasts can look very similar to GARCH forecasts, as shown in Figure 8.2. In currency markets the RiskMetrics forecasts are similar but generally tend to be too "persistent". In equities, the RiskMetrics forecasts

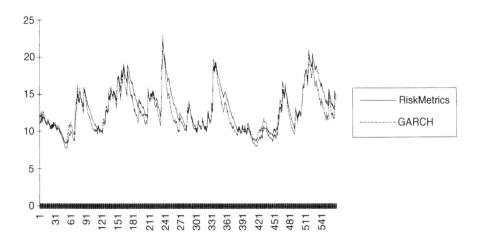

Figure 8.2 Daily volatility forecasts for DEM/USD rate: January 91 to December 92

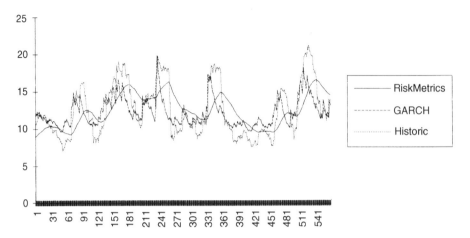

Figure 8.3 Monthly volatility forecasts for DEM/USD rate: January 91 to December 92

can be much smoother than the GARCH forecasts, indicating that the smoothing constant should perhaps be less than 0.94.

The RiskMetrics forecasts of volatility over the next *month* behave in a rather strange fashion, and may indeed be changed in a later edition. The EWMA is applied to a series x_t, as usual, and this time with a value $\lambda = 0.97$. But now x_t is taken to be the 25-historic volatility (see Section 8.2.1) which is a series which suffers from "ghost features". The effect of applying an EWMA to such a series is to *augment* the original ghost feature, and not to diminish it as was their original intention. Indeed RiskMetrics monthly forecasts will *peak* exactly 25 days *after* a major market movement (see Figure 8.3). For more details see Alexander (1995b). The RiskMetrics monthly forecasts should be used with caution, until a better forecasting method is being employed by J.P. Morgan in later editions of *RiskMetrics*.

8.3 GARCH

The unfortunate acronym "GARCH" is nevertheless essential, since it stands for *generalized autoregressive conditional heteroskedasticity*! *Heteroskedasticity* means "changing variance", so *conditional* heteroskedasticity means changing conditional variance. A time series displays conditional heteroskedasticity if it has highly volatile periods interspersed with tranquil periods, so there are "bursts" or "clusters" of volatility. Most financial time series display conditional heteroskedasticity, with the exception of fixed exchange rates and some daily bond returns of course, and a typical example of conditionally heteroskedastic returns in high frequency data is shown in Figure 8.4. *Autoregressive* means "regression on itself", and this refers to the method used to model conditional heteroskedasticity in GARCH models.

The first ARCH model, introduced by Rob Engle (1992) was later generalized by Tim Bollerslev (1986). The Bollerslev formulation has been found to be sufficiently general to capture most types of conditionally heteroskedastic behaviour, and many variations on his basic normal GARCH model have been introduced in the last ten years. For excellent reviews of the enormous literature on GARCH models in finance see Bollerslev et al. (1992) and (1994).

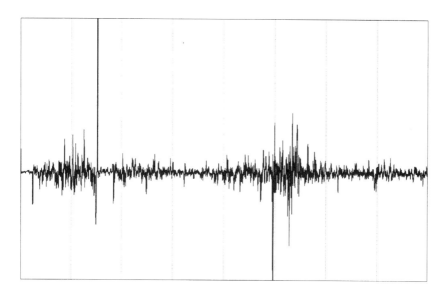

Figure 8.4 A conditionally heteroskedastic time series

8.3.1 Conditional and Unconditional Moments

The mean and variance are the first two moments of a returns distribution. GARCH does not model higher moments directly, like the skewness and kurtosis (weight in tails) and their properties are entirely defined by the theoretical characteristics of the assumed distribution of returns. For example, if we assume that returns are normally distributed then they have zero skew and kurtosis equal to 3 (variance)^2. So in this section we just look at conditional and unconditional means and variances — of stationary time series. Without the assumption of stationarity unconditional means and variances are not finite constants.

The *unconditional mean* of a stationary time series $y_t (t = 1, 2, \ldots T)$ is a single number, a constant. It is denoted $E(y_t)$ or μ, and is usually estimated by the sample mean

$$\bar{y} = \sum_{t=1}^{T} y_t / T \tag{8}$$

Standard regression techniques provide a model for the *conditional mean* of a time series. A common time series regression model is the autoregressive model of order 1, or AR(1) model, where

$$y_t = \alpha + \rho y_{t\,} + \varepsilon_t \tag{9}$$

To estimate the model parameters α and ρ efficiently we need to make some assumptions about the error term ε, for example that it is independent and identically distributed (i.i.d.). We can then use an appropriate method of estimation, such as ordinary least squares, to get the fitted model

$$\hat{y}_t = \hat{\alpha} + \hat{\rho} y_{t-1} \tag{10}$$

The estimated value of y_t — which is denoted $\hat{y}_t$ — is then used to estimate the time-varying conditional mean. Clearly different regression models give different estimates, but they are all estimates of the same conditional mean of the true distribution of y_t. This true conditional mean is denoted $E_t(y_t)$ or μ_t or $E(y_1|\Omega_t)$, where Ω_t is the information set available at time t (so Ω_t includes y_{t-1} and any other values which are known at time t). The last notation makes explicit how the conditional distribution is constructed on the assumption that all data up to that point are known, deterministic variables. On the other hand the unconditional mean assumes *all* observations are realizations of an i.i.d. random process.

These constructs are illustrated in Figure 8.5(a), where the unconditional mean is a constant, estimated using a standard formula such as the sample mean (8). The conditional mean is time-varying, and needs a model for its estimation — different models give different estimates, and not all models are regression models. In fact, neural networks and genetic algorithms are often used to estimate conditional means.

We now extend these idea to conditional and unconditional variances. The unconditional variance of a stationary time series y_t is a constant, denoted $V(y_t)$ or σ^2, the square of the unconditional standard deviation. An unbiased estimate of σ^2 is the sample variance

$$s^2 = \sum_{t=1}^{T}(y_t - \bar{y})^2/(T-1) \tag{11}$$

We subtract 1 from the sample size T because one parameter (the mean) has to be estimated (by $\bar{y}$) before s^2 can be calculated. That is, one degree of freedom is lost. However, we sometimes assume that $E(y_t) = 0$, in which case an unbiased estimate of $V(y_t)$ is

$$\hat{\sigma}^2 = \sum_{t=1}^{T} y_t^2/T \tag{12}$$

The true conditional variance of a time series y_t is denoted $V_t(y_t)$ or σ_t^2 or $V_t(y_t|\Omega_t)$. It is itself a time series (as is the conditional mean) representing the variance of the conditional

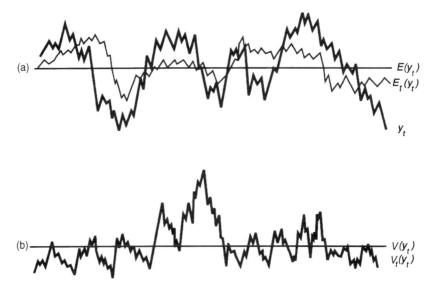

Figure 8.5

distribution of y_t. The difference between conditional and unconditional variances is illustrated in Figure 8.5(b). But how can we estimate the conditional variance?

The idea of GARCH is to add a second equation to the standard regression model — an equation which models the conditional variance. Therefore an equation such as (9) is called the conditional mean equation to distinguish it from the second equation, the conditional variance equation, whose form depends on the particular GARCH model employed.

8.3.2 The Conditional Mean and Variance Equations of GARCH Models

The dependent variable in GARCH conditional mean equations is the asset return y_t. Efficient markets imply that asset returns are i.i.d. — that is, they are instantaneously mean-reverting and have zero autocorrelation. So we may expect little success if we try to predict the conditional mean return (but see Section 8.5.3). Of course we can put whatever predetermined variables we want in the conditional mean equation of a GARCH model, but should err on the side of parsimony if we want the model estimation procedure to converge properly (see Section 8.3.3). And however many explanatory variables are used, we should not expect a good fit from the conditional mean equation — indeed it is common to use either a constant or, just to capture any autocorrelation in returns, the AR(1) model (9). After all, the emphasis of GARCH modelling is estimation and forecasting of the conditional variance, not the conditional mean.

When the conditional mean equation is just a constant plus error, the errors are just the returns in mean deviation form. If other explanatory variables are included, the errors are the unexplained components in returns. In practice, whenever predetermined variables are used in the conditional mean equation for returns, the conditional distribution of returns y_t is determined by the conditional distribution of its error process ε_t, and it is usual to define the conditional variance on these, namely

$$\sigma_t^2 = V_t(\varepsilon_t)$$

The difference between various GARCH models lies in their specification of an equation to model σ_t^2 — and their assumption about the shape of the conditional distribution of the errors. The two most common assumptions about this distribution are normal and t-distributions. In normal GARCH models we assume that ε_t is conditionally normally distributed: $\varepsilon_t | \Omega_t \sim N(0, \sigma_t^2)$. The unconditional returns distributions will then be *leptokurtic* — that is, have fatter tails than the normal — because the changing conditional variance allows for more outliers or unusually large observations. However, in high frequency data there may still be insufficient leptokurtosis in normal GARCH to capture the full extent of kurtosis in the data, and in this case a t-distribution should be assumed (Baillie and Bollerslev (1989)).

Very many different types of GARCH models have been proposed in the academic literature, but only a few of these have found good practical applications. We now review the seven most important univariate GARCH models: ARCH, GARCH, IGARCH, AGARCH, EGARCH, the "Components Model" and "Factor ARCH".

(i) ARCH

The original model of autoregressive conditional heteroskedasticity introduced in Engle (1982) has the conditional variance equation

$$\sigma_t^2 = \alpha_0 + \alpha_1 \varepsilon_{t-1}^2 + \cdots + \alpha_p \varepsilon_{t-p}^2$$

$$\alpha_0 > 0, \qquad \alpha_1, \ldots, \alpha_p \geq 0 \tag{13}$$

where the constraints on the coefficients are necessary to ensure that the conditional variance is always positive. This is the ARCH(p) conditional variance specification, with a memory of p time periods. This model captures the conditional heteroskedasticity of financial returns by using a moving average of past squared errors: if a major market movement in either direction occurred m periods ago ($m \leq p$) the error square will be large, and assuming its coefficient α is non-zero the effect will be to increase today's conditional variance. This means that we are more likely to have a large market move today, in either direction. Hence "large movements tend to follow large movements ... of either sign" — an observation made by Benoit Mandelbrot in 1962 and which today we call conditional heteroskedasticity.

Square rooting the conditional variance and expressing it as an annualized percentage in the usual way yields a time-varying volatility estimate. Unlike the moving average methods just described, the estimate is *not* the forecast. But a single estimated model can be used to construct forecasts of volatility over any time horizon, and not just from now. For example, when valuing Asian options, volatility options, or measuring risk capital requirements it is often necessary to forecast forward volatility, such as a one-month volatility but in six months' time. This flexibility is one of the many advantages of GARCH modelling over the moving average methods just described, advantages which will be revealed as we track deeper into the world of GARCH. But we are jumping ahead of ourselves — back to the description of basic GARCH models.

(ii) GARCH

The generalization of Engle's ARCH(p) model by his student Bollerslev (1986) adds q autoregressive terms to the moving averages of squared errors: it takes the form

$$\sigma_t^2 = \alpha_0 + \alpha_1 \varepsilon_{t-1}^2 + \cdots + \alpha_p \varepsilon_{t-p}^2 + \beta_1 \sigma_{t-1}^2 + \cdots + \beta_q \sigma_{t-q}^2$$

$$\alpha_0 > 0, \qquad \alpha_1, \ldots, \alpha_p, \beta_1, \ldots, \beta_q \geq 0 \tag{14}$$

This is the GARCH(p, q) conditional variance. The parsimonious GARCH(1,1) model, which has just one lagged error square and one autoregressive term, is in fact sufficient for most purposes, since it has infinite memory. (Below we show that it is equivalent to an infinite ARCH model, with exponentially declining weights on the past squared errors.) Such a constraint makes sense because we would expect more recent events to have a bigger influence on the conditional variance. That is, $\alpha_1 \geq \alpha_2 \geq \ldots \geq \alpha_p$. To see that this is the case we write the GARCH(1,1) as an infinite ARCH:

$$\sigma_t^2 = \alpha_0 + \alpha_1 \varepsilon_{t-1}^2 + \beta_1 \sigma_{t-1}^2$$

$$= \alpha_0 + \alpha_1 \varepsilon_{t-1}^2 + \beta_1 (\alpha_0 + \alpha_1 \varepsilon_{t-2}^2 + \beta_1 (\alpha_0 + \alpha_1 \varepsilon_{t-3}^2 + \beta_1 (\ldots$$

$$= \alpha_0 / (1 - \beta_1) + \alpha_1 (\varepsilon_{t-1}^2 + \beta_1 \varepsilon_{t-2}^2 + \beta_1^2 \varepsilon_{t-3}^2 + \cdots)$$

The above assumes that the GARCH lag coefficient β_1 is less than 1. In fact a few calculations show that the *un*conditional variance corresponding to a GARCH(1,1) conditional variance is

$$\sigma^2 = \alpha_0 / (1 - \alpha_1 - \beta_1) \tag{15}$$

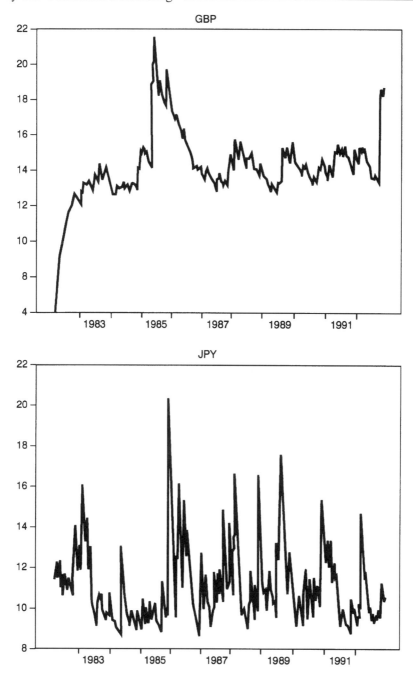

Figure 8.6 Annualized GARCH(1,1) volatilities

and so not only must the *GARCH error* coefficient α_1 be less than 1 also, the sum $\alpha_1 + \beta_1 \leq 1$.

In financial markets it is common to find GARCH lag coefficients in excess of 0.7 but GARCH error coefficients tend to be smaller. The size of these parameters determines the shape of the resulting volatility time series: large GARCH lag coefficients indicate that shocks to conditional variance take a long time to die out, so volatility is persistent; large GARCH error coefficients mean that volatility is quick to react to market movements, and volatilities tend to be more spiky. Figure 8.6 shows US dollar rate GARCH(1,1) volatilities for sterling and the Japanese Yen. Cable volatility is more persistent (its lag coefficient is 0.931 compared with 0.839 for the JPY/USD) — the JPY/USD is more spiky (its error coefficient is 0.094 compared with 0.052 for Cable). See Alexander (1995a) for more details.

(iii) IGARCH

When $\alpha_1 + \beta_1 = 1$ we can rewrite the GARCH(1,1) model as

$$\sigma_t^2 = \alpha_0 + (1 - \lambda)\varepsilon_{t-1}^2 + \lambda\sigma_{t-1}^2 \qquad 0 \leq \lambda \leq 1 \qquad (16)$$

Note that the unconditional variance (15) is undefined — indeed we have a non-stationary GARCH model called the *Integrated GARCH* model. Our main interest in the IGARCH model is that it is equivalent to an infinite EWMA, such as those used by RiskMetrics. This may be seen by repeated substitution in (16):

$$\sigma_t^2 = \alpha_0 + (1 - \lambda)\varepsilon_{t-1}^2 + \lambda(\alpha_0 + (1 - \lambda)\varepsilon_{t-2}^2 + \lambda(\alpha_0 + (1 - \lambda)\varepsilon_{t-3}^2 + \lambda(\ldots$$

$$= \alpha_0/(1 - \lambda) + (1 - \lambda)(\varepsilon_{t-1}^2 + \lambda\varepsilon_{t-2}^2 + \lambda^2\varepsilon_{t-3}^2 + \cdots) \qquad (17)$$

Comparing the EWMA model (7), the representation (17) is equivalent when $\alpha_0 = 0$. We shall see in Section 8.3.5 that GARCH forecasts do not converge in an IGARCH model, so if one tries to forecast from EWMAs rather than just take the current estimate as their forecast, one would run into problems!

(iv) AGARCH

The normal GARCH(1,1) does not always fully account for the skewness and kurtosis properties of empirical financial returns. The kurtosis may be increased by using a *t*-distributed error process instead of a normal one, and skewness is easily accommodated by introducing just one additional parameter in the conditional variance specification: this is the *Asymmetric GARCH(1,1)* model, which has conditional variance equation

$$\sigma_t^2 = \alpha_0 + \alpha_1(\varepsilon_{t-1} - \xi)^2 + \beta_1\sigma_{t-1}^2 \qquad \alpha_0 > 0, \qquad \alpha_1, \beta_1, \xi \geq 0 \qquad (18)$$

In this model, negative shocks to returns ($\varepsilon_{t-1} < 0$) induce larger conditional variances than positive shocks. The AGARCH model is therefore appropriate when we expect more volatility following a market fall than following a market rise — and this is indeed a common feature of financial markets, particularly equities. It is known as the *leverage effect*.

(v) EGARCH

The non-negativity constraints of the GARCH models considered so far can unduly restrain the dynamics of conditional variances so obtained. Nelson (1991) eliminates the

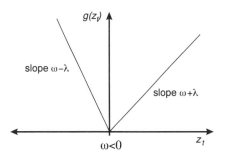

Figure 8.7

need for such constraints in his *exponential GARCH* model by formulating the conditional variance equation in logarithmic terms

$$\log \sigma_t^2 = \alpha + g(z_{t-1}) + \beta \log \sigma_{t-1}^2 \tag{19}$$

where $z_t = \varepsilon_t / \sigma_t$, so z_t is standard normal, and

$$g(z_t) = \omega z_t + \lambda \left(|z_t| - \sqrt{\frac{2}{\pi}} \right) \tag{20}$$

The asymmetric response function $g(.)$, which is illustrated in Figure 8.7, provides the leverage effect just as in the AGARCH model.

(vi) The Components Model

In practice, estimation of a GARCH model over a rolling or expanding data window will each time generate a term structure of volatility forecasts which, as the maturity increases, converge to a "baseline" level of volatility (see Section 8.3.6). This "baseline" corresponds to the unconditional variance of the GARCH model, such as equation (15). So as the data window is rolled or expanded different "baselines" will be estimated, corresponding to different estimates of the GARCH parameters and the "baseline" volatility level changes over time. Thus when the end of the data window suddenly includes a particularly volatile period, the "baseline" increases.

The components model extends this idea of time-varying "baseline" volatility to allow variation *within* the estimation period. This construction aids computation of forecasts in markets which produce non-stationary GARCH models: when $\hat{\alpha}_1 + \hat{\beta}_1 = 1$ forecasts do not converge as they should (see Section 8.3.6). So in these markets (and currency markets are particularly prone to this problem) a components model should be used. To understand the components model of Engle and Lee (1993a, b), note that when $\alpha_1 + \beta_1 < 1$ the GARCH(1,1) conditional variance may be written

$$\sigma_t^2 = (1 - \alpha_1 - \beta_1)\sigma^2 + \alpha_1 \varepsilon_{t-1}^2 + \beta_1 \sigma_{t-1}^2$$
$$= \sigma^2 + \alpha_1(\varepsilon_{t-1}^2 - \sigma^2) + \beta_1(\sigma_{t-1}^2 - \sigma^2) \tag{21}$$

where σ^2 is defined by equation (15). We now define the "baseline" variance level as a permanent component in conditional variance:

$$q_t = \omega + \rho(q_{t-1} - \omega) + \phi(\varepsilon_{t-1}^2 - \sigma_{t-1}^2) \tag{22}$$

and then equation (21) becomes

$$\sigma_t^2 = q_t + \alpha_1(\varepsilon_{t-1}^2 - q_{t-1}) + \beta_1(\sigma_{t-1}^2 - q_{t-1}) \tag{23}$$

Equations (22) and (23) together define the components model. If $\rho = 1$, the permanent component — to which long-term forecasts mean revert — is just a random walk. In the many cases that Salomon Brothers (New York) have employed this model the estimate of ρ turns out to be very close to 1 indeed.

(vii) Factor ARCH

In the standard one factor CAPM or APT framework individual asset or portfolio returns are related to market returns M_t in a conditional mean regression equation

$$r_{it} = \alpha_i + \beta_i M_t + \varepsilon_{it} \qquad i = 1, 2, \dots, n \tag{24}$$

Factor ARCH allows individual volatilities and correlations to be estimated (or forecasted) using only the estimated (or forecasted) GARCH volatility of the market: denoting by σ_{it} the standard deviation of asset i at time t and by σ_{ijt} the covariance between assets i and j at time t, equation (24) yields

$$\sigma_{it}^2 = \beta_i^2 \sigma_{Mt}^2 + \sigma_{\varepsilon_{it}}^2$$
$$\sigma_{ijt}^2 = \beta_i \beta_j \sigma_{Mt}^2 + \sigma_{\varepsilon_{it}\varepsilon_{jt}} \tag{25}$$

From a simultaneous estimation of the n linear regression equations in (24) we get estimates of the factor sensitivities β_i and the error variances and covariances. These, and the univariate GARCH estimates (or forecasts) of the market volatility σ_M, are used in equation (25) to generate individual asset volatilities and correlations. The idea is easily extended to a model with more than one risk factor and this construction is very usefully employed in variance–covariance VAR models (see Section 8.5.3).

8.3.3 Maximum Likelihood Estimation of Model Parameters

Most of the models described above are available as pre-programmed procedures in econometric packages such as TSP, EVIEWS and MICROFIT, and in GAUSS and RATS, GARCH procedures can be written, as explained in the manuals. The method used to estimate GARCH model parameters is maximum likelihood estimation (MLE), which is a powerful and general statistical procedure, widely used because it always produces consistent estimates.

The idea is to choose parameter estimates to maximize the likelihood of the data under an assumption about the shape of the distribution of the data generation process. For example, if we assume a normal data generation process with mean μ and variance σ^2 then the likelihood of getting returns $r_1, r_2, \dots, r_T$ is

$$L(\mu, \sigma^2 | r_1, r_2, \dots, r_T) = \prod_{t=1}^{T} f(r_t) \tag{26}$$

where

$$f(r) = \frac{1}{\sqrt{2\pi\sigma^2}} \exp\left\{ -\frac{1}{2}\left(\frac{r - \mu}{\sigma}\right)^2 \right\} \tag{27}$$

Choosing μ and σ^2 to maximize L (or equivalently to minimize $-2 \log L$, which is easier) yields the maximum likelihood estimates of these parameters.

In GARCH models there are more than two parameters to estimate, and the likelihood functions are more complex (see Engle (1982) and Bollerslev (1986)) but the principle is the same. Problems arise though, because the more parameters in the likelihood function the "flatter" it becomes, and therefore more difficult to estimate (see Section 8.3.7). For this reason the GARCH(1,1) model is preferred to an ARCH model with a long lag, and parameterizations of conditional mean equations are as parsimonious as possible — often we use just a single constant in the conditional mean.

8.3.4 Choosing an Appropriate GARCH Model

Most empirical studies have focused on whether normal GARCH, IGARCH or EGARCH fits the in-sample data better, and the consensus opinion is that EGARCH leads to better estimates of volatility because of the leverage effect (Taylor (1994), Heynen et al. (1994) and Lumsdaine (1995)). A more informative comparison is between AGARCH and EGARCH. AGARCH models can underestimate the leverage effect, but they converge more easily particularly when the data contain large market movements (see Section 8.3.3). Another difference between these models is the ease with which forecasts can be constructed in AGARCH compared to EGARCH. A GARCH forecast can easily be generated using the iterative procedure described in Section 8.3.6, but EGARCH forecasts are much more complex.

It is possible to test for the presence of ARCH effects in returns by looking at the autocorrelation in the time series of squared returns. Standard autocorrelation test statistics may be used, such as the Box-Pierce $Q \sim \chi^2(p)$:

$$Q = T \sum_{n=1}^{p} \varphi(n)^2 \tag{28}$$

where $\varphi(n)$ is the nth order autocorrelation coefficient in squared returns

$$\varphi(n) = \frac{\displaystyle\sum_{t=n+1}^{T} r_t^2 r_{t-n}^2}{\displaystyle\sum_{t=1}^{T} r_t^4} \tag{29}$$

One of the main specification diagnostics in GARCH models is to standardize the returns, dividing by the estimated GARCH standard deviation, and then testing for autocorrelation in squared standardized returns. If it has been removed, the GARCH model is doing its job.

But what if several GARCH models account equally well for GARCH effects? In that case choose the GARCH model which gives the highest likelihood, either in-sample or in post-sample predictive tests (see Section 8.3.8).

8.3.5 GARCH Correlation

Before getting to one of the most useful properties of GARCH models (the production of a continuous volatility term structure) we first describe how multivariate GARCH models may be used to estimate (and forecast) correlation.

We begin with the bivariate case where we are only interested in the correlation between two returns series, r_1 and r_2. There will now be *two* conditional mean equations, which can be anything we like, for example the AR(1) formulation

$$r_{1,t} = \varphi_{11} + \varphi_{12}r_{1,t-1} + \varepsilon_{1,t}$$

$$r_{2,t} = \varphi_{21} + \varphi_{22}r_{2,t-1} + \varepsilon_{2,t}$$

(30)

But the need for parsimony is even greater in multivariate GARCH models and it is common to drop the autoregressive terms, leaving just one parameter to be estimated in each equation. Now the unconditional variance of a multivariate process is a positive definite matrix, called the covariance matrix, or variance–covariance matrix, with variances of each variable along the diagonals and covariances on the off diagonals. The conditional variance of a multivariate process is a time series of matrices, one matrix for each point in time. It is not surprising therefore that estimation of these models can pose problems!

In a bivariate GARCH there will be three conditional variance equations, one for each conditional variance and one for the conditional covariance; in a trivariate GARCH there are six equations for the conditional variances and covariances, and so on. Since all parameters will be estimated simultaneously in one huge likelihood, it can get *very* flat indeed, so we need to use as few parameters as possible. In the diagonal vech parameterization, where each equation is a GARCH(1,1), there are only nine parameters — three in each equation:

$$\sigma_{1,t}^2 = \alpha_{10} + \alpha_{11}\varepsilon_{1,t-1}^2 + \beta_{11}\sigma_{1,t-1}^2$$

$$\sigma_{2,t}^2 = \alpha_{20} + \alpha_{21}\varepsilon_{2,t-1}^2 + \beta_{21}\sigma_{2,t-1}^2$$

(31)

$$\sigma_{12,t} = \alpha_{30} + \alpha_{31}\varepsilon_{1,t-1}\varepsilon_{2,t-1} + \beta_{31}\sigma_{12,t-1}$$

As usual, constraints on the coefficients in equation (31) are necessary to ensure positive definiteness of the covariance matrices. To obtain time series of GARCH correlations we simply divide the estimated covariance by the product of the estimated standard deviations, at every point in time (see Figure 8.8).

Matrix notation will become essential when we consider systems with more than two returns series. Usually it is essential to take all relevant series together in one big GARCH model, because pairwise estimation cannot guarantee positive definiteness of the whole covariance matrix. The matrix form of equation (31) is

$$\text{vech}(\mathbf{H}_t) = \mathbf{A} + \mathbf{B}\,\text{vech}(\boldsymbol{\xi}_{t-1}\boldsymbol{\xi}_{t-1}') + \mathbf{C}\,\text{vech}(\mathbf{H}_{t-1})$$

(32)

where $\mathbf{H}_t$ is the conditional variance matrix at time t, $\boldsymbol{\xi}_t = (\varepsilon_{1t}, \varepsilon_{2t})'$, $\mathbf{A} = (\alpha_{10}, \alpha_{20}, \alpha_{30})'$, $\mathbf{B} = \text{diag}\,(\alpha_{11}, \alpha_{21}, \alpha_{31})$ and $\mathbf{C} = \text{diag}\,(\beta_{11}, \beta_{21}, \beta_{31})$. Now the generalization to a multivariate diagonal vech parameterization is obvious.

There are severe cross-equation restrictions in the diagonal vech model, for example the conditional variances are not allowed to affect the covariances and vice versa. A much more general formulation, which involves the minimum number of parameters whilst imposing no cross-equation restrictions *and* ensures positive definiteness for any parameter values is the BEKK model (after Baba, Engle, Kraft and Kroner who wrote the preliminary version of Engle and Kroner (1993)). This parameterization is given by

$$\mathbf{H}_t = \mathbf{A}'\mathbf{A} + \mathbf{B}'\boldsymbol{\xi}_{t-1}\boldsymbol{\xi}_{t-1}'\mathbf{B} + \mathbf{C}'\mathbf{H}_{t-1}\mathbf{C}$$

where $\mathbf{A}$, $\mathbf{B}$ and $\mathbf{C}$ are general nxn matrices ($\mathbf{A}$ is triangular).

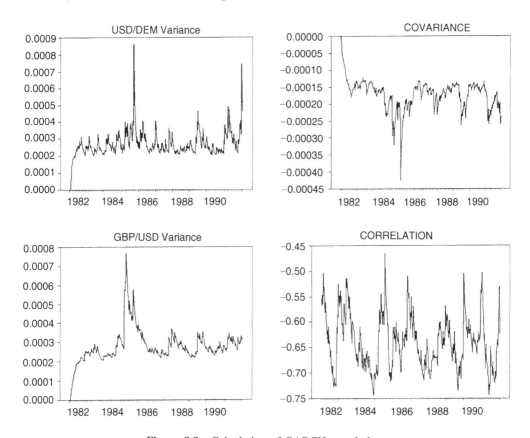

Figure 8.8 Calculation of GARCH correlation

The BEKK parameterization for a bivariate model involves 11 parameters, only two more than the diagonal vech. But for higher dimensional systems the extra number of parameters increases, and completely free estimation becomes very difficult indeed. Often it is necessary to let **B** and **C** be scalar matrices, to reduce the number of parameters needing estimation and so improve the likelihood surface and, hopefully, achieve convergence. More details are given in Bollerslev et al. (1994).

8.3.6 Construction of a Term Structure of GARCH Forecasts

One of the beauties of GARCH is that volatility and correlation forecasts for any horizon can be constructed from the one estimated model. Let's begin with volatility forecasts, and first define some notation. Let $R_{t,n}$ be the (logarithmic) return at time t over the next n periods, so that $R_{t,1} = r_{t+1}$ and

$$R_{t,n} = \sum_{j=1}^{n} r_{t+j}$$

GARCH models give us forecasts of instantaneous volatility, that is the volatility of r_{t+j}, made at time t and for any step ahead j. However, we can use these to get forecasts of volatility over the next n periods, since

$$V_t(R_{t,n}) = \sum_{i=1}^{n} V_t(r_{t+i}) + \sum_i \sum_j \text{cov}_t(r_{t+i}, r_{t+j}) \tag{33}$$

Hence the GARCH forecast of n-period variance is the sum of the instantaneous GARCH forecast variances, plus the double sum of the forecast autocovariances between returns. This double sum will be very small compared to the first sum on the right-hand side of equation (33). For example in an AR(1)–GARCH(1,1) model with autocorrelation coefficient ρ in the conditional mean, equation (33) becomes

$$\hat{\sigma}_{t,n}^2 = \sum_{i=1}^{n} \hat{\sigma}_{t+i}^2 + \hat{\sigma}_t^2 [\rho(1 - \rho^n)/(1 - \rho)]^2 \tag{34}$$

and the first term clearly dominates the second. Hence we ignore the second, autocovariance term, and construct n-period volatility forecasts simply by adding the j-step-ahead GARCH variance forecasts (and then square-rooting and annualizing in the usual way).

The instantaneous GARCH forecasts are calculated in a natural way: for example, in the GARCH(1,1) model

$$\hat{\sigma}_{t+1}^2 = \hat{\alpha}_0 + \hat{\alpha}_1 \varepsilon_t^2 + \hat{\beta}_1 \sigma_t^2 \tag{35}$$

and the j-step ahead forecasts of forward 1-day variances are computed iteratively as

$$\hat{\sigma}_{t+j}^2 = \hat{\alpha}_0 + (\hat{\alpha}_1 + \hat{\beta}_1)\hat{\sigma}_{t+j-1}^2 \tag{36}$$

In this way we can also construct any sort of forward volatility forecasts, such as three-month volatility but for a period starting six months from now.

Correlation forecasts are calculated simply by iterating conditional covariance forecasts in a similar fashion to equations (35) and (36), summing these to get n-period covariance forecasts, and then dividing by the product of n-period volatility forecasts. To see this, note that

$$\text{cov}_t(R_{1,t,n}, R_{2,t,n}) = \sum_{i,j=1}^{n} \text{cov}_t(r_{1,t+i}, r_{2,t+j})$$

but non-contemporaneous covariances are ignored, so

$$\hat{\sigma}_{12,t,n} = \sum_{i=1}^{n} \hat{\sigma}_{12,t+i} \tag{37}$$

and finally

$$\hat{\rho}_{t,n} = \hat{\sigma}_{12,t,n}/\hat{\sigma}_{1,t,n}\hat{\sigma}_{2,t,n} \tag{38}$$

The principles illustrated in equations (35)–(38), for GARCH(1,1) and multivariate GARCH, are easily generalized to other GARCH models, such as the AGARCH. Of the GARCH models described in Section 8.3.2, the EGARCH model is the most difficult to use for forecasting, because the asymmetric response function $g(\cdot)$ is complicated to iterate.

Figure 8.9 shows ten-day and 60-day volatility forecasts for the FTSE. Note how the forecasts converge to the "baseline" volatility level (given by equation (15) in GARCH(1,1)) as the forecast horizon increases. This is because the instantaneous j-step-ahead forecasts (of forward 1-day volatilities) converge to the same baseline level,

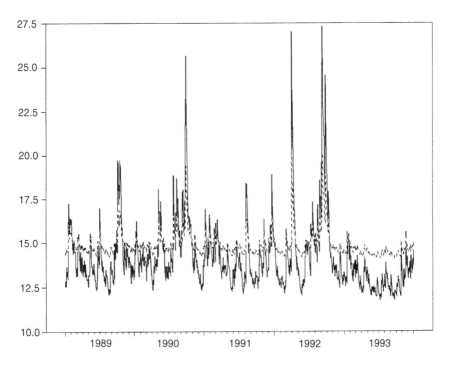

Figure 8.9 Ten-day and 60-day GARCH(1,1) forecasts of the FTSE

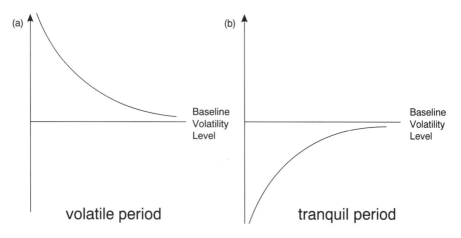

Figure 8.10 Forward volatilities

as can be seen from equation (36) if $\hat{\alpha}_1 + \hat{\beta}_1 < 1$. So if the last data point in the estimation of the GARCH model is above this baseline, j-step-ahead forecasts will converge as in Figure 8.10(a) and if it is below the baseline they converge from below, as in Figure 8.10(b). If $\hat{\alpha}_1 + \hat{\beta}_1 = 1$ we can see from equation (36) that forecasts do not converge at all, as already discussed in Section 8.3.2.

8.3.7 Convergence Problems and Data Considerations

Convergence problems in the numerical optimization procedures used to estimate GARCH parameters can arise with very flat likelihood surfaces, and we have already stressed the need for parsimony in parameterizations of GARCH models. But other convergence problems may still arise, because of inappropriate starting values for the iterative method used in maximum likelihood, or insufficient ARCH effects in the data. When starting values are near a boundary (such as $\alpha_1 = 0$ or $\beta_1 = 1$) it is possible that the iteration will go off the boundary and convergence will never be achieved. Hitting a boundary can even happen when starting values are very good, because of a local gradient in the likelihood surface. In such cases it often helps to change the data, if only by chopping some of the data off the beginning of the period.

The two important considerations in choosing data for GARCH modelling are the data frequency and the data period. It is usual to employ intraday, daily or weekly data since convergence problems could be encountered on any lower frequency data due to insufficient ARCH effects. If daily data are used then deterministic daily dummies in conditional mean and variance equations will identify any "weekend" effects in mean returns or returns volatility (see Baillie and Bollerslev (1989)). If tic data are used the time bucket should be sufficiently large to ensure there are no long periods of no trades. And by the same token interest rate data can be a problem if the rates remain fixed for too long.

When it comes to choosing the amount of historical data for estimating GARCH models, the real issue is whether you want major market events from several years ago to influence your forecasts today. For example, including Black Monday in equity GARCH models has the effect of raising long-term volatility forecasts by several per cent. This is because the parameter estimates used to calculate the unconditional volatility, such as equation (15), are changed substantially by major market events, and this has the effect of altering the "baseline" volatility level to which all forecasts converge.

8.4 "IMPLIED" VOLATILITY AND CORRELATION

Implied volatility and correlation are those volatilities and correlations which are implicit in the prices of options. When an explicit analytic pricing formula is available (such as the Black–Scholes formula) the quoted prices of these products, along with known variables such as interest rates, time to maturity, exercise prices and so on, can be used in an implicit formula for volatility. The result is called the implied volatility. It is a volatility forecast — not an estimate of current volatility — the volatility forecast which is implicit in the quoted price of the option. The forecast horizon is therefore given by the maturity of the option.

We shall also see how related implied volatilities can (sometimes) be used to calculate implied correlations. These volatilities and correlation forecasts differ from the other forecasts which have been reviewed in this chapter. They use much more than the historical returns data considered so far, and in many respects should be treated as prices rather than volatilities since, *ceteris paribus*, the two are interchangeable. In fact, rather than viewing implied volatility and the other methods as complementary forecasting procedures, when implied volatilities are available they should be taken alongside the other forecasts. For example in Salomon Brothers "Gift" (GARCH index forecasting tool) the relationship between implied volatility and GARCH volatility is used to predict future movements in prices — see Chew (1993).

8.4.1 Black–Scholes Implied Volatility

The Black–Scholes formula for the price of a call option with strike price K and time to maturity t on an underlying asset with current price S and t-period volatility σ is

$$C = SN(x) - Kr^{-t}N(x - \sigma\sqrt{t}) \tag{39}$$

where r denotes the "risk-free" rate of interest, $N(.)$ is the normal distribution function and

$$x = \ln(S/Kr^{-t})/\sigma\sqrt{t} + \sigma\sqrt{t}/2$$

See Cox and Rubinstein (1985).

If C is known, and so also are S, K, r and t, then equation (39) may be used instead to calculate σ, the implied volatility of the asset. But typically there will be several options of different maturities and strikes on any one asset, and different options will give different answers for the same implied volatility. In general at-the-money (ATM) options yield lower implied volatilities than in-the-money (ITM) or out-of-the-money (OTM) options, and this is called the volatility *smile*. The smile occurs because ATM options are the most sensitive to volatility and so a smaller volatility spread is required for them to achieve the same profit or risk premium as OTM options. The smile is particularly noticeable in Black–Scholes implied volatilities (possibly because of the inappropriate assumptions underlying the Black–Scholes model — see Hull and White (1987)) and tends to increase as the option approaches maturity: if a short-dated OTM option is to make any profit, a large movement will have to occur in the underlying asset price. Hence a much larger volatility must be implicit in its price.

The smile may also be *skewed*, particularly in equity markets, where options with lower strike prices attract higher volatilities. This may be because of the leverage effect — that volatility increases more following large market falls than following large market rises. To see this consider an OTM put: when the asset price falls volatility increases more because of the leverage effect and the put could go back out-of-the-money. So a bigger price fall is needed before the put goes safely ITM.

If a single implied volatility for the underlying asset is required, rather than the whole smile, it is usual to take a vega weighted average of all volatilities across the smile, and therefore deep ITM and OTM options are more or less excluded.

Volatility cones are graphic representations of the term structure of volatility, used for visual comparison of current implied volatility with an empirical historical distribution of implied volatilities. To construct a cone, fix a time to maturity t and estimate a frequency distribution of implied volatility from all t-maturity implied volatilities during the last two years (say), recording the upper and lower 95 per cent confidence limits. Repeat for all t. Plotting these confidence limits yields a cone-like structure because the implied volatility distribution becomes more peaked as the option approaches maturity. Cones are used to track implied volatility over the life of a particular option, and under- or overshooting the cone can signal an opportunity to trade. Sometimes cones are constructed on "historic" volatility because historic data on implied volatility may be difficult to obtain. In this case cones should be used with caution, particularly if overshooting is apparent at the long end: differences between long-term "historic" and implied volatility are to be expected, due to transactions costs.

8.4.2 Implied Correlation

The increase in derivatives trading in OTC markets enables implied correlations to be calculated from three implied volatilities by rearrangement of the formula for the variance of a difference (or, equally well, a sum):

$$V(x - y) = V(x) + V(y) - 2\ \text{cov}(x, y)$$

So if we denote by ρ the correlation between x and y

$$\sigma_{x-y}^2 = \sigma_x^2 + \sigma_y^2 - 2\sigma_x\sigma_y\rho \tag{40}$$

or

$$\rho = \frac{\sigma_x^2 + \sigma_y^2 - \sigma_{x-y}^2}{2\sigma_x\sigma_y} \tag{41}$$

Putting implied volatilities in equation (41) gives the associated implied correlation — we just need traded options on three associated assets or rates X, Y and $X - Y$. For example, X and Y could be two USD FX rates (in logarithms) so $X - Y$ is the cross rate. Then returns to these three assets, (first differences of the logarithms) are denoted x, y and $x - y$ in the above formulae, which yields the implied correlation between the two currencies. Another case in which implied volatilities can be used to calculate implied correlations is when an optionable stock is traded on two exchanges, for example Cable and Wireless in New York and London. Denote the log prices by X and Y respectively, so $X - Y$ is the log sterling/dollar FX rate. Implied volatilities on these three are put in equation (41) to yield the implied correlation between the Cable and Wireless price in GBP and its price in USD. Similar calculations can be used for *equity implied correlations*. Assuming the correlation between all pairs of equities in an index is constant allows this correlation to be approximated from implied volatilities of stocks in the index — see Kelly (1994). Of course, the assumption is very restrictive and not all equities will be optionable, so the approximation is very crude and can lead to implied correlations which are greater than 1. Another way in which implied correlations can be obtained is by inverting the quanto pricing formula (see Section 3.2.2). When we know the quanto price, the interest rate, the equity and FX implied volatilities and so on we can invert the Black–Scholes quanto pricing formula to obtain an implied correlation between the equity and the FX rate.

8.5 ESTIMATION AND FORECASTING FOR MARKET RISK MEASUREMENT

8.5.1 Hedge Ratios and Market Sensitivities

A regression hedge ratio is found by dividing the covariance between the returns to the hedge instrument and the returns to the underlying by the variance of the hedge instrument (returns). A similar formula applies to estimating a regression beta when there is a single market risk factor, but for more general portfolios a general linear regression framework

Figure 8.11 Time-varying beta for BT vs. FTSE

should be employed. The formulae are more complicated, but they still use only variances and covariances of portfolio and market returns — see Alexander (1996).

Since a bivariate GARCH model yields time-varying covariances and variances, these may be used to calculate time-varying hedge ratios (and market betas). These conditional deltas will not only be more accurate estimates of the quantities with which we are genuinely concerned, they can be used to estimate gamma in a natural way (by regressing the time-varying delta on the price of the underlying). An example of a GARCH beta is shown in Figure 8.11.

8.5.2 Forecasting the Variance–Covariance Matrix for VAR Calculations

Current recommendations of the Basle committee (April 1995) are that 99 per cent VAR (value at risk) measures be calculated over a holding period of ten working days. The heart of any VAR model will be accurate forecasts of variances and covariances for the required holding period whether the variance–covariance matrix or Monte Carlo simulation methodology is used. Of all the forecasting procedures reviewed in this chapter I would recommend using GARCH forecasts, except when the holding period is more than a few months, in which case the simple unconditional variance–covariance matrix — over a long and appropriate data period — should be used.

Although GARCH forecasts give increased accuracy over shorter time horizons, the programming problems inherent in attempting to estimate variance–covariance matrices of large dimensions are insurmountable. However, it is possible to use principal components analysis on the returns to all factors within a given risk category. This is done not — as is usually the case — necessarily to reduce dimensions — although some reduction in dimensionality will occur. Rather, the principal components will be orthogonal, so their unconditional correlations will be zero. An unconditional variance–covariance matrix of principal components is therefore diagonal, by definition. The conditional matrix will only be approximately diagonal in general, but nevertheless forecasts of the off-diagonal elements of this matrix will converge to zero.

Hence a way forward in the use of GARCH forecasts for VAR models is to use univariate GARCH forecasts of the principal components of the returns to all risk factors in a given category. These are then aggregated across risk categories assuming zero correlations, as recommended by the Basle committee.

8.5.3 Evaluating Volatility and Correlation Forecasts

Different models can be ranked according to how much better they perform according to a certain benchmark. But what do we mean by "better", and what should be taken as a "benchmark"? I like to take the unconditional standard deviation over a very long data period as the benchmark against which to test different volatility forecasting models — if a model cannot improve upon this there is no point in using it!

However well a model fits in-sample (i.e. within the data period used to estimate the model parameters) the real test of its forecasting power is in out-of-sample (usually post-sample) predictive tests. A certain amount of historic data is withheld from the period used to estimate the model, and then forecasts made from the model are evaluated in some way. Some of the literature uses root mean square errors to evaluate volatility and correlation forecasts, but this appears to be a misguided procedure. Why? Because volatility and correlation forecasts are good if variance and covariance forecasts are good; variance is a parameter of the returns distribution function, covariance is a parameter of the joint returns distribution, and a prediction of a parameter can only be assessed by seeing how well the out-of-sample data fit the predicted distribution. This means that we should be measuring the likelihood of the out-of-sample data under the predicted distributions: better predictions yield higher likelihoods. Now, the root mean square error criterion comes from a normal likelihood function — minimizing the sum of squared differences between the actual observations and the predicted means will maximize the normal likelihood when volatility is constant (see equation (27)). Hence root mean square errors are applicable to mean predictions rather than variance or covariance predictions.* But where is the statistical theory which shows that one can evaluate volatility forecasts using root mean square errors between volatility forecasts and *ex-post* estimates of "volatility" (whatever that is)?

Whatever the forecasting procedure used, short-term volatility forecasts will be more accurate than long-term volatility forecasts. That is just about the only definitive answer that can be given to the question of relative effectiveness of different forecasting procedures. One reason for this is that it is difficult to compare different forecasts because they refer to different time horizons. For example, "historic" volatility is usually only used for long-term forecasts, say of a month or more, implied volatility is difficult to compare with other forecasts because the maturity of its forecast is continually changing, and

---

* Of course, a variance is a mean, but the mean of the *squared* random variable, which is chi-squared distributed, not normally distributed, so the likelihood function is totally different and does not involve any sum of squared errors.

RiskMetrics (Third Edition) provides only one-day ahead and one-month ahead forecasts (although ten-day forecasts may be added to later editions). In fact, of all the volatility and correlation forecasting methods in common use, only GARCH models provide the entire term structure of forecasts, from one-day ahead upwards. Another reason for the different results on relative efficiency of forecasting procedures is the inappropriate use of root mean square errors as a method of comparison, as mentioned above. For more details, see Alexander (1995b).

8.6 NEW DIRECTIONS

This chapter has covered three methods of volatility and correlation forecasting: moving averages, GARCH and implied. These are the most established and most widely used models, but there are new methods in financial forecasting which, once established, could possibly offer improved volatility and correlation forecasts.

An interesting method devised by Tompkins (1995) divides historical data into high and low volatility regions, taking these two regions as the sample space. The volatility forecast is taken to be the expected volatility (proportion of high volatility periods × average volatility in high periods + proportion of low volatility periods × average volatility in

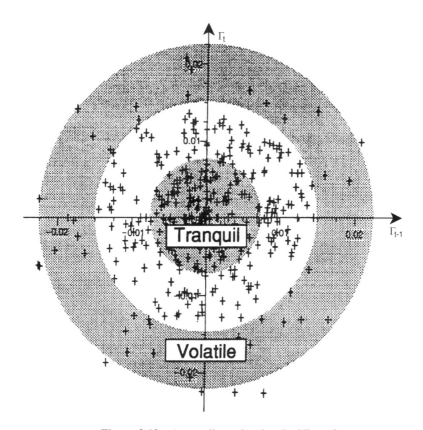

Figure 8.12 A two-dimensional embedding of returns

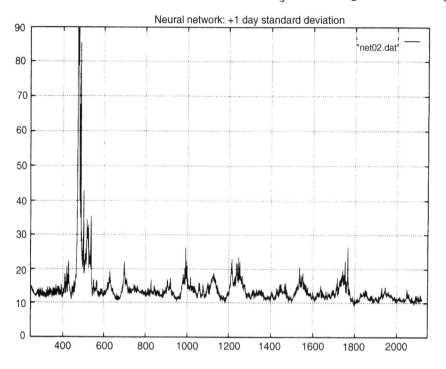

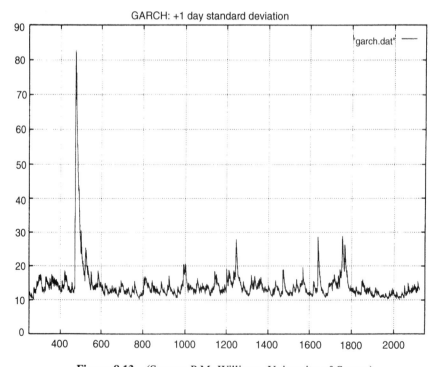

Figure 8.13 (Source: P.M. Williams, University of Sussex)

low periods). The empirical evidence that he presents indicates an astonishing degree of accuracy of these forecasts but it is very limited and, presently, more empirical work needs to be done in this area.

Tompkins' method is related to nearest neighbour techniques, which have their roots in the theory of chaos (Casdagli (1992)). These methods begin with a multidimensional *pattern recognition* stage, where a time series (or several associated time series) is embedded in n-dimensional Euclidean space. Instead of a single line through time (or several lines through time) we view the time series as a pattern in n-dimensional space: one n-dimensional point for every time period. The point to be forecast is then embedded within this pattern and its nearest neighbours are located. These nearest neighbours identify the historic data points which show similar "configurations" to the current point to be forecast and only these data points are used in the second stage — prediction.

Time-delay embedding methods go back to a theorem of Takens (1981), which states that it should be possible to reconstruct a strange attractor of a chaotic time series when the embedding is $(x_t, x_{t-k}, x_{t-2k}, \ldots, x_{t-nk})$, provided n is at least as great as the dimension of the attractor. For volatility forecasting, an embedding such as $(x_t, x_{t-1}, x_{t-2}, \ldots, x_{t-n})$ on returns would enable the pattern recognition stage to identify high and low volatility regions. Figure 8.12 plots current returns against yesterday's returns to the FTSE 100, marking those pairs which indicate high and low volatility. This is for illustration purposes only — an embedding dimension much higher than 2 would be necessary to reveal the dynamics of any strange attractor.

The limited research which has been done on the effectiveness of these methods for volatility forecasting does not reveal much success. In contrast, nearest neighbour techniques can be most useful for short-term mean forecasting in very high frequency financial data (see Alexander and Giblin (1995)).

Finally, neural networks with more than one output can be used for volatility and correlation forecasting. Standard neural network packages for financial markets output just a single quantity and iterate on the root mean square error. But if two outputs are regarded as the mean and variance of a normal distribution, and the network converges by optimizing the whole likelihood function, the network will provide volatility as well as mean forecasts. Figure 8.13 shows the volatility forecasts for the FTSE derived from the neural network of Williams (1995a), compared with standard GARCH(1,1) forecasts (Section 8.3). In Williams (1995b) these ideas are extended to multivariate networks and applied to covariance and correlation forecasting.

This concludes the review of volatility and correlation forecasting methods for financial markets. It is a huge area, of which the present text represents only a survey. For an in-depth coverage of this and other areas of financial time series analysis, see Alexander (forthcoming).

8.7 REFERENCES

Alexander, C.O. (1994) "History debunked". *Risk*, **7**, no. 12, 59–63.
Alexander, C.O. (1995a) "Common volatility in the foreign exchange market". *Applied Financial Economics*, **5**, no. 1, 1–10.
Alexander, C.O. (1995b) "On the variance–covariance matrices used in VAR models" (Mimeo)
Alexander, C.O. (forthcoming) *Time Series Analysis for Financial Markets*, Chichester UK, Wiley.
Alexander, C.O. and Giblin, I. (1995) "Multivariate embedding methods: Forecasting high-frequency data in the first INFFC" (*Submitted to Neurove$t, February 1995*).

Andersen, T.G. (1994) "Stochastic autoregressive volatility: A framework for volatility modelling". *Mathematical Finance*, **4**, vol. 2, 75–102.

Baillie, R.T. and Bollerslev, T. (1989) "The message in daily exchange rates: a conditional-variance tale". *Journal of Business and Economic Statistics*, **7**, no. 3, 297–305.

Bollerslev, T., Chou, R.Y. and Kroner, K.F. (1992) "ARCH modelling in finance". *Journal of Econometrics*, **52**, 5–59.

Bollerslev, T., Engle, R.F. and Nelson, D.B. (1994) "ARCH models" in *Handbook of Econometrics*, vol. 4, R.F. Engle and D.L. McFadden (eds), North Holland.

Bollerslev, T. (1986) "Generalized autoregressive conditional heteroskedasticity". *Journal of Econometrics*, **31**, 307–27.25.

Casdagli, M. (1992) "Chaos and deterministic vs stochastic non-linear modelling". *JRSS series B*, **54**, 303–28.

Chew, L. (1993) "Summer of content", *Risk*, **6**, no. 8, 28–35.

Cox, J.C. and Rubinstein, M. (1985) *Options Markets*. New Jersey, Prentice Hall.

Engle, R.F. (1982) "Autoregressive conditional heteroskedasticity with estimates of the variance of United Kingdom inflation". *Econometrica*, **50**, no. 4, 987–1007.

Engle, R.F. and Kroner, K.F. (1993) "Multivariate simultaneous generalized ARCH". Department of Economics, University of California at San Diego, USA.

Engle, R.F. and Lee, G.G.J. (1993a) "Long run volatility forecasting for individual stocks in a one factor model". Department of Economics, University of California at San Diego, USA.

Engle, R.F. and Lee, G.G.J. (1993b) "A permanent and transitory component model of stock return volatility". Department of Economics, University of California at San Diego, USA.

Heynen, R., Kemna, A. and Vorst, T. (1994) "Analysis of the term structure of implied volatilities". *Journal of Financial and Quantitative Analysis*, **29**, vol. 1, 31–56.

Hull, J. and White, W. (1987) "The pricing of options on assets with stochastic volatilities". *Journal of Finance*, **42**, 281–300.

Kelly, M. (1994) "Stock answer". *Risk*, **7**, no. 8, 40–3.

Lumsdaine, R.L. (1995) "Finite sample properties of the maximum likelihood estimation in GARCH(1,1) and IGARCH(1,1) models: a Monte Carlo investigation". *Journal of Business and Economic Statistics*, **13**, vol. 1, 1–10.

Nelson, D.B. (1991) "Conditional heteroskedasticity in asset returns: a new approach". *Econometrica*, **59**, no. 2, 347–70.

Takens, F. (1981) "Detecting strange attractors in fluid turbulence", in *Dynamical Systems and Turbulence*. D. Rand and L.-S. Young (eds), Springer.

Taylor, S.J. (1994) "Modelling stochastic volatility". *Mathematical Finance*, **4**, no. 2, 183–204.

Tompkins, R. (1995) "Answers in the cards". *Risk*, **8**, no. 6, 55–8.

Williams, P.M. (1995a) "Bayesian regularization and pruning using a Laplave prior". *Neural Computation*, **7**, 117–43.

Williams, P.M. (1995b) "Using neural networks to model conditional multivariate densities". *Cognitive Science Research Report*, CSRP 371, University of Sussex.

9
Credit Risk
ROBERT JARROW AND STUART TURNBULL

9.1 INTRODUCTION

We consider two facets of credit risk. First, the pricing of derivatives written on assets subject to default risk. An example is the pricing of derivatives written on corporate bonds, where there is a positive probability that default may occur on the part of the issuer of the bonds. Second is the pricing of derivatives where the writer of the derivative might default. Consider an over-the-counter option written on a Treasury bond. There is no default risk arising from the underlying asset — the Treasury bond. However, there is default risk arising from the fact that the writer of the option may not be able to honour the obligation if the option is exercised. This form of risk is referred to as *counterparty risk*. In the over-the-counter market counterparty risk is a major concern to financial institutions and regulatory bodies. We will describe a simple approach to the pricing and hedging of both forms of credit risk. We will give a number of examples: the pricing of options on credit risky bonds, the pricing of over-the-counter caps, and the pricing of credit default swaps.

9.2 PRICING CREDIT RISKY BONDS

Firms are allocated to particular risk classes AAA, AA, etc. on the basis of their current creditworthiness. A typical set of term structures is shown in Figure 9.1. A firm in credit class AAA is assumed to have the least credit risk among corporate firms. Firms of lower credit than AAA, such as those in credit class AA, trade at a lower price and are thus higher yield.

Suppose we want to price a derivative written on a zero coupon bond issued by a firm with credit rating ABC. We must price this derivative in such a way that it is (i) consistent with the absence of arbitrage; (ii) consistent with the relevant initial term structures of interest rates; and (iii) consistent with a positive probability of default. We do this by first constructing a lattice of one period interest rates to model the term structure of default-free Treasury bills. This is described in Jarrow and Turnbull (1995). Next we consider zero coupon bonds for the firm belonging to the particular risk class, ABC.

The Handbook of Risk Management and Analysis. Edited by Carol Alexander
© 1996 John Wiley & Sons Ltd

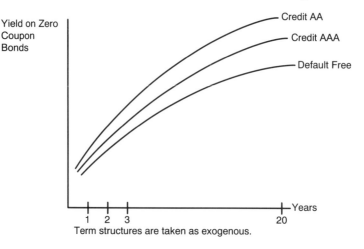

Figure 9.1 Term structures

9.2.1 Lattice of Default-free Interest Rates

The prices of default-free zero coupon bonds are given in Table 9.1. Following Black, Derman and Toy (1991), it is assumed that spot interest rates are log-normally distributed. The lattice is shown in Figure 9.2. The value of the one-year default-free bond, face value 100, is

$$B_F(0, 1) = 100 \exp(-0.047175) = 95.3921$$

The value of the two-year default-free zero coupon bond, face value 100, at year one is

$$B_F(1, 2) = 100 \exp(-0.053810) = 94.7612$$

if the spot rate is 5.3810 per cent, and

$$B_F(1, 2) = 100 \exp(-0.048689) = 95.2477$$

if the spot rate is 4.8689 per cent.

We know from Black, Derman and Toy (1991) that normalized prices are a martingale under the martingale probabilities. It is assumed that the martingale probability of the spot interest in an up-state is 0.5. Therefore,

$$B_F(0, 2) = \exp(-0.047175)(0.5 \times 94.7612 + 0.5 \times 95.2477)$$
$$= 90.6267$$

Table 9.1 Prices of zero coupon bonds

Maturity Years T	Default-Free $B_F(0, T)$	Credit Class ABC $v(0, t; \overline{D})$
1	95.3921	95.0486
2	90.6264	89.7056
3	85.7820	84.1008

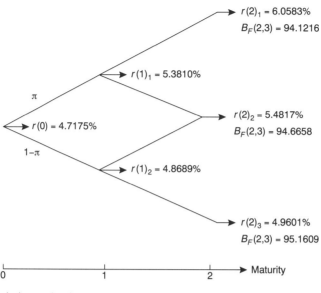

$r(2)_1 = 6.0583\%$
$B_F(2,3) = 94.1216$

$r(1)_1 = 5.3810\%$

π

$r(0) = 4.7175\%$

$r(2)_2 = 5.4817\%$
$B_F(2,3) = 94.6658$

$1-\pi$

$r(1)_2 = 4.8689\%$

$r(2)_3 = 4.9601\%$
$B_F(2,3) = 95.1609$

0   1   2   Maturity

π is the martingale probability of an up-state ($\pi = 0.5$).
$1 - \pi$ is the martingale probability of a down-state ($1 - \pi = 0.5$).
Volatility is 5 per cent.

Figure 9.2 Default-free spot interest rates

which equals the number in Table 9.1, ignoring a small round-off error. Extending this analysis gives $B_F(0, 3) = 85.7820$.

9.2.2 Risky Debt

We want to value a zero coupon bond for a firm belonging to the credit class ABC. Let $v(t, T; DS_t)$ denote the value at date t of a zero coupon bond issued by the firm. The debt matures at time T and the bondholders are promised the face value of the bond at maturity. Let the face value be USD 100. There is a positive probability that the firm might default over the life of the bond. If default occurs, the bondholders will receive less than the promised amount. The symbol DS_t is used to denote the default status of the bond at date t:

$$DS_t \equiv \begin{cases} \overline{D}; \text{ default has not occurred at date } t \\ D; \text{ default has occurred at or before date } t \end{cases}$$

As the symbol DS_t indicates, there are two possibilities. One, default does not occur before or at date t, denoted $\overline{D}$; and two, default does occur before or at date t, denoted D.

We can always view the pricing of credit risky bonds in terms of a foreign currency analogy. Imagine a hypothetical currency, called ABCs. In terms of this currency, we can view the debt issued by the firm as default-free. Indeed, at maturity, the bondholder is issued the face value of debt in ABCs. But, this currency is useless to the bondholder, so we need to define an exchange rate which converts this hypothetical currency to dollars. After all, the bondholders are interested in the dollar value of their ABCs. If default has not occurred before or at date t, then the exchange rate is unity. If default did occur, it is assumed that we get some fraction, δ, of a dollar for each ABC. This is the same as being paid the fraction δ of the face amount of the debt. The fraction δ is also called the *pay-off ratio* or *recovery rate*. Defining $e(t)$ as the date t exchange rate per ABCs, we have:

$$e(t) \equiv \begin{cases} 1; \text{ with probability } 1 - \mu(t)h \text{ if } DS_t = \overline{D} \\ \delta; \text{ with probability } \mu(t)h \text{ if } DS_t = D, \end{cases} \tag{1}$$

where $0 \leq \delta < 1$; h denotes the time interval and $\mu(t)h$ is the martingale probability of default occurring, conditional upon no default at or before date $t - h$. We are interested in the martingale probabilities of default because we want to develop pricing formulae which are arbitrage-free.[1] If default has occurred at or before date $t - h$, then it is assumed that the bond remains in default and the pay-off ratio constant at δ dollars,

$$e(t) \equiv \delta \tag{2}$$

The conditional martingale probabilities of default can be estimated using the observed term structures of interest rates. We will discuss how to do this below.

To simplify the analysis, we are going to assume that the default process is independent of the level of the default-free rate of interest. This implies that if interest rates are "high" or "low" this has no effect on the probability of default. It is a useful first approximation, and its relaxation is discussed in Jarrow and Turnbull (1995b).

9.2.3 Credit Risky Debt

In Table 9.1 we are given two sets of prices for zero coupon bonds. The first is for default-free bonds and the second is for bonds belonging to credit class ABC. The default-free bonds at each maturity are seen to be more valuable than the equivalent maturity bond issued by the firm in credit class ABC. This difference reflects the likelihood of default. We want to estimate these implicit martingale probabilities of default.

Before we can do this, however, we must first specify the pay-off ratio δ in the event of default. This value comes from our credit risk analysts, who estimate that given the nature of the debt, we expect to receive USD 0.40 on the dollar in the event of default.[2]

Consider first the one-year bond. For simplicity, we take the interval in the lattice to be one year. At maturity, the credit risky bond's value is:

$$v(1, 1, DS) = 100 \begin{cases} 1; \text{ probability } 1 - \mu(0)h \text{ if } DS_1 = \overline{D} \text{ (No Default)} \\ \delta; \text{ probability } \mu(0)h \text{ if } DS_1 = D \text{ (Default)} \end{cases} \tag{3}$$

where $h = 1$ and $\delta = 0.40$. The face value of the bond is 100.

The default process is shown in Figure 9.3. Given that default has not occurred at date $t = 0$, the conditional (martingale) probability that default occurs at $t = 1$ is denoted by $\mu(0) \times h$, where h is the time interval. In this example $h = 1$. The conditional (martingale) probability that default does not occur is $1 - \mu(0)h$. We can use the term structures of interest rates for default-free bonds and for credit class ABC bonds to infer the value of $\mu(0)$.

The expected value of the pay-off is

$$100\{1 \times [1 - \mu(0)] + \delta \times \mu(0)\}$$

and discounting at the risk-free rate gives, using Table 9.1

$$v(0, 1, \overline{D}) = 0.9539 \times 100\{1 \times [1 - \mu(0)] + \delta \times \mu(0)\} \tag{4}$$

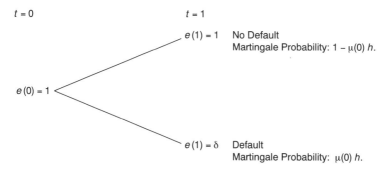

$\mu(0).h$ is the martingale probability that default occurs at date $t = 1$, conditional that default has not occurred at date $t = 0$.

Figure 9.3 One-period credit risky debt default process

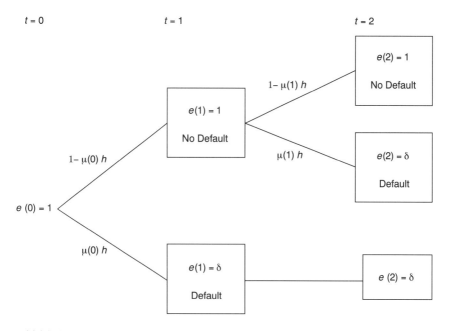

$\mu(1)\ h$ is the martingale probability that default occurs at date $t = 2$ conditional that default has not occurred at date $t = 1$

Figure 9.4 Two-period credit risky debt default process

From Table 9.1, we know that $v(0, 1, \overline{D}) = 95.0401$. Therefore

$$95.0486 = 0.9539 \times 100\{[1 - \mu(0)] + 0.40\mu(0)\} \tag{5}$$

Solving for martingale probability of default gives

$$(1 - 0.40) \times \mu(0) = 1 - (95.0486/0.9539)/100$$

or

$$\mu(0) = 0.006$$

The pricing of the two-period zero coupon bond is slightly more complicated because at the end of the first period both interest rates and the default status of the firm are uncertain. The default process is shown in Figure 9.4. If default has occurred at date $t = 1$, the bond is assumed to remain in default. If default has not occurred at date $t = 1$, then one period later at date $t = 2$ either default occurs or it does not. The martingale probability of default occurring at date $t = 2$ conditional upon the fact that default has not occurred at date $t = 1$ is $\mu(1)h$. The conditional (martingale) probability that default does not occur at date $t = 2$ is $1 - \mu(1)h$. Figure 9.4 is combined with Figure 9.2 and the possible states are shown in Figure 9.5. The same argument is used to determine the conditional martingale probability of default $\mu(1)$.

Let us start at State A, at date $t = 1$. The value of a default-free bond, face value of 1, that matures at $t = 2$ is

$$B(1, 2)_d = \exp(-0.0487)$$

The subscript "d" refers to the "down" state for the default-free spot rate of interest.

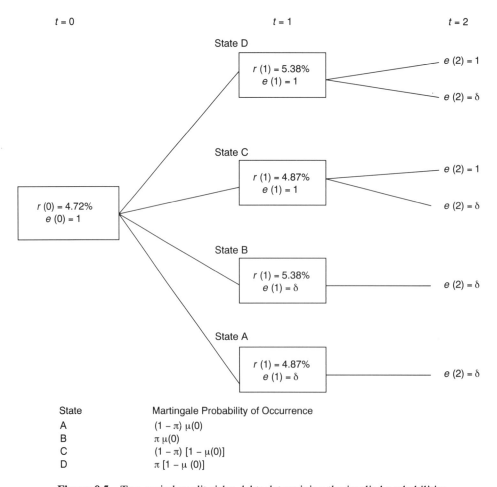

State	Martingale Probability of Occurrence
A	$(1 - \pi)\,\mu(0)$
B	$\pi\,\mu(0)$
C	$(1 - \pi)\,[1 - \mu(0)]$
D	$\pi\,[1 - \mu(0)]$

Figure 9.5 Two-period credit risky debt: determining the implied probabilities

Default has occurred at date $t = 1$, so the pay-off to the bond at date $t = 2$ is

$$v(2, 2; D) = 100\delta$$

The value in State A at date $t = 1$ is

$$v_A(1, 2; D) = \exp(-0.0487)(100\delta)$$
$$= B(1, 2)_d(100\delta)$$

A similar argument applies if State B occurs:

$$v_B(1, 2, D) = \exp(-0.0538)(100\delta)$$
$$= B(1, 2)_u(100\delta),$$

where $B(1, 2)_u$ is the value at date $t = 1$ of a one-period default-free bond and is equal to

$$B(1, 2)_u = \exp(-0.0538)$$

The subscript "u" refers to the "up" state for the default-free spot rate of interest.

If State C occurs, the argument is more interesting. In State C default has not occurred, so that one period later, at maturity, one of two possible states can occur:

$$v(2, 2, DS) = 100 \begin{cases} 1; \text{ probability } 1 - \mu(1) \text{ if } DS_2 = \overline{D} \text{ (no default)} \\ \delta; \text{ probability } \mu(1) \text{ if } DS_2 = D \text{ (default)} \end{cases}$$

Therefore, in State C the value of the bond is

$$v_C(1, 2, \overline{D}) = B(1, 2)_d 100\{[1 - \mu(1)] + \delta\mu(1)\}$$

In State D a similar argument applies:

$$v_D(1, 2, \overline{D}) = B(1, 2)_u 100\{[1 - \mu(1)] + \delta\mu(1)\}$$

The value of the credit risky bond today, $v(0, 2, \overline{D})$, is determined by calculating the expected value of the bond at date $t = 1$ using the martingale probabilities and discounting at the risk-free rate of interest. Referring to Figure 9.5, there are four possible states. Therefore

$$v(0, 2; \overline{D}) = 0.9539 \times [(1 - \pi)\mu(0)v_A(1, 2; D) + \pi\mu(0)v_B(1, 2, D)$$
$$+ (1 - \pi)[1 - \mu(0)]v_C(1, 2, \overline{D}) + \pi[1 - \mu(0)]v_D(1, 2, \overline{D})]$$

Substituting the values of the bond in the four different states gives

$$v(0, 2; \overline{D}) = 0.9539 \times [(1 - \pi)\exp(-0.0487) + \pi\exp(-0.0538)]\mu(0)(100\delta)$$
$$+ 0.9539 \times [(1 - \pi)\exp(-0.0487) + \pi\exp(-0.0538)]$$
$$\times [1 - \mu(0)]100\{[1 - \mu(1)] + \mu(1)\delta\}$$

The above calculation can be simplified by considering the pricing of a two-period default-free zero coupon bond. Consider the value of the default-free bond at $t = 1$:

$$B(1, 2) = \begin{cases} \exp(-0.0538); \text{ martingale probability } \pi \\ \exp(-0.0487); \text{ martingale probability } 1 - \pi, \end{cases}$$

and the value of the default-free bond today at $t = 0$ is

$$B(0, 2) = 0.9539 \times [(1 - \pi)\exp(-0.0487) + \pi \exp(-0.0538)]$$

Therefore

$$v(0, 2; \overline{D}) = B(0, 2)[\mu(0)(100\delta) + [1 - \mu(0)]100\{[1 - \mu(1)] + \mu(1)\delta\}] \qquad (6)$$

From Table 9.1 we have $B_F(0, 2) = 90.6264$, $v(0, 2, \overline{D}) = 89.7056$ and $\delta = 0.40$. We have estimated $\mu(0) = 0.006$. Therefore, substituting these values into equation (6) and solving for $\mu(1)$ gives

$$\mu(1) = 0.011$$

The martingale probability of default at time 1, as implied by the bond prices, is almost twice that of default at time 0. Given $\mu(0) = 0.006$ and $\mu(1) = 0.011$, the pricing of the two-period credit risky debt is summarized in Figure 9.6.

Repeating this argument for the three-year zero coupon bond gives

$$\mu(2) = 0.016$$

Equation (5) can be written in the form

$$v(0, 1, \overline{D}) = B_F(0, 1)E_0^Q[e(1)] \qquad (7)$$

where the expected pay-off is

$$E_0^Q[e(1)] = 1 - \mu(0) + \delta\mu(0)$$

$$= 0.9964$$

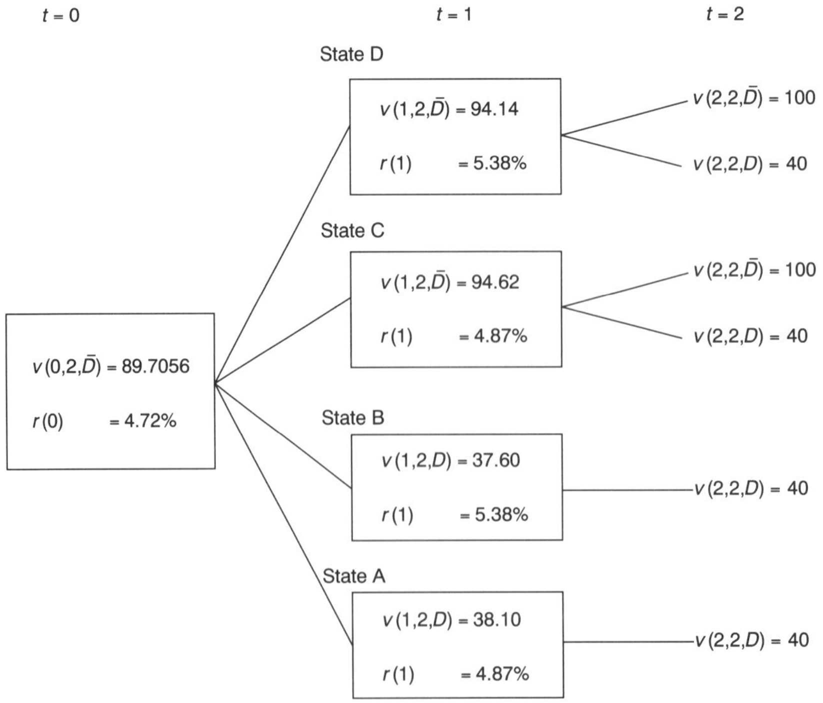

Figure 9.6 Two-period credit risky debt: summary of results

Hence

$$B_F(0, 1)E_0^Q[e(1)] = 95.3921 \times 0.9964$$

$$= 95.0486$$

which agrees with Table 9.1.

Equation (6) can be written in the form

$$v(0, 2, \overline{D}) = B_F(0, 2)E_0^Q[e(2)] \tag{8}$$

where the expected pay-off is

$$E_0^Q[e(2)] = [1 - \mu(0)][1 - \mu(1) + \delta\mu(1)] + \delta\mu(0)$$

$$= 0.989840$$

Hence

$$B_F(0, 2)E_0^Q[e(2)] = 90.6264 \times 0.989840$$

$$= 89.7056$$

which agrees with Table 9.1.

In general one can write

$$v(0, T; \overline{D}) = B_F(0, T)E_0^Q[e(T)|\overline{D}] \tag{9}$$

Equation (9) gives the value of the zero coupon bond if the firm is not in default. Equation (9) is an important and intuitive result. It is important because (i) it provides a practical way of computing the martingale probabilities of default using market data, and (ii) it can be used for pricing derivatives on credit risky cash flows. It is intuitive because the second term in equation (9), $E_0^Q[e(T)|\overline{D}]$, can be interpreted as the date 0 present value of the promised pay-off at date T. We can rewrite equation (9) in the form

$$E_0^Q[e(T)|\overline{D}] = v(0, T, \overline{D})/B_F(0, T), \tag{10}$$

where the right side can be interpreted as a credit spread.

9.3 PRICING OPTIONS ON CREDIT RISKY BONDS

Consider a put option written on debt issued by the ABC company. The maturity of the option is one year. At maturity the option allows you to sell, for a strike price of 94, a two-year bond with a coupon of USD 3 paid annually and face value of USD 100, issued by the ABC firm. To price this option, we start by considering the value of the option at its maturity date. For simplicity of exposition, we maintain our assumption that the length of the lattice interval is one year, so that we can use all the results summarized in Figure 9.6. In practice, one would use intervals of shorter length than a year.

At the maturity of the option, at date $t = 1$, there are four possible values of the underlying bond depending on interest rates and whether default has occurred or not. If default has not occurred, then the value of the coupon bond is

$$v_c(1; \overline{D}) \equiv 3B(1, 2)E_1^Q[e(2)|\overline{D}] + (3 + 100)B(1, 3)E_1^Q[e(3)|\overline{D}]$$

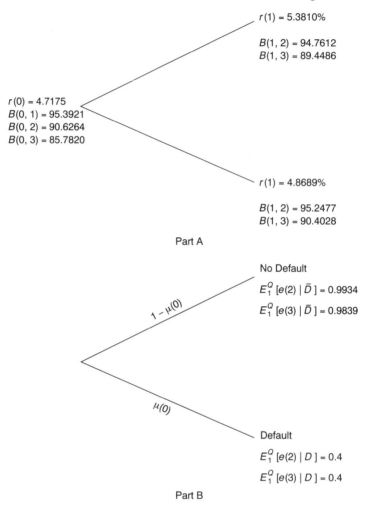

$r(1)$ = 5.3810%

$B(1, 2)$ = 94.7612
$B(1, 3)$ = 89.4486

$r(0)$ = 4.7175
$B(0, 1)$ = 95.3921
$B(0, 2)$ = 90.6264
$B(0, 3)$ = 85.7820

$r(1)$ = 4.8689%

$B(1, 2)$ = 95.2477
$B(1, 3)$ = 90.4028

Part A

No Default

$E_1^Q[e(2) \mid \bar{D}]$ = 0.9934

$E_1^Q[e(3) \mid \bar{D}]$ = 0.9839

$1 - \mu(0)$

$\mu(0)$

Default

$E_1^Q[e(2) \mid D]$ = 0.4

$E_1^Q[e(3) \mid D]$ = 0.4

Part B

Figure 9.7 Part A: default-free term structure, Part B: default/no default states

using equation (9), where $B(1, T)$ denotes the value at date 1 of receiving one dollar for sure at date T. If default has occurred, then the value of the coupon bond is

$$v_c(1; D) \equiv 3B(1, 2)E_1^Q[e(2)|D] + (3 + 100)B(1, 3)E_1^Q[e(3)|D]$$

Relevant values are shown in Figure 9.7.

The values of the coupon bond in the four possible states are shown in Figure 9.8, along with the values of the put option. To determine the option value today, we must calculate the expected value of the option at date $t = 1$ and discount back at the risk-free rate of interest.

In States A and B default has occurred on the underlying ABC zero coupon bond. The value of the option varies over these two states because the value of the underlying asset varies due to the interest rate risk. In States C and D the underlying asset at $t = 1$ is not

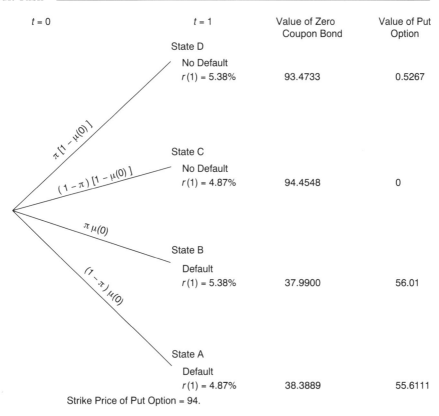

Strike Price of Put Option = 94.

Figure 9.8 Pricing a put option written on credit risky debt

in default. The value of the option today is

$$p(0) = 0.9539 \times \{[1 - \mu(0)][\pi 0.5267 + (1 - \pi)0]$$
$$+ \mu(0)[\pi 56.01 + (1 - \pi)55.6111]\} \qquad (11)$$

Given that $\pi = 0.5$ and $\mu(0) = 0.006$ then

$$p(0) = 0.9539 \times \{[1 - \mu(0)]0.2634 + \mu(0)55.8105\}$$
$$= 0.5692$$

This methodology can easily be extended to price American options on credit risky bonds.

9.4 PRICING VULNERABLE DERIVATIVES

This section studies the pricing of vulnerable derivatives. *Vulnerable derivatives* are derivative securities subject to the additional risk that the writer of the derivative might default. Consider an example of an over-the-counter (OTC) option written on a Treasury bill. There is no default risk associated with the underlying asset — the Treasury bill. However, the writer of the option is a financial institution which may default, so that

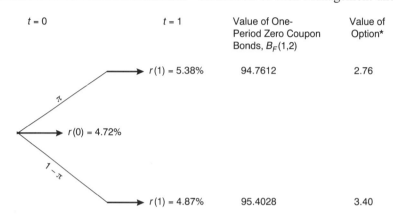

	t = 1	Value of One-Period Zero Coupon Bonds, $B_F(1,2)$	Value of Option*
	$r(1) = 5.38\%$	94.7612	2.76
$r(0) = 4.72\%$			
	$r(1) = 4.87\%$	95.4028	3.40

* Strike Price is 92 where $\pi = 0.5$ represents the martingale probability of an up-state.

Figure 9.9 Pricing a default-free Treasury bill call option

there is the risk that if the option is exercised the writer may be unable to fulfil the obligation to make the required payment to the option owner. The methodology that we have developed can handle this problem. A simple example is used to illustrate the procedure.

First, let us assume there is no risk of the writer defaulting. Consider a call option written on a Treasury bill. The maturity is one year, and at expiration the option holder can purchase a one-year Treasury bill at a strike price of 92. The option is valued using the information summarized in Figure 9.9. The lattice of interest rates comes from Figure 9.8. The date 0 value of the call option is

$$c(0) = 0.9539[0.5 \times 2.76 + 0.5 \times 3.40]$$

$$= 2.94$$

Now assume that the financial institution that wrote the option belongs to the ABC risk class. When the option matures there are four possible states depending on whether interest rates go up or down and whether the writer defaults. The four states are shown in Figure 9.10. This figure is similar in nature to Figure 9.8. In States A and B the writer defaults. By assumption, claim holders receive as a pay-off ratio 40 per cent of the value of their option.

The value of the vulnerable option today is

$$c_V(0) = 0.9539 \times \{[1 - \mu(0)][\pi 2.76 + (1 - \pi)3.40]$$

$$+ \mu(0)[\pi 2.76 + (1 - \pi)3.40] \times 0.40\}$$

Given that $\pi = 0.5$ and $\mu(0) = 0.006$, then

$$c_V(0) = [1 - \mu(0)]2.94 + \mu(0)2.94 \times 0.40$$

$$= 2.93 \tag{12}$$

The difference in the option prices is small, only 1 cent, which is to be expected given that the martingale probability of default is small.

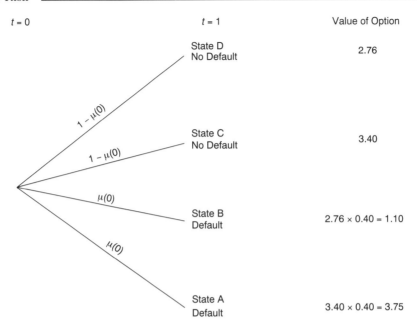

Where $\mu(0) = 0.006$ represents the martingale probability of default occurring at date $t = 1$, conditional upon not being in default at date $t = 0$.

Figure 9.10 Pricing a vulnerable call option

9.4.1 Formalization

This section formalizes the analysis in the previous example. This involves little more than replacing numerical values with symbols. Let $c(1)$ represent the value of the option at date $t = 1$ in the absence of default on the part of the writer, and $c_V(1)$ the value of the vulnerable option. At maturity the pay-off to the option holder is

$$c_V(1) = \begin{cases} c(1); \text{ no default} \\ \delta c(1); \text{ default} \end{cases}$$

where δ represents the pay-off fraction of the option the holder receives if default occurs. The date 0 value of the option in the absence of default is $c(0)$ and the value of the vulnerable option is, using equation (12),

$$c_V(0) = [1 - \mu(0)]c(0) + \mu(0)\delta c(0)$$
$$= E_0^Q[e(1)]c(0) \tag{13}$$

because $E_0^Q[e(1)] = (1 - \mu(0)) + \mu(0)\delta$.

This result has an important implication. Given that there is a positive probability of default, then

$$E_0^Q[e(1)] < 1$$

which implies that a vulnerable option must always be worth less than a non-vulnerable option,

$$c_V(0) < c(0) \tag{14}$$

Equation (14) generalizes in a natural way for a European option that matures at date T:

$$c_V(0) = E_0^Q[e(T)]c(0) \qquad (15)$$

Using equation (9) this can be written in the form

$$c_V(0) = [v(0, T; \overline{D})/B_F(0, T)]c(0) \qquad (16)$$

This form of the expression is useful in practice because it involves pricing a vulnerable option in terms of a credit risk spread for the writer, and the price of a non-vulnerable option.

9.4.2 Example

A firm wants to buy a five-year interest rate cap on the six-month default-free interest rate. Three institutions offer to sell the firm a cap. The institutions, however, have different credit ratings. Institution A belongs to credit class A, institution B belongs to credit

Table 9.2 Pricing a vulnerable cap

Part A: Term structure data

Maturity (Years)	Default-Free	Credit Class A	Credit Class B	Credit Class C
0.5	97.7098	97.4460	97.4069	97.2334
1.0	95.3513	94.8364	94.7542	94.4131
1.5	92.9414	92.1883	92.0598	91.5571
2.0	90.4954	89.5169	89.3397	88.6816
2.5	88.0269	86.8356	86.6079	85.8011
3.0	85.5478	84.1563	83.8770	82.9279
3.5	83.0689	81.4894	81.1579	80.0733
4.0	80.5994	78.8440	78.4602	77.2466
4.5	78.1475	76.2278	75.7919	74.4562

Part B: Pricing the caplets

Maturity (Years)	Value of Caplet*	Credit Class A	Credit Class B	Credit Class C
0.5	70	69.81	69.78	69.66
1.0	1,092	1,086.10	1,085.16	1,081.26
1.5	3,212	3,185.97	3,181.53	3,164.16
2.0	5,877	5,813.45	5,801.95	5,759.21
2.5	8,709	8,591.14	8,515.19	8,488.79
3.0	11,484	11,297.20	11,259.71	11,132.30
3.5	14,094	13,826.01	13,769.77	13,585.75
4.0	16,472	16,113.25	16,034.81	15,786.79
4.5	18,593	18,136.26	18,032.55	17,714.76
Total	79,603	78,119.19	77,750.45	76,782.60
Difference		1,483.81	1,852.55	2,820.32
		1.86%	2.33%	3.54%

*Volatility	1.2 per cent
Volatility Reduction Factor	0.15
Cap Rate	7.00 per cent
Principal	USD 10 million

class B, and institution C belongs to credit class C. Credit class A has a lower risk of default than credit class B and credit class B has a lower risk of default than credit class C.

The term structure details are given in Table 9.2, Part A for default-free interest rates and the three credit classes. The value of the caplets, assuming no counterparty risk, is calculated using the Heath, Jarrow and Morton (1991) model, assuming interest rates are normally distributed. The prices of the caplets are given in Table 9.2, Part B.

To incorporate the effects of counterparty risk, equation (16) is used. Consider the last caplet. The value in the absence of counterparty risk is USD 18,593. For institution A, belonging to credit class A, using the figures from the last row of Table 9.2, Part A:

$$v_A(0, 4.5, \overline{D})/B_F(0, 4.5) = 76.2278/78.1475$$

$$= 0.9754$$

Therefore using equation (16) the value of the caplet is

$$\text{USD } 18,593 \times 0.9754 = \text{USD } 18,136.26$$

as shown in Table 9.2, Part B. The values of the other caplets are calculated in a similar way. For institution A, its credit risk lowers the value of the cap by approximately 1.86 per cent; for institution B, 2.33 per cent; and for institution C, 3.54 per cent.

9.5 CREDIT DEFAULT SWAP

We now examine the pricing of a simple credit default swap. Consider a one-year credit default swap referenced to two credits. The basic structure is shown in Figure 9.11. The bank is buying protection from the counterparty on the first of two credits to experience a default. The counterparty has a liability to pay the bank in the event that one of the two reference credits defaults. The counterparty's exposure is to two names or reference credits and the exposure is limited to the first name to default. After the first default, any exposure to subsequent defaults is terminated. In the event of a default by one of the two names, the counterparty pays a fixed amount to the bank. In return for this default insurance, the bank pays a premium to the counterparty.

To illustrate how to price this form of swap, the data in Table 9.2 will be used. It is assumed that the counterparty belongs to credit class A and the two reference credits belong to credit class C. Conditional on no defaults by the two reference credits at date $t-1$, payment by the counterparty at date t is described by one of four mutually exclusive and exhaustive events:

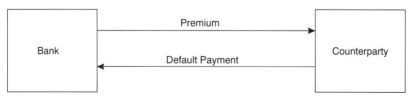

Nominal Principal: $60 million
Default Payment: Nominal Principal × (1 − Recovery Rate)
Recovery Rate: 30 per cent

Figure 9.11   A simple credit default swap

1. First credit defaults, second credit does not default.
2. First credit does not default, second credit defaults.
3. First credit defaults, second credit defaults.
4. First credit does not default, second credit does not default.

If one of the first three events occurs the counterparty makes a fixed payment, F, to the bank. If event four occurs, no payment occurs. The probability that first (second) credit does not default at date t, conditional upon no default at date $t-1$ is $[1 - \mu_c(t-1)h]$, where $\mu_c(t-1)$ is the (martingale) conditional probability of default occurring at date t for a firm in credit class C, conditional upon no default at date $t-1$, and h is the length of the interval between dates $t-1$ and t. Assuming independence between the event of default for the first credit and the second credit, the conditional probability of event four occurring is $[1 - \mu_c(t-1)h]^2$.

To summarize the payment by the counterparty to the bank, it will prove useful to define the following indicator function. Conditional upon no default at date $t-1$,

$$e_1(t) \equiv \begin{cases} 0; & \text{probability } [1 - \mu_c(t-1)h]^2 \\ 1; & \text{probability } 1 - [1 - \mu_c(t-1)h]^2 \end{cases} \tag{17}$$

If $e_1(t) = 0$ at date t, this implies event four has occurred and no payment is made by the counterparty to the bank; if $e_1(t) = 1$ at date t, this implies that either event one, two, or three has occurred and the counterparty makes a payment, F, to the bank. If a default has occurred at or prior to date $t-1$, define

$$e_1(t) \equiv 0, \tag{18}$$

implying that the counterparty's exposure is terminated. In this example the credit swap has maturity of one year. For the sake of simplicity, we have divided the one year into two half year intervals. In practice, shorter intervals would be used. The default payment process over the two intervals is shown in Figure 9.12.

Referring to Figure 9.12, if no defaults have occurred at date $t = 1$, the value of the swap is

$$V(1; \overline{D}) \equiv B(1, 2)[0 \times q_1 + F \times (1 - q_1)], \tag{19}$$

where $B(1, 2)$ is the value at date $t = 1$ of a default-free zero coupon bond that pays one dollar at date 2. If one or more defaults occur at date $t = 1$, then

$$V(1; D) \equiv F \tag{20}$$

Today the value of the swap is

$$V(0; \overline{D}) = B(0, 2)q_0[0 \times q_1 + F \times (1 - q_1)] + B(0, 1)(1 - q_0)F \tag{21}$$

Using the values in Tables 9.2 and 9.3

$$V(0; \overline{D}) = F\{0.9049 \times 0.9858 \times (1 - 0.9854)\} + F\{0.9535 \times (1 - 0.9858)\}$$

$$= F0.0266$$

This analysis implicitly assumes that the counterparty does not default. This assumption can be relaxed using the analysis given in Section 9.4.

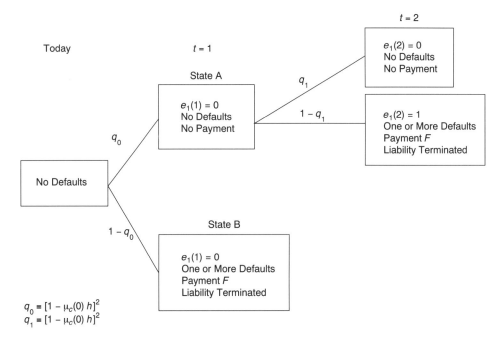

Figure 9.12 Default payment process

Table 9.3 Implies martingale conditional probabilities of default

Maturity (Years)	Credit Class A	Credit Class C
0.5	0.01	0.0143
1.0	0.01	0.0147

$$q_0 = (1 - 0.0143 \times 0.5)^2 = 0.9858$$
$$q_1 = (1 - 0.0147 \times 0.5)^2 = 0.9854$$

9.6 SUMMARY

We take as exogenous the term structure of zero coupon corporate bonds for firms within a given risk class and the term structure of zero coupon default-free bonds. Using standard arguments, we show how to extract the conditional martingale probabilities of default. Given these probabilities we show how to price options on credit risky bonds, how to price vulnerable options, and how to price credit default swaps.

We have made the simplifying assumption that the martingale default probabilities are independent of the martingale probabilities for the default-free spot interest rates. This assumption can be relaxed and generalized in numerous ways. Jarrow, Lando and Turnbull (1994) let the default probabilities for firm ABC be dependent on a current credit rating given by an external agency, such as Standard & Poors, Inc. or Moody's. This creates a Markov chain in credit ratings, in which historical default frequency data can be utilized. Lando (1994) allows the default probability to be dependent on the level of spot interest rates. This last modification appears promising in the area of Eurodollar contracts (see Jarrow, Lando and Turnbull (1995)).

9.7 ENDNOTES

1. The existence and uniqueness of these martingale probabilities of default is discussed in Jarrow and Turnbull (1995).
2. For different types of bonds, average recovery rates are given in Moody's Special Report (1992).

9.8 REFERENCES

Black, F., Derman, E. and Toy, W. (1990) "A one factor model of interest rates and its application to Treasury bond options". *Financial Analyst Journal*, **46**, 33–9.

Heath, D., Jarrow, R.A. and Morton, A. (1992) "Bond pricing and the term structure of interest rates: A new methodology for contingent claims valuations". *Econometrica*, **60**, 77–105.

Jarrow, R.A., Lando, D. and Turnbull, S.M. (1993) "A Markov model for the term structure of credit risk spreads". Unpublished manuscript, Cornell University (Forthcoming, *Review of Financial Studies*).

Jarrow, R.A., Lando, D. and Turnbull, S.M. (1995) "The pricing of Eurodollar contracts". Work in progress.

Jarrow, R.A. and Turnbull, S.M. (1995) "Pricing options on derivative securities subject to credit risk". *Journal of Finance*, **50**, 53–85.

Lando, D. (1994) "Three essays on contingent claims pricing". Ph.D. thesis, Cornell University.

PART 3
Risk Management

10
Emerging Markets
MARK FOX

10.1 INTRODUCTION

10.1.1 Definition of Emerging Market Investment

The term "emerging market" has become a fashionable one among investors and market participants alike. This has occurred as part of the trend throughout the 1980s in the search among global investors for a progressively wider range of countries to invest in.

For example, the Spanish and Italian bond markets were regarded as "exotic" in the early 1980s but had become mainstream by the late 1980s, and were included in major government bond indices by the 1990s. Both countries now appear in all but the most restrictive of global fixed income and equity indices. The rationale for investment in a progressively wider range of countries is simple: greater opportunity for higher performance and successful investment in those countries that are less "discovered" by global capital flows than in those economies that had achieved maturity. Moreover the possibilities for risk reduction through diversification are greater, as different investment considerations apply.

The search for an ever expanding range of newer economic opportunities that have not yet been exploited is a continuing feature of global investment. At the same time institutions like the IMF and World Bank have increased their efforts to direct investment flows into the world's poorer nations. These two trends together led to progressively greater investor attention being paid to what became described as "emerging markets".[1] There now exist substantial flows of money available for investment in emerging markets around the world. Private money now forms the largest source of investment for emerging countries, although the amounts invested through equity and bond flows form only a small part of the total (see Figure 10.1).

In fact the term "emerging market" is commonly used to cover a wide variety of different forms of risk, and has become a blanket term for a wide spectrum of investment activity without due consideration as to the specific nature of the investment type or its risks.

The Handbook of Risk Management and Analysis. Edited by Carol Alexander
© 1996 John Wiley & Sons Ltd

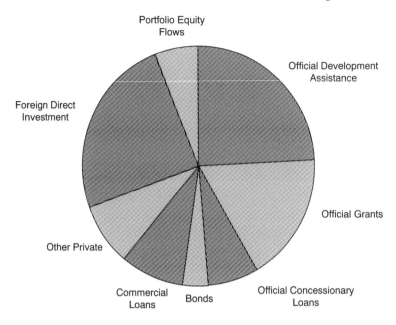

Figure 10.1 Resource flows to emerging markets (Source: IFC Handbook)

A broad divide can be drawn between those investments which are made in a developed market, but seeking to gain from the emergence of a particular country, either through improving credit, or growing corporate earnings, and those investments which are made in a market which is itself emergent within a country. Both types of risk are colloquially referred to as emerging market risk. Examples of the former are investments in Eurobonds issued by Latin American or Eastern European credits or in a US company which derives a significant proportion of its earnings from China. An example of the latter would be the purchase of Venezuelan bolivar denominated Treasury bills or shares on the Jakarta stock exchange. Clearly an investment in a developed market which it is hoped will benefit from an emerging economy has different risk considerations from investment in an undeveloped market, with all the accompanying problems described further below. This chapter will seek to describe both types of investment, but highlight the differences between them.

10.1.2 Size of Emerging Markets

Emerging markets now form a sizeable part of global investment markets. According to the Emerging Markets Traders Association,[2] 1993 debt trading volumes reached USD 1.98 trillion. Within that number unrestructured loans were only 13.2 per cent of the total, Brady bonds making up the bulk of the rest. Euro- or corporate bonds trading levels are typically around 8 per cent of the trading volumes in Brady bonds of any single country. The report does not detail separately the volumes for local market trading other than the largest Latin American countries. The two largest are Mexico where volumes reached around USD 70 billion and Argentina slightly over USD 100 billion. In both cases the bulk of the debt is US dollar denominated, albeit that it is issued and traded locally.

In terms of outstanding debt, the largest Brady bond issues by debtors such as Mexico, Venezuela, Argentina and Brazil are in the region of USD 10–15 billion. The largest corporate/Eurobond issues are very much smaller, around USD 1 billion, and consequently very much less liquid.

The aggregate capitalization of emerging world equity markets as at the end of 1993 totalled USD 1.636 trillion compared with USD 14.1 trillion for all world equity markets[3]. The largest of these markets such as South Africa, Malaysia and Taiwan are capitalized at around USD 200 billion. The ten stock markets with the highest turnover as a percentage of their capitalization include only two developed markets, the remainder all being emerging markets. In the case of Taiwan, the market with the highest turnover, the ratio is 235.5 per cent of capitalization.

10.1.3 Defining an Emerging Economy

The definition of an emerging economy that is most widely cited is that of the World Bank which defines an emerging market as that of a country which has a GNP per capita between USD 635 and USD 7,909. By employing GDP per capita the relative wealth of the country rather than its size becomes the key criterion. Switzerland, a very small country, is clearly beyond emerging, whereas, India, a very large country cannot be described as mature, but is still emerging. A GDP per capita definition also captures another important point. Emerging economies typically tend to have a much faster population growth rate than mature economies. GDP growth of 3 per cent per annum which might be very respectable for a mature economy, is inadequate for a country with population growth of 4 per cent per annum. Focusing on GDP per capita growth neutralizes differing population growth rates and makes economic performance comparisons between economies more meaningful.

Low GDP per capita is, however, only one of a number of factors that can be said to constitute an emerging economy. Economic and political stability and consistency also matter. Some of the oil rich Middle Eastern states which have a very high GDP per capita, but where this has only been the case for a relatively short period of time, could arguably still be classified as emerging. Other measures such as the high proportion of GDP spent on construction and infrastructure in the Middle East are another sign that the area is still emerging. Distribution of income, reliance on primary commodities rather than industrial activity and concentration of economic activity in one sector are all factors that are can be considered when deciding whether or not an economy is fully developed.

The method of economic management and the political structure behind it as well as the economic numbers themselves are also pertinent to the definition of an emerging economy. Emerging economies frequently have a high degree of government management that is only liberalized as the economy develops. Excessive control of economic sectors regarded as of strategic importance, protectionism, and overregulation are all commonly found in emerging economies. Wider political judgements also often colour judgement as to whether an economy is emerging. Stability of the political structure, racial tensions within a country and the degree of democratization are all relevant factors, as is the existence of an educated executive to implement the reforming policies. Thailand, for example, is generally considered to be an emerging market despite a considerable period of strong economic performance because it has until recently experienced a succession of military coups; whereas Italy, which has suffered deteriorating economic performance for some time, is now usually regarded as developed because of its highly developed political structure and long stature as a major economic power.

Ultimately a subjective investor judgement has to be made as to whether a particular economy is emerging or developed, and opinions do vary sharply. Thailand or Greece will be differently regarded according to the investor. Some investors attach great significance to OECD membership. Under such a definition Mexico has joined the league of developed rather than emerging nations. Portugal and Greece are two countries which are on the cusp of emerging vs. developed nations. For many investors EC membership is sufficient to make them developed, whereas others continue to class them as suitable for investment only as part of an emerging markets investment. Whilst opinions differ at the margins, there does, however, seem to be broad general agreement as to how to identify an emerging rather than a developed economy.

10.1.4 Characteristics of Emerging Markets

Investment directly into the local equity or fixed income markets of any of the emerging economies requires consideration of factors additional to those which affect the investor view of the emerging economy. Emerging markets usually display at least some of the characteristics described below:

1. Limited available information and research, often only available locally.
2. Limited access to the market.
3. High volatility.
4. Heavy concentration in the hands of a small number of players.
5. Poor settlements procedures.
6. Inadequate regulation.
7. Greater performance sensitivity to political relative to economic considerations than developed markets.
8. Greater performance sensitivity to other extraneous considerations such as the commodity cycle.

Before an investor embarks upon investment in emerging markets each of these hurdles has to be addressed. Another frequently cited indicator is low capitalization. This has been excluded from the above list because there are a considerable number of markets commonly thought of as emerging which actually have quite high capitalization (for example the local bond markets of India and Taiwan), but one or more of the other listed characteristics leads to them being thought of as emerging.

10.1.5 Do Emerging Markets Constitute a Separate Asset Class?

Emerging markets are frequently treated as a separate asset class by investors. Institutional and private investors alike regard the portion of their assets invested in emerging markets as high risk/high reward investment, the success of which is dependent on factors specific to the underlying markets rather than upon the general factors that drive global developed markets. Many investment managers have "emerging markets" teams that run money dedicated to those markets. Yet it has been suggested above that the term "emerging markets" covers many different types of investment. As well as the divide between emerging economies and markets, there is the divide between fixed income and equity investment within these markets. It is also the case that assets linked to either emerging economies or markets are used by investors to achieve widely varying objectives.

At one extreme investors seek simply to gain the maximum possible total return from high performance economies or markets. Investors buy either individual holdings or invest in emerging markets funds to achieve this. Equity, fixed income and balanced variants of these funds exist. At the other end of the spectrum are the "yield funds" that are particularly popular in the US and that seek low NAV volatility but a yield uplift over US rates. These funds invest in emerging market assets as part of a diversified strategy investing across a range of assets such as low grade corporate bonds or mortgages in order to achieve their yield objective. Somewhere in between, many funds, both equity and fixed income, are invested primarily in developed markets, but invest a proportion of their funds in emerging economies or markets either for diversification or, more frequently, in the hope of achieving an increase in performance beyond that which they hope to achieve in developed markets.

Emerging markets should probably be regarded as a separate asset class in that there is a broad consensus that the investment process that is deemed necessary for investment in emerging economies or markets does differ from the processes employed by many of the large institutional investors for their developed investments. The process utilized for emerging markets investment seeks to control and evaluate the differing risks that are a function specifically of the differences between emerging and developed markets elaborated in the previous section. An informal survey of a number of the larger investors suggests that investors do analyse those risks separately, usually with the fixed income and equity teams that invest in emerging markets working at least as closely together as each group does with their developed market counterparts.

There is now a considerable body of literature on the performance of emerging markets compared with their developed counterparts, examining the validity of the claims of both the diversification benefits and excess returns over developed markets that are claimed by adherents of emerging markets investors.[4] The evidence is not decisive, although it is the case that individual markets or assets in emerging markets have offered some spectacular opportunities for gains. However, as is to be expected, performance varies widely, as do the correlations both relative to their developed counterparts and to each other. There are conflicting claims as to the degree to which emerging markets provide excess returns, or merely diversification benefits.

Is the range of performance and investment objectives so wide that it cannot be said that emerging markets form a distinctive group? There are common elements that can be said to identify emerging market investment, notwithstanding that the nature of the risk may vary.

For an investment to be defined as emerging market investment, it will usually display at least some of the following characteristics:

1. The performance of the asset must at least partly be tied to the fortunes of a country that is not usually associated with global capital investment flows.

2. Whilst the country may have a satisfactory credit rating, it is believed that there is greater risk of political instability than is normally expected of a country that is being invested in.

3. Information flows are poorer than would be expected from a developed country or market.

4. Short-term volatility is expected to be greater than that of a similar asset that is tied to the fortunes of a developed country or market.

5. It is believed that part of the outperformance of the asset relative to similar assets tied to developed countries will result from a good economic performance by the country, or greater political stability.

The individual types of emerging markets will now be examined.

10.2 NON-PERFORMING LOANS

10.2.1 Introduction

In the 1970s a common misconception among commercial bankers held that sovereign nations could never go "bankrupt" in the same manner as private enterprises, and that it was safe to lend large sums of money to countries rather than corporations as countries would never default on money lent to them. This belief ignored the experiences of earlier generations of bankers who had suffered sovereign default. The 1980s Mexican debt crisis was, in fact, the third time this century that Mexico had defaulted on its debt. Nonetheless there was a lending explosion to less developed countries through the 1970s such that by the 1980s many countries found themselves unable to service the debt that they had accumulated. During the 1980s default on sovereign debt became commonplace for the poorer nations of Latin and Central America, Africa and Eastern Europe.

Once loans became non-performing many banks wished to sell those loans rather than keep them on their books, and they sought ways of liquidation. Others were willing to buy such loans in the belief either that the defaulting borrower would recommence servicing the loan at a future date, and ultimately pay it back, or that the borrower would be willing to renegotiate the terms of the original loan and service the renegotiated loan. Thus a market grew up between buyers and sellers of non-performing loans. Initially a significant part of this market constituted banks swapping loans with each other to create a book of loans more suited to each bank's needs. Each deal was by lengthy negotiation and involved considerable transaction costs.

Over time commercial banks set up specialist departments with the specific purpose of buying and selling loans in default. These gradually developed into full sales and trading operations buying and selling loans in default other than those which the departments had inherited solely through loans originally made by the bank.

10.2.2 Anatomy of the Market

Commercial banks are still the major participants in the loans market. The loans market remains, however, a relatively specialist market. This is particularly so as most of the larger nations that defaulted on their debt have already restructured their debt through Brady or similar plans, and it is the debt of smaller countries that remains to be restructured. Few institutions have the resources to carry out detailed credit work on countries where there may be only a small amount of debt outstanding, and such debt will never be very liquid because of lack of supply anyway.

The majority of large investors shy away from investing in loans, concentrating instead on Brady and Eurobonds. There are a number of reasons for this. First, defaulted loans remain very much less liquid than their performing Brady and Eurobond counterparts. Second, whilst a particular country may have a large amount of defaulted debt outstanding, the banks that are the holders of this debt have tended only to sell a part of their total holdings. Thus often only a small proportion of the original loans are available as a tradeable float, even where the country was large enough to have a substantial amount of debt outstanding. In many jurisdictions it is undesirable for a bank's balance sheet to sell non-performing loans. Only once the loans are converted to Brady bonds does it become attractive to do so. Thus a proper tradeable float of paper is created once a Brady plan is complete.

The loans market also has only a limited number of participants because the price performance of defaulted loans is heavily dependent on the prospects of a successful outcome to negotiations between the creditor commercial banks and the debtor country for restructuring the defaulted debt so that it becomes performing once more. As the borrower is in default the valuation of the loans must necessarily be based totally on the likelihood of the borrower paying any income or principal payments in part or in whole to the creditors at some future date. Those banks which are part of the negotiating process will have inside knowledge of the probability of payments being made by the borrower and can buy and sell part of the outstanding float based on their inside knowledge. In theory Chinese walls have been erected to prevent insider dealing by those commercial banks that are active in buying and selling loans rather than simply seeking to sell down their position acquired when loans were originally made. It is widely believed that, particularly in the early days of loans trading, insider knowledge was relied upon by many of the participants in the market. Those without access to such knowledge therefore choose to avoid these assets.

Settlements procedures are a further deterrent to wide-scale investment in loans. A performing bond represents evidence of entitlement to a known set of future cash streams. A non-performing loan represents only the entitlement to participate in negotiations with the borrower in the hope of achieving future cash streams. In order to validate a claim to any future cash streams that are forthcoming it is necessary to trace the right to the original creditor. Thus each time a loan is sold an assignment has to be made from the seller to the buyer so that the negotiation rights attached to the loan can continue to be traced to the original creditor. Whilst there has been considerable progress towards the standardization of assignment procedures, it remains the case that settlement requires lawyers to process each assignment.

Furthermore, as different loans may specify different assignment procedures lawyers need to check the validity of each previous assignment in order to check that the line of assignees can be traced and added to in a valid manner. Such a procedure is a major deterrent to many investors. The complexity of the process is such that three weeks is normally specified for settlement of a purchase or sale of loans in order to give each party's lawyers time to complete their work. Even so, many loan transactions settle late, often two or three months after the three-week period that has been specified as standard by the Emerging Markets Traders Association ("EMTA"). Such extended settlement periods create considerable counterparty risk, and this too acts as a deterrent.

10.2.3 Special Considerations for Loans

Loans differ from other emerging market assets in that there is no standardization of the nature of the rights being purchased. An investor who purchases a bond is purchasing a standardized security with known terms. No such standardization exists in the case of loans, as each loan will have been separately negotiated by the original counterparties. Loans in default may have been made either to a state or any one of numerous sovereign agencies. The same borrower might have negotiated slightly differing terms on loans with different banks all taken out at the same time. There is no guarantee that in a restructuring all loans will be accorded equal treatment. The original loans will have been for varying time periods, and with differing levels of interest payments. The different borrowers may have defaulted at different times, also giving rise to varying levels of unpaid interest.

The EMTA has sought to standardize loan types for each of the countries where trading in non-performing loans has become active in order to facilitate ease of trading. However, substantial differences within each standard class can exist.[5] In the case of loans where the borrower defaulted a long time ago the amount of cumulative unpaid interest may be notionally worth as much or more than the original loan itself. In this case trading is made still more complex by considerations as to the likely treatment of interest in debt restructuring negotiations. Rights to unpaid interest have usually, but not always, been separated from rights to the loan principal for both trading and negotiations purposes. The outcome of negotiations on unpaid interest (usually referred to as past due interest or "PDI") has varied widely. In some cases past interest has simply been written off. In other cases a percentage has been paid, and in yet others all outstanding interest, however much it may have varied as between differing non-performing loans, has been equalized for the sake of ease of settlement of outstanding claims made by partial payment of interest during the period after default.

Countries in default have often shown preferential treatment to holders of certain classes of loans in default. Partial payments of interest on only particular loans outstanding have sometimes been made. Partial payments too complicate the proper evaluation of outstanding loans, and the task of estimating likely future cash streams. Nor is it the case that all debt holders will necessarily be treated in the same manner. Quite apart from the different classes of debt being treated differently in a restructuring, governments have allowed certain classes of loans to be eligible for swaps into privatizations of state entities, often at a level above that at which the loans were trading prior to the government offer. Debtor governments may be seeking to target early retirement of particularly troublesome classes of loans, either for administrative ease, or because a particular class of loan is likely to prove more expensive to refinance. Thus they are willing to offer some incentive to holders of those loans. Obviously such treatment will affect the value of particular loans.

In evaluating loans a study of the terms upon which a restructuring into performing bonds will occur is also essential. For example, the percentage of outstanding loanholders that is required to approve a particular restructuring is also an important consideration in understanding the loans market. An unusual but important precedent was set by Brazil when a wealthy family (the Dart family) sought to buy sufficient of Brazil's outstanding debt to provide it with a veto on whether or not Brazil's debt restructuring would be completed, thereby hoping to obtain more favourable terms. Brazil, with the consent of the banks which held 94 per cent of the outstanding debt, simply ignored the original terms of the restructuring and proceeded with the issuance of new bonds in exchange for retirement of its loans in default. At the time of writing the Dart family are challenging the validity of the action taken by Brazil and its creditor banks.

10.3 BRADY BONDS

10.3.1 Description

Brady bonds are bonds resulting from a debt restructuring and securitization of sovereign debt in default where the redemption value of at least some of the bonds resulting from that restructuring has been guaranteed by the US Treasury. In some cases the income payments may also have been guaranteed by a holding of US Treasury zero coupon bonds in exchange for the restructuring.

Brady bonds, resulting from Brady plans, came about in the following manner. During the 1980s Mexico, along with several other emerging countries, became unable to service its debt. The amount of money owed to the US commercial banks was sufficiently large that failure to seek some form of solution to the crisis could have led to a major breakdown of confidence in the whole banking system. Clearly action had to be taken. Nicholas Brady, the US Secretary of the Treasury at the time, sponsored a debt restructuring scheme for outstanding Mexican debt modelled upon a floating rate bond structured and brought to the market in March 1988 for the United States of Mexico by J.P. Morgan.

The bond issued in 1988 was structured so that both the ultimate redemption value and a rolling 18-month income guarantee were guaranteed by holdings of US Treasury zeros.[6] The guarantee was achieved by the simple but ingenious device of purchasing US Treasury zeros that would mature on the date of maturity of the debt. Zeros do not pay a coupon but earn income for the holder by rising in price each year towards their eventual redemption value of par. Zeros that mature in 20 years' time can be purchased at a very substantial discount, as payment will not be made for 20 years. Therefore the amount of money that had to be laid out initially in order to achieve the guarantee that the zeros would eventually pay off the principal was relatively small.

The attraction of applying the J.P. Morgan structure to all of Mexico's debt was that it could serve both debtor and creditor well. Mexico succeeded in extending the due date of its debt by some 20 years (i.e. the maturity of the bond in the case of the J.P. Morgan structure), and at the end of that time would not have to pay the principal of the debt. The banks were able to avoid a write-off of the debt and acquire an asset guaranteed by the US Treasury. Such an asset was saleable, thereby creating liquidity for the banks. Mexico was also able to persuade the banks to write off some of its debt in exchange for providing US Treasury zeros and therefore liquidity for their debt.

The key components of the deal between Mexico and its creditor banks sponsored by Brady were that in return for the banks writing off 35 cents of each dollar that was owed to them and their agreement to extend payment of the outstanding principal for 30 years US Treasury zeros would be added to the Mexican debt. A single bond, which combined the deferred Mexican debt with the accruing US Treasury zeros was to be created, thereby securitizing the debt, and providing banks with a liquid instrument that they could sell if they wished to do so. The money for purchase of the zeros was provided by Mexico itself, but the cost of the zeros was subsidized by the US Treasury in order to ensure successful completion of the deal. The bonds that resulted from the securitization became known generically as "Brady" bonds. All resulted from the Brady plan, although a number of different bond structures were created as a result of the plan, seeking to match as far as possible within the overall structure of the scheme the needs of the various creditor banks. In one case a bond created under the plan did not have a US Treasury guarantee (see Table 10.1).

Table 10.1 Bonds created by the Mexico Brady plan

Pars	USD 22.3 billion of bonds maturing December 2019
	Fixed coupon 6.25 per cent, bullet capital payment at maturity
	Rolling collateral guarantee of 18 months' interest
	Two series, each with detachable oil recovery rights
	Currency: USD, SwFr, Dfl, F fr, Lira, yen
Discounts	USD 12 billion of bond maturing 31/12/2019
	Coupon floating at Libor +13/16 per cent, bullet payment at maturity
	Rolling collateral guarantee of 18 months' interest
	Four series, each with detachable oil recovery warrants
	Currency: USD, CD, Dfl, F fr, yen
New money	USD 500 million
	Coupon floating at Libor +13/16 per cent, amortizing semi-annually from 28/09/97
	No collateral guarantee
	One series, no oil warrant, USD only

The variety of bonds created arose from the differing needs of the various creditor banks in order to minimize the impact on them of the partial write-off of their Mexican debt. Brady bonds were issued in several currencies as well as varying structures reflecting the needs of the original lending banks. If a French bank, for example, had lent French francs it might not wish to receive a US dollar denominated bond as it would create a currency translation problem which would not be experienced by a US bank. A Brady bond denominated in French francs overcame this problem. Whilst Brady bonds in several currencies addressed a specific problem at the time, it has left many creditor banks with holdings of very illiquid bonds. Trading in Brady bonds denominated in currencies other than US dollars remains very poor.

The different fixed/floating structures resulted from various groups of banks seeking to provide the debt forgiveness in ways that minimized the impact on their balance sheets according to the accounting practices in their home countries. In each type of bond the forgiveness of debt was made in a different form, albeit that the blended level of forgiveness of 35 cents was consistent across the plan.[7] Par bonds were ideal for banks wishing to avoid a write-down of the original debt, as the original debt would still be repaid at full par value in 30 years' time. Forgiveness came in the form of lower income service payments (i.e. the coupon on the bond) than prevailing interest rates.[8] Discount bonds created an initial write-down of the debt for the banks, i.e. the debt was exchanged for bonds issued at a discount, but met the requirements of many of the banks of maintaining stable income from their portfolio, the bond continuing to pay Libor plus a margin set at market levels. Finally New Money bonds were created for those banks willing to lend additional funds to Mexico at the new margin over Libor. Such banks, of course, had faith in Mexico's future ability to service its debt, and therefore did not require a rolling interest guarantee.

Several other countries have restructured and securitized their debt using the Mexican model of debt extension into long dated bonds backed by US Treasuries.[9] The majority of the resulting bonds have the feature that they are bonds that have a blended credit risk of more than one borrower, namely the US Treasury and the country that has restructured its debt. There have, however, also been a number of bonds that have been created within each Brady plan that do not have any form of US government guarantee.[10] These bonds are also commonly described as Brady bonds, and fall within the above definition. New types of Brady bond continue to be created in order to satisfy the requirements of borrowers and lenders alike as each new plan is completed, and no two plans are identical as each country negotiates with its creditors a variant of debt restructuring acceptable to both sides. An appendix of differing forms of Brady bonds appears at the end of this chapter.

The credit blend of all those bonds which do have a US guarantee at maturity have a similar pattern to their credit mix, with the US Treasury guaranteed component gradually rising towards maturity. The following graph illustrates the credit make-up of the Mexican par bond as of its creation. The top segment of each column represents the Mexican risk. Initially the US Treasury zero component was worth almost nothing. Over time the value of the US zero gradually rises as illustrated by the rising lower segment. Eventually the whole bond is guaranteed by the US Treasury as illustrated by the rising lower segment. There is rolling income guarantee on this bond of 18 months of income as well as the principal guarantee. Notice this illustrated as the middle segment in each column. It diminishes to nothing well before the maturity of the bond. This is because the net present value of the income guarantee rapidly diminishes in successive years.

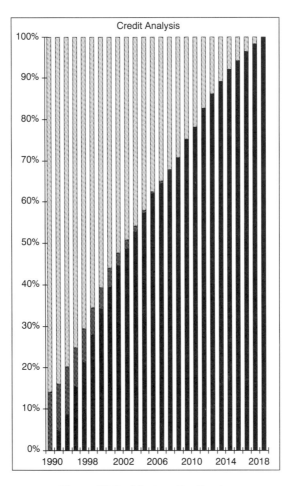

Figure 10.2 Mexican Par Bonds

10.3.2 Evaluation of Brady Bonds

The present value of conventional bonds is usually evaluated by one of two measures, namely yield to maturity or current yield. An investor seeking to evaluate the performance characteristics of a bond in a changing interest rate environment will look at either the average life of the bond or, more accurately, its duration. The same measures are usually applied to Brady bonds, save that it is also necessary to calculate the value of the exposure to the emerging credit stripped of the US Treasury collateral embedded within most Brady bonds to discover the true yield offered for taking the credit risk on a particular emerging credit. The problem of stripping the US Treasury component does not, of course, occur where there is no such collateral.

The overall yield to maturity and current yield are calculated in the same way as those for any other bonds. In order to compare floating coupon with fixed rate bonds floaters are normally shown swapped to a fixed income stream, again a standard evaluation procedure carried out for all bonds. The complications begin when seeking to strip out the US collateral in order to look at the pure emerging market yield. Different Brady bonds offer varying mixes of US and emerging country credit, and in order to carry out the desired comparison it becomes necessary to develop a methodology for stripping out the value of the US collateral consistently in each bond. The yield offered by a Brady bond after the US guaranteed component has been removed is referred to as the "stripped yield". In the case of floating rate bonds that have been first swapped to fixed rates the yield is known as the "swapped stripped yield". A stripped yield is simply the measure of the yield of the emerging credit portion of any Brady bond, and therefore enables different yields on emerging market credits to be compared, regardless of the variations of the US collateral in different bonds.

There are two forms of collateral in Brady bonds: (i) the collateral for guaranteeing principal repayment and (ii) the collateral for guaranteeing rolling interest payments. The US zero coupon curve provides a benchmark valuation of the net present worth of a US Treasury payment of USD 100 at a given date in the future, and the yield to maturity of that payment at present prices. It is a simple matter to strip out the net present worth of the principal guarantee. The remainder of the current price of the bond is the price paid for a known income stream from the emerging market credit (subject to the second form of collateral).

Most Brady bonds offer some form of income guarantee for 12–18 months' worth of income. In order accurately to make a valuation of the emerging market credit risk alone, the income guarantee needs to be stripped out of the calculation too. There are a number of ways of achieving this. The simplest would be to treat the number of future payments that are covered by the guarantee as being US risk alone, and all payments beyond that as being the emerging credit risk. This would understate the value of the rolling nature of the guarantee. A more common method is to apply a probability of default to all future income payments, and then treat the guarantee as an option that provides protection in the event of default. This method accords with the practice that is now very popular of treating a variety of forms of event risk contained within bonds as options, which can be valued as such, and the value offered by a bond adjusted for the cost or benefit of the option.

The options adjusted method is open to several criticisms. That the calculation of default risk either depends on a high degree of subjectivity or, if it is derived from the yield on the principal amount compared with the yield on a riskless asset such as a US treasury, it is ignoring a large number of other factors that may influence the value of a Brady bond such as relative liquidity. It has been argued that as Brady bonds collateralized by special US Treasury issues have an express prohibition against stripping the collateral out anyway, the whole exercise of stripping is sufficiently theoretical to make it fruitless to carry out very precise option valuations on future income streams.[11] Such an approach is somewhat defeatist, after all the calculation of conventional yields to maturity on bonds rely on certain assumptions about the present valuation of future cash flows. Some form of valuation for comparative purposes is better than none. Options adjusted spreads arguably offer spurious precision, but do provide some evaluation of income guarantee. Stripped yields calculated by the majority of market participants do include a value of this guarantee, which is calculated by whichever one of the different models of OAS valuation the investor chooses to follow.

Apart from yield both of the blended credit and specifically of the emerging market credit, investors will wish to look at the duration characteristics of a Brady bond. Ordinary or modified duration measures the price sensitivity of a bond to interest rate changes. This is calculated in the same way as that of any other bond. There is, however, another dynamic measure of a Brady bond's sensitivity to a changing market environment that is unique to Brady bonds because of the blended credit. A new measure, "stripped swapped duration", has been devised to measure the price sensitivity for any change in the stripped spread that may occur in a given Brady bond. As a borrower's credit improves or deteriorates, this will be reflected in the spread offered by bonds issued by that borrower to an equivalent maturity US Treasury. According to how much US Treasury credit and how much emerging country credit is blended within a given Brady bond, the overall sensitivity of any given Brady to a credit spread change due to the emerging country's credit altering will differ. It is a useful measure that will help the investor to choose an appropriate Brady bond from any particular plan according to how strong a view he may wish to take on the credit of the country that completed that plan. In summary, duration measures interest rate sensitivity, stripped duration measures credit spread sensitivity.

Table 10.2 is an illustration of a typical Brady bond evaluation sheet.

Table 10.2   Brady bond evaluation sheet

Mexico Par Bond 6.25 per cent 31/12/19 As of 1st July 1994	
Price:	64
Current Yield:	9.80%
Yield to Maturity:	10.29%
Weighted Average Life:	25.5 yrs
Modified Duration:	10.56 yrs
Stripped Yield:*	11.81%
Stripped Duration:*	5.44 yrs

*Swapped and stripped in the case of floating rate bonds

10.3.3 Anatomy of the Brady Market

Few markets have changed in character as dramatically or as rapidly as the Brady bond market has in the last five years. In the early stages most transactions were by negotiation. The dominant players were the commercial banks which had inherited Brady bonds as a result of the renegotiations of original sovereign loans, and were selling or swapping loans on their own behalf. By 1993 both the nature of the transactions and the market participants had changed dramatically.

One of the major attractions of Brady plans for the original lenders of loans was the creation of marketable securities which could then be sold off their balance sheets. This has been achieved with a vengeance. According to the issue being transacted upon, liquidity can be comparable to highly liquid government bond markets. Mexican and Argentine par bonds, the most liquid bonds, are quoted on a quarter point spread. The nature of the transactions has also changed. The majority of activity is investment related rather than originating from commercial banks. New pools of money for the purpose of investment in Brady bonds along with other emerging market bonds have been created. These funds have become increasingly run along the same lines as other bond portfolios by fund managers, switching allocations between different Brady bonds and country credits, thereby creating transactions motivated by different considerations from those which originally dominated the market. A division between market-makers and principal investors has also arisen as the Brady market has become an investment driven market. All the major investment banks now make markets in Brady bonds as well as a small number of the original commercial banks that made the original loans that were subsequently converted into Brady bonds.

Current practice is that market-makers are only obligated to make markets in USD 2 million lots to each other, but will often trade in USD 5-10 million blocs. However, greater liquidity exists for end investors such as the large mutual funds which may be able to transact in USD 25 million lots without disturbing the price. At the other extreme, some of the smaller Brady plans gave rise to small, highly illiquid issues that continue to trade only once every few months. An active market in these bonds cannot develop because market-makers are unable to risk shorting such issues as the shorts may be impossible to replace. Such issues continue to trade through negotiation.

As the market has developed into a full investment market, other features that typify such markets have arisen. There are now a number of Brady bond indices that seek to provide data on the performance of the market, and offer a benchmark for investors.[12] Derivatives have become commonplace. For example, special purpose vehicles swapping fixed into floating assets and vice versa have been constructed, as have vehicles enabling investors to take pure emerging markets credit, stripping away the US collateral. Active options markets exist in all the more actively traded bonds; these are typically one month to six months in maturity. Baskets on various country combinations of Brady bonds have been created, and so have warrants on individual bonds. There is also an active rentals and repurchase market in Brady bonds, enabling market-makers temporarily to borrow short bonds, thereby assisting in providing greater liquidity to the underlying cash market.

As the number of countries that have completed Brady plans has continued to grow, the depth and range of the market has continued to expand. Figure 10.3 shows the liquid Brady bonds of each country by market capitalization as of May 1994. It will be seen at once that the addition of Brazil to the Brady market in April 1994 caused a considerable adjustment to the universe of Brady bonds available. Brady bonds from Jordan, the Dominican Republic and Uruguay have been excluded because they are illiquid. At the time of writing Poland, Bulgaria and Ecuador are all completing Brady plans, and will further change the universe of investable Brady bonds.

At present the Brady market is heavily weighted towards Latin America as it is in that region that the greatest progress has been made in negotiating Brady deals. The

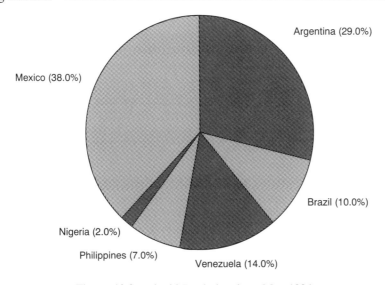

Figure 10.3 Liquid Brady bonds — May 1994

addition of eastern Europe will add further geographic diversification. So far the only Asian country that has defaulted and which has subsequently negotiated a plan is the Philippines. Possible future Brady candidates include Vietnam and Laos. The only African country to have successfully completed a plan is Nigeria, but there are numerous other potential candidates for the future. In the Middle East Jordan has completed a small plan, Iraq and Iran both have defaulted sovereign debt outstanding.

10.3.4 Trading Strategies Unique to the Brady Market

The sophistication of possible trading strategies has ballooned. This is particularly true in relation to countries that do not yet have Brady bonds, but are expected to in the near future. In the earlier plans, the only way to buy bonds expected to be issued under future Brady plans prior to completion was to purchase the non-performing loans that would be cancelled in favour of new Brady bonds when a deal was complete. Now the Brady market itself provides the means either to participate in future plans, or simply to take a view on the likelihood of a plan being completed, independent of the merits of the country that is near to completing a plan.

As a new country negotiates a Brady plan it has become standard market practice for "when-and-if" Brady bonds to be traded, on the assumption that negotiation of a plan will be completed by a certain date. This date is known as the "drop dead" date. In the event of a Brady plan not being successfully negotiated by the drop dead date all trades completed on a when-and-if basis are cancelled. All Brady plans to date have led to several different bonds being created. When-and-if trading takes place in each of the major types of Brady bonds that are expected to follow from the plan. Purchase of a when-and-if Brady bond achieves investment in future bonds if they come into existence, but it does not provide a way of betting solely upon the likelihood of a plan being completed.

It is also possible to take a graduated view upon the prospects of completion of any plan rather than the value of the bonds that result from a plan. As well as when-and-if trading in bonds expected to be created by future plans, trading can also occur in future

Brady bonds on what is somewhat confusingly called a "cash" basis. In the case of a cash trade, the trade will be valid regardless of whether or not the Brady plan is completed by a set date. However, the nature of the instrument received by the buyer is dependent on the outcome of the negotiations. If a plan is in place by the drop dead date, the buyer receives the Brady bond. If the plan is not completed, he receives the original loan that would have become a particular type of Brady bond in the event of the plan going ahead.

Investors can buy a when-and-if Brady bond, which has an embedded put option through the drop dead clause, but then sell the cash Brady bond against it so that they deliver away any Brady bond that is received through the when-and-if purchase. The price spread between when-and-if Brady bonds and the cash bonds effectively represents the value of the put option. The less certain the market is that a new Brady plan will be successfully completed, the less the premium that the when-and-if bond should command over the cash bond. Prior to the completion of the Brazil Brady plan Brazil Capitalization bonds were traded heavily on both a when-and-if basis and a cash basis. The premium of when-and-if bonds was as high as ten points over the cash bonds at times when investors were willing to pay a high premium for the embedded put option. As the market became more certain that Brazil would complete its deal, investors became increasingly reluctant to pay a premium for the when-and-if clause with the drop dead clause which ensured that they had no Brazilian exposure in the event of a plan not being completed. Eventually the two types of future Brazil Capitalization bond traded at an identical price with each other, as would be expected once it became clear that the deal would definitely go ahead.

10.4 EUROBONDS

If a country has defaulted on its obligations the international capital markets are generally closed to it until such time as a satisfactory agreement has been reached on the outstanding debt in default. Moreover would-be corporate borrowers based in the jurisdiction of a country in default are usually also unable to access international markets. This is because the ratings agencies place a "sovereign ceiling" on the ratings of any corporate issuer in any country, that a corporate cannot receive a higher credit rating than its country of domicile, even if the majority of its operations are outside its domicile.

As each emerging country has successfully renegotiated its debt in default and signed a Brady plan, the capital markets were reopened for it. For example, once Mexico had negotiated a Brady plan, it became possible for Mexico and subsequently a large number of Mexican corporate borrowers to raise funds through borrowing on the international bond markets. As other nations in default have renegotiated their debt they too have returned to the capital markets, raising funds in developed currencies. Figure 10.4 shows debt issuance in capital markets by emerging countries in the last two years since Brady plan restructuring opened up other capital markets for them. It has not been necessary in every case for a signed Brady plan to be complete before countries have commenced issuing debt. Clear intention to negotiate a settlement of past defaults has been enough to persuade bond investors to purchase bonds from countries such as Argentina and Brazil sovereign agencies prior to the completion of Brady plans.

The bulk of emerging country Eurobonds have been denominated in US dollars, but Deutschmarks, sterling, yen, French francs, Italian lira and Spanish pesetas have all been used.

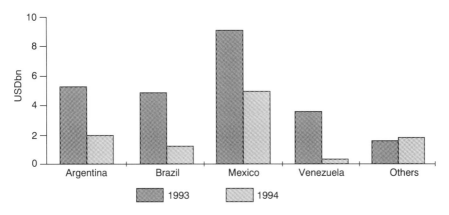

Figure 10.4   Eurobond issuance

Sovereign borrowers have historically accorded a much higher level of priority in servicing their foreign debt held in the form of bond issues than they have in servicing outstanding loans to commercial banks. Thus, for example, in the 1980s neither Mexico nor Venezuela ever defaulted on their Eurobond issues, despite defaulting on their bank debt.[13] Knowledge of this has been one of the factors that has led investors to be willing to lend money through Eurobond issues prior to a renegotiation of defaulted debt being complete.

It is not intended to dwell on the Eurobond market for emerging market credits at length other than to highlight those features of this sector of the Eurobond market that are unique to emerging credits. In most respects Eurobond practice is similar in the field of emerging credits to the operation of the market for bonds issued by developed borrowers. The average size of issue by emerging credits is, however, significantly smaller than the average size for developed borrowers, reflecting the smaller pool of investors willing to purchase issues with lower credit ratings. To date only two issues of USD 1 billion have been launched, the majority of issues being in the USD 80–150 million range. This in turn has led to poor liquidity in many issues, especially during periods of weak markets. It is common practice for secondary markets to be made only by the lead manager, and for market-makers to refuse to make markets to each other.

Investors contemplating the purchase of emerging market Eurobonds should consider carefully a number of issues before purchase. Liquidity can be very poor in many emerging credit Eurobonds, generally much poorer than, for example, in Brady bonds issued by the same borrower. Second, many Eurobonds, especially by Brazilian banks, have "dollar constraint" or "convertibility" clauses. Unlike developed markets, it cannot be taken for granted that the currencies of emerging countries will be freely convertible. Some borrowers domiciled in emerging countries, especially Brazilian banks, have therefore inserted clauses allowing them to repay hard currency debt in local currencies in the event of suspension of convertibility, rather than the bond being puttable, and the borrower repaying the bondholder in dollars. Finally, checking the creditworthiness of corporate borrowers needs to be carried out with more than usual thoroughness, as accounting and corporate governance regimes tend to be much laxer in emerging countries than in developed ones.

10.5 LOCAL FIXED INCOME MARKETS

Investment in local bond and money markets tends to occur in those countries that are some way towards becoming fully economically and/or politically developed, lagging after local equity investment, or purchase of the credit in developed currency fixed income markets. There are several reasons for this. Local equity investment is often considered relatively early on because individual companies may perform well long before the whole economy is stable. In most emerging countries faith in individual enterprises is established long before faith in the government, government policy and the local currency are secured. Whereas taking local currency exposure is seen as an unfortunate incidental necessity to achieve large equity returns, investors will only be confident in the currency itself once the whole economy is on a fairly firm footing.

Those who wish to buy the credit story of an emerging country are usually able to do so earlier through bonds issued in developed currencies. Local currency bond market investment develops later. This is because currency returns are typically a far larger component of fixed income investment than of equity investment. Moreover many emerging country governments strongly discourage or ban external investment in the local bond and money markets, which they perceive to be foreign speculation seeking short-term gains through high yields[14], whereas they encourage equity investment which is seen as long-term investment in the country's industrial and commercial base.[15]

Conversations with fund managers suggest that the following are among the additional criteria that need to be satisfied before a fixed income investor is likely to make the leap from buying a credit in a developed currency to buying the same credit in the local currency:

1. Government permission to purchase local debt instruments.
2. A commitment to permanent convertibility of the currency.
3. A responsible attitude towards the currency, encouraging neither high overvaluation for "macho" purposes, nor overly aggressive depreciation to stimulate exports.
4. Sufficient foreign exchange reserves to provide a degree of comfort as to the prospects for the currency, not merely sufficient reserves to service debt.
5. Stability of policy on currency and monetary targets.
6. A stable tax regime for local instruments.

Additionally a local capital market of sufficient depth and sophistication to handle local fixed income borrowings will have to exist. This will occur at a later stage than a local equity market because fixed income transactions tend to be much larger in size. The capital needed to be a market-maker in fixed income instruments, or even to act as an agency broker, may not be readily available. Issues such as counterparty credit also become far more important in view of the larger size of the transactions and there may be a limited number of local brokers who satisfy the necessary minimum standards. As a local debt market develops it will have to satisfy the same range of criteria that any market, debt or equity has to satisfy. These include a degree of liquidity and a workable, even if not efficient, settlements procedure.

Whilst it is understandable in view of the factors described above why it is that international investors tend to invest in local debt instruments relatively late on in the cycle, that approach should not be taken for granted as being the right one. Local debt markets tend to be more highly rated by credit ratings agencies than borrowings of the same government in foreign currencies.[16] This is explained by the rating agencies as being because the only relevant question that needs to be considered from a pure credit as opposed to investment desirability standpoint is whether the government both currently and historically has been inclined to pay its domestic debt holders. An impecunious government is always able to print more currency to repay its debt holders if there is a shortage of finance, albeit that in the process it may make that currency worthless, whereas a government's ability to repay foreign or developed currency debt depends on a large number of financial considerations.

Other reasons exist why investment in local currency instruments should be considered early on in a country's economic cycle. Investors who place a high premium on risk diversification will be attracted to the diversification potential offered by a different interest rate environment, with different inflationary, monetary and fiscal dynamics from developed markets. Moreover the players in an emerging local market, both brokers and investors, are more likely to be different than the major global players that dominate most developed markets. Investing in truly emerging local markets will provide greater diversification benefits than buying an emerging market credit in a developed bond market where only a change in the perception of the credit relative to other credits in the developed market will offer diversity of performance. Local instruments are also often short in duration, and therefore more likely to be stable in price than, for example, Brady bonds.

The evolution of local debt markets has followed strikingly similar patterns across the world. The first and often only issuing credit for some time will be the government or government agencies. Governments will generally borrow in their own currencies rather than in other currencies as soon as they are able to do so, that is, when investors are willing to buy the credit of that government in the local currency. This is done because they necessarily have ultimate control over local currency denominated markets, and in order to promote a local financial development. It may, however, be a long time before a government is able to fund its entire borrowing requirements in its own currency.[17]

Borrowings are usually in the form of Treasury bills of relatively short maturity. Gradually bills of longer maturity are issued, although initially the size of the longer dated bill issues tends to be much smaller, and the longer bills consequently less liquid. Over time the government begins to issue bonds. These are generally taken to mean securities longer than one year and issued at par with a coupon rather than at a discount, but there is no strict rule about this. Mexico, for example, has two-year Treasury bills. The bond market grows in depth and liquidity, and a full yield curve with liquid bonds along the whole spectrum of maturities develops. Derivatives and futures develop as well.

An interim step to a fully developed bond market is the issuance of bonds linked to the performance of an external developed currency. Mexico, for example, has issued bonds linked to the performance of the US dollar/Mexican peso exchange rate, and Greece has issued bonds exchanged linked to the ECU. Many emergent economies experience high inflation which damages confidence in the currency, hence this need for an external link. Another common interim measure in the process of creating a local bond market adopted by governments seeking to increase investor comfort in their bond markets is to issue index linked bonds, thereby overcoming investor concerns that inflation will erode either the yield offered by the bonds or the real value of the currency.

Corporate and other non-governmental borrowers will gradually enter the market. The largest and best known names will be first, followed by a broader range of borrowers over time. Private placement of debt rather than fully public offerings is often the first stage of a non-governmental market developing, with small issues placed with a few knowledgeable investors. This is because corporate credit assessment of local borrowers in emerging markets cannot be achieved with the same ease as such analysis in developed markets, and therefore the pool of investors willing to buy such debt is limited by the number who have resources to make a full study of emerging corporate credit. Most corporates will be unrated by the major credit agencies. Accounting standards in emerging countries may be poor or non-existent. There may be no local credit agencies, or if they do exist, their skills and impartiality may be open to question. Frequently potential buyers of locally issued emerging market debt will turn to their equity colleagues for help, as equity investors in emerging markets are more familiar with assessment of the worth of an enterprise on poor information.

Some large liquid local bond markets are sometimes referred to as "emerging" because they are still closed to foreigners or just beginning to open. As described above attitudes towards foreign investment in local bond markets can often be ambivalent or even hostile. Foreign investment in local equities is perceived to be desirable investing in the long-term growth and enterprise of a nation, whereas foreign investment in local bond markets is seen as "speculative". The local currency is allowed to be freely purchased for equity investment, which is perceived to be for the long-term benefit of the economy, but not for the purchase of local fixed income investment, which is perceived to be "speculation" by foreigners. Only foreign government pressure finally forces open these closed bond markets. More subtle barriers to local market participation than outright bans may also exist. Withholding tax, turnover tax, or registration requirements are common features of emerging markets. Administrative overregulation rather than regulation seeking to tackle substantive problems such as price manipulation is frequently encountered.

Investment in local debt markets presents many additional considerations for investors. However precisely because local markets can be problematic and are therefore not efficient, opportunities are available. Mexico offers the best case history of the development of a local market. By December 1993 outstanding debt stood at around USD 80 billion, of which approximately half was owned by foreigners. Brazil as well as many of the Asian markets, once they are opened up, offer similar potential for the future.

10.6 EMERGING EQUITY MARKETS

10.6.1 Introduction

Investment specifically in equity markets said to be "emerging" rather than developed as a distinctive discipline can be traced back rather further than fixed interest emerging market investment. Governmental organizations such as the IFC were investing equity into emerging markets as part of government assistance programmes long before private investors became involved. The genesis of investment in emerging equity markets is rather different from that of fixed income investment. The fixed income markets grew rapidly almost by accident as an increasing amount of defaulted debt was restructured as tradeable bonds. Emerging equity investment grew more systematically because of the obvious philosophical fit between the rationale for taking an equity stake in an enterprise that is perceived to have good growth prospects and seeking to participate in the rapid growth of a developing country. During the course of this century the majority of countries have experienced positive GNP growth most of the time. Those countries which are thought of as emerging are countries which, starting from a poorer base, have experienced sustained periods of above average growth, and above average stock market growth, as can be seen in the growth of emerging stock market capitalization relative to developed markets (see Figure 10.5).

In equity markets as in fixed income markets the term "emerging" can be applied either to the nature of the underlying country, or to the market itself. Frequently, as with fixed income, a nation will have made sufficient progress to have an adequately functioning equity market accessible to locals, but access to foreigners has not yet been opened up either through regulatory restriction or through lack of foreign familiarity with the local market.[18] Some of these equity markets, such as Taiwan, have very sizeable capitalization (in Taiwan's case, in excess of USD 100 billion). At the other extreme the market capitalization of markets such as Uruguay is only USD 500 million. The emergence of a sizeable equity market and equity market capitalization is not, of course, merely a function of size of GDP. The market capitalization of Jordan is around seven times that of Uruguay, but Jordan's GDP is less than half the size. A trading or entrepreneurial culture within a country will tend to lead to a more active stock market at an earlier stage.

The state tends to dominate economic activity in many emerging countries. As countries seek to develop, the encouragement of entrepreneurial activity becomes normal, and businesses developing upon multiple ownership are founded. Equities are usually created as a convenient way of creating multiple transferable ownership of business ventures. Equity stakes also provide a quantifiable way for outside sponsors such as the IFC or EBRD to participate in the creation of ventures. Co-operative ventures between foreign corporations seeking to exploit an emerging market and local businesses seeking products and know-how are also common. Once more equities provide the ideal vehicle for defining the ownership and operation of the co-operative venture.

Equity markets in emerging markets can often be traced to informal private transfers of business stakes. In both China and Russia governments have found that they have had to introduce a regulatory framework following the creation of equity markets rather than leading them, as private citizens have begun buying and selling equity stakes in local ventures. In other cases governments have brought in consultants from stock exchanges in developed countries specifically to foster the creation of a domestic equity market.

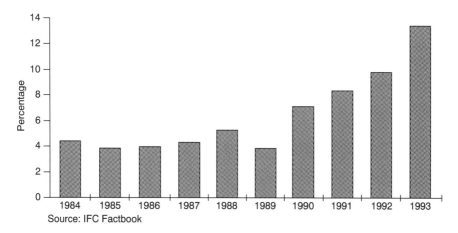

Figure 10.5 EMG stock cap as percentage of developed cap

10.6.2 Anatomy of Emerging Equity Markets

At the beginning of the chapter some general features of emerging markets were identified. Certain characteristics specific to equity markets can also be identified as features common to those equity markets which can be said to be emerging rather than developed.

1. Total market capitalization is small.
2. A limited number of stocks dominate trading.
3. Manipulation is common.
4. Volumes are usually small, with a limited number of trading hours.
5. Concentrated ownership of stocks, together with a high degree of cross-holdings.
6. Limited number of business activities represented in the market.
7. Corporate accounting standards do not accord to a common code, and fall short of developed accounting standards.
8. Poor equity registration and settlements procedures.
9. Foreigners restricted from ownership of some equities or of certain voting classes of equities.

Early supply of equities to emerging markets comes from two principal sources. Usually there are a small number of larger enterprises that are sufficiently well known locally that they have been able to issue equities. Second, there will be a stream of privatizations as the governments of emergent countries gradually cede control of economic activity to private ownership. The classic function of developed equity markets, to support the fund raising activities of new businesses will usually only develop later as the economy settles down into regular development patterns. At the earliest stage, the country and prospects of the existing businesses provide as much risk as the majority of investors wish to take.

Direct equity investment through venture participation rather than through the purchase of equities on the local stock market remains the major form of investment in most emerging countries until the local market develops the depth and liquidity to sustain reasonable volumes. Moreover direct venture participation can also often prove the only route to investing in the specific area of activity within the developing economy that an investor may wish to be exposed to. Once such participation has taken place, of course, the incentive to list shares in the concern on the local emergent stock market grows considerably.

An intermediate step between direct venture participation and a fully functional stock market is often single country investment funds listed on a developed stock exchange, but which invests in and seeks to reflect the performance of the emerging corporate sector. Country funds are a close equivalent of emerging market debt in a developed currency. By utilizing the market mechanisms of developed markets the risks of inefficient emerging markets are minimized, whilst the investor can still take advantage of the opportunities offered by the emerging country, and spread stock selection risk.

10.6.3 Evaluating Emerging Stock Markets

Correct evaluation of emerging stock markets is an extremely difficult task, given the inefficiencies described above. Are the rewards higher? Theory suggests that the fortunes

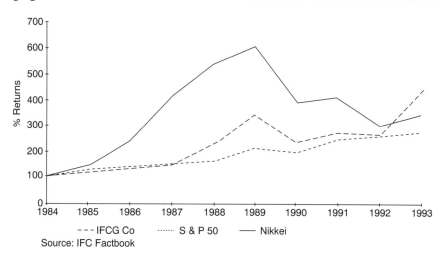

Source: IFC Factbook

Figure 10.6 Performance of emerging stock markets

of equity markets are more closely linked to faster economic growth in an economy than those of bond markets. Whilst faster growth can lead to better credit prospects for a country and its borrowers, for bond investors fast growth also raises concerns of rising inflation and rising bond yields. Thus fast growing economies offer more ambiguous advantages for bond investors than equity investors. For equity investors inflation, for example, can be a positive factor. Moreover equity investors are potentially more highly rewarded through profits growth than fixed income investors, and therefore the former have a greater incentive to take risk than the latter. Institutional equity investors have generally been more willing to invest in emerging equity markets than their fixed income counterparts and have begun to utilize emerging markets earlier.

Emerging markets equity indices have been compiled for longer than bond indices, and it is possible to test whether theory has translated into reality, with the caveat that emerging market indices by their very nature will tend to hide greater individual stock performance dispersion than developed indices. Figure 10.6 shows the performance of the IFC Composite Emerging Stock Market Index since inception compared with some of the developed market indices. It will be seen that the evidence suggests that the theory of investing in emerging stock markets generically is far from proven. However, the dispersion in performance between different markets, and indeed between different stocks, will tend to be far wider than in the developed markets. It is inherent in the nature of new markets both that the failure rate of new enterprises will be high, but that those which succeed will do so very spectacularly. Academic work on dispersion analysis of markets, sectors and stocks in emerging markets vs. developed markets has yet to be carried out.

10.7 CONCLUSION

The term "emerging markets" embraces a wide range of investment strategies and asset types. The growth of emerging market investment is still sufficiently early and rapid that a disciplined methodology for analysing risk in these markets has yet to be fully developed. Issues such as whether or not emerging markets should be classified as a truly separate asset class and whether better performance can be achieved through investment in emerging markets have yet to be resolved. There is every indication that the growth of emerging market investment is an irreversible process. Turnover in emerging market debt has grown from almost zero in the late 1980s, estimated at around USD 1.5 trillion. Both the needs of the world's emergent economies and the willingness of investors to seek opportunities through the globalization of investment flows suggest that this is an area of investment that will continue to experience the dramatic growth that has occurred in the last decade into the future.

10.8 ENDNOTES

1. Margaret Price in her book *Emerging Stock Markets* describes the term "emerging market" as having been coined in 1981 by Antoine W. van Agtmael when he served at the IFC.
2. *EMTA 1993 Trading Volume Survey*, available from EMTA, 37 Wall Street, 17th Floor, New York, NY 10260.
3. *Emerging Stock Markets Factbook 1994*, IFC, 1850 I Street N.W., Washington DC 20433.
4. A few examples of the claims made can be found in the literature listed in the bibliography. Indices for the performance of emerging markets are relatively recent, and the difficulty in obtaining reliable backdata has prevented the index compilers from creating a long historic database.
5. For example, Ecuador "Consolidated" loans was split into seven tranches. The terms of the tranches varied as to whether the interest, which was unpaid, was set against Libor or Treasury bills as a benchmark, and the margin varied between $\frac{7}{8}$ per cent and $2\frac{1}{4}$ per cent, yet no specification as to tranche was usually made between counterparties who traded this loan. The cumulative amount of unpaid interest over eight years varied widely between the different tranches. If Ecuador had paid a pro rata amount relative to the unpaid interest as part of its debt restructuring rather than treat all interest rate claims equally, similarly holders of the different tranches would have received considerably varying amounts of unpaid interest, despite the failure to specify which tranche was being traded.
6. The so-called "Aztec" bond, totalling some USD 2.56 billion, maturing 31st March 2008.
7. The overall blended level of forgiveness of debt that is agreed in each case has become a highly sensitive political matter, with different debtor countries striving to achieve higher levels of forgiveness than each other. For example, Bulgaria achieved 47.1 per cent, Poland 42.5 per cent, but the latter achieved a greater write-off of interest.
8. Prevailing 30-year Treasury interest rates were 8.4 per cent. Obviously the prevailing market yield for Mexican paper would have been considerably greater, quite aside from the debt restructuring under way.
9. As at the time of writing these were Argentina, Brazil, Costa Rica, Dominican Republic, Nigeria, Philippines, Uruguay and Venezuela. Ecuador, Bulgaria and Poland are about to achieve similar plans.
10. The main examples are Argentina FRBs, Brazil C bonds, Phase-in bonds, Costa Rica Principal B bonds, Venezuela DCBs.
11. I am indebted to Ken Telljohanns's article "Stripped yield madness" (published 14th February 1994 by Lehman Brothers Research) for this point and a much fuller exposition of the debt surrounding the correct evaluation of collateral guarantees of income.
12. Salomon Brothers, J.P. Morgan and Lehman Brothers have all produced Brady indices. These can be split geographically, or between floating and fixed Brady bonds. Whilst Brady bonds form a distinctive class of bond and as such require separate study, few investors have funds dedicated solely to Brady bonds, but usually utilize them in conjunction with other benchmark indices.
13. An interesting question is how a defaulting borrower would accord seniority of repayment between Brady bonds, i.e. recycled sovereign loans and Eurobonds. One of the justifications given for Eurobonds usually trading much more expensively than Brady bonds, and the ratings

given to Brady bonds by Moody's, which is usually one notch below a Eurobond rating of the same borrower notwithstanding the US guarantee is the alleged seniority of Eurobonds. The author doubts that Eurobonds would be given preferential treatment over Brady bonds.

14. This may appear an obvious point, but see note 15.

15. Taiwan, South Korea, Malaysia, Brazil and Colombia have banned or restricted investment in local instruments because they feared large inflows of foreign money seeking to take advantage of high local yields coupled with currency stability or a currency appreciating in real terms against the major traded OECD currencies. The ban is or was ostensibly to prevent the inflationary effects of such inflows as excess liquidity flowed into their markets. In fact such inflows would force their currencies to appreciate sharply, thereby providing a countervailing deflationary effect through lower import prices and dampening exports. The restrictions keep their currencies artificially cheap, thereby helping to achieve large export surpluses.

16. For example Mexico's foreign debt rating is BB+, whereas peso denominated debt is rated AA−. The same rationale for higher rating of domestic debt described here is also applied by the agencies to developed governments, for example Italy has only an AA rating for its foreign debt, but its lira debt is AAA rated.

17. See "Aspects of barriers to international integrated securities markets". *Journal of International Securities Markets*, vol. 6, Autumn 1992 for a full discussion of motives and limitations of governments seeking to develop their own domestic bond markets.

18. The average GDP per capita of those emerging markets included in the MSCI Emerging Markets Equity Index is USD 3100 compared with USD 20,535 for the developed markets covered by the MSCI Equity Index which covers the major developed equity markets. The IFC defines low income economies as those having a GNP per capita below USD 672 in 1992, middle income economies as USD 672–USD 8,355, and high income as USD 8,356 or more. Thus those countries that have equity markets which satisfy the criteria for inclusion in the MSCI Emerging Markets Equity Index tend to be middle to upper income emerging countries, rather than those that still have a very low GDP per capita.

10.9 REFERENCES

Dym (1994) "Identifying and measuring the risks of developing country bonds". *Journal of Portfolio Management*, Winter.
Emerging Bond and Money Market Guide–1994 Edition. Kleiman International Consultants Inc.
Errunza (1994) "Emerging markets: some new concepts". *Journal of Portfolio Management*, Spring.
IFC. *Emerging Stock Markets Factbook 1994* ISBN 0-8213-2820-4.
Price *Emerging Stock Markets*. McGraw Hill, ISBN 0-07-051049-0.
Wilcox (1992) "Global investing in emerging markets". *Financial Analysts Journal*, January–February.

Each of the above contains a substantial bibliography of further reading.

APPENDIX:BRADY BOND GLOSSARY

Each Plan has been separately negotiated, and led to differing bonds. Below is only intended as a generalized description. Detailed handbooks can be obtained from the major market participants.

Par Bonds "Pars"	Debt exchanged $ for $. Fixed rate set at outset below market levels. Coupon may be stepped. No amortization. Principal and rolling income guarantee. Usually most liquid Brady for any country. Example countries: Mexico, Argentina, Brazil, Venezuela, Philippines, Nigeria.

Discount Bonds "Discos"	Debt exchanged at a discount. Floating rate at market. No amortization. Principal and rolling income guarantee. Very liquid for Mexico and Argentina. Reasonable liquidity Brazil. Poor for Venezuela
Front Loaded Interest Bearing Bonds "FLIRBs"	Floating rate, with fixed coupon that steps up in first few years.
Debt Conversion Bonds "DCBs"	Debt exchanged at a discount. Floating at market. Unlike Discount bonds, no guarantee. No amortization. Usually very liquid. Example countries: Venezuela, Philippines, Uruguay, Poland.
New Money Bonds "NMBs"	Debt plus new cash. Floating rate at market. Principal amortization. No guarantee. Liquidity patchy. Example countries: Mexico, Venezuela, Brazil.
Principal Note/Fixed Rate/Bonds	Debt exchanged $ for $. Fixed rate at outset, below market levels. No amortization. Principal and rolling income guarantee. Illiquid. Example countries: Costa Rica, Uruguay.
Floating Rate Bonds "FRBs"	Debt exchanged at a discount. Floating at market levels. Principal amortization. No collateral. Very liquid.
Eligible Interest/Interest Due Unpaid/Past Due Interest "EI/IDU/PDI"	All issued against unpaid interest. All float at market levels. All have amortization. None have principal amortization. Variable liquidity. Example countries: Brazil, Bulgaria, Dominican Republic, Ecuador, Poland.
Capitalization Bonds "Cs"	Capitalised interest converted into further Brady bonds. Principal amortization. No collateral. Very liquid. Brazil only.

11

Credit Enhancement

LEE WAKEMAN*

11.1 INTRODUCTION

At the birth of the derivatives market in the early 1980s, credit officers quite often took the extremely conservative view that a swap was as risky as a loan. As the derivatives market grew, the pendulum swung toward the opposite view that the credit exposure on derivatives products was generally so much smaller than on loans, and often so well balanced by counterparty, that it could safely be ignored for both pricing and credit risk management purposes. More recently, defaults in the derivatives markets (especially that of the Borough of Hammersmith and Fulham) have convinced most observers that, although the potential default loss of a single swap is considerably less than that of a loan, default losses can be substantial for a portfolio of derivatives.

This reassessment of the default risks involved, combined with on-going, significant increases in the number, average size and maturity of derivative deals outstanding, has led credit officers to consider techniques for mitigating these risks. Each of these techniques is already in use in either the banking industry or on the organized exchanges, but generally they have been used separately. This paper describes a "credit enhancement" approach, currently in use in the derivatives industry, which uses several of these techniques in combination, in a manner which explicitly models their interactions. Although this approach cannot guarantee the abolition of credit risk, its proper implementation can alleviate the fear of long-dated derivatives, reduce both expected and "stressed case" credit losses, and free up credit lines to be used elsewhere.

In order to discuss techniques for mitigating credit risk, we must first discuss the methods used to measure credit risk. This chapter therefore starts, in Section 11.2, with a brief overview of the process used by credit officers to model potential credit losses. The next four sections then discuss how each of the main elements of such a credit model can be modified to incorporate the various techniques which reduce potential credit losses. Several examples of the efficacy of such techniques are provided in Section 11.7, and the

* I am indebted to Tom Francois, Douglas Lucas, Charles Smithson and Stuart Turnbull, who have considerably enhanced my understanding of credit management techniques.

The Handbook of Risk Management and Analysis. Edited by Carol Alexander
© 1996 John Wiley & Sons Ltd

trade-off between the benefits and the costs of implementing these credit enhancement techniques is outlined in Section 11.8. The chapter concludes with a discussion of the changes in the roles of both marketers and credit officers that are engendered by the adoption of this credit enhancement approach.

11.2 THE BASIC CREDIT MODEL

The standard approach to measuring the potential credit loss of a portfolio of derivatives contracts is based on the models of potential credit loss used in the banking industry. These models generally have three main elements: calculating the potential credit exposure profile of a loan until it matures, assessing the probability that the borrower will default whilst the loan is outstanding, and estimating how much of the loan can be recovered if the borrower does default.

A general model of potential credit loss would incorporate the correlations between these three main elements into a joint distribution function. This approach would model, for example, the fact that a slowing economy could increase both credit exposure and default probability, and that the probability of default and the recovery rate can both be affected by a change in a counterparty's credit rating.[1] However, there are serious data deficiencies involved in estimating this multivariate probability distribution of potential losses. Most models implemented in the banking and derivatives industries therefore concentrate their firepower on analysing these three main elements independently.

Given these three elements, credit enhancement techniques can be simply viewed as efforts to reduce both credit exposures and default probabilities and to increase recovery rates.

11.3 CREDIT EXPOSURE MODIFIERS

Before detailing the techniques used to reduce the credit exposure to a counterparty, we need to discuss the alternative techniques currently used in the derivatives industry for measuring counterparty credit exposure.

11.3.1 Modelling Credit Exposure

Although the concepts of default probabilities and recovery rates translate reasonably well from the banking industry to the derivatives industry, the concept of credit exposure does not. Why not? Because the paradigm underlying credit exposure in the banking industry is inappropriate for the derivatives industry.

The credit exposure for a given loan is normally stable over time, varying only slightly around the amount of the loan, and is always significantly positive. Another loan or line of credit to the same counterparty can only add to the exposure. In these circumstances, using the sum of the projected loan balances to estimate a potential credit exposure profile is both simple and relatively accurate. By contrast, derivatives transactions generally have exposures which are a small proportion of the notional amount, may be negative as well as positive, and can be quite unstable over time.

For example, consider a USD 250 million notional ten-year interest rate swap in which we receive a fixed rate of 7.1 per cent and pay the semi-annual London Interbank Offering Rate (Libor), and assume that the Libor term structure of interest rates is rising from its

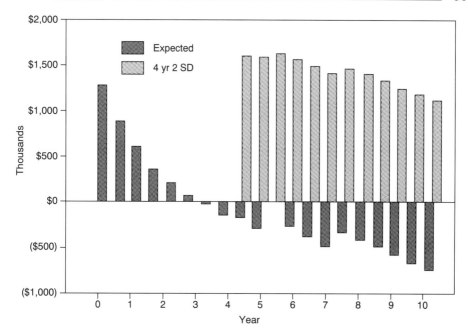

Figure 11.1   Receive fixed net cash flows: expected and four-year 2 SD

current 6.0 per cent. The 20 semi-annual expected cash flows associated with this swap
are set out in Figure 11.1. If this swap is initiated at the current market rate, it would
first be marked-to-market at zero and would therefore have no current credit exposure.
After we receive the first payment of approximately USD 1.3 million in six months' time,
the expected present value of the remaining cash flows becomes negative, and the swap
therefore has negative credit exposure. Only if interest rates fall does the swap become an
asset and create credit exposure to the counterparty. To illustrate this point, assume that
the Libor curve falls two standard deviations per year for the next four years. We would
then expect to receive the 12 semi-annual cash flows which start in year 4 in Figure 11.1,
creating a credit exposure exceeding USD 10 million at year 4.

   Currently, the most widely used approach to measuring counterparty credit risk in the
derivatives industry is the Bank for International Settlements (BIS) model, which is used
to assess the capital required to be held by OECD banks against their derivative portfolios.
Credit exposure in this model is calculated as the sum of a deal's mark-to-market and
its potential exposure — a measure of how much the deal's value can change over its
remaining life.

   For simplicity, potential exposure is calculated in the BIS model as a percentage of the
deal's notional principal outstanding, ranging from 0 per cent to 15 per cent, depending
on the type of deal and its remaining maturity. Unfortunately, the gain in simplicity
is more than offset by the loss in accuracy. Take, for example, a long-dated fixed rate
currency swap — in which the counterparties agree to exchange, at maturity, principal
amounts which reflect the current exchange rate. Unless the forward exchange rate equals
the current exchange rate, there will be a considerable one-way expected exposure at
maturity (approximately equal to the swap's notional amount times the difference between
the swap's fixed rate times the swap's maturity), depending on which currency is expected

to strengthen over the life of the deal. Yet the BIS model assigns exactly the same potential exposure, regardless of whether the counterparty is paying the strengthening currency or the weakening currency.

For a counterparty with several deals outstanding, the BIS model now applies a netting factor, based on the netting effect of current exposures, to the sum of the deals' potential exposures. But netted potential exposures can vary considerably from netted current exposures, and it is therefore relatively easy for the BIS model to greatly overstate the potential exposure to such a counterparty.

Given the inability of the BIS model to reflect the nuances of all but the simplest of derivatives portfolios, most dealers have turned to estimating the distribution of potential exposures directly. The general approach taken is quite simple: identify the risk variables affecting the value of a derivatives portfolio, model the distribution of these variables and then map from this distribution to a distribution of values for the portfolio.

Because a counterparty's credit exposure profile is a function of the potential mark-to-market values of the deals currently outstanding with that counterparty, it depends in large part on exactly the same variables that impact the market risk of a derivatives portfolio: interest rate, equity and commodity yield and volatility curves, foreign exchange rates, and the correlations between these variables.

If there are only a few relevant risk variables, negligible correlations, and the value of the deals are computed from the underlying risk variables using simple, monotonic formulae, scenario analysis is sufficient to model the potential exposure. Take, for example, a portfolio of swaps, caps and floors executed in one currency. The "stressed case" potential exposure (defined for this example as the 95 per cent 2 tail confidence interval) at any future time, t, can be modelled by first valuing the deals in the counterparty's portfolio with an "upward shift" forward interest rate curve in which each expected forward rate from t onwards is increased by 2 times the volatility appropriate for that maturity. If netting is appropriate, the deals' values are summed to create the portfolio's value at time t under this scenario. If netting is inappropriate, all negative deal values are first set to zero, and then the deals' values are summed. The process is then repeated with a similarly constructed "downward shift" curve. The higher of these two portfolio values is then taken as the potential exposure of the portfolio at time t. Repeating this procedure over the remaining life of the portfolio of derivatives creates a potential exposure profile for a counterparty. This scenario analysis is remarkably simple to implement, is generally adequate for most single currency derivative portfolios and can be adapted to portfolios containing derivatives denominated in two currencies which are correlated.

This stressed case approach becomes increasingly inaccurate whenever the assumption of a monotonic link between risk variables and deal value becomes tenuous. For example, if a portfolio consists of range forward notes, the stressed case exposure will not occur on either of the upward or downward interest rate shift paths, but on some "interior" interest rate path. This particular problem can be successfully addressed by using the same binomial or trinomial lattice framework that prices such "exotics" to model credit exposure,[2] but even lattice pricing becomes increasingly burdensome when correlated variables are involved.

As the number of relevant risk variables increases, the importance of modelling the correlation between those variables increases, and the simplified approaches discussed above give way to a Monte Carlo simulation approach. This approach first models the joint distribution of movements in the term structures of interest rates, foreign exchange rates and equity indices. The value of the portfolio is then calculated at every time point in each simulation. Finally, the stressed case criteria are applied to the simulated distribution of portfolio values for each time point to create the potential exposure profile.[3]

Given that a potential exposure profile has been created for a counterparty, we now turn to the techniques that can be used to reduce this profile — collateralization and recouponing.

11.3.2 Collateral Arrangements

In order to trade on a futures exchange, an investor has to put up initial margin. The amount required is an estimate of what the investor would lose if there were a serious adverse move in the underlying price the next day. In addition, on days when the investor loses money, the margin account has to be "topped up" by the payment of variation margin (which is returned on days when the investor gains). This concept of the marking-to-market of a position on a regular basis, together with the related posting and return of collateral, has been adapted to the derivatives markets, albeit with several small changes.

The first change is that, for derivatives trades, dealers rarely require posting of initial margin if the deal's value is close to zero, and normally agree to require the posting of variation margin only if the mark-to-market exceeds a predetermined exposure limit. Agreeing on the appropriate exposure limits for two counterparties can involve some interesting discussions, especially when their assessments of a counterparty's creditworthiness differ. One solution to this problem is for the counterparties to agree on exposure limits which are a function of published credit ratings. They might, for example, agree to post margin if current exposure exceeds USD 20 million for an AAA counterparty, USD 15 million for an AA+ counterparty, etc.

The second change is that, rather than marking-to-market the position on a daily basis, the counterparties can agree on a longer period, such as a month or a quarter, between remarkings. The trade-off is that, although the operational costs are reduced by lengthening the remarking period, the probability of exceeding the exposure ceiling at the next remarking increases. This probability is explicitly recognized by many derivatives dealers, who set the counterparty's exposure ceiling equal to the contracted ceiling plus an amount reflecting how much that counterparty's portfolio could move between remarkings.

The third change is that, although an individual investor is normally required to post cash as margin, counterparties to exposure ceiling agreements often agree to post securities as collateral, with the amount posted increasing with increasing market and credit risk. For example, an agreement may specify a "haircut" of 100 per cent for cash, 101 per cent for short-term governments, 103 per cent for medium-term governments and 108 per cent for longer-term governments and shorter-term, AA or higher rated corporate debt.

The impact of this exposure limitation technique can be quite powerful. For example, consider a USD 100 million ten year interest rate swap in which we receive the floating rate. If, after one year, the yield curve drops 100 b.p. we expect to receive an additional USD 1 million a year for nine years, creating an additional credit exposure of approximately USD 7 million. If interest rates drop a further 100 b.p. in the next year, the annuity rises to USD 2 million a year for eight years, creating a credit exposure of approximately USD 12 million. If yields continue to drop, the annuity continues to rise, but, at some point, the decrease in the remaining life outweighs this annuity effect, and the credit

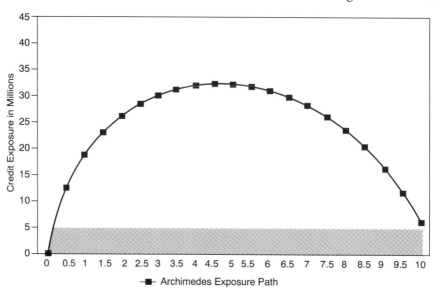

Figure 11.2 USD 100 million ten-year interest rate swap

exposure begins to drop. This 2 standard deviation potential exposure, or "Archimedes",[4] profile is illustrated in Figure 11.2, which shows the stressed case exposure for an uncollateralized deal reaching USD 30 million in year 4. Now assume that the counterparty agrees to post collateral if, at the end of any day, the mark-to-market exceeds USD 5 million. Then, although the new Archimedes exposure path rises to USD 5 million in the first year, it remains constant at USD 5 million thereafter, and therefore reduces the maximum potential exposure to the counterparty by a factor of 6.

Although collateral arrangements are used in short-dated interest rate swaps only for counterparties with poor credit ratings, they are increasingly used, even by counterparties with high credit ratings, for longer-dated interest rate swaps, commodity swaps (with their higher volatilities) and currency swaps which have an exchange of principal at maturity.

11.3.3 Recouponing

An alternative to providing collateral is to recoupon. The main similarity between the two methods is that, after a remarking, cash is exchanged. The main difference is that the deal's interest and/or exchange rates are reset at that time so that the value of the deal is either brought within an agreed range, or more commonly, reset to zero. Although this approach can cause some liquidity problems (in that it may require the sale of securities at short notice to provide the cash required), it is gaining popularity, especially in jurisdictions where there is uncertainty as to the rights afforded holders of collateral in bankruptcy (the motto for recouponing could be "Better to have a small, uncollateralized exposure than a large, collateralized one") and among counterparties which have restrictions on pledging assets. Given the certainty that cash will be exchanged at each remarking under this system, the remarking periods chosen are usually longer, and it is common for them to be set quarterly.

11.3.4 Netting

Although netting is generally not considered as a specific credit enhancement technique, it can be a very powerful tool for reducing potential exposure. Its impact on current exposure is illustrated by the survey of US intermediaries active in the derivatives market published in *Swaps Monitor* on 18th May 1992. The gross mark-to-market on the USD 1,920 billion in notional principal booked by these intermediaries was USD 64 billion. Netting reduced this value to USD 27 billion — a 58 per cent reduction.

The impact on a counterparty's potential exposure profile can be even more dramatic. Consider first a counterparty that is paying floating on a USD 100 million, ten year interest rate swap. As illustrated in Figure 11.2, its potential exposure profile rises to more than USD 30 million in year 4. Now assume that the same counterparty pays fixed on another USD 100 million for a similar maturity. Its Archimedes profile will collapse to almost zero. Why? As noted in Section 11.3.2, a 100 b.p. one-year drop in the yield curve will increase the credit exposure of the first swap by approximately USD 7 million. But that same 100 b.p. one-year drop in the yield curve will decrease the credit exposure of the second swap by an offsetting USD 7 million. More reasonably, assume that the counterparty pays fixed on a USD 100 million, seven year swap. Then, although the two swaps have considerably different maturities, the portfolio's Archimedes exposure at year 1 will still be significantly reduced, since the credit exposure of the swap with six years remaining decreases by approximately USD 5 million. This offset will decrease over time as the second swap runs off, but, as can be seen in Figure 11.3, the portfolio's potential exposure will decrease for every year until the maturity of the shorter swap.

In general, the larger the number of deals outstanding with a given counterparty, the closer their maturities, and the more evenly balanced the portfolio between receiving and paying in each currency, the larger the reduction in potential exposure to that counterparty created by netting.

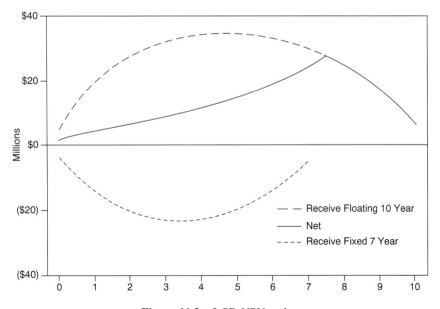

Figure 11.3 2 SD NPV paths

As discussed at the beginning of Section 11.3, the BIS exposure model does a rather simplistic job of modelling netting, and usually underestimates its impact on potential exposure significantly. Both scenario and simulation analysis can analyse the impact of netting on a counterparty's potential exposure profile quite accurately, and therefore are preferred to the BIS model by sophisticated derivatives credit officers.

11.4 DEFAULT MODIFIERS

In order to calculate the distribution of credit losses that would be suffered if a counterparty defaulted, the probability that the counterparty will default before the outstanding deals mature must be assessed.

Traditionally, in the absence of any external data on defaults, bank credit officers have had to rely on internal credit models to assess the probability that a counterparty will become insolvent whilst a deal is outstanding. Recently, both Moody's and Standard & Poor's have published studies of the history of bond defaults in the US in the last 25 years, and have classified their results by the senior, unsecured bond rating of the defaulting company.[5] For example, although no corporation has defaulted whilst it had a triple A rating, there are cases of defaulted companies which at some earlier point in their histories had a triple A rating, and these cases have been used to calculate cumulative probabilities of default over time for a company whose senior unsecured bond is currently rated triple A. The cumulative default rates for companies with Moody's ratings over the period 1970–1994 are graphed in Figure 11.4,[6] and they show that, apart

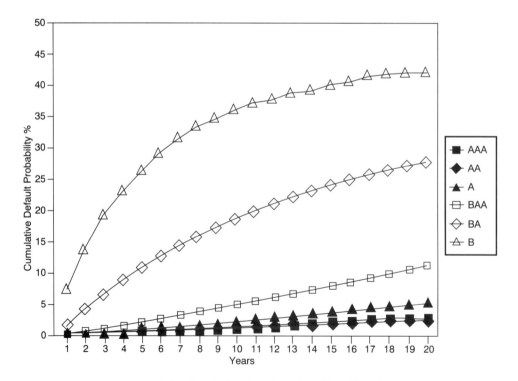

Figure 11.4 Cumulative default probabilities 1970–1994

from a slight inconsistency beyond 15 years (where the samples are quite small) for the AAA and AA rating groups, there is a strong correlation between Moody's ratings and default rates.

If you believe that the results drawn from the samples used by Moody's and Standard & Poor's are valid for your counterparties, then you can use these studies to estimate the probability that a rated counterparty will default in each of the next T years. First, break down the published cumulative probabilities (which are presented by year) into the appropriate marginal annual probabilities using:

$$\text{prob(default)}_t = \sum \text{prob(default)}_{t+1} - \sum \text{prob(default)}_t$$

Then, modify (using artistic licence) the relatively coarse rating class groupings used in these studies to reflect the finer gradations currently used by the rating agencies. An example of this approach is set out in Table 11.1.[7] Several points are of interest in this table. First, the first year default probabilities approximately double each time you move from AAA (0.009 per cent) to AA2 (0.022 per cent) to A2 (0.06 per cent) to BAA2 (0.16 per cent), but then tentuple as you move out of the investment grades to BA2 (1.79 per cent). Second, the marginal annual default probabilities for the higher ratings classes increase with time, rising, for example, for an AA1 rated company from 0.015 per cent in year 1 to 0.15 per cent in year 10. The explanation for this phenomena is quite simple. It is remarkably rare for a highly-rated company to be downgraded more than once in a given year, and therefore the 0.015 per cent reflects the probability of defaulting in the next year given that the company starts the year with an AA1 rating. On the other hand, the 0.15 per cent reflects the probability that a company will default in the next year, given that it had an AA1 rating nine years ago. There is a tendency for the ratings of highly-rated companies to drift downwards, rather than upwards, over time, so that the average rating of a group of companies initially rated AA1 will erode over the nine years to approximately a BAA2 rating, with a consequently higher marginal probability of defaulting in year 10. Conversely, the marginal default probabilities decrease with time for

Table 11.1 Marginal default probabilities

Years	1	2	3	4	5	6	7	8	9	10
AAA	0.01%	0.02%	0.03%	0.03%	0.07%	0.07%	0.11%	0.12%	0.14%	0.15%
AA1	0.02%	0.05%	0.07%	0.08%	0.10%	0.10%	0.11%	0.12%	0.13%	0.15%
AA2	0.02%	0.08%	0.12%	0.12%	0.14%	0.12%	0.11%	0.11%	0.13%	0.15%
AA3	0.03%	0.08%	0.13%	0.14%	0.17%	0.15%	0.12%	0.16%	0.19%	0.22%
A1	0.05%	0.09%	0.14%	0.16%	0.21%	0.18%	0.14%	0.20%	0.24%	0.28%
A2	0.06%	0.09%	0.15%	0.18%	0.24%	0.20%	0.15%	0.24%	0.30%	0.35%
A3	0.09%	0.18%	0.23%	0.30%	0.33%	0.30%	0.31%	0.38%	0.42%	0.42%
BAA1	0.13%	0.27%	0.31%	0.43%	0.42%	0.40%	0.47%	0.51%	0.53%	0.50%
BAA2	0.16%	0.36%	0.40%	0.55%	0.51%	0.49%	0.63%	0.64%	0.65%	0.57%
BAA3	0.70%	1.11%	1.11%	1.19%	1.15%	0.98%	0.93%	0.91%	0.90%	0.84%
BA1	1.25%	1.85%	1.82%	1.84%	1.80%	1.47%	1.22%	1.17%	1.15%	1.11%
BA2	1.79%	2.59%	2.53%	2.48%	2.44%	1.96%	1.51%	1.44%	1.40%	1.39%
BA3	3.96%	3.90%	3.53%	3.12%	2.71%	2.60%	1.81%	1.75%	1.50%	1.47%
B1	6.14%	5.21%	4.54%	3.75%	2.98%	3.25%	2.11%	2.05%	1.60%	1.55%
B2	8.31%	6.52%	5.54%	4.39%	3.24%	3.90%	2.41%	2.35%	1.70%	1.64%
B3	15.08%	6.82%	5.21%	3.80%	3.14%	4.43%	2.58%	1.69%	2.54%	2.01%

Source: Extrapolated from Moody's data.

the lowest rating classes, falling, for example, for a B2 rated company from 8.31 per cent in year 1 to 1.64 per cent in year 10. This suggests that a "survivorship bias" is present in that, although some companies initially rated B2 will struggle and default, others will flourish, be upgraded, and default thereafter with significantly lower frequency, so that the average rating of a group of companies initially rated B2 will improve over the nine years to approximately a BA2 rating.

These data are not complete — they cover only US corporations and a relatively short time period — but they are the best currently publicly available, and can serve as the basis for a credit rating system which can then be "tweaked" by the credit department. Several companies use a ratings based system, but modify a company's rating to reflect additional information. For example, it is common practice to raise the ratings of US municipalities (even after the Orange County debacle) to reflect a perceived lower rate of defaults.

Several academics have published studies showing that discriminant analysis, using up to three years of prior profit and loss statements and balance sheets, can successfully predict bankruptcy several years beforehand.[8] For example, Altman's study scans a series of financial ratios, such as the current and the debt/equity ratios, for matched samples of 50 bankrupt and 50 non-bankrupt firms, in order to find ratios that differentiate between companies that subsequently default and companies that do not. Discriminant analysis, by first choosing appropriate weights for each of these ratios and then summing these weighted ratios, constructs a formula which maximizes the difference between the formula values for the bankrupt sample and the non-bankrupt sample. Altman's model is generally regarded as being successful in that, using this formula, it correctly predicts 80 per cent of both the bankrupt and the non-bankrupt firms in a "hold out" sample of 50 bankrupt and 50 non-bankrupt firms.

But such a model could present problems when applied to companies that are well rated. Given the numbers presented in Table 11.1, a random sample of 10,000 companies rated A2 or above would include no more than ten that would default in the next two years. If the discriminant model's prediction accuracy was maintained, it would correctly predict eight of these bankruptcies, but would also incorrectly predict that 1998 of the healthy companies would default. Unless the costs of rejecting 1998 healthy counterparties are less than the costs of accepting ten counterparties that will default, using this model will provide results which are inferior to those provided by a model which extends credit to any counterparty rated A2 or above.[9] This implies that the ratings of more widely known and generally higher-rated credits (where the rating agencies have access to the best quality credit information available) should generally be accepted and that credit evaluation resources should be concentrated on lower-rated companies (especially if there is only one rating) and on companies that lack ratings.

An alternative approach to estimating default probabilities is to "unwind" them from the prices of a company's securities trading in the markets. Several examples of this approach are presented in a recent paper by Jarrow and Turnbull,[10] presented as Chapter 9 in this book. In this paper they describe a model which, in its simplest form, adds a series of independent coin tosses, to model default, at each node in a binomial or trinomial term structure model. Although this approach is conceptually rigorous, it requires as many instruments as there are nodes. It is therefore difficult to implement for a particular company because of the relative paucity of traded instruments issued by that company. This deficiency should not, however, limit the use of the model to estimate default probabilities for a ratings class.

11.4.1 Credit Guarantees

The simplest way to reduce the probability of default for a counterparty is to have a guarantee from another company. To the extent that these companies are entirely independent, such a guarantee can reduce the probability of default dramatically. For example, the cumulative default probability over five years for a company rated BA by Moody's is 11.1 per cent. If its performance is guaranteed by an entirely independent A rated company, with a cumulative default probability of 0.6 per cent, the joint probability of default is reduced to 0.07 per cent — less than the 0.1 per cent probability for an AAA company. There are cases where the independence assumption appears justified — an American energy company posting collateral in the form of lines of credit from a European bank, for instance — but generally guarantees are provided by parent organizations to subsidiaries. In these cases, it is usual to replace the subsidiary's rating with the parent's (higher) rating in the calculation of potential losses.

11.4.2 Credit Triggers

ISDA Master Agreements for longer-term derivative transactions now frequently contain a ratings downgrade clause, which permits a party to terminate all outstanding transactions (on the basis of "market quotation" and "full two way" payments) if the credit rating of the other party falls below a specified level. Typically these termination rights are referenced to the lowest of the ratings assigned by the rating agencies, and failure to maintain a rating gives rise to a termination event.

Ratings downgrade triggers can significantly reduce counterparty default probabilities. For example, if all outstanding transactions can be immediately terminated when a counterparty's rating falls below A3, the exposure to that counterparty becomes a function of the probability that the counterparty will default whilst rated A3 or higher. Default probabilities should therefore be adjusted downward in situations where such downgrade triggers exist.

To quantify this reduction, single stage Markov chain analysis can be used to create a rating transition matrix. One-year transition matrices have been published by both Moody's and Standard & Poor's,[11] and can be used for the purpose of calculating the impact on default probabilities of alternative downgrade triggers.[12] Table 11.2 illustrates this analysis. The rows beginning with a single rating (AAA, AA, etc.) report the cumulative default probabilities over time for that rating which are implied by Standard & Poor's one-year transition matrix. The rows beginning with a double rating (AAA/A, AAA/B, etc.) report the cumulative default probabilities assuming that, at the end of any year in which a counterparty finally "drifted" from the first rating to the second rating, all transactions are terminated and the drift process stops. The "% Reduction" rows show that the cumulative default probabilities are reduced substantially, with the percentage reduction being greater the higher the ratings trigger.[13]

For example, an AA rated counterparty has a cumulative default probability over ten years of 0.81 per cent. Given that the counterparty agrees to terminate the derivatives contract if, at the end of any year, its rating falls to BB or below, the cumulative default probability falls 72 per cent to 0.23 per cent. As the table shows, a higher downgrade trigger reduces the default probability even further. But there is a trade-off, since the higher downgrade trigger also increases the probability that a deal that would have otherwise run to its planned maturity will be prematurely terminated.

Two further caveats, in addition to those raised concerning the quality of the data underlying the rating agencies' analyses, should be mentioned. The first is that it is quite

Table 11.2 Impact of ratings downgrade triggers on cumulative default probabilitites

Years	1	3	5	10	15	20	25
AAA	0.00%	0.01%	0.04%	0.27%	0.73%	1.37%	2.13%
AAA/A	0.00%	0.00%	0.00%	0.00%	0.00%	0.00%	0.00%
% Reduction	0.00%	100.00%	100.00%	100.00%	100.00%	100.00%	100.00%
AAA/BBB	0.00%	0.00%	0.01%	0.04%	0.09%	0.14%	0.20%
% Reduction	0.00%	100.00%	82.94%	85.47%	87.70%	89.47%	90.78%
AAA/BB	0.00%	0.00%	0.01%	0.07%	0.17%	0.30%	0.43%
% Reduction	0.00%	100.00%	74.27%	75.03%	76.64%	78.35%	79.83%
AA	0.00%	0.06%	0.19%	0.81%	1.73%	2.77%	3.80%
AA/A	0.00%	0.00%	0.00%	0.00%	0.00%	0.00%	0.00%
% Reduction	0.00%	100.00%	100.00%	100.00%	100.00%	100.00%	100.00%
AA/BBB	0.00%	0.01%	0.04%	0.12%	0.21%	0.27%	0.32%
% Reduction	0.00%	76.47%	79.23%	84.67%	88.06%	90.15%	91.48%
AA/BB	0.00%	0.02%	0.06%	0.23%	0.42%	0.60%	0.75%
% Reduction	0.00%	66.27%	67.68%	72.16%	75.84%	78.43%	80.21%
A	0.07%	0.31%	0.69%	2.07%	3.65%	5.08%	6.27%
A/BBB	0.07%	0.19%	0.28%	0.43%	0.51%	0.56%	0.60%
% Reduction	0.00%	40.43%	60.21%	79.44%	85.94%	88.89%	90.46%
A/BB	0.07%	0.22%	0.38%	0.73%	0.99%	1.18%	1.32%
% Reduction	0.00%	28.27%	45.18%	64.86%	72.76%	76.69%	78.90%
BBB	0.25%	1.09%	2.21%	5.19%	7.55%	9.16%	10.24%
BBB/BB	0.25%	0.63%	0.90%	1.30%	1.51%	1.63%	1.71%
% Reduction	0.00%	41.98%	59.23%	74.92%	80.00%	82.20%	83.31%

Rating to right of slash is rating at which termination can be elected.
Methodology: Markov Analysis applied to S&P's average one-year transition matrix from May 1995 study.

difficult to reproduce a rating agency's table of cumulative defaults by rating at different maturities using that agency's one-year transition matrix. The second, related caveat is that the assumption underlying single stage Markov chain analysis — that the probabilities of a company transitioning from its current state (rating) in the next period are independent of its state in the previous period — appears to be suspect. Recent research[14] at Moody's suggests that, for corporations with a BAA or lower rating, the probability of a downgrade in the next year is a function not only of the current rating, but also of last year's rating. For example, the marginal probability of being downgraded in the next year from BAA is 6.3 per cent (including a 0.1 per cent probability of defaulting). But the probability of being downgraded from BAA, given that the company was upgraded to BAA this year, is only 3.2 per cent, and the probability of being downgraded from BAA, given that the company was downgraded to BAA this year, is 11.5 per cent. Given this evidence, it may be necessary to expand the analysis to two stage Markov chain analysis if downgrade triggers are implemented at the lower ratings.

11.5 MUTUAL TERMINATION OPTIONS

One credit enhancement technique which combines potential exposure reduction with default probability reduction is the mutual termination option, or time put. This clause

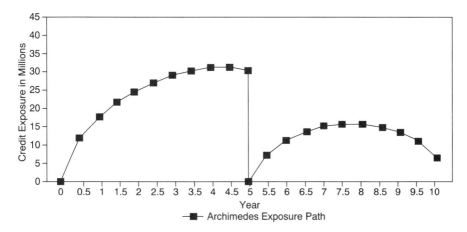

Figure 11.5 Termination option at 5 years

permits either counterparty to terminate unconditionally each of the derivative transactions covered by the ISDA Master Agreement on one or more dates before its maturity, using a pre-agreed formula to value the transaction at these times. For example, an agreement could permit termination of each transaction on its fifth anniversary and on each subsequent deal anniversary until maturity. This early termination option reduces the possibility that a company will have to stand by helplessly as a counterparty's credit standing deteriorates, and can possibly lessen the maximum potential exposure to a counterparty.

Apart from the problems of agreeing on the "pre-agreed formula" (which often includes an "Olympic" system of throwing away the high and the low "mid-market" quotes and averaging the remaining quotes), and worrying about the costs of finding a new, acceptable, and accepting counterparty, mutual termination options create conceptual problems for reserving unless there is a clear policy regarding exercise. If, for example, we state that we will always exercise this option at the first exercise date, the potential exposure profile is truncated at that date. If, however, we agree to recoupon the swap to zero at the mutual termination option date, the potential exposure profile begins again at zero on the option date. Figure 11.5 illustrates the impact on the potential exposure profile of a ten-year interest rate swap of an option either to terminate, or to continue with recouponing to zero, after five years.

More reasonably, the decision to terminate on an option date will be a function of the counterparty's rating and the effect of the deal's mark-to-market on the counterparty's current exposure at that time, and is best handled by simulation.

11.6 RECOVERY RATES

The third element in estimating the potential losses in a derivatives transaction is the recovery rate. It has been common practice in the past to ignore this element of potential loss, which implicitly assumes that there will be no recovery of sums owed in the event of a default by the counterparty. Whilst this may be a reasonable assumption for terminating triple A structured derivatives product companies, it appears rather inappropriate for ongoing companies which can wait the estimated two years to recover some of the moneys owed.

Both of the rating agencies have studied recovery rates, from differing viewpoints, and have come to similar conclusions regarding the factors affecting the distribution of recovery rates. The main conclusion, as stated in the S&P study of recovery rates for defaulted bonds, published in the 20th July 1992 edition of Creditweek is that "loss experience, on average, varied according to the obligation's rank". Derivative claims generally rank equally with senior unsecured debt obligations in insolvency, and therefore can be treated as such for the purposes of modelling recovery rates. Although the least conservative measure of the losses on the 78 senior unsecured debt issues, "L1" (which measures the loss of principal only), implied a mean recovery rate of 79 per cent, the most conservative measure, "L3" (which also includes the foregone compounded interest), implied a mean recovery rate of 45 per cent.

The Moody's study of corporate bond defaults (referenced in Section 11.4) produces remarkably similar results. Using the market prices of these bonds one month after default, it finds that "the 246 senior unsecured bonds sold for $44.62 on average". But this study raises some interesting points. The first is that Chart 9 in the study, "Distribution of Defaulted Senior Unsecured Bond Prices", shows a distribution that is not concentrated around the mean, but is quite uniformly distributed between 0 per cent and 90 per cent. The second, and probably related point, is that the study's Table 1, "Recoveries for Senior Unsecured Bonds by Rating before Default", shows that the recovery rate is not uniform across rating classes. For defaulted bonds that were rated CAA one year before default, the recovery rate was less than USD 31, while the recovery rate for bonds rated BAA one year before default was over USD 71. These points suggest, specifically, that modelling of downgrade triggers should link the recovery rate to the downgrade trigger and, generally, that joint simulations of interest rates, exchange rates and default probabilities should keep track of prior rating for simulations that end in default.

11.7 EXAMPLES

To illustrate the usefulness of these techniques, first assume that we operate with two limits:

- the "Archimedes" limit, which constrains a counterparty's Archimedes exposure (the maximum recovery-adjusted potential exposure to that counterparty), and is set as a function of the counterparty's rating, and

- the "PASCAL" limit, which constrains a counterparty's PASCAL exposure (the Probability Adjusted Stressed Case Anticipated Loss, which equals the stressed case replacement cost at time k times the marginal default probability at time k times $(1 -$ recovery rate), present valued and summed over k), and is set at a single level for all counterparties,

and then assume that we hold two reserves:

- the Credit reserve, calculated as the expected replacement cost at time k times the marginal default probability at time k times $(1 -$ recovery rate), present valued and summed over k, for each counterparty, and

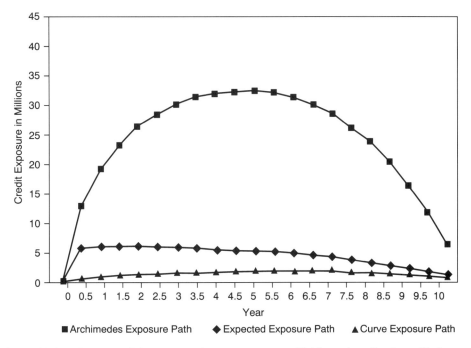

Figure 11.6 USD 100 million ten-year interest rate swap: TMG receives floating with five year recouponing to zero MTM

- the Equity reserve, calculated as a return on the equity that needs to be held to cover the difference at each point in time between the credit reserve and the PASCAL exposure to a counterparty

Then consider a USD 100 million interest rate swap in which the counterparty pays fixed for ten years. Figure 11.6 illustrates the three exposure paths usually considered:

- the curve exposure path, which calculates the value of the swap assuming that the forward rates remain at their expected level
- the expected exposure path, used to calculate the credit reserve, and
- the Archimedes (stressed case) exposure path, used to calculate the PASCAL exposure.

Table 11.3 illustrates the impact on the limits and on the reserves of using exposure limits ("Credit Caps"), mutual termination options ("Time Puts"), and downgrade triggers ("Termination below A3") both separately and jointly, assuming a constant recovery rate of 40 per cent. Let us first examine the results for an AA2 rated counterparty.

The credit cap affects the credit reserve only slightly, since it is set at USD 5 million, which is only slightly exceeded by the expected exposure, but reduces the equity reserve considerably, since, by limiting the stressed case potential exposure (Archimedes drops from USD 19,430 to USD 3,000), it lowers the PASCAL exposure from USD 121,200 to USD 23,600.

The time put at five years does not reduce the Archimedes exposure, since it does not occur before the point of maximum potential exposure, but since, for this example, we

Table 11.3 USD 100 million ten-year swap — TMG receives floating (numbers in thousands of dollars)

Aa2 Rating				
Enhancement	Archimedes	Pascal	Default Reserve	Equity Reserve
None	19,430.1	121.2	20.8	4.5
Credit Cap*	3,000.0	23.6	19.5	0.4
Time Put**	19,430.1	72.3	13.0	6.1
Both	3,000.0	12.7	11.8	0.3
With Termination				
Below A3	19,430.1	56.9	10.7	2.0
With the Works	3,000.0	7.3	7.1	0.1
A2 Rating				
Enhancement	Archimedes	Pascal	Default Reserve	Equity Reserve
None	19,430.1	202.5	33.9	7.6
Credit Cap*	3,000.0	40.9	32.1	0.8
Time Put**	19,430.1	108.2	19.5	9.7
Both	3,000.0	18.9	17.7	0.4
With Termination				
Below A3	19,430.1	70.4	13.7	2.3
With the Works	3,000.0	9.3	8.9	0.1

*USD 5 million.
**At five years.

assume that the time put is exercised, the exposure paths all drop to zero at year 5, and therefore the credit reserve is significantly reduced, from USD 20,800 to USD 13,000. Although the credit reserve and the PASCAL exposure have been reduced by similar amounts, the credit reserve now runs off proportionally faster, and therefore the equity reserve has to increase slightly, from USD 4,500 to USD 6,100, although the total reserves still decrease, from USD 25,300 to USD 19,100.

The downgrade trigger set below A3 only affects default probabilities in this example, so the Archimedes exposure remains unchanged. But the reduction in default probabilities does reduce the PASCAL exposure and both the credit and equity reserves, which now total USD 12,700.

The combination of the three credit enhancement techniques ("With the Works") is quite powerful. The Archimedes and PASCAL exposures are reduced by 85 per cent and 90 per cent respectively, and the total reserves are reduced by 70 per cent to USD 7,200.

Now consider a counterparty with an A2 rating. As one would expect, the impact on the Archimedes exposure is the same as for the AA2 counterparty. The credit cap and the time put still reduce the PASCAL exposure and the total reserves, but a more major role is now played by the downgrade trigger, which is now considerably closer to the initial rating, and therefore exerts a proportionally stronger downward influence on the probability of default. The combination of the three credit enhancement techniques reduces the PASCAL exposure by 95 per cent and the total reserves by almost 80 per cent, from USD 41,500 to USD 9,000.

11.8 IMPLEMENTATION

The examples described in Section 11.7 illustrate that these credit enhancement techniques can significantly reduce the potential credit losses from derivatives transactions. There are, however, two considerations which must be addressed when considering the use of such techniques: are they legally enforceable, and do their potential benefits outweigh the costs of implementing them?

11.8.1 Legal Considerations

The techniques that raise the fewest legal warning flags are time puts, recouponings and credit downgrade triggers. Time puts are generally considered to be a normal part of contract law, and few questions, if any, have been raised concerning the recapture of sums paid when a time put is exercised if one of the counterparties subsequently goes into receivership. The treatment of recouponing payments is less well researched, but the conclusions are similar. Downgrade triggers are conceptually akin to the covenants included in traditional commercial lending, such as minimum net worth and coverage ratios, and are generally accorded the same legal standing.

The situation becomes more cloudy when one turns to collateral arrangements. For simplicity, assume that a counterparty who has posted collateral to us becomes insolvent. In an "ideal" situation, this insolvency would not affect the enforceability of the collateral arrangement. The receiver would recognize that we had a first priority perfected security interest in the collateral, and would not attempt either to avoid or to stay the liquidation of that collateral for our benefit. Assuming that the "haircut" was sufficient to cover the liquidation costs (an inaccurate assumption in the case of the 1994 insolvency of Askin Capital Management's portfolio of principal-only strips and inverse floaters, which were liquidated at prices substantially below their "fair economic value"[15]), our claim would be fully enforced, and in a timely manner.

The jurisdiction that comes closest to this ideal state is the US, where amendments made to the Bankruptcy Code in 1990 place swaps counterparties in a better position than ordinary secured creditors in that swap participants now enjoy an exemption from the automatic stay and preferential transfer clauses of the Code. The situation in other jurisdictions is less clear, and both Moody's and Standard & Poor's have raised concerns about the enforceability of collateral agreements in insolvency.[16]

These rating agencies have also raised questions about the ability of netting agreements to withstand the desire of a trustee or debtor in possession to "cherry pick" among contracts, and at present consider close-out netting provisions to be unambiguously enforceable only in Australia, the UK and the US. At this point, rather than continuing to pontificate on matters which are well beyond my competence, it seems appropriate simply to state that it is important, when contemplating the use of these credit enhancement techniques, to obtain legal advice on the laws governing insolvency in the counterparty's country of incorporation.

11.8.2 Economic Considerations

The resources required to monitor time put and downgrade trigger clauses are minimal, and therefore the decision to use them should be quite simple. But concerns have been raised about the potential adverse impacts that could be triggered by the exercise of such clauses. For example, if a 17-year aircraft lease-related swap is terminated after five years, there is no assurance that a substitute 12-year swap will be available in the market at a price close to the "mid-market" valuation agreed to by the counterparties. The main worry, however, is that the downgrading of a counterparty could create a "domino" effect on a counterparty's liquidity, and thereby cause that company to become insolvent. To illustrate this point, consider the case of a company, with derivatives trades outstanding to several counterparties, whose downgrade triggers a termination event. Those counterparties owed money will generally exercise their option to terminate their deals and demand payment. Unless the downgrade trigger requires the termination of all transactions (which is not customary), it is not clear that counterparties who owe money will exercise the option to terminate (although a counterparty may decide to make the payment in order to ensure that it is not owed money by the downgraded company at a later date). In these circumstances, there could be a serious cash drain on the downgraded company. (This drain is exacerbated if the downgrade trigger clause applies on a deal-by-deal basis, rather than on a master agreement basis, since a counterparty can then "cherry pick" and only terminate those trades which are "in-the-money".)

Although these concerns are recognized in the derivatives industry, the current consensus is that the potential benefits of time put and downgrade trigger clauses outweigh their potential costs.

Considerably more resources are required to implement recouponing and collateral arrangements. Not only must the value of the portfolio of deals outstanding with a given counterparty be calculated and compared with the appropriate limit on a frequent basis, but transfer costs may be involved. For recouponing agreements requiring the transfer of cash on an infrequent basis (for example, quarterly), these costs are generally small (although concerns have been raised about selling relatively illiquid assets to provide the cash). But collateral arrangements which involve both frequent (for example, daily) valuations and tight exposure limits can engender a considerable number of transfers of collateral. Furthermore, the required form of the posted collateral can create costs. For example, if a collateral agreement requires the posting of government securities as collateral, interest will be forgone by any counterparty that usually invests in securities which offer a higher return.

There is therefore an interesting trade-off between the costs and the potential benefits in a collateral agreement. Increasing the valuation frequency and decreasing the exposure limit raise the monitoring and potential transfer costs involved, but at the same time decrease the potential exposure at the next valuation date. Complete models for this decision have yet to be published, but will, in addition to the parameters discussed above, incorporate both the volatility of the value of the portfolio of derivative transactions outstanding with a given counterparty and the probability of default of that counterparty.

11.9 CONCLUSION

Traditionally, after the initial enquiries to the credit officers from the marketers as to whether or not the proposed counterparty is acceptable have been satisfactorily answered, there has been little interaction over time between them. Only if a counterparty's credit exposure exceeds limits and necessitates remedial action will marketers consider the dynamic nature of the credit, and thus capital, costs imposed on the company.

This wilful ignoring of the inter-relationships between the credit exposure profiles of deals in a counterparty's portfolio, and the widespread tendency to think in terms of a deal's current, static exposure rather than in terms of the impact of dynamic markets on a portfolio's potential credit exposure, can lead to significant errors in estimating the potential losses involved with derivatives transactions. Take, for example, a simple "off-market" asset swap involving a four-year bond issued with a detachable equity warrant and a low coupon of approximately 2 per cent. In order to compensate us for receiving the under-market fixed rate of 2 per cent and paying the current on-market floating rate, we would expect to receive a terminal payment of approximately 15 per cent of the deal's notional amount. Although the initial mark-to-market, and therefore the current exposure, of the swap will be approximately zero, the present value of the deal will undoubtedly increase over the next four years to approximately 15 per cent of its notional amount. Paying fixed and receiving fixed on such an asset swap should therefore have very different associated credit reserves, yet the BIS methodology currently used by many participants in the derivatives industry assigns the same 0.5 per cent of the notional amount as potential exposure to both sides of this swap.

But despite the potential for errors, the move toward an integrated, dynamically based approach to credit risk management has been quite slow.

One deterrent to the acceptance of such a credit system is the accounting policy most widely used in the derivatives industry until quite recently — the practice of creating profit and loss statements by marking derivatives deals to mid-market without taking specific reserves against future credit, hedging and operating costs. Specifically, this policy books to the profit and loss statement the present value of the future gross revenues whilst ignoring the future costs involved in running the derivatives portfolio until the deals mature. This policy is justified by assuming that the annual interest "earned" as the future revenues come a year closer will be sufficient to cover that year's costs. This assumption is becoming increasingly dubious for "vanilla" derivatives as gross profit margins are being squeezed whilst operating costs are steadily rising.

11.9.1 Incentives for Marketers

The most obvious impact of this accounting policy is on the marketing area, where it provided the incentive to assume that the difference between the transaction price and the mark-to-mid-market value is the "profit", rather than only the present value of the future revenues, of a deal. This non-recognition of expected future costs led to the obvious mind-set among marketers that, once a deal was done, it could be forgotten. This mentality could normally prevail for extended periods, until some deals, whose overlooked future risks were at least commensurate with the large "profits" booked, defaulted or, more usually, generated current credit exposures which were sufficiently high to preclude further trades with those counterparties.

Further, only the first deal with a new counterparty will definitely invoke potential credit losses. Thereafter a prospective deal can incur either positive or negative expected future credit costs, depending on whether or not it reduces an existing counterparty's credit exposure. If an accounting policy ignores a prospective derivative deal's impact on a counterparty's potential credit loss, it increases the probability that the net profit contribution of that deal will be seriously misestimated.

More recently, as noted in the 1994 ISDA survey, many derivatives dealers are changing their accounting policies to hold explicit reserves against potential credit losses, and some are incorporating credit enhancement techniques into their credit management processes. If a system incorporating these points is put in place, the incentives provided to the marketers change quite dramatically, in that they are encouraged to work with the credit officers to correctly price the potential credit losses (positive or negative) involved in a prospective deal and motivated to work with the counterparty to minimize total credit management costs over time.

11.9.2 Role of the Credit Officer

The adoption of a credit system incorporating explicit credit reserves and modelling the impact of credit enhancement techniques will lead to a difference in the way that the credit management function is performed. Credit officers will shift their focus from the static calculation of current exposures to the dynamic nature of counterparty credit over time, mapping a counterparty's expected and "stressed case" exposures over the remaining life of the deals currently outstanding and incorporating explicit default probability and recovery rate assumptions into their credit management model to create that counterparty's potential credit loss profile over time.

Given this modelling capability, they will then not just passively respond to marketers' credit enquiries, but will keep them informed not only of a counterparty's current exposure, but also of future "orange" and "red" light potential credit loss situations. This modelling capability will further allow the credit officers both to guide the marketers to seek new deals, or negotiate credit enhancements to current deals that will reduce these potential losses, and to provide estimates of the reduction of reserves that can be attained thereby.

If the marketers and credit officers do interact in this manner, the growth of credit reserves can be seriously constrained, increasing both profits and bonuses.

11.10 ENDNOTES/REFERENCES

1. For a discussion of such a general model, see Mark, R.M. (1995) "Integrated Risk Management", Chapter 8, pp. 109–139, in *Derivative Credit Risk: Advances in Measurement and Management*. Risk Publications.
2. To implement this approach, first iterate backwards through the lattice, setting any negative value at a node to zero. Then, for any time t, collate the node values and their attendant probabilities into a probability mass function and identify the appropriate stressed case exposure value in the right tail.
3. For a more extended treatment of these points, see Rowe, D.M. (1995) "Aggregating Credit Exposures: The Primary Risk Source Approach", Chapter 1, pp. 13–31, and Lawrence, D. (1995) "Aggregating Credit Exposures: The Simulation Approach", Chapter 2, pp. 23–31, in *Derivative Credit Risk: Advances in Measurement and Management*. Risk Publications.
4. When we were implementing our first derivatives credit system at Chemical Bank in 1985, our concerned credit officers noted that, whilst our system calculated probability adjusted losses, the bank's credit committee would be far more interested in "how much of a bath we could take" if a counterparty did default. Hence "Archimedes".
5. Brand, L., Kitto T.C. and Bahar, R. (1994) "Corporate Default, Rating Transition Study Results", Standard & Poor's, and Carty, L.V., Lieberman D. and Fons, J.S. (1995) "Corporate Bond Defaults and Default Rates, 1970–1994", Moody's Investors Service.
6. This graph was prepared from data presented in Carty, L.V., Lieberman D. and Fons, J.S. (1995) *op. cit.*
7. This table was prepared by D. Lucas when he was the credit officer for TMG Financial Products. A more complete description is set out in Lucas, D. (1995) "Measuring Credit

Risk and Required Capital", Chapter 7, pp. 99–108, in *Derivative Credit Risk: Advances in Measurement and Management*. Risk Publications.

8. See, for example, Altman, E.I. et al., (1993) "Credit Scoring Applications", in *Application of Classification Techniques in Business, Banking and Finance*. JAI Press.

9. Using Bayes' theorem, we can write the probability of bankruptcy, given bankruptcy is forecast, as:

$$p(B|FB) = \frac{p(FB|B)p(B)}{p(FB|B)p(B) + p(FB|B')p(B')}$$

If the model predicts with 80 per cent accuracy, then $p(FB|B) = 0.8$ and $p(FB|B') = 0.2$. For a matched sample, $p(B) = p(B') = 0.5$. Then

$$p(B|FB) = (0.8)(0.5)/\{(0.8)(0.5) + (0.2)(0.5)\} = 0.8$$

i.e. 80 per cent of the companies forecast to go bankrupt will go bankrupt. For the A2 sample, $p(B) = 0.001$ and $p(B') = 0.999$. Then

$$p(B|FB) = (0.8)(0.001)/\{(0.8)(0.001) + (0.2)(0.999)\} = 0.004$$

i.e. 99.6 per cent of the companies forecast to go bankrupt will remain solvent.

10. Jarrow, R.A. and Turnbull, S.M. (1995) "Pricing derivatives on financial securities subject to credit risk". *Journal of Finance*, vol. 50, no. 1, 53–85.

11. Moody's matrix is published in Carty, L.V. and Fons, J.S. (1993) "Measuring Changes in Corporate Credit Quality", Moody's Investors Service. Standard & Poor's matrix is published in its 1995 "Special Report on Corporate Defaults".

12. These matrices include a "Withdrawn Rating" column. It is common practice to redistribute a probability in this column proportionally over the other columns, but since rating withdrawals are associated with debt retirements and exchange offers and not with defaults, it would be better either to reapportion this probability over the non-default probabilities or explicitly to model "Withdrawn Rating" as a non-defaulting "sink" state.

13. The one-year default probabilities show no decrease because of the one-year "transition step" used in the transition matrix. Experiments with one-month transition matrices produce, as one would expect, greater reductions in default probabilities.

14. Fons, J.S. and Carty, L.V. (1995) "Probability of Default: A Derivatives Perspective", Chapter 3, pp. 36–47, in *Derivative Credit Risk: Advances in Measurement and Management*. Risk Publications.

15. See Smithson, C.W. "Managing Financial Risk: 1995 Yearbook". Chase Manhattan Bank, pp. 15–16.

16. Bahar, R. and Gold, M. "Structuring Derivative Product Companies: Risks and Safeguards", Chapter 11, pp. 173–188, and Curry, D.A., Gluck, J.A., May W.L. and Backman, A.C. "Evaluating Derivative Product Companies", Chapter 12, pp. 189–203, in *Derivative Credit Risk: Advances in Measurement and Management*. Risk Publications.

12
Trading Volatility

M. DESMOND FITZGERALD

12.1 INTRODUCTION

Essentially there are two types of derivative trading. The first is position trading where the trades are based on expectations of where prices are going, but are consistent with the current market assumed level of volatility. The other type of trading is based on taking a view on market volatility different from that contained in the current set of market prices. The market forecast of volatility over the life of a derivative is obviously one of the prime determinants of derivative prices. If, therefore, for whatever reason, the trader believes the market forecast of volatility is incorrect, he can put in place trades which will make profits if his forecast is realized. Such trades will be designed to insulate the trader from underlying price movements distinct from those induced by changes in volatility.

However, one has to be very careful when talking about volatility trading to distinguish between different types of volatility and different sources of volatility trading profits. Figure 12.1 illustrates the different types of volatility: historical volatility, implied volatility, and realized volatility. Previous chapters in this book have extensively discussed alternative volatility forecasting procedures using historical information to analyse subsequent realized volatility. Historical and realized volatilities are both measures of observed price volatility. Implied volatility is a measure of how variable option traders expect the underlying asset price to be over the life of the option. Changes in both types of volatility will influence the profitability of an options volatility trade where the position is kept broadly delta neutral. Profits and losses will accrue as underlying prices move and the position is rebalanced to maintain delta neutrality. Profits and losses will also accrue as changes in market prices influence and change option traders' views of likely volatility over the remaining life of an option.

The easiest way to consider these different profits is to identify the precise sources of profit to a delta neutral trade through time. These can be listed as follows.

$$\text{Time Decay profit:} \quad \text{Position gamma} \times \frac{(\text{Asset price})^2}{2} \times (\text{Implied volatility})^2$$

The Handbook of Risk Management and Analysis. Edited by Carol Alexander
© 1996 John Wiley & Sons Ltd

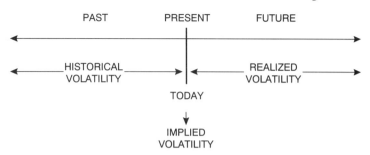

Figure 12.1 Three types of volatility

The realization here is that in simple option models, theta pays for gamma, and the rate of theta profit depends on the implied volatility at which the option was originally sold or purchased.

$$\begin{matrix} \text{Net profit from} \\ \text{realized volatility:} \end{matrix} \begin{matrix} \text{Position} \\ \text{gamma} \end{matrix} \times \frac{(\text{Asset price})^2}{2} \times \left[\left(\begin{matrix} \text{Realized} \\ \text{volatility} \end{matrix} \right)^2 - \left(\begin{matrix} \text{Implied} \\ \text{volatility} \end{matrix} \right)^2 \right]$$

This profit is accounted for by the rebalancing of the position to maintain delta neutrality. If the option position has high gamma, then if daily price changes are significantly different to those needed to cover time decay (changes consistent with original implied volatility), profits and losses on the book will be created. Although this might technically be referred to as gamma trading by derivatives traders, its profitability is still based on realized market volatility.

$$\begin{matrix} \text{Net profit from changes} \\ \text{in implied volatility:} \end{matrix} \quad \text{Vega} \times \left[\begin{matrix} \text{Current implied} \\ \text{volatility} \end{matrix} - \begin{matrix} \text{Original implied} \\ \text{volatility} \end{matrix} \right]$$

This profit is accounted for by the impact of a change in implied volatility on the current price of the option. This could be the result of a volatility term structure effect, or a change in implied volatility occasioned by market developments. The process of attempting to make profits from predicting changes in implied volatility would be termed vega trading.

It should be noted that these two different types of volatility trading are not necessarily independent. An abrupt rise in realized volatility versus original implied volatility (as occasioned, for example, by a market crash) is also highly likely to lead to a reassessment upwards of subsequent implied volatility by market traders. The ability of individual derivatives positions to realize profits from gamma and vega trading, however, is crucially dependent on the average maturity and degree of moneyness of the derivatives book. This is because although the level of vega and gamma are both highest at-the-money, vega and gamma sensitivities are mirror images of each other with respect to maturity. This is well illustrated in Figures 12.2 and 12.3. For at-the-money options it can be seen that long maturity options display high vega and low gamma: short maturity options display low vega and high gamma. By contrast for out-of-the-money options, long maturity options display lower vega and higher gamma, and short maturity options higher vega and lower gamma. Hence designing a position with exactly the combination of vega and gamma exposure desired by a specific trader will be a complex and dynamic process.

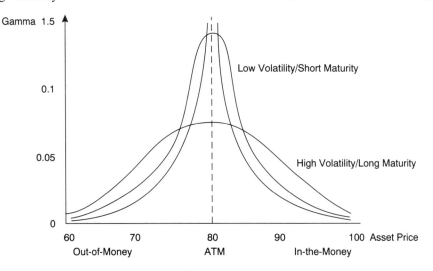

Figure 12.2 Option gamma

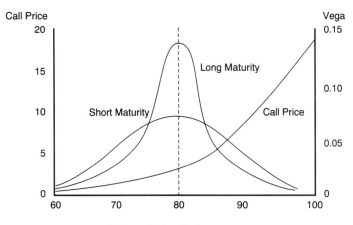

Figure 12.3 Option vega

Certain fundamental points concerning the balance between gamma-based and vega-based volatility trading may be noted, however.

1. If a trader desires high gamma but zero vega exposure, then a suitable position would be a large quantity of short maturity at-the-money options hedged with a small quantity of long maturity at-the-money options.

2. If a trader desires high vega but zero gamma exposure, then a suitable position would be a large quantity of long maturity at-the-money options hedged with a small quantity of short maturity at-the-money options.

3. For either of the previous positions, a significant movement in the underlying asset price could reverse the degree of exposure, and necessitate major rebalancing to restore the original position.

There is one further general point that needs to be mentioned before going on to the technical details of designing volatility trades and that is the implication of using simple option models to calculate vega sensitivities. It is well known that one of the main assumptions underlying the Black–Scholes and related models (including binomial models) is that the asset price process is a constant variance diffusion process. Many commentators have previously pointed out the apparent inconsistency in asking a model based on constant variance to provide risk parameters with respect to changes in volatility. However, for volatility trading the use of such models causes greater difficulties. We have mentioned before that in standard simple models theta pays for gamma, yet there is no mechanism within such models for any payment for vega exposure. This does not affect the pricing of at-the-money options since at-the-money options are linear in volatility across a wide range of models, and linear bets have no value. However, out-of-the-money and in-the-money options are certainly not linear with respect to volatility, and hence it would appear that there should be some trade-off between the level of vega and the level of theta. Hence in practice it would not be too surprising if the pattern of time decay suggested for specific options by a regular Black–Scholes or binomial model was not an accurate predictor of the actual evolution of the option price. Modelling the true impact of vega risk on time decay patterns could significantly improve the expected profitability of volatility term structure trading. We will return to this point below.

Another general volatility point that should be mentioned is the relationship between the best historical forecast volatility and implied volatility, and the relationship between diffusion volatility components and jump volatility components. This is because different volatility assumptions will give rise to different delta and gamma measures, which in turn will have considerable impact upon the dynamic risk management of the position. In essence, the first problem arises because of the unknown nature of the process of determination of implied volatility. We could imagine two extreme cases. The first is one of market efficiency where at-the-money implied volatility is the best forecast of subsequent realized volatility. The second is where the best historical based forecast is indeed the market's forecast, but the market is short volatility to customers. Hence by assigning a suitable margin for the cost of hedging and for expected profit, the final implied volatility is generated. Thus the situation might be as follows.

Historical forecast	12%
+	
Cost of hedging	3%
+	
Required profit margin	1%
=	
Observed implied volatility	16%

If the trader accepted this view of implied volatility generation, then he would also face interesting questions as to which is the "best" volatility estimate to adopt in determining the delta and gamma sensitivities of the position. It would surely not be 16 per cent since this includes a simple profit margin add-on unrelated to market risk. Should it be 12 per cent or 15 per cent? It would appear that using 15 per cent would produce a dynamic hedging strategy that would minimize day-to-day P/L fluctuations, but if the 12 per cent forecast truly explains the realized volatility of the underlying price, then this strategy would not be the *risk* minimization hedge. On the other hand, the risk minimization hedging strategy may induce undue fluctuations in day-to-day P/L, which could cause concerns within senior management about the trading book.

The second hedging question that arises is in the situation where the realized volatility of an asset price process is best described not as that of a diffusion process but as that of a jump-diffusion process. Many observers, for example, of precious metal price processes are of the opinion that a jump-diffusion process is a better description of daily price movements. Now suppose we observed gold price volatility (implied) at 11 per cent, and came to the conclusion that around 6 per cent was attributable to the jump process. We also know that a dynamic hedging strategy (delta-based strategy) cannot hedge P/L fluctuations due to the jumps. Such P/L fluctuations can only be hedged using other option positions. Then the important question arises as to what volatility number should be used to dynamically hedge the position. There appears to be a strong case for saying that since only the diffusion component is dynamically hedgeable, it is only the volatility associated with that process that should be used to define the deltas used in the hedging process. Hence this would imply hedging strategies based on a volatility input of 5 per cent. This could have a very major impact upon the amount of hedging carried out during the progress of a volatility trade.

The fundamental message, therefore, before we talk about the technical details of volatility trading is that the inputs into trading profits and losses can be relatively complex. First, we have to distinguish between volatility profits due to gamma exposure, due to vega exposure, and due to gamma–vega correlation exposure. Second, we have to analyse the term structure and degree of moneyness of trades very carefully to determine the precise structure of gamma and vega sensitivities. Third, we have to be aware that the reliability of the reported vega exposures from simple option models needs to be considered carefully. Fourth, the exact volatility inputs to be used in determining delta and gamma levels for dynamic hedging of volatility positions need to be very carefully analysed. Only after all these matters are considered, should a volatility trade be actually implemented.

12.2 BASICS OF VOLATILITY TRADING

Let us take the simplest type of volatility trading. A trader believes that the current implied volatility in at-the-money options is lower than he expects to be realized over the life of the option. Hence he wishes to acquire a delta neutral, gamma positive position. He does not wish to concern himself with vega exposure because he intends to run the position all the way through to maturity if necessary.

Clearly the simplest trade on day 0 would be to buy a straddle: a combination of an at-the-money call and an at-the-money put with zero delta. This is the position A shown in Figure 12.4. The P/L profile shown in the figure represents the position one day later on day 1. We can easily identify the size of the daily movements up and down that are required to offset the impact of time decay and realize a net profit on rebalancing the position to delta zero one day later. Such price changes are naturally consistent with the original implied volatility at which the option was purchased. In our case, let us imagine at the end of day 1 that the price has moved to a level consistent with point B on the P/L profile. This has obviously generated a significant profit to the simple volatility trade. Assuming the trader is running a pure volatility position, then he will desire to restore his delta neutral position at B by selling five futures contracts.

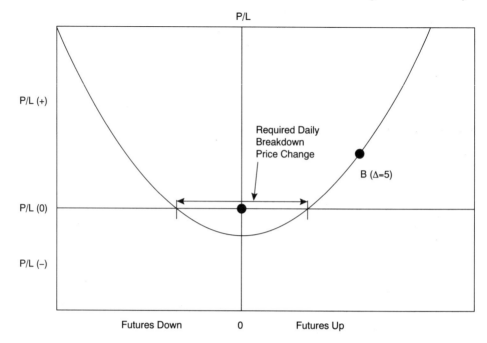

Figure 12.4   Long volatility position (Day 1)

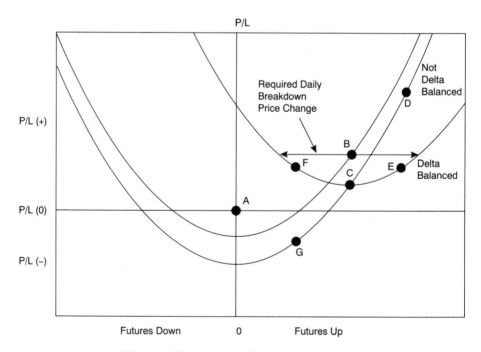

Figure 12.5   Long volatility position (Day 2)

Figure 12.5 shows the result of the rehedged position one day later on day 2. This is the curve marked F-C-E. It is interesting to compare the new hedged P/L profile with the P/L profile resulting from an unhedged position marked G-C-D. However, the important point to note is the changing nature of the volatility trade as a gamma trade. If we examine the required breakeven price change successively on Figures 12.4 and 12.5, then the change is slightly larger on day 2 than on day 1. This is natural because we are now creating a delta neutral position with an in-the-money call and an out-of-the-money put. Hence the overall gamma of the position has diminished, as indeed has the vega exposure. If the trader wishes to maintain the original degree of gamma exposure, then the alternative strategy might be to roll the position up into the current at-the-money straddle. The message here, of course, is that simply delta hedging the original gamma position does not result in an unchanged realized volatility exposure, and the trader needs to think carefully about whether to delta hedge the original position or to establish a new position more in keeping with his original volatility view at the new price level.

Further insights into this trade-off can be garnered by looking at Table 12.1 which shows the P/L of the position for various combinations of price and volatility changes. We can see the interplay of the gamma and vega aspects of volatility changes. The theta of the position is USD 6,000 per day, and it requires a DM rate change up and down of around 1 per cent per day to cover that cost of carry. That equates to an annualized volatility of around 16 per cent. It is also interesting to observe the degree of vega risk with this position, whereby a 1 per cent change in implied volatility would produce a daily profit/loss of USD 16,000. Hence a 1/2 per cent rise in volatility would be enough to offset the impact of time decay even if the asset price failed to move.

However, it is also worth noting the possible impact of correlation between price movements and implied volatility movements. If a 2 per cent price movement up or down convinced the market to raise its implied volatility 2 per cent from 15.8 per cent to 17.8 per cent, then the position would show a realized profit of USD 46,000. Similarly if a zero price change resulted in a reduction in volatility of, say, 1 per cent, the daily theta loss of USD 16,000 would be dramatically increased to USD 28,000.

Any serious volatility trader needs to be fully aware of the potential implications of the correlation between extreme price movements and changes in implied volatilities.

The relationship between the gamma and vega aspects of volatility can be further examined via Figures 12.6 and 12.7 representing the P/L profiles for a 15-day maturity

Table 12.1   Value of long DM volatility position after 1 day*

| | | Futures Change from 0.5500 | | | | |
		−0.0110	−0.0055	0	+0.0055	+0.0110
	+2%	301	285	281	286	301
	+1%	287	270	265	271	287
Implied						
Volatility	0%	272	255	249	255	273
Change						
From	−1%	258	240	233	240	259
15.8%	−2%	244	225	217	225	245

*Position: Long 100 55   Calls
           Long 100 55   Puts
           Short 2   Futures
Original Cost = USD 255 Thousand

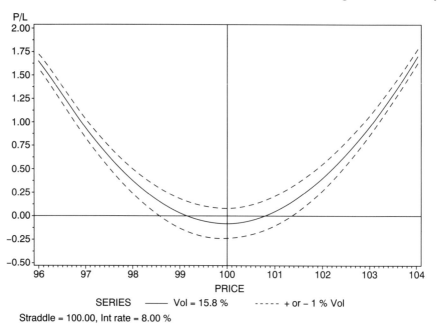

Figure 12.6 Potential P/L for long straddle (calendar days to expiration = 15)

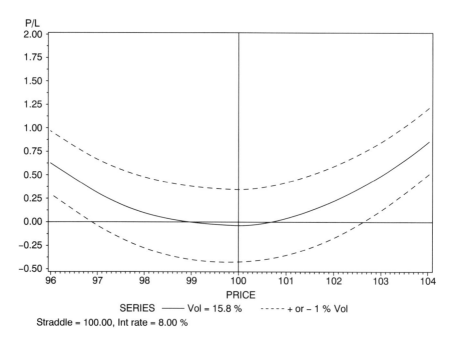

Figure 12.7 Potential P/L for long straddle (calendar days to expiration = 90)

straddle and a 90-day maturity straddle. If we look at the 15-day straddle, we can see the relatively narrow price movement required for a daily breakeven, but additionally the relatively limited impact of a 1 per cent volatility change up or down. The 90-day straddle reveals a much wider breakeven range (lower gamma) but a very much greater responsiveness to a volatility change.

The alternatives to the traditional straddle as pure volatility trades would be various forms of strangle and butterflies. Remember a strangle involves the purchase or sale of a combination of out-of-the-money puts and calls. The butterfly involves any one of three combinations of option positions. We illustrate these via long volatility positions.

Call butterfly: Sell ITM call, buy 2 ATM calls, sell OTM call

Put butterfly: Sell ITM put, buy 2 ATM puts, sell OTM put

Iron butterfly: Buy OTM put, buy ATM put, buy ATM call, buy OTM call

If we now examine Table 12.2, which shows the characteristics of various volatility trades, including the 55 straddle discussed previously, we can immediately see that the positions offer all sorts of combinations of vega and gamma exposures at various prices to the volatility trader. Indeed one useful thing to do for any volatility trader would be to produce a gamma and vega value index for each position: in other words, to identify how much exposure per unit of theta is obtained for each position. Table 12.3 shows these index values.

What is interesting about this table is how different positions give such different bangs for the buck for different risk measures. Thus if we take the short-term volatility positions, we can see how the various straddles and strangles provide virtually the same volatility exposure per dollar of theta, but the out-of-the-money strangle provides by far the largest gamma exposure per dollar of theta. By contrast if we look at the longer-term option positions, the apparently low risk butterfly position provides both the highest vega and highest gamma exposure per dollar of theta. Hence the automatic assumption that straddles provide the maximum "volatility" exposure is not necessarily entirely accurate.

Table 12.2 Characteristics of straddles, strangles and butterflies*

Contract Month	Position			
	55 Straddle	54/56 Strangle	53/57 Strangle	53/55/57 Butterfly
SEP				
Cost	$2550	$1500	$800	$1750
Gamma	0.0030	0.0028	0.0024	0.0006
Vega	$160	$150	$119	$41
Theta	$40	$37	$29	$11
DEC				
Cost	$4925	$3800	$2862	$2063
Gamma	0.0016	0.0016	0.0014	0.0002
Vega	$314	$307	$288	$26
Theta	$19	$19	$18	$1

*Assume DM futures at 0.5500 for both SEP and DEC and that SEP options have one month to expiration.

Table 12.3 Gamma and vega value indexes

	55 Straddle	54/56 Strangle	53/57 Strangle	53/55/57 Butterfly
September				
Gamma	75.0	75.7	82.8	54.5
Vega	40.0	40.5	41.0	37.3
December				
Gamma	84.2	84.2	77.8	200.0
Vega	165.3	161.6	160.0	260.0

The second thing to remember about even relatively simple volatility trades is that they are inherently dynamic. Rarely does a trader manage a volatility position by mechanical delta hedging as discussed earlier. As an example, it is useful to refer to an actual volatility trade carried out in the OEX stock index options. We will follow this trade through in detail.

June 7 The trader's volatility forecast over the life of the July option, with approximately six weeks to go to maturity, was 15.5 per cent. Implied volatility in the July 330–355 strangle was 18 per cent, so the trader sells 2,500 units of this strangle. He is happy with the volatility differential and with a breakeven index range of 322.85 to 362.15, around the current index level of 341.00 — this is something like a 10 per cent range for a six-week period.

					Cash Flow
Sold	2,500	July	330 Puts	2.95	+USD 737,500
Sold	2,500	July	355 Calls	4.205	+USD 1,051,250

The structure of the risk position can be seen in Figure 12.8(a).

June 11 The trader observed quite a significant rise in the market and decided to hedge the call side by buying 2,500 July 365 calls. At the same time he bought some cheap June downside protection with out-of-the-money puts.

					Cash Flow
Bought	2,500	July	365 Calls	2.25	−USD 562,500
Bought	1,045	June	330 Puts	0.62	−USD 64,790
Bought	100	June	325 Puts	0.375	−USD 3,750

The changed structure of the risk position can be seen in Figure 12.8(b).

June 14 The trader seized the opportunity offered by a further rise in the market to close all the put positions, leaving the effective position as short 2,500 July 355–365 call spreads at an effective level of 1.95 (4.205 − 2.25).

					Cash Flow
Bought	2,500	July	330 Calls	1.5625	−USD 390,625
Sold	1,045	June	330 Puts	0.0715	−USD 7,471
Sold	100	June	325 Puts	0.0625	−USD 625

The adjusted risk position is shown in Figure 12.8(c).

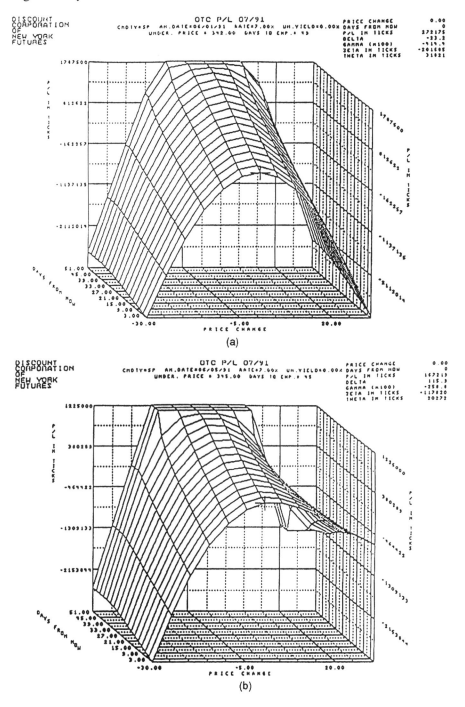

Figure 12.8 P/L profiles for a dynamic volatility trade

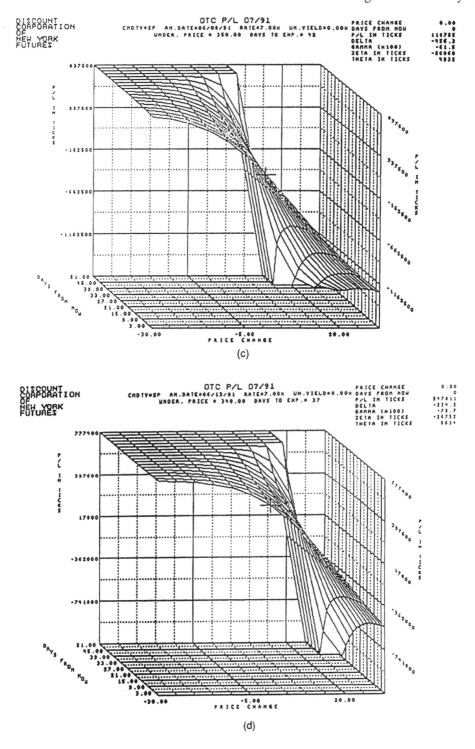

Figure 12.8 *(continued)*

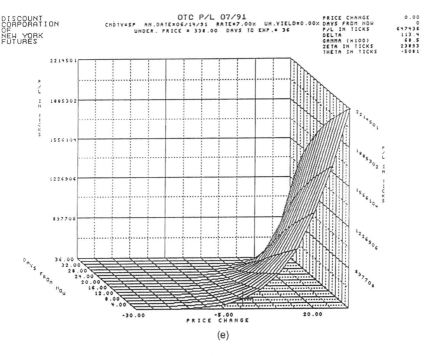

Figure 12.8 *(continued)*

June 16   The trader took the opportunity of a fall in the market to buy back 601 of the call spreads at an all-in price of 1.00.

					Cash Flow
Buy	601	July	355 Calls }	1.00	−USD 50,100
Sell	601	July	365 Calls }		

The adjusted risk position is shown in Figure 12.8(d).

June 18   The trader on a slight fall in the market bought back 1,899 July 355 calls at a price of 1.128 leaving a final speculative out-of-the-money call position effectively in the book at zero cost.

					Cash Flow
Buy	1,899	July	355 Calls	1.128	−USD 214,207

The final risk position is shown in Figure 12.8(e). This position was run through to expiration as a pure punt and expired worthless.

If we now add up the cash flows, we can see that the final position on June 18th was

Net Cash Flow   +USD 500,874
Final Position
Long 1899 July 365 Calls
At Zero Cost

This was clearly a very satisfactory volatility trade, although ironically if the trader had simply held the volatility position through to maturity and done no hedging or rebalancing, the entire premium income would have been retained. The important point to note, however, is that the dynamic nature of the hedging is pretty much independent of delta hedging theory. Also note the willingness of the trader to close and open positions in the reverse direction to apparent trends in the market — the mirror image of normal delta hedging.

This interplay of short and long volatility positions is often referred to in terms of "volatility overlay" strategies. Thus some typical volatility strategies might be:

1. Take advantage of lower expected volatility by selling short-dated strangles. Protect the ends of the position by buying longer-dated strangles. Here the trader should benefit from differential time decay on the shorter-dated options if the market displays low realized volatility, but gets protection from the longer-dated strangles if there is a big market movement. Furthermore if a big market move leads to an increase in implied volatility, the longer-dated options will differentially benefit the trader through higher vega exposure. Typical individual positions and the combined position for this strategy are shown in Figures 12.9(a), (b) and (c).

2. Take advantage of higher expected realized and implied volatility by buying longer-term straddles. Cover some of the cost of running the position by selling at-the-money short-term butterflies. The extreme time decay features of the short-dated butterfly should cover much of the cost of financing the longer-dated straddle position, whilst retaining many of the benefits of a large price move because of the limited risk characteristics of the butterfly position. Typical individual positions and the combined

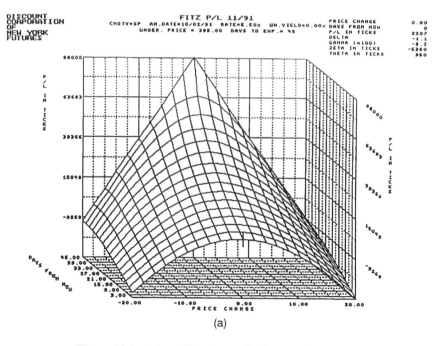

(a)

Figure 12.9 P/L profiles for a volatility overlay strategy

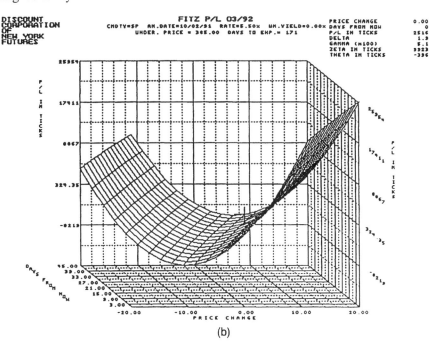

(b)

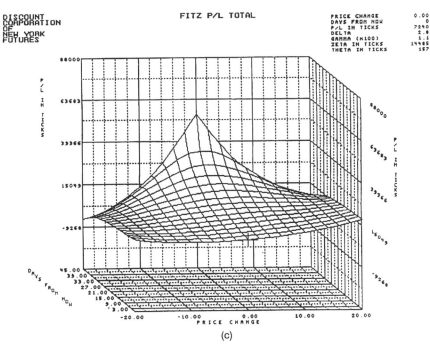

(c)

Figure 12.9 *(continued)*

position for this strategy are shown in Figures 12.10(a), (b) and (c). Note that in this case the pattern of market prices has enabled the trader to generate an extremely attractive combined position.

12.3 ANALYSING VOLATILITY PATTERNS FOR TRADING

So far we have discussed the basic principles of volatility trading and how the standard volatility trades are implemented and managed. The next question is what would determine an active volatility trader to institute a trade. Clearly the answer is: if his view on realized volatility or subsequent implied volatility is significantly different to the current implied volatility. Many volatility traders utilize volatility cones to examine the term structure of volatilities for individual contracts and identify anomalies. Such volatility cones, which could be created using historical volatilities or implied volatilities, are designed to illustrate the mean volatility and appropriate confidence limits for different option maturities. A typical cone can be seen in Figure 12.11, which is a typical page of volatility analysis from a major US broker: the diagram marked "Maturity Structure of Volatility" represents the volatility cone. As can be seen the US Treasury bond volatility term structure shows a modest tendency to rise from the one-month maturity with a mean of 8.743 per cent to one year with a mean of 9.622 per cent. The pattern of confidence limits illustrates the widely different volatilities of volatility at the short end (very high) and the long end (relative low).

Obviously the intent of cone-based volatility trading is to identify periods when the implied volatility of the options lies outside the confidence limits for a significant period

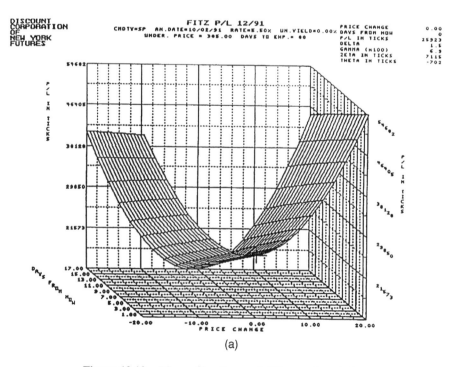

(a)

Figure 12.10 P/L profiles for a volatility overlay strategy

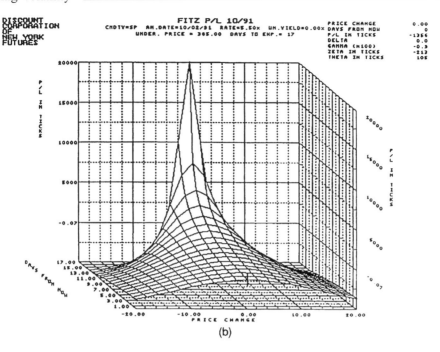

(b)

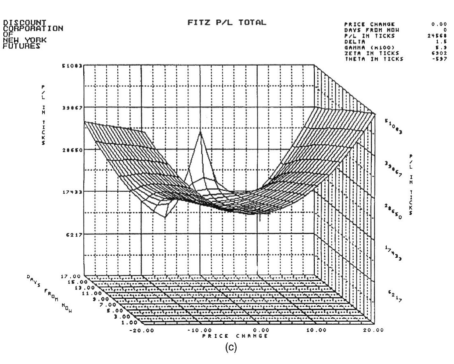

(c)

Figure 12.10 *(continued)*

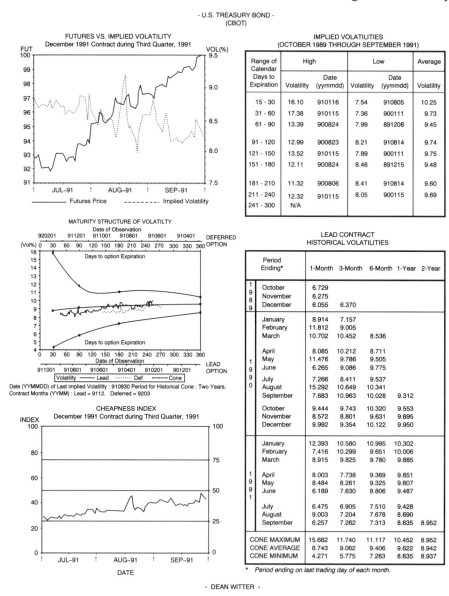

Figure 12.11 (Reproduced by permission of Dean Witter Institutional Futures)

of time, and buy or sell volatility accordingly. Obviously the timing of such volatility trades is important because a 90-day volatility purchased outside the confidence bounds could easily be inside the confidence bounds as a 60-day volatility, without the volatility actually changing. Hence there is a need for the trader to monitor the speed of mean reversion displayed by implied volatility, as well as simply its current relationship to the cone. In the Treasury bond cone in question, we can observe the pattern of implied volatility for the current lead and next to lead contract superimposed on the cone. In this case, although implied volatilities have been trading somewhat cheap to the volatility mean, they are well within the 95 per cent confidence bonds so that no volatility trade is suggested.

To give an illustration of how volatility cones can be used to suggest successful volatility trades, however, we use one of the most famous examples of yen–dollar volatility back in 1988 — old but good as the saying goes. This is actually one of the more renowned volatility trades. Figure 12.12 shows the volatility cone and superimposed implied volatility and 30-day historical volatilities as of 13th June 1988. It will be observed that both implied and 30-day historical volatilities have traded well outside the confidence bounds. Moreover they are sufficiently far outside the current bounds to be still undervalued over the next 30 days. Hence the trader is likely to feel comfortable in buying a straddle. Figure 12.13 shows the classic result: over the next 30 days implied and 30-day historical volatilities trade back towards the mean. The total rise in implied volatility over 30 days was from around 7.5 per cent to 12 per cent, representing a significant volatility trading opportunity. Although trades will not always work out as successfully as this, volatility cones are useful tools for suggesting suitable trades. Similar techniques could be used to study the relationship between volatilities on different assets by superimposing their volatility cones and centring the means of the cones at zero.

The other features that option traders often make use of in designing volatility trades are skews and smiles in the pattern of implied volatilities. Volatility smiles reflect the phenomenon that out-of-the-money options often display generally higher volatility than at-the-money options when implied volatilities are calculated using standard Black–Scholes and binomial models. Figure 12.14 shows a typical volatility smile for DM/USD implied volatility. Note how the shape of the smile becomes accentuated as

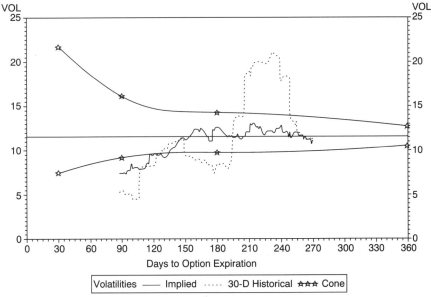

Date of Last Implied Volatility Reading: 13th June 1988
Time Period for Historical Cones: May-1986 through Apr-1988
Source : DCNYF Research Group.

Figure 12.12 Maturity structure of September 1988 Japanese yen volatility: implied volatility vs. 30-day historical volatility

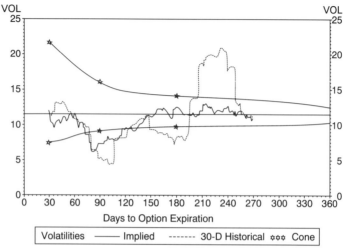

Time Period for Historical Cones: May-86 through Apr-88
Source : DCNYF Research Group.

Figure 12.13 Maturity structure of September 1988 Japanese yen volatility: implied volatility vs. 30-day historical volatility

we move from options with 60–90 days to maturity to 1–7 days to maturity. There is a general consensus among volatility traders that the smile probably reflects the inadequacy of simple standard models to deal with the fat middles and long tails (high kurtosis) displayed by many underlying return distributions. Such distributions are often the result of the underlying distribution being characterized as generated by a jump-diffusion process rather than a pure diffusion process. Mean reversion effects in volatility would also be likely to generate smile effects as discussed earlier in this volume.

Nevertheless although the smile effect may be primarily due to the inadequacy of the model used to derive implied volatilities, it does have an impact on the design of traditional volatility trades. Clearly straddles and strangles will react differentially to movements up and down the smile. For instance, consider a trader purchasing a straddle. Suppose there is then a significant movement upwards in the underlying asset price. Then the call will move into the money and benefit from the increased volatility embedded in the smile, and the put will move out-of-the-money and do the same. Hence the smile effect will boost the profitability to a successful straddle trade considerably. In the case of the strangle, the out-of-the-money call will move down the smile to become at-the-money and suffer from the reduced implied volatility, whilst the out-of-the-money puts will become further out-of-the-money. Although technically they will benefit from the smile, the value is likely to be so small anyway that it will be dominated by the adverse call effects. Hence the strangle will be adversely effected by the smile effect if the market moves substantially. Therefore a low risk volatility trade if the trade expects major market movements might be to sell strangles and buy straddles with the same maturity.

The other volatility phenomenon is that of skewness, meaning differential patterns of implied volatility between out-of-the-money calls and out-of-the-money puts. Figure 12.15 shows a typical pattern of skewness for various FX options — note the skewness phenomenon is often known as a pattern of risk reversal in the foreign exchange options market. Note in Figure 12.15 the extreme pattern of skewness for the peseta/dollar options,

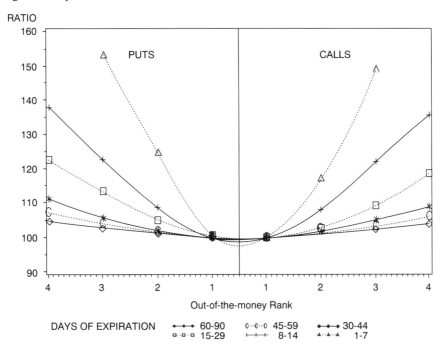

Figure 12.14 Average skewness in DM lead implied volatility (with different days to expiration): 1st January 1990 to 12th November 1991

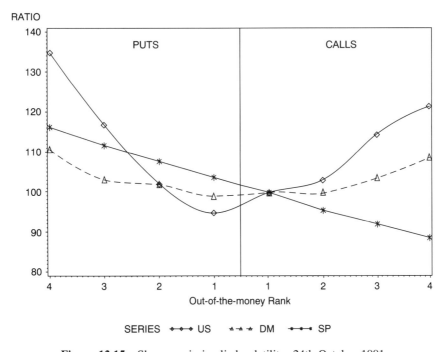

Figure 12.15 Skewness in implied volatility: 24th October 1991

where calls display lower and lower volatility as they move further out-of-the-money whilst the puts display higher and higher volatilities as they move further out-of-the-money. One can debate the reasons for the existence of this phenomenon. Traders often argue that this pattern of skewness reflects market forecasts of underlying asset price movements: in other words the pattern of peseta skewness suggests the market expects the currency to rise significantly against the dollar. Alternatively one could argue that if there is an underlying jump process, the chances of a jump and its size are greater in one direction than another. In any case clearly different volatility trades will react differently to skewness in the market.

It is important, however, to be careful in interpreting actual patterns of volatility in practice. As an example of this, Tables 12.4 and 12.5 show the volatility pattern after a substantial shift in the FTSE market on 27th May 1994. Table 12.4 shows the patterns of implied volatilities for the June FTSE options, whilst Table 12.5 shows the closing levels

Table 12.4

Assume Index 93.8/yr Div. UKX						OPTION HORIZON ANALYSIS JUN OPTIONS ON FT-SE 100 INDEX MARKET CLOSED TODAY					
			TRADE DATE 2966.4				7 DAYS LATER 2966.4 unch				
OPTION PRICING:	Tickr			Tickr			Volat=Same			Volat=Same	
	CALLS			PUTS			CALLS			PUTS	
STRIKE	Prc	Del	I.Vol	Prc	Del	I.Vol	Prc	Chg	%Chg	Prc	Chg	%Chg
2800	b.int			11.0s	0.13	22.56				5.5	−5.5	−50%
2850	b.int			20.5s	0.22	22.65				12.5	−8.0	−39%
2900	75.5s	0.83	10.20	36.5s	0.33	22.33	71.5	−4.0	−5%	26.0	−10.5	−29%
2950	48.5s	0.58	13.49	58.5s	0.44	22.98	41.0	−7.5	−15%	46.5	−12.0	−21%
3000	27.0s	0.39	14.21	87.5s	0.55	24.99	19.5	−7.5	−28%	75.5	−12.0	−14%
3050	16.0s	0.24	15.78	127.5s	0.64	28.21	9.5	−6.5	−41%	115.0	−12.5	−10%
3100	7.5s	0.13	15.92	172.5s	0.70	32.20	3.5	−4.0	−53%	159.0	−13.5	−8%
3150	3.0s	0.06	15.85	220.5s	0.73	36.73	1.0	−2.0	−67%	206.5	−14.0	−6%
Fri	5/27/94 (21days Expr)			4.88%Fin			Fri	6/3/94 (14days Expr)		4.88%Fin	

OPTION PRICING:	T - "Tickr" price	s - "Same" volatility
	M - Trade "Match" volatility	12.5% (or any other volat.)
Source : Bloomberg.		

Table 12.5

			FT - SE 100 INDEX AS OF CLOSE: FRI 5/27								
	Exchange :		1 (GO) FOR YESTERDAY n (GO) FOR n DAYS AGO 0 (PAGE) FOR LATEST				BID/ASK N				
London Futures Exchange							-- AS REPORTED 5/27 --				
Red date = option trading								57811	20896	Previous	
Symbol		Last	Chg	Time	High	Low	Tic	OpenInt	TotVol	Close	
1) UKX	spot	2966.4	−53.3	11:30	3033.7	2959.0	1024	0	0	3019.7	
2) X M4	Jun94	2940.0s	−67.0	Close	3024.0	2932.0	4680	50090	20222	3007.0	
3) X U4	Sep94	2953.0s	−68.5	Close	3035.0	2945.0	90	7470	674	3021.5	
4) X Z4	Dec94	2964.0s	−67.0	Close			4	251	0	3031.0	

Source : Bloomberg.

of the FTSE and relevant FTSE futures contracts. Remember the implied volatilities are calculated using a standard option model with the cash value of the index as an input since these are options on cash rather than options on futures.

At first sight, the most observable phenomenon is the high level of skewness between the puts and calls, with at-the-money volatility trading at 24 per cent for the puts and only 14 per cent for the calls. However, observe the pattern of cash and futures prices in Table 12.5. Because of the rapid fall in the market, futures closed extremely cheap relative to cash — indeed cash was at 2,966.4 whilst the June future was at 2,940.0. Since most volatility traders and market-makers use futures rather than cash positions to hedge, then they tend to price the options off the hedging instrument rather than the model prices based on cash. Given the cash index level of 2,966.4, a dividend yield over 21 days of 3.16 per cent and a financing rate of 4.88 per cent, the fair forward would appear to be 2,969.30 compared with the futures price of 2,940.0. By using the fair forward to compute the implied volatilities instead of the futures, the effect is to dramatically increase apparent implied put volatility and decrease implied call volatility.

After adjusting for the effect of mispricing, however, the actual pattern of volatility skews and smiles remains interesting. The usual skew in stock index contracts is declining volatility for out-of-the-money calls and increasing volatility for out-of-the-money puts. This probably represents the observed phenomenon of higher probabilities of extreme jumps on the downside in stock markets. In Table 12.4, however, we observe the reverse: increasing volatility for out-of-the-money calls from around 13.5/14.0 per cent at-the-money to 16 per cent 100 points plus out-of-the-money. By contrast the puts show declining volatility as they go out-of-the-money and increasing volatility as they go in-the-money. If one ignores arguments of market efficiency, then it might be argued that the market is expecting a market reversal (that is, the fall in the index will not continue) and hence is not assigning extra value to the out-of-the-money puts. If, however, one expects a return to the more usual pattern of volatility behaviour, then this could represent an excellent opportunity to sell out-of-the-money call volatility and buy out-of-the-money put volatility, delta hedging the resultant position with index futures.

One final point on volatility analysis that may be mentioned is the role of different types of volatility forecast in the dynamic hedging of these volatility positions once they have been instituted. Elsewhere in this book, the forecasting of volatility and correlation is discussed in great detail. We have already mentioned the distinction between using implied volatilities and historically based forecasts in determining risk sensitivities for volatility positions. We reshow in Table 12.6 some results for straddle trading for the S + P 500 and the Nikkei-Dow, where the hedging is based on a variety of volatility forecast estimates.

The main points to note are that all the volatility trading strategies, including the most naive, are profitable. This is because of the strong tendency in implied volatilities to overreact to asset price changes and then to regress to the mean. Obviously the best strategy in terms of profit is when the hedging is carried out using the subsequent realized volatility (not possible in practice) but note that the profits are not that much larger than for the next best strategies. Nor is there significant evidence that mean reverting volatility models and GARCH type models are any better or worse than naive strategies based on constant or simple historical forecasts. In other words, it may not make too much difference in terms of realized results to volatility trading which volatility estimate is used to determine risk sensitivities.

Table 12.6   Straddle trading*

	MR	LOG MR	GARCH	EGARCH	S&P 500 HISTORICAL	REALIZED	CONSTANT
gain 1	0.65	0.59	0.62	0.82	0.48	0.48	0.00
gain 2	1.96	3.54	3.21	2.40	3.16	3.29	−0.15
gain 3	2.76	2.30	4.99	0.03	1.09	2.97	1.65
gain 4	2.88	2.52	0.00	2.51	2.13	3.53	2.08
gain 5	0.44	0.60	0.04	0.24	0.89	0.72	1.00
gain 6	4.96	5.44	3.64	4.46	4.62	4.98	3.36
gain 7	3.06	2.58	2.77	2.75	1.81	4.15	1.31
gain 8	2.66	2.61	2.96	2.12	3.95	2.78	2.93
total	19.36	20.18	18.23	15.34	18.14	22.90	12.16
transactions	283	292	262	278	221	243	158

	MR	LOG MR	GARCH	EGARCH	NIKKEI HISTORICAL	REALIZED	CONSTANT
gain 1	0.13	0.21	−0.26	0.17	0.34	0.40	0.18
gain 2	0.69	0.69	−1.14	1.17	1.27	1.10	1.48
gain 3	0.05	0.05	0.05	0.05	0.27	0.00	0.00
gain 4	9.05	8.62	8.68	9.57	10.68	17.69	5.40
gain 5	8.47	14.36	4.74	13.14	4.76	21.62	11.17
gain 6	28.03	26.94	33.02	29.39	28.22	41.40	37.42
gain 7	30.37	25.10	49.18	25.30	20.16	24.33	20.39
gain 8	21.40	12.85	0.00	13.58	30.02	30.68	28.67
total	98.17	88.83	94.25	92.35	95.73	137.22	104.70
transactions	692.00	779.00	491.00	707.00	643.00	641.00	600.00

*Thanks are due to Jacques Pézier of Credit Agricole-Lazard for this table.

In practice many traders adopt a much more robust approach to the dynamic hedging of volatility positions. We would, for example, when selling a strangle suggest an ad hoc approach whereby no hedging is done until halfway to the at-the-money point, with a full hedge only being created if either the put or the call option becomes at-the-money. For instance, suppose a trader sold a 3,300–3,500 FTSE strangle when the current market is at 3,400. Then a possible dynamic hedging strategy might be no hedging in the range 3,350–3,450, and as the index moves outside this level gradually increase the hedge to a full delta hedge at index levels of 3,300 or 3,500. This hedge strategy seems to work quite well for distributions with high degrees of kurtosis.

12.4 RELATIVE VOLATILITY TRADING

As well as outright volatility trading based on analysis of skews, smiles and the term structure of volatility, there has been considerable interest of late in so-called relative volatility trading. That is, trading anomalies between the volatilities of options defined on different but related assets. Such trades could be between different stock indexes in a single economy (OEX vs. SPX), between different equities (BP vs. SHELL), between different interest rates (sterling vs. Deutschmark) and so on. The methods of analysis would broadly be the same as for standard volatility trades, save that we would attempt to establish confidence bounds on the relative volatility indexes and volatility spreads.

DISCOUNT
CORPORATION
OF
NEW YORK
FUTURES

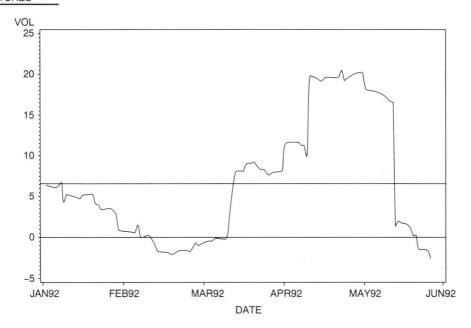

Figure 12.16 03-M sterling vs. EuroDM September 1992 historical (20-day) volatility spread

Figures 12.16 and 12.17 show one of the more famous relative volatility patterns of recent years. They show the relative volatility spread between short sterling and EuroDM September implied volatility in the period up until 18th May 1992. We can observe the peak relative volatilities in April as the first difficulties with sterling's position in the ERM became apparent, and the subsequent decline to a negative spread of sterling volatility over DM volatility in May. This was apparent on both historical and implied volatility calculations, and compared with a normal position spread of around 4 per cent. Hence this appeared to represent an excellent opportunity to buy sterling volatility and sell DM volatility in a hedged position. At the time volatility on sterling was 7.4 per cent with a cheapness index of 12.6, and DM volatility was 8.6 per cent with a cheapness index of 67.9. Remember the cheapness index represents cheapness or dearness relative to the mean of the volatility cone and is centred at 50.0.

Obviously, therefore, the trader will buy short sterling at-the-money straddles and sell DM at-the-money straddles. The aim would be to unwind the position when the current negative volatility spread of −1.2 per cent returns to a positive volatility spread of +4.0 per cent. To construct the trade we want to create equal and opposite exposures to changes in implied volatilities — that is, equal and opposite vegas expressed in a single currency. The risk sensitivities of the options available are shown in Table 12.7. We can see from this table (note the Dean Witter system we are using happens to refer to vega as zeta) that we will have equal dollar vegas if we sell 147 EuroDM September 90.50

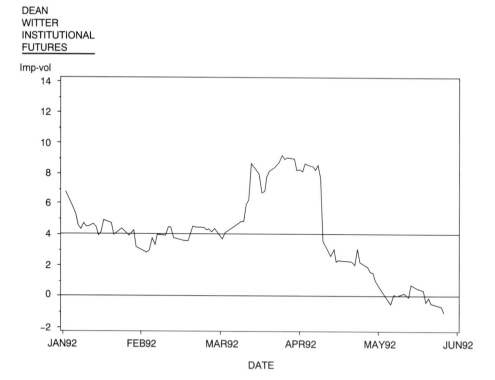

Figure 12.17 03-M sterling vs. EuroDM September 1992 implied volatility spread

straddles and buy 100 Short Sterling September 90.25 straddles. The structure of the trades is illustrated below.

Activity: 28th May 1992

1. Establish vega neutral options position, using at-the-money straddles.

    Vega ratio, using common currency:

    (Short Sterling/EuroDM): (USD 92.82/USD 63.28) = 1.47

    Need 1.47 times as many EuroDM as Short Sterling.

    | Short Sterling: | Buy 100 of the Sep-92 90.25 straddle |
    | EuroDM: | Sell 147 of the Sep-92 90.50 straddle. |

2. Make delta neutral.

    | Short Sterling: | Delta of 1 straddle = 0.20 |
    | | Delta of 100 straddles = $0.20 \times 100 = 20$ |
    | | Sell 20 Sep-92 futures @ 90.36 |
    | EuroDM: | Delta of 1 straddle = 0.06 |
    | | Delta of -147 straddles = $0.06 \times -147 = -8.82$ |
    | | Buy 8 Sep-92 futures @ 90.54 |

Table 12.7

Conversion Rates: May 28, 1992
$/£ 1.8010 DM/$: 1.6338 DM/£: 2.9425

EURODM

(c) 1993 Dean Witter Reynolds Inc.

COMMOD RU	MO/YR (Days) UNDERLYING		09/92 110 90.54		00/0 0 0.00		00/0 0 0.00	
			Call	Put	Call	Put	Call	Put
Date 05/28/92	90.50	Price	0.20	0.16				
		Vol	8.64	8.64				
		Delta	0.53	−0.47				
Int rate 0.00%		Gamma	0.89	0.89				
		Zeta	51.69	51.69				
		Theta	−2.03	−2.03				
Yld rate 0.00%	90.75	Price						
		Vol						
		Delta						
		Gamma						
Gamma × 100		Zeta						
		Theta						
	91.00	Price						
		Vol						
Zeta and		Delta						
Theta		Gamma						
in DM		Zeta						
		Theta						

Zeta of 90.50 EuroDM Straddle
ticks: 4.14   BP: 35.13   DM:103.38 $: 63.28

SHORT STERLING

(c) 1993 Dean Witter Reynolds Inc.

COMMOD RL	MO/YR (Days) UNDERLYING		09/92 112 90.36		00/0 0 0.00		00/0 0 0.00	
			Call	Put	Call	Put	Call	Put
Date 05/28/92	90.25	Price	0.22	0.11				
		Vol	7.42	7.42				
		Delta	0.60	−0.40				
Int rate 0.00%		Gamma	0.97	0.97				
		Zeta	25.77	25.77				
		Theta	−0.86	−0.86				
Yld rate 0.00%	90.50	Price						
		Vol						
		Delta						
Gamma × 100		Gamma						
		Zeta						
		Theta						
	90.75	Price						
		Vol						
Zeta and		Delta						
Theta		Gamma						
in BP		Zeta						
		Theta						

Zeta of 90.25 Short Sterling Straddle
ticks: 4.12   BP: 51.54   DM: 151.66 $: 92.82

Trade Ratio: Zeta Neutrality
Ratio (Short Sterling/EuroDM) (in $): (92.82/63.28) = 1.47
Therefore: Sell 147 EuroDM Sep 90.50 straddles
Buy 100 Short Sterling Sep 90.25 straddles

356 Handbook of Risk Management and Analysis

Note that, of course, the position will have to be rebalanced at regular intervals whilst the trade is held to keep it neutral with respect to overall rather than relative volatility movements, and most importantly to maintain delta neutrality on both the sterling side and the DM side.

Moving ahead, Figures 12.18 and 12.19 show the movements of the relative volatility during the period through September 1992. It will be observed that by early July 1992, the relative volatility spread has moved back to its long-term mean of 4 per cent and hence the position would be unwound. We show below the results of the trade: remember the P/L reflects a considerable amount of dynamic hedging during the period the trade was held.

Activity: 13th July 1992

Lift trade.

Date	Implied Volatility		Spread = Short Sterling− EuroDM	P/L (USD)
	Short Sterling (cheapness index)	EuroDM (cheapness index)		
28th May 1992	7.4% (12.6)	8.6% (67.9)	−1.2%	0
13th July 1992	11.9% (46.3)	6.1% (34.3)	+5.8%	78,251

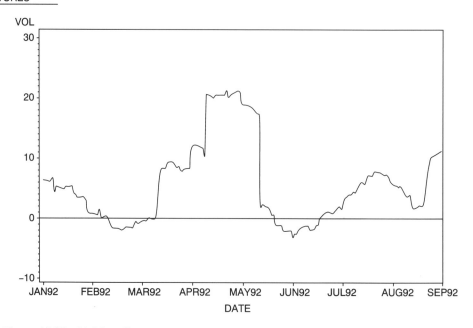

Figure 12.18   03-M sterling vs. EuroDM September historical (20-day) volatility spread

Imp-vol

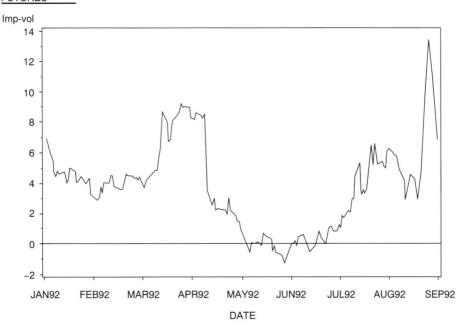

Figure 12.19   03-M sterling vs. EuroDM September 1992 implied volatility spread

This is a classic example of a successful relative volatility trade triggered by apparent anomalies in the volatility spreads in the market.

In practice, traders try to establish relative volatility confidence limits for many related assets. Figure 12.20 shows a typical relative volatility analysis for British Gas vs. British Telecom on 25th May 1995. This shows relative historical volatilities and relative implied volatilities for the period 4th May 1993 to 25th May 1995, together with the current 95 per cent confidence limits for relative implied volatilities. Currently relative implied volatilities lie around the centre of the bounds, but the analysis would have suggested the purchase of relative volatility earlier in the year. In general, the trader would have purchased British Gas straddles and sold British Telecom straddles in proportion so as to create equal and opposite sterling vega positions. Rather than hedge the delta of each position separately with the stock, the trader is more likely to work out the net market exposure of the entire position and hedge the net sterling delta with FTSE index futures. Individual exposures to British Gas and British Telecom will be monitored on a continuous basis, however.

Many other forms of relative volatility trading can be identified. We give some ideas of types of trades below.

1. *Stock index vs. stock index*
    The US has long been trading stock index futures including price-weighted and value-weighted indexes, narrow and broad indexes, and basket indexes. Since many index

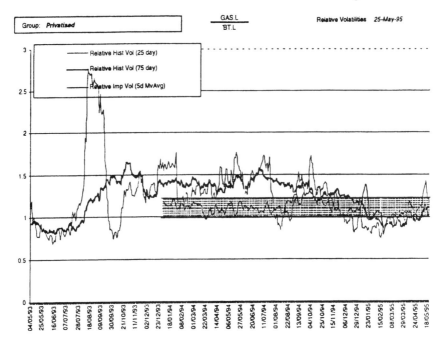

Figure 12.20

constituents are common, it may be possible to establish relative volatility bounds to monitor. Typical trades would be the Major Market Index vs. the OEX, a group of basket indexes vs. the OEX or SPX, and so on.

2. *Embedded options vs. traded options*

Many futures contracts are known to contain embedded options — for instance, one of the most famous is the cheapest to deliver switch option in the US Treasury bond contract. If the implied volatility in the embedded options is significantly different to the implied volatility in the equivalent exchange traded futures options, then a relative volatility trade may be successfully implemented.

3. *Interest rate term structure relative volatility trading*

A very active area of interest rate research currently is the use of term structure models to ensure consistent pricing of all interest rate products and related derivatives. The prices derived from such models can then be reprocessed through standard Black models, widely used to price caps, floors and swaptions, to determine required patterns of implied volatilities. If these consistent patterns are violated in the market, then relative volatility trading opportunities may well exist.

12.5 SUMMARY

What we have tried to do in this chapter is outline various aspects of volatility and relative volatility trading, and explain on what basis traders in the market institute such trades. It is important to remember that most volatility trading in practice is hardly pure, and may be biased by the trader's directional view. He may choose to hedge more often in one direction than another, or put in protection via options in one place and not in another and so on. Nevertheless there are certain principles which seem to summarize most volatility trading.

1. Traders need to be aware of the crucial difference between gamma (realized volatility) based volatility trading and vega (implied volatility) based volatility trading.

2. Reliance on simple Black–Scholes and binomial models is likely to lead to misguided decisions for the potential profitability of vega based volatility trading.

3. Dynamic hedging strategies for volatility trades depend crucially on the right option model, but hardly at all on the type of volatility forecasting procedure.

4. Sophisticated analysis of skews, smiles and volatility term structures is essential for successful volatility trading.

5. Relative volatility trading may be capable of generating higher risk adjusted profit margins than outright volatility trading.

Index